SCHOOLDAYS
ON THE BANKS OF THE BANN

COLERAINE
ACADEMICAL
INSTITUTION

1860 - 2010

Published 2010

© Joe Cassells & Len Quigg

Designed & Printed by
Impact Printing
Coleraine & Ballycastle

ISBN: 978 1 9066 89 23 0

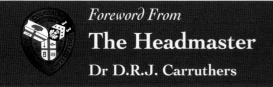

Just after taking up post as the eighth Headmaster in 147 years of Coleraine Academical Institution I was surprised to find that a history of the school had not yet been written. I learned from a few articles that the school was planned in the 1840s, but its foundation was delayed by many factors including The Great Famine. I also learned how the school had grown physically and in reputation and of the central role it has played in the Coleraine area for so many years.

The sesquicentenary is a wonderful opportunity to produce a timely history of the school and, as it approached, Mr Joe Cassells and Mr Len Quigg seemed natural choices to write this book; Joe taught History at C.A.I. and Len taught English. Both started their teaching careers in 1971, with Joe leaving in 2006 and Len, who was of course my predecessor as Headmaster, in 2007. You will see as you enjoy this history, that both men bring scholarship, enthusiasm and humour to their task.

From my perspective, 150 years of history seem to make my three years look very short, and I find it extraordinary that the second Headmaster, T.G. Houston, was in post for forty five years. However, it is possible even in three years to experience many of the highs and lows, joys and challenges of school leadership, and quite a number of these have not changed over the years.

Seeing pupils and teachers grow and develop together in a symbiotic learning relationship is an eternal element of education. Seeing pupils achieve in terms of university entrance, A level, AS or GCSE grades or in terms of their own improvement is our essential purpose. Sporting and cultural achievement go hand-in-hand with academic success, and this school has a long and proud record of participation and achievement in extra curricular activities.

As for the challenges, many current head teachers would concur with the following: "the conduct of some boys away from school is not as good as we desire, particularly boys travelling in the buses and those coming from the neighbouring seaside resorts. Too many seem out of parental control." Or again: "I cannot get the boys to wear their caps away from school. In view of this I am giving them permission to dispense with caps in the summer term – provided they wear a school blazer." These are not my words, though sometimes they could be. No, the quotation is from William White to the governors in the 1930s.

Today, in an era when part-time jobs are all too common amongst pupils, consider this: "Boys everywhere, nowadays, seem to have too much money, and to devote this to outside amusement... A change of outlook, a more pleasure loving outlook, on the part of the boys has contributed to a deterioration in exam results." A comment on the "swinging sixties" perhaps? Or even on the "Noughties" decade just past? No – this was the Headmaster's analysis of the Northern Ireland teenager of 1945!

My own view is that while some themes are unchanging in school life, the world in which teenagers are growing up today is a rapidly changing and challenging place. At C.A.I. we strive to equip boys with the knowledge and skills they need for 2010 and beyond.

It is a privilege to be Headmaster of this great school and it is with great pleasure that I commend this book to you.

The story of the founding of Coleraine Academical Institution and its development over these 150 years is remarkable, and one which I trust you will enjoy reading.

Many of us for whom the Inst. was our Alma Mater, will find our minds going back to our own days at the school. For some this is a fairly recent memory whilst for others the memories will take them quite a way back into the last century. Many of those reminiscences will be of camaraderie and contest; of the joy of winning, as well as the pain of defeat. Inevitably, the memories of friends who once walked the Castlerock Road with us, or who shared a classroom or dorm and are no longer with us, may cause us to reflect on the frailty of life.

Our founding fathers, wishing to make provision for the education of the sons of Coleraine and district, were greatly encouraged and generously supported by The Honourable The Irish Society and The Worshipful Company of Clothworkers. We acknowledge, with gratitude, the fundamental role which they each played in the formation of the school. There has been much development

of the school over its 150 years; nevertheless the original building of 1860 still dominates our magnificent Castlerock Road site as testament to those who pursued their vision all those years ago.

Education in Northern Ireland faces many uncertainties at present, and Coleraine Inst. is not immune to their effects. I trust that something of the dedication and courage which characterised our founding fathers, and many of their successors, will be found in those with the responsibility of taking this great school forward and that, under their wise leadership, the provision of high quality education for the sons of the Coleraine area will be secure for many generations to come.

I commend the authors, and those who supported them, for the vast amount of effort which they have expended in bringing this history of Coleraine Inst. to fruition and I trust that, whatever your link with the school, you will derive great enjoyment from your reading of it.

I count it a great privilege to be associated with the school at such a significant time as this.

iv

Introduction
Joe Cassells & Len Quigg

In September 1971, two fresh-faced young men began their teaching careers at Coleraine Inst. In the days before interview panels, power point presentations and specimen lessons, their futures had been decided at one of Dr George Humphreys' memorable interviews. At some stage in the encounter, he may have given them to understand that they were coming to the best school in the world, and he certainly extolled the merits of free accommodation in the boarding department. They in their turn were glad to have found friendly colleagues among whom to begin their careers, and an expanding school, which offered ample scope for career development. Although they spent the next three and a half decades working harder than they would ever have dreamed, the two authors of this book remained happily at the Inst. for the rest of their careers. And when they retired, Joe Cassells and Len Quigg were rather easily persuaded to undertake the task of writing the school's history as its sesquicentenary began to appear on the horizon.

The task seemed daunting, but as our researches began, fear gave way to fascination and the work proved engrossing and enjoyable. We aimed, of course, to include all the usual things which local historians cover: a coherent chronology of the school; the major features of its development; some consideration of the political and economic context; the impact of government education policy; the effect of curriculum development and reform. But as we worked, the past came almost eerily alive, and we began to sense that if we confined ourselves to a purely factual recital, we would not really be writing the history of the school in its fullest sense.

Coleraine Inst. has always been a living community, and through its portals over the last 150 years have passed generations of boys who stayed for longer or shorter periods of time. Some of them loved the school, others loathed it, but the apparently mundane details of their daily lives are just as revealing and interesting as the 'high politics' of the boardroom, the headmaster's office or even the staff room. We have tried to keep our touch light, to bring the past to life, to recall the experience of being teachers or pupils through several generations, to share at least some of the anecdotes that have come our way, and sometimes just to let photographs and illustrations tell their own stories. So this book is more a celebration of a community than a work of profound scholarship, and readers will look in vain for glossaries, bibliographies or copious footnotes. Neither, of course, is this book the work of a single hand. At the outset we divided the work chronologically, with 1927 as the dividing point. When we finished, we found to our surprise that we had produced two sections of almost identical length. We trust that, running through our natural differences of style and approach, readers will discern a common synthesis and a common love of our subject.

As two men who were privileged to spend the whole of our professional lives at the Inst., we want to wish Dr David Carruthers and today's school community every success in the coming years. We want to pay tribute to the colleagues whose companionable fellowship in past years enhanced our professional development and helped us not to take ourselves too seriously. And we want to pay a very special tribute to the hundreds of young men who sat in our classrooms during thirty-six years, sometimes amusing us, occasionally exasperating us, usually bringing the best out of us, and certainly enriching our lives through their company.

To the many generations of old boys, and not least to those with whom we had personal contact, this book is affectionately dedicated.

Acknowledgements

Compiling the history of Coleraine Inst. has been a daunting task. At its conclusion, the authors, if not necessarily wiser, judge themselves to be at least somewhat better informed, much more computer literate, and very heavily indebted to many people who have helped to lighten their burden.

From the 1940s until the early 1960s, the late Albert Clarke produced a serial history of the school in successive issues of the school magazine, and we have mined deeply into the huge seam of factual material which that devoted servant of the school preserved for the benefit of future generations. Then, in the 1970s, the late David Edmiston took responsibility for the annual magazine of the Coleraine Old Boys' Association. Under his editorship, successive editions produced treasure troves of information and reminiscence, and his own work on the foundation and early history of the school have been particularly useful to us. In his lifetime, David always sternly insisted that no material from the C.O.B.A. Magazine should be reproduced without first asking his permission. Since we can no longer seek that consent, we are glad at least to express a debt of gratitude to an unforgettable character, and to the fruit of his lifelong researches into the history of the school he loved, and latterly served as a Governor, and as Secretary to The Institution.

We have benefited from the memories of a large number of people who – in some cases quite unwittingly - have helped to bring some fresh air into what might have been an arid historical record. Of our former colleagues, Richard Adams, Jim Foote, Jim Flanagan, Donald McKay, Hugh Montgomery and Jimmy Shaw were particularly helpful in this respect. Their suggestions, reminiscences and corrections, together with the precise and relentless proof-reading of Jim Flanagan, Frank Rogers and Jimmy Shaw, are deeply appreciated. Within the current school community, Mrs Sharyn Griffith, Patrick Allen, Robert Kane and Willie McCluskey helpfully identified errors and answered queries which clarified several issues in the final chapter. The Rev. John Faris (an old boy of 'the other Inst.'), was most obliging in translating a Greek inscription on the school sundial.

Many old boys have also encouraged us in our researches into the school which clearly meant much to them. Mr Edward Simpson and Mr Rodney Adams kindly contributed memories of boarding in the 1930s and the 1950s, which have added considerably to the value of this history. Two men who sadly died during 2009 deserve special mention. Mr Brian Smyth and the Rev. Fergus Marshall, two of the last survivors of the 1939 Schools' Cup team, gave generously of their personal memories for this history, and of their treasured memorabilia for the school museum. Brian and Fergus took a real interest in the writing of the school's history: we trust that the end product is something of which they would have approved.

From the outset, Mr Gordon Knight, the school bursar, has given us enthusiastic encouragement and taken on himself much of the initial work involved in seeing this book through to publication. To two former schoolmasters, woefully innocent of the world of business, Gordon's practical expertise has been quite invaluable. Dr George Hull of the Geography department at C.A.I. has developed an instinctive empathy with the project. We are particularly grateful to him for his help with illustrations, as well as clarifying several matters dealing with rowing in the school.

The Governors of the school have been unfailingly encouraging in their support, and our particular thanks are due to the President, Mr James Smyth, and those members of the Executive Committee of the Board of Governors who read and commented on the manuscript before it went into print.

Mr Smyth and the Headmaster, Dr David Carruthers, have kindly contributed forewords, and we greatly appreciate their interest in the tradition into which they have themselves entered.

From the outset, our printers, Impact Printing of Ballycastle, have been both enthusiastic and helpful in the production of this book. The whole project has been particularly gratifying to Tommy McDonald and Nigel Johnston of Impact, both old boys of the school.

Except where otherwise stated, the illustrations are from the C.A.I. Museum Archive, and from a large collection of contemporary photographs of the school community which Dr George Hull is currently developing. The authors are indebted to other individuals, named in captions where appropriate, for making photographs available, and to Lilian Davis Photographic Studios in Coleraine for permission to reproduce some of their pictures.

As with almost everything which emanates from the school, this project owes much to the assistance, encouragement and willing co-operation of the school office staff. It might be appropriate here to mention particularly the senior member of the team, for Mrs Gwen Reavey has now made C.A.I. history by serving no less than five of the school's nine principals as Headmaster's Secretary. Her knowledge of the school in modern times has proved to be both encyclopaedic and instantly accessible.

To all who have helped us we offer our sincere thanks, and to any whose names have been unintentionally omitted we offer our sincere apologies. It goes without saying that any omissions or errors which remain in the book are the joint responsibility of the authors alone.

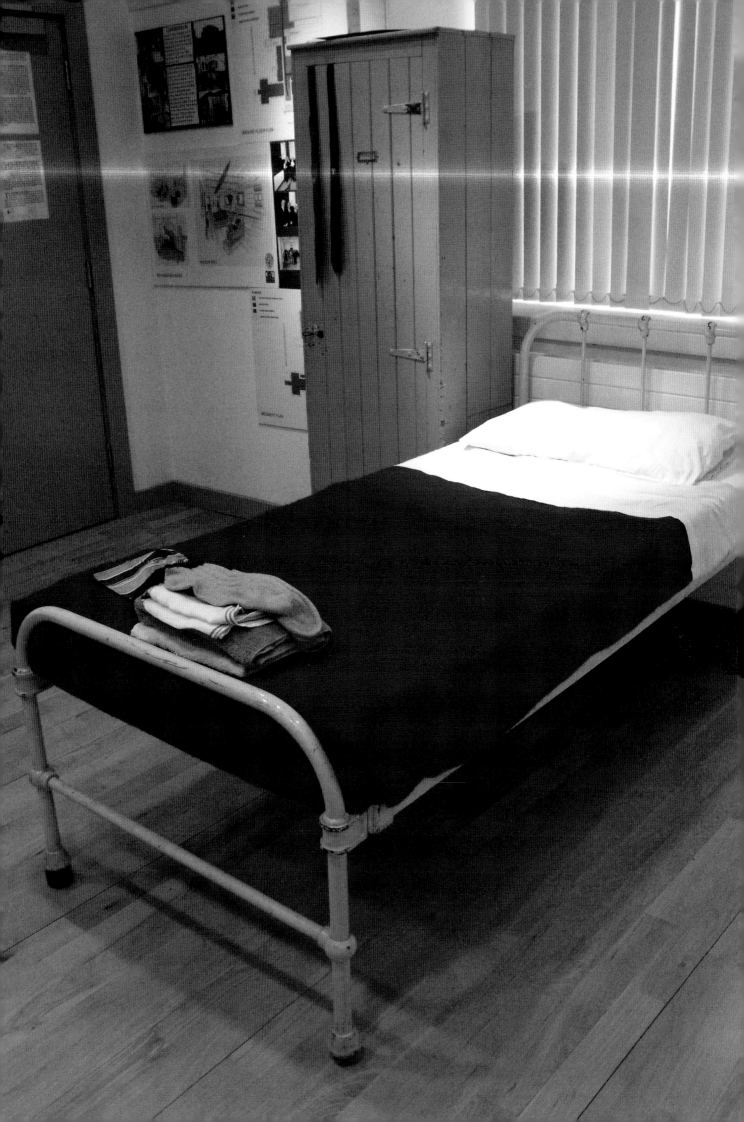

Contents

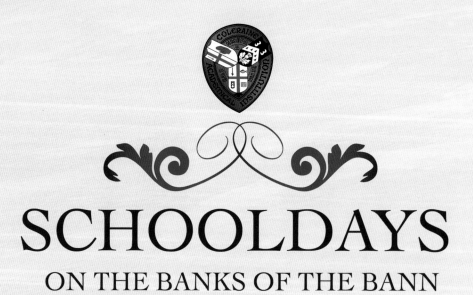

SCHOOLDAYS

ON THE BANKS OF THE BANN

Today, even with all the advantages of 21st century technology, expertise, vast financial resources (when eventually tapped!) and the 'assistance' of an all-powerful Department of Education, new schools certainly do not appear overnight. The process of moving to 'new-build' stage is lengthy and complex, involving much form-filling, endless negotiating with government and education board officials, making planning applications, commissioning 'feasibility studies' and 'environmental impact assessments', consulting with a wide range of supposedly interested parties, and deciding on architecture, accommodation, facilities and health and safety features. It can be an exhausting and often frustrating burden for those most closely involved in the process, but the prize at the end is to see all the dreams and the plans realised, and the glittering, new, educational establishment awaiting its first intake of pupils.

So it was with Coleraine Academical Institution in the middle years of the 19th century, a time when severe economic and social problems in Ireland made progress towards the dream of a modern 'intermediate' school in Coleraine particularly slow. Fortunately, amongst the many local people who expressed an interest in promoting such a venture, there were several committed and faithful individuals who had the vision, energy, patience and persuasive or practical skills to see the dream of a school for the boys of Coleraine and district, situated on a 'commanding situation' on a hill just west of the town, come to fruition.

Why did the people of Coleraine and district feel the need for a school such as "The Inst."? There were other schools, both public (free) and private in the area, but all these schools provided a basic education in the traditional 'three Rs', at what we would now term primary school level. The reasonably well-off business, professional or farming classes had to send their sons to board at distant public schools, often in England, or employ private tutors, if they wanted them to obtain the necessary qualifications to take them to university and to appropriate careers beyond.

At the formal opening of the school on 23 May 1860, the secretary of the management committee stated: *"So long ago as the year 1846, the state of Coleraine, as to its means of education, for the middle and upper classes in its neighbourhood, was made the subject of anxious consideration by a few who took an interest in its social progress. The working class were well provided by means of the National and other free schools, but what is now known as 'intermediate education' was imperfectly and with uncertainty obtained."* We have long moved on from the rigid class divisions of Victorian society; we now live in one-time Prime Minister John Major's so-called 'classless society' and the current school of course welcomes pupils from all walks of life, irrespective of class, colour, religion, nationality, or race. (In this matter, it is interesting to note that the school's joint top prize-winners in the 2009 A-Level examinations, each with four A grades, were local boy Michael Griffith, Tom He, whose parents came to Coleraine from China, and Markus Taeubert, who has joint Paraguayan and German nationality.)

It was the visit in 1846 of a deputation from The Honourable The Irish Society, the major land and property owner in the area at the time, which first gave encouragement to those who felt the need for a school capable of providing higher education for the boys of the town and neighbourhood. The feeling was that the powerful, London-based Irish Society could be persuaded to provide a substantial amount of the funding for such an establishment. What exactly was (and is!) The Honourable The Irish Society? It was, to put it simply, very much a part of the 'Plantation' of Ulster in the seventeenth century and in many ways the story of the development of the town of Coleraine is the story of The Irish Society.

When the English Crown, in the person of Sir Arthur Chichester, Lord Deputy of Ireland, with the cognisance of the monarch, James the First, decided that the north-west of Ireland was vulnerable to the chief enemy of the day, the King of Spain, it was agreed (circa 1609/1610) to colonise or to "plant", as it was then called the County of Coleraine, later to become County Londonderry. There being no money in government coffers for such an enterprise, the necessary finances were provided by the rich London companies or merchant 'Guilds', for example, the Clothworkers, who were given large grants of land in and around Coleraine, the Drapers (the origin of Draperstown), the Grocers and the Ironmongers. (The large, Georgian building situated on the west side of the River Bann, just across the Old Bridge, is still known, from an inscription on its second floor, as 'The Clothworkers' Building'.) These London companies formed what might be termed today a holding company to look after their financial interests in Ireland and this body was called 'The Society of the Governor and Assistants, London, of the New Plantation in Ulster, within the realm of Ireland', to become known eventually as 'The Honourable The Irish Society'.

Of course, those London merchant adventurers of the seventeenth century and later were quite simply our modern capitalists and their main aim was to extract the maximum amount of profit from their Irish holdings. They were not by inclination philanthropists, but at least the more far-seeing or liberal amongst them saw the value in ploughing back some of their profits into schemes such as promoting the education of those young men who might well assist in the consolidation, expansion and further prosperity of their Irish enterprises.

The Honourable The Irish Society has, over the centuries, done much to advance the well-being of the people of Coleraine and district and has focused particularly on promoting the education of the young. As examples, one of the town's most successful primary schools is known as 'The Irish Society's Primary School' and the most prestigious prize (£250) annually awarded to the top student at Coleraine Inst. is 'The Irish Society's Prize', kindly donated by

the Society. Both schools still receive occasional visits by deputations from The Honourable The Irish Society, usually including the Governor of the Society, or his/her deputy. The Society still has significant economic interests in the Coleraine area, including, as local fishermen well know, the ownership of all fishing rights on the lower River Bann, and the local headquarters of the Society is based at Cutts House, Coleraine. The Society still exercises its right under the school's Management Scheme to have one representative on the Inst. Board of Governors, and his or her input into the deliberations and decisions of the Board is much appreciated.

First Committee Appointed

As a result of the 1846 visit by some distinguished (and no doubt lavishly-robed!) members of The Honourable The Irish Society and the hopes raised by it, a large and enthusiastic meeting of influential local citizens was convened in the Town Hall on Wednesday 6 September 1846, Henry Richardson, Esq., D.L., J.P., of Somerset, Coleraine, presiding. The purpose of the meeting was to *consider the propriety of presenting a Memorial to The Honourable The Irish Society for the Establishment and Endowment of a Clerical and Mercantile school in this place.*" It is interesting to note the emphasis on a 'clerical and mercantile school', reflecting the focus the committee placed on the education of the sons of the local business and merchant classes. On the proposal of Hugh Lyle, Esq., J.P., seconded by A. Orr, Esq., J.P., it was unanimously resolved to compose and present this 'Memorial', and a committee was appointed to carry out the scheme. This committee consisted of prominent citizens of the district with the clergymen of the town as ex-officio members.

For the record, the twenty-eight members of that original committee were:
H. Richardson, Esq., H. Lyle, Esq., A. Orr, Esq., J. Orr, Esq., H. Kyle, Esq., Jas. Lyle, Esq., S. Lawrence, Esq., W.N. Rowan, Esq., R. Sharpe, Esq., A. Neill, Esq. , S.W. Knox, Esq., H.B. Mackey, Esq., Dr Cavin, Dr Babington, Dr Carson, Dr McCaldin, Mr A. McElwaine, Mr W. Young, Mr McCarter, Rev. Edwd.

Harvey, Rev. Wm. Richey, Rev. Jas. O'Hara, Rev. Wm. McGill, Rev. W.W. Sillito, Rev. Dr Appleby, Rev. Mr Heathcote, Rev. Mr Eccles, Rev. Mr Fullerton.

This committee was a large and potentially cumbersome body and it did have its problems at times: not all meetings were harmonious, there were several resignations and new appointments, and the attendance rate at meetings was often poor. However, a sufficient number of dedicated members of the committee worked tirelessly over the next fourteen years to ensure that the dream of a prestigious new school for Coleraine became a reality.

At that very first meeting on 6 September 1846, as well as the decision to proceed with the 'Memorial', there were three further resolutions:
1. *"that the fullest information on the subject of a new school be obtained from various educational establishments throughout the country,"*
2. *"that warm acknowledgements be conveyed to The Honourable The Irish Society for their deep interest in the cause of education,"*
3. *"that Dr McCaldin should be appointed Convenor of Committee."*

The third resolution later proved to be a very wise decision, as Dr McCaldin effectively became the Secretary to the General Committee and all other sub-committees which would be set up to steer this challenging educational project through to its construction, furnishing, opening, and indeed beyond. Dr McCaldin was a Coleraine man born and bred, a son of the manse, his father, the Rev. A. McCaldin, being minister of First Coleraine Presbyterian Church. He quickly established himself as the pivotal force within the committee and saw the scheme through to its completion. Without the faithful commitment of Dr McCaldin over these years, Coleraine Academical Institution might well not exist today.

The next meeting of the general committee took place on Friday 22 September 1846, in the Commissioners' Boardroom in the Town Hall, with Samuel Lawrence, J.P., in the chair. This meeting confirmed Dr McCaldin as its secretary, set up a sub-committee to draw up the 'Memorial' to The Irish Society and to seek advice from various schools throughout the country as to the setting up of an educational institution in Coleraine. When they met again, on 2 October 1846, the Memorial had been prepared, was duly adopted as appropriate, and a small deputation, including the secretary, was appointed to present the Memorial to The Irish Society's agent, W.F. Green, Esquire. Dr Boyd, the Member of Parliament for the area, was to be asked to attend the relevant meeting of the board of The Honourable The Irish Society in London at which the Memorial would be presented, presumably to add his personal support to the appeal from the Coleraine committee.

Also at the 22 September meeting of the committee, the secretary read communications from other schools in response to the requests for advice and information. These schools were: Dungannon, Londonderry, Portora, Ennis, Belfast, The High School Edinburgh, and Glasgow. There is no record of the precise advice, information or assistance which they offered, but presumably the Coleraine committee found these communications most useful when they came to the difficult practical matters involved in the setting up their new school.

A couple of months elapsed before The Irish Society's formal response to the Memorial arrived in Coleraine and that response was favourable. The Society promised an annual endowment of £100, a considerable sum in those days, and a sum of £500 towards the building fund, provided that a further £1,500 was raised by public subscription, and that the £2,000 thus acquired would be spent on construction of the school. The Irish Society had thus thrown out a challenge to the local committee, a challenge which was later taken up most enthusiastically by the public-spirited citizens of Coleraine. Self-help was of course very much a feature of Victorian society. When the Coleraine committee next met, on 29 December 1846, with Hugh Lyle, Esquire, in the chair, the members were obviously very satisfied with this liberal grant and a letter of thanks was sent off to the Society.

Despite this promising start to the committee's efforts, the economic and social problems of this time, in particular the horrors of the Great Irish Famine of the 'Hungry Forties', delayed progress on the venture. Although Coleraine escaped comparatively lightly in the disasters of these years, the committee felt it would be useless to appeal for funds at a time of such distress and suffering. Seven years were to elapse before the committee felt that the time was right to raise this educational project again.

By 1853, the committee had resumed its labours; on Thursday 17 February of that year, the 'Endowed School Committee', as this body was now termed, met at 12 noon in the Commissioners' Room in the Town Hall. The Reverend James O'Hara was in the chair and, for the record, the committee now consisted of: A. Orr Esq., S. Orr Esq., H. Kyle Esq., Jas. Lyle Esq., S. Lawrence Esq., W.N. Rowan Esq., R. Sharpe Esq., Dr Cavin, Dr Babington, A. Neill Esq., Dr Carson, S.W. Knox Esq., W.B. Mackey Esq., A. McElwaine Esq., Mr Wm. Young, Mr McCarter, Dr McCaldin, Rev. Wm. Richey, Rev. Jas. O'Hara, Rev. Joseph McDonnell, Rev. J.A. Canning, Rev. W.W. Sillito, Rev. W. McMullan, Rev. Mr McKee, Rev. Mr Young, John Cromie Esq. Added to these names were those of subscribers of £50 and upwards towards the building fund, as having a vote in deliberations: T. Bellas, H. Bellas, Jas. Moore, C.J. Knox, D. Gailey, Curtis Hemphill, Rev. J. Martin, W.W. Campbell and Thomas Bennett Esq., Rock House.

At this first meeting for seven years, the Rev. Wm. Richey revealed that he had been to London and had had interviews with the Clothworkers' Company and The Irish Society. The latter had reaffirmed their promise of £500 and £100 yearly, while the Clothworkers gave reason for the committee to expect generous aid from them. So at least some members of the committee had been working quietly behind the scenes during the past seven years and the dream of a new 'clerical and mercantile school' was still very much alive. It was decided to draft and send Memorials to the Clothworkers' Company and to all other public companies having an interest in the Coleraine area.

During the year 1853, the various local gentlemen with the interests of the proposed school at heart met no less than fifteen times, either in full committee or in sub-committees. The first essential, as with all ambitious building projects, was money. The Irish Society had promised a down payment of £500, provided the locals could raise £1,500, so a powerful committee was appointed to raise funds in the Coleraine area. This fund-raising committee included a number of clergy – Rev. J. O'Hara, Rev. W. Richey, Rev. J.A. Canning, Rev J. McDonnell, Rev. W. McMullan and Rev. W.W. Sillito – along with Dr Cavin, A. Orr, R. Sharpe, W.N. Rowan, A. McElwaine, S.W. Knox and the ever-present secretary, Dr McCaldin. By May 1853 they had obtained or been promised £530 and by 28 June 1853 this figure had risen to £1,425, including £210 and a promise of five acres of land for the site of the school from the Clothworkers' Company. The Rev. Richey's no-doubt eloquent appeal at that earlier London meeting with the Clothworkers had not fallen on deaf ears.

Meanwhile, the obviously very busy general committee drew up a school 'Prospectus' and also a set of rules which was adopted as *"the fundamental and unalterable basis of the Institution"*. This set of rules, though not 'unalterable', eventually developed into the school's 'Constitution', which will be referred to in detail in the next chapter. Hugh and Thomas Bellas, who would play prominent roles in the project as a whole, were brought in on the planning of the new school at this time (June 1853), being subscribers of £50 or more. A group of committee members, led by the secretary, made an official approach to Charles J. Knox, solicitor in the town and agent for the Clothworkers' Company, to gain possession of the promised five acres of land. This they managed some eight months later, on 13 February 1854.

In the meantime, the committee remained very busy and solidly focused on its objective. In June 1853, the first Trustees of the new Institution were appointed – W.F. Green, agent for The Irish Society, Charles J. Knox, agent for the Clothworkers' Company, A. McElwaine, Hugh Bellas, Dr Canning, Henry

Kyle and Joseph McCarter. It is interesting to note that the powerful London companies, as well as contributing generously to the building fund for the new school, shrewdly maintained an influence on developments through the appointment of their local representatives as Trustees.

At the same time, Messrs. Bellas, Mackey and the secretary set about obtaining plans and specifications for the new building, even though they did not as yet have formal possession of the land on which to put it. As a result of an earlier advertisement, no less than eight designs for a new school were submitted by: Mr Isaac Farrell, Dublin, Mr Duncan Ferguson, Dublin, Mr Lyons, Dublin, Mr Boulger, Dublin, Mr Barre, Newry, Mr Boyd, Belfast and Mr Hurley, Coleraine. After 'lengthy deliberations at three successive meetings' the premier award of £20 went to Isaac Farrell (and with this the eventual contract for the design of the building). Second place and £5 was given to Mr Boyd of Belfast. The Clothworkers' Company, which had still not formally released the five-acre site, approved Farrell's design in September 1853. A further letter was received from The Irish Society, also approving the plans for the new building.

This was the time for sub-committees to supervise the impending construction, to prepare the Trust deed and to develop the permanent Constitution. Their first task was to employ James Lithgow, a local surveyor, to produce a detailed map of the ground on which the building was to be sited. He submitted this map on 3 October 1853 and received ten shillings for his services. October 1853 was a busy month. Lengthy rules were drawn up for the filling of committee and office bearer vacancies and updated lists were produced of those who had subscribed £50 or over, those subscribers having a vote in the Committee's deliberations.

Rows And Resignations

However, the year 1853 was not all sweetness and light in the affairs of the committee. Dr Thomas H. Babington resigned on 6 May 1853 and a letter of resignation from Rev. W.W. Sillito

was received at a meeting on 22 September. The reasons for these two resignations are not clear but a third resignation letter on 29 September, from Andrew Orr, revealed that relationships between some members of the committee were, to say the least, somewhat strained:

Millhouse
Sept. 29, 1853

Dear Sir,
Your letter of 24th I only read at one o'clock. The present is to state that I must decline the honour of holding any office in the new intended Academical Institution. It is only of late I have been obliged to resign and give up attending the large school and Savings Bank, having been publicly insulted by a person who is master of the one and Secretary of the other. This took place in the Diamond of Coleraine on a Saturday about 12 o'clock and no notice has been taken of it since. On the contrary Canning's salary has been raised, I should suppose in consequence of his rudeness to me. Under these circumstances I am determined to have nothing to do with any Public Institution for the future in Coleraine.

Andrew Orr

One can only speculate as to the nature of the incident which 'took place in the Diamond of Coleraine on a Saturday about 12 o'clock', but Mr Orr's rage is still simmering in this letter! It is of course only natural that, after years of intense and no doubt sometimes heated discussions, coupled with the frustrations arising from the protracted nature of the project, personal disagreements amongst the members of the committee could sometimes develop. Further resignations took place in 1854 and these revealed some of the frustrations which individual members of the committee felt. The Rev. James O'Hara wrote on 27 September 1854 to say, *"As railways will soon bring other localities which afford a better opening for good tutors and masters within easy reach of Coleraine will you have the goodness to take my name from the Committee of the proposed school intended to be built in Killowen Parish."* Whether this was an excuse for leaving the committee or not, Rev. O'Hara certainly had a point – in 1853 the railway line between Londonderry and Coleraine had been

5

completed, thus making access to other parts of the country much easier. Another resignation letter, from Dr Carson, showed how at least some of the committee had lost faith in the whole project:

Coleraine, 30ᵗʰ November 1854

My dear Sir,
As I have lost all hope of seeing the projected endowed school brought to a satisfactory or speedy issue, I have to request that you remove my name from the subscription list as well as from the list of the Committee.

Yours very truly,
J.C.L. Carson

However, returning to 1853, there were sufficient numbers on the committee who had the conviction, determination and energy to press ahead with the venture, no matter how slow or frustrating the pace of developments. By December, S.J. Knox, the solicitor, had been instructed to draw up the Trust Deed for the new school and Mr Farrell, the prize-winning architect, had been asked to specify on his designs that the building be finished in best hard brick, with quoins, corniches, etc, in 'Roman cement'. He was also asked to provide an estimate of the difference in expense between cement quoins and freestone. The committee was obviously determined that the building be constructed of the best possible materials, but at a reasonable price.

On the matter of money, an amusing minor hiccup occurred at this time. The occupier at the time of the promised five-acre site, one Patrick Kennedy, requested £12 in return for the manure he had spread on it, if and when the ground was handed over by the Clothworkers. No doubt the eyebrows of the committee members were considerably raised by this liberal estimate of the cost of manure in 1853, but Mr Kennedy was obviously as shrewd a businessman as those on the committee, in pressing his claim! The five acres were eventually handed over on 13 February 1854 and Patrick Kennedy did receive £12 for his special, expensive manure!

The year 1854 started off well. Isaac Farrell's specifications for the design of the building were accepted and advertisements for tenders by builders were inserted in the *Coleraine Chronicle*, the *Belfast Whig* and *Newsletter*, the *Derry Standard* and *Sentinel* and the *Dublin Advertiser*. But only one tender was received, from a Mr S. Kilpatrick, and at a much higher figure than the committee had been expecting. Even though Mr Farrell was asked to make some economical changes to his specifications, with the builder's agreement, the committee decided that they needed more money. As a consequence, another Memorial was prepared for The Irish Society and the Clothworkers' Company and Mr McCarter and Dr Cavin were delegated to go to London in May, to plead the case for further funds. They returned triumphantly, apparently having received promises of further generous assistance and an article in the *Coleraine Chronicle* of that week praised the efforts of all concerned. The thanks of the Committee were conveyed to Sir J. Musgrove, Governor of The Irish Society, George Harker Esquire, Deputy Governor, and to Mr Kirk, the local M.P.

However, by September, problems arose, mainly because The Irish Society had concerns about parts of the draft Constitution for the new school. Also, the Committee was unhappy with The Irish Society's desire to introduce their own veto on some of the clauses in the Constitution. This matter had to be sorted out before further funds were made available.

A deputation from The Irish Society was actually staying in Davock's Hotel, Coleraine, on 13 September 1854, so several members of the Committee waited upon them at their meeting to: *"disabuse their minds of an erroneous impression which they have taken up with regard to the sectarian character of the Institution and to endeavour to ascertain their views upon the veto on the several clauses of the Constitution."* The 'sectarian character' of the Constitution which troubled the Irish Society was presumably clause 3, which required:
"all members of the Committee of Management, all trustees, and all teachers in the Institution to be persons holding the principles set forth in outline of Christian truth, adopted by the Evangelical Alliance."

The full details of this clause, and the rest of that original Constitution will be shown in the next chapter.

Things did not go well for the Committee members at the Davock's Hotel meeting. At the next Committee meeting, on 18 September 1854, the motion before them was a suggestion from the Irish Society:

"That in the event of the Irish Society and the Clothworkers' Company co-jointly erecting the building, entirely at their own expense, they should retain it as their own property and be allowed a veto in the management of the Institution as regards the appointment of masters; but that the veto claimed by them should, in no instance, infringe on the Constitution already recognised and accepted by the two bodies."

Whilst favourably disposed towards this motion, especially the implication that The Irish Society and the Clothworkers' Company might erect the building 'entirely at their own expense', the Committee members felt that they could not take a mere suggestion to the existing subscribers. They needed a firm commitment from these powerful, London-based bodies and in asking The Irish Society for this they also asked for a similar decision on the Memorial presented by Mr McCarter and Dr Cavin in May last. The sense of euphoria generated by the apparently favourable response at that time had by now diminished.

Ongoing Frustrations

The present mood of disappointment and frustration was evident when the Committee next met on 14 May 1855. By then the subscribers to the building fund were getting restive and impatient; the Committee wanted to know, from The Irish Society and the Clothworkers' Company, whether or not they should go ahead and build with the funds currently raised or if any further financial help could be expected from London. The Committee members felt they were being pressurised and would therefore need an immediate reply, as H.M. Commissioners on Endowed Schools were demanding answers to certain queries about the proposed Institution.

The mood of frustration continued throughout the rest of the year 1855. The Irish Society maintained its uncompromising stand, so the Committee resolved to go ahead with the building operation, if the architect could amend his plans to fit the available finances. Mr Farrell did some further tinkering with his specifications and although the builder, Mr Kilpatrick, was asked if he could adjust his estimates accordingly, the Committee decided to put the contract out to tender again, in the hope of reducing expenditure. Most obvious throughout these proceedings were (a) the Committee's constant focus on keeping costs down and (b) the remarkable patience of both the architect and the builder.

The second advertisement for a builder resulted in three tenders: Mr Kilpatrick estimated £2,692–14s–6d with outside plastering and £2,563 without, Mr Con Dornan, on the same basis, £2,340 and £2,133 and Messrs J. Esdale and Boyd estimated £2,780 and £2,573. It was initially decided to accept the lowest tender, Mr Dornan's, subject to certain guarantees on both sides. Mr Dornan must have refused to give the necessary guarantees, for the contract was eventually awarded (again!) to the ever-faithful Mr Kilpatrick.

Meanwhile, the question of the terms of the lease of the site for the school was still unresolved and despite further correspondence between the Committee secretary, Dr McCaldin, and Mr Towse, the Clerk of the Clothworkers' Company, this remained the case at the end of 1855. The air of gloom was still present when the Committee next met on 28 February 1856. At this meeting Hugh Bellas and Archie McElwaine moved that the entire scheme be abandoned as the Clothworkers had decided in September 1855, and reaffirmed on 11 January 1856, not to grant a lease on the site on such conditions as would justify the Committee in proceeding with the undertaking. The subscribers were to be informed of this and a survey made of the Institution's financial position. The result of these drastic proposals was another appeal to the Clothworkers' Company, reiterating the views of the Coleraine Committee and their current difficulties, but containing nothing new. This appeal was met with the same response – the Committee's proposals regarding the lease were *"not in accordance with the wishes of the Company"*.

To compound the problem, on 7 November 1856 Hugh Bellas and five fellow Committee members were confronted by Charles J. Knox, local agent of the Clothworkers' Company (and also a member of the General Committee – double-jobbing existed in the 1850s as well as today!), who, through his bailiff, was demanding re-possession of the five acre site, under threat of eviction proceedings. This led to a meeting of the Committee and subscribers on 12 November, actually attended also by Charles J. Knox, who must have felt rather like Daniel in the lions' den! The meeting was indeed rather tense, but the outcome was not as catastrophic for the promoters of the new Institution as some might have feared. It was unanimously agreed that the undertaking should go forward and all present undertook to pay their subscriptions on the condition that the overall sum promised by local subscribers, £2,000, be paid. All subscribers not attending the meeting were to be contacted on their willingness to pay. At this point, Charles J. Knox, on behalf of the Clothworkers, demanded the formal surrender of the five acres. This led to a formal agreement that, if the full sum of £2,000 were not paid, the land would indeed be surrendered.

With this threat hanging over the project, things moved onwards with considerable urgency and by 26 November £1,800 had been guaranteed, exclusive of offers by Thomas Wilson Campbell, Mr Beck (Ironmongers' Company Clerk) and R.B. Towse (Clothworkers' Company Clerk) totalling £200. The target figure of £2,000 had been reached and the Committee members could therefore breathe more easily. With this more cheerful prospect, the contractor, Mr Kilpatrick, was asked (yet again!) if he could reduce his estimate and re-state his terms and conditions of work.

When the Committee next met, on 5 December 1856, with Hugh Bellas in the Chair, £2,002 had been guaranteed and the builder's estimate divided into two parts: £1,708-15s-10d for

the construction and covering of the building and the balance for the finishing. To give the builder the necessary security, the contract was signed by all present: C.J. Knox, S. Bennett, Hugh Bellas, Joseph McCarter, Alexander Cuthbert, Edward Gribbon, John Adams, H.B. Mackey, Samuel W. Knox, Thomas Bellas, James Moore, William Warke, Robert Thompson, Daniel Taylor, John Lusk, William Cavin, J.J. McCaldin. Finally, in an attempt to secure overall funding sufficient to construct the new Institution, the secretary was to write to The Irish Society asking for their promised subscription of £500, with a similar letter to the Clothworkers' Company.

By the end of 1856, the cloud of gloom and despondency was now lifting and the Committee members could have some hope that their long-cherished dream could become a reality in the not-too-distant future. On 21 January 1857, a newly appointed Building Sub-committee, with the Clothworkers' local representative Charles J. Knox in the chair, was giving the contractor, Mr Kilpatrick, the exact position on which the building was to be constructed. By 19 March, the question of the laying of a Foundation Stone had arisen and it was decided that the ceremony should be performed by none other than the Clothworkers' agent, Charles J. Knox. In addition, the Committee members, as always on the lookout for new support and funding, agreed that Hugh Anderson, agent for the Ironmongers' Company, should become a member of the Committee (which was by now really the Governing Board of the proposed Institution), on the payment of a £50 subscription. In due course, a sum of £50 was placed to the agent's credit in the Provincial Bank, Coleraine, to be paid to the Trustees when the building was deemed to be sufficiently advanced.

Foundation Day

The work of the Committee now focused on arrangements for the laying of the Foundation Stone and the date of 4 June 1857 was chosen. It was decided that the following items be placed in a sealed container within the Foundation Stone:
- A copy of the *Coleraine Chronicle*

- *The Belfast Almanac*
- The School Constitution and Rules
- A List of Subscribers and Donors
- A List of the General Committee
- A List of the Trustees
- Copies of the Grants of The Irish Society and the Clothworkers' Company
- The Names of the Architect and Builder
- One each of the several coins of the Realm

The order of procedure for the day's events would be:

1. The Committee would meet and proceed to the site.
2. Copies of the Documents to be deposited to be read by the Secretary with a Report of the Origin and Progress of the Institution.
3. The architect to exhibit the plans.
4. A portion of Scripture to be read by Rev. James A. Canning.
5. A Prayer to be offered up by Rev. Wm. Richey.
6. The Documents to be deposited and a Silver Trowel to be presented to Mr Knox.
7. Mr Knox to lay the stone and to give an Address.
8. The Chairman of the Committee to give an Address.
9. Prayer and Benediction by Rev. Joseph McDonnell.

These events certainly indicate a lengthy ceremony, with an obviously daunting task for the Secretary under item 2 of the list – one wonders if he did read *all* of the edition of the *Coleraine Chronicle* as well as the other documents! Of course due ceremony and appropriate ritual were important features of formal events in Victorian times.

The Committee decided that the Foundation Ceremony would be followed by a 'Dejeuner' (lunch) in Davock's Hotel, with the following important guests being invited: the Governor, Secretary and Agent of The Irish Society, the Master and Secretary of the Clothworkers' Company, the County Surveyor with the two County Members and the borough Members, the Bishop of Down and Connor, the Bishop of Derry, the Moderator of the General Assembly, the President of Queen's College, Belfast, the President of Faculty, Presbyterian College, the Inspector General of National Schools, and the District Inspector of National Schools.

The Dejeuner menu, as arranged with Mr Davock himself, included *"hot soup, fish and potatoes, with the remainder cold, and ale, porter and a half-bottle of wine for each guest"*. The charge was to be ten shillings and six pence each (a tidy sum in those days!) and the guests' tickets were to be paid for by the Committee members, out of their own pockets. The menu indicates something much more than the usual 'nibbles' or 'bun-feasts' accompanying similar events today and one can imagine the grimaces of perhaps some Committee members as they reluctantly plumbed the depths of 'their own pockets' to entertain the guests! One also hopes that all these distinguished personages, especially the clerical gentlemen, were able to consume their personal allocation of ale, porter and wine without in any way compromising the dignity of their offices!

At this time it was also decided that W.W. Campbell should be appointed permanent Chairman of the Committee of Management, in other words the first Chairman of the Board of Governors. The work of the General Committee continued and indeed intensified. This was a crucial time in the development of the project and the committee felt that it was time for all members to pull their weight, the attendance rate of some members being poor. On 7 May 1857, J.A. Canning presented a motion, directed at non-attending and non-contributing Committee members, to the effect that: *"the time has come when serious responsibilities are to be undertaken by members of Committee and to beg of such parties to inform the Secretary, in writing, whether they wish their names to be continued on the Committee"*. The message here was quite clear – the heat was on! Perhaps as a result, five days later a letter of resignation was received from Dr Robert Sharpe; he stated that *"on the grounds of absence from home and other reasons"* he had been unable to attend Committee meetings.

By 8 October 1857, progress on the new building had reached the stage where the architect, Isaac Farrell, could recommend that the builder, Mr Kilpatrick, should be paid the first instalment of the contract price, £569-10s-0d. The treasurer, Dr Cavin, was authorised to pay the architect's own fee of £23-19s-6d

COLERAINE ACADEMICAL INSTITUTION

The original school building 1860, from a woodcut of the time.

covering the same period. On 13 November, Thomas Bennett and Daniel Gailey were made Committee members in lieu of Dr Robert Sharpe (resigned) and A. Neill (deceased).

Another New Year arrived and by 25 January 1858, the second instalments to the architect and the builder were overdue. The Treasurer was authorised to pay whatever he could of these but it was 1 April before there was any action. By this time £400 was due but the Committee had only £354 in the coffers. So a bill for £200 was drawn on the Provincial Bank, Coleraine, and the Treasurer was instructed to overdraw and pay the debts. The problem of an overdraft, and especially the interest charged on it, remained a problem for the school for many years.

In the meantime, an urgent call had gone out to subscribers for the fourth instalment of their promised subscriptions. An interesting minor, but welcome, development at this time was the offer (immediately accepted) by the proprietor of the journal, *Architect, Engineer and Builder'* to provide a woodcut of the building, at £3. Also, the architect had recommended a 'balustrade' to run to the basement of the building, at the

cost of five shillings per foot, total cost £40. This balustrade was apparently shown on the woodcut, so it must be assumed that his recommendation was approved.

In March of 1858, the architect got authorisation to *"carry up The Observatory as laid out in his Plans"* and on 4th June persuaded the Committee that the observatory roof should be of glass and not slate. This increased the builder's price from £73-10s-0d to £85. For once, a degree of extravagance was creeping into the decisions of the Committee! The nature and location of this 'Observatory' is not clear today, but it may well have been the fourth floor room known as "The Crow's Nest" above the main hallway leading into the old boarding school. There was also agreement on the construction of an outside stair *"to communicate between the Lecture Room, and the basement Classrooms."*

Finance continued to be the main worry of the Committee, so in April, Hugh Bellas and Joseph McCarter went round a special list of subscribers (those who had not paid anything so far!) and Charles J. Knox was instructed to urge the Clothworkers to provide their long-promised £210. In June 1858, one year after the foundation stone was laid, a survey of accounts showed that the sum of £719-12s-0d was needed to complete the first part of the contract and there was very little in the kitty. Another round of begging calls had to be made. Lord Naas and the Clothworkers, amongst others, were again approached and Archie McElwaine was asked for his £50 so that his name could be entered in the Trust Deed. This Deed and legal counsel's observations on it were being considered through the offices of solicitor Samuel W. Knox.

Within the Committee itself there were more changes. Thomas Bellas and Rev. James Martin were elected members in place of W.W. Campbell (deceased) and Samuel Lawrence (resigned). Rev. William Richey was elected to represent the late W.W. Campbell as a '£50 and upward subscriber' and to exercise the vote which went with that subscription.

Arm-twisting Necessary!

When the accounts were again reviewed, it was found that the sum of £490 was available, made up of £210 from the Clothworkers' Company (at last!), £250 from the Irish Society and £100 from other subscribers, with an outstanding bill for £70. The Treasurer was instructed to pay part of the instalment now due to the builder and to issue him with a promissory note, signed by those who had guaranteed the original contract, for the balance.

In October 1858, with this worrying cash-flow problem, the Committee decided to put serious pressure on defaulters to the building fund. The secretary was instructed to write to eleven subscribers who had ignored all previous communications and to inform them that if they did not pay their promised amounts by 1 November the matter would be put into the hands of the Committee's solicitor for collection. The amounts they owed ranged from £2–10s-0d to £50. Demanding (but perhaps less threatening) letters were also sent to subscribers who had already paid something, reminding them that further instalments of their promised subscriptions were now due. Amongst those approached was no less a person than Lord Naas, for his second

instalment, and also The Irish Society, for an outstanding £250. These serious measures met with some success, with, in particular, the Secretary to The Irish Society writing to say that he had the £250 ready to be handed over on receiving a receipt. It was decided to draw up a contract with Mr Kilpatrick for the completion of the building at £953. This sum was to be guaranteed by twenty individuals at £50 each. Once again the various arm-twisting techniques of the Committee had succeeded in keeping the dream of an educational Institution alive.

Turning to more mundane practical matters, the work on the five-acre site at Ballycairn continued and the matter of sanitation was obviously viewed as important. It was decided that there should be a 'water closet' in the Headmaster's house (on the south side of the building) on the small landing above the bedroom floor. The 'soil pipe' from this water closet was to run south to the boundary ditch of the 'Commissioner's field', where it would empty into a 'cesspool' covered over with planks and earth and not requiring to be opened more than once or twice a year. The soil pipe from the 'School department and the boys' privies' was to be carried down to the north-east corner of the grounds, also terminating in a 'Tank' covered over in the same manner.

Other minor details of the construction decided upon included bells: there was to be one in the Assistant Master's bedroom, one for the hall door of the School department and no less than five in the headmaster's house – one in the parlour, one in the drawing room, one in each bedroom and one for the Hall door. These bells were not intended for signalling the end of classes, as with most schools today, but instead to summon servants from the nether regions of the building. Down in the kitchen, instead of the originally planned *"open range and hot hearth"* there was to be a *"close range (six feet) with a high pressure malleable iron boiler with steam valves and hot-water pipe carried up to a high level, the hot-water pipe to the scullery to be omitted."* One wonders what this marvellous piece of Victorian technology, with its 'malleable iron boiler' actually looked like. There was to be a serving hatch between the kitchen and the dining hall and (presumably another cost-cutting measure) 'a shelf to serve as a sideboard.' In the building, it seems that no space was wasted; in the Headmaster's house a vacant space below the stairs was to be enclosed to make a 'china cabinet', to be entered from the Headmaster's parlour.

Financial problems continued. By May 1859, the patient, amiable Mr Kilpatrick had still not been paid the first instalment on the second contract. Committee members had to sign a 'bill' (another overdraft agreement) with the Provincial Bank to get the £492-19s-3d to pay him. Although progress on the construction of the building was now well advanced, another potential problem was that the Clothworkers' Company had not as yet formally granted a lease on the school site.

Appointing A Headmaster

However, there were obviously men of great faith, determination and conviction on the Committee, for at this stage they commenced the process of appointing a Headmaster for the Institution. An advertisement was placed, three times, in the following newspapers: *Coleraine Chronicle, Belfast Whig, Derry Sentinel, Dublin Express* and *Edinburgh Witness*. 'Applications for particulars' of the position had to be with the secretary of the Committee by 1 July 1859, but there were few enquiries and indeed the process of finding a Headmaster became almost as frustrating as raising funds for the construction of the building. Further advertisements were placed in the *Coleraine Chronicle, Belfast News Letter, Derry Standard*, another Dublin paper, and the *Glasgow Courier*, with the deadline date for enquiries extended to 28 July. By 20 September, four applicants had been selected for further enquiry: Mr Ball of Rathgar, Dublin, Rev. McCorken, Stranraer, Mr O'Meara, Dublin and Mr Rodgers, Enniskillen. Dr Cavin and the secretary were authorised to visit these gentlemen and report back. They went to Dublin and Enniskillen but on 26 October noted that a visit to Stranraer was not necessary.

While this was happening, and to make clear some of the financial remunerations for the first headmaster, the following Scale of Fees for pupils was adopted by the Committee:

- First Elementary (Junior) English, including Reading, Grammar, Writing and Geography - per quarter fifteen shillings.
- Second Thorough (Senior) English, comprising Grammar, Geography, Arithmetic, History, Composition, Writing, Mathematics, Algebra and Elementary Science – per quarter £1-1s-0d.
- The above branches with Classics, the elements of Natural History, Nat. Philosophy, ancient and modern History and the use of Globes – per quarter £1-15s-0d.
- French and German – each £1-1s-0d per quarter.
- Boarding, with the highest branches of English and classical education, French, German and Drawing – per year £40.

Education at the new Institution would certainly not be free!

Presumably not fully satisfied with the four applicants so far, the post of headmaster was advertised again in the *Coleraine Chronicle, General Advertiser, Evening Mail, Belfast Morning News*, a Cork paper and the *Glasgow Herald*. The Principal of the Institution was to be offered the endowment of £100 a year besides 'other things', this being likely to "*attract eminent men to apply.*" By 2 December 1859, thirty-three applications for the post had been received, four of which were ineligible because the applicants did not have university degrees. The list of applicants was further narrowed to those with Degrees in Arts, namely Mr Young, Mr Heagle, Dr Hare, Rev. Wm. Charters, Rev. Mr Faringdon, Mr Matthews, Mr Samlilands, Mr A. McClean, Rev. McMaster, Mr T.C. Bryce, Rev. M.A. McCully, Rev. Mr Witherow, Mr Hall and Mr Daly. The Committee eventually selected a short list of three – Mr Young, Mr Heagle and Rev. McCully.

The Committee would meet on 20 December 1859, at twelve noon in the Commissioners' Room in the Town Hall, for the 'Election' of a Headmaster. The Secretary was to write to the three candidates, telling them that their expenses for attendance would not be paid by the Committee. It was further decided that the scale of fees already proposed should stand, subject to the approval of the selected Principal. Also, after the deduction of whatever percentage might be necessary for the incidental expenses of the Institution, the remainder of the fees raised should go to the Principal, who would choose and pay his own Assistants, subject to the approval of the Committee. This financial package, giving the Principal considerable access to the funds coming into the school, certainly seemed attractive.

The final arrangements for the Election were made on Monday 19 December 1859, by a small sub-committee consisting of Rev. J.A. Canning, Joseph McCarter, Hugh Bellas, Thomas Bellas, Dr Cavin and the Secretary, Dr McCaldin. Each candidate would be interviewed separately and asked the following questions:

1. *What experience have you had in teaching and in what branches?*
2. *How are you at present occupied?*
3. *Are you aware of the position and responsibilities of the Principalship?*
4. *How would you organise the school both as regards classes and masters?*
5. *Have you read the Constitution and are you prepared to subscribe it?*
6. *In what relation would the Masters stand to each other?*
7. *What length of time would the School occupy?*
8. *How would you occupy the time out of School of the Boarders?*
9. *How would you provide for the matroning of the establishment?*

It would also be made clear that the only servant to be paid for by the Committee would be the Porter. Finally, the sub-committee decided that the election would be by 'Leet', meaning that committee members would vote, *viva voce,* for the candidate of their choice at the end of the interviews, with the one having the fewest votes being struck off and a vote being taken again for the remaining two.

At the meeting on 20 December, the General Committee, with £50 subscribers to the original £1,500, met in the Town Hall, with Thomas Bennett in the Chair. With him were the Revs. Wm. Richey, James A. Canning and George Vance and Messrs. H.B. Mackey, Thomas Bellas, Hugh Bellas, Wm. Young, Joseph McCarter, Samuel W. Knox, Henry Kyle, Dr Willam Cavin and the secretary. They began by turning down an application from Mr Gowdy, the headmaster of another school in the town (known locally as 'Gowdy's Academy') because it was 'informal' and so could not be received. They went on to look at the scale of fees and increased the Junior English from fifteen shillings to £1, Senior English to £1-10s-0d and highest Classical to £2. French, German and Drawing would be extras at £1-1s-0d each. The rate for Boarders would remain at £40. The right to admit pupils to the school would be left to the Principal, to whom all applications would be made, and he would report on all cases to the relevant Committee meeting.

At the conclusion of the interviews and the voting, Mr Alex Waugh Young, B.A., Andrews Scholar of University College, London, was elected the first Principal of Coleraine Academical Institution, by a large majority. Mr Young was a Londoner and had been educated at the City of London School. He came from a clerical background, his father being a Scottish theologian celebrated for his religious writings, one of which was "The Christ of History", and his grandfather, Rev. Dr Alexander Waugh, being one of the founders of the London Missionary Society. The school's first Principal was an excellent Classical scholar and an example of his skills can be seen in his detailed contribution to *'The Classical Review'* in 1905.

Mr Young always insisted on being referred to officially as Alex Waugh Young, the inclusion of his middle name being a personal tribute to his grandfather. As a matter of interest, in recent correspondence with Mrs Angeline Phillips (nee Young), Mr Young's great-great-grand-daughter, it has been discovered that he was related to the celebrated novelist, Evelyn Waugh, (of *'Brideshead Revisited'* fame): A.W. Young's grandfather, the Reverend Alexander Waugh, was also the great-great-grandfather of Evelyn Waugh.

Following the 'Election' of the Principal, and overturning their previous decision, the Committee paid the expenses of the two unsuccessful candidates, out of their own pockets - £3 to Mr Heagle and £2 to Rev. McCully. At the conclusion of the meeting, they agreed that the outstanding debt of £1,200, to pay off the builder and the architect, should be honoured by the Committee, on their personal security, by a bill of overdraft at 4% interest.

The Headmaster Commences Work

Mr Young wasted no time in taking up his responsibilities; just two days later, on 22 December 1859, he had his first meeting with the Managing Committee. This meeting focused especially on the provision of equipment for the new school but also dealt with a number of other practical matters. Desks were to be ordered, having cast iron feet and wooden tops divided into compartments, as were wooden forms (benches), again with iron feet, both desks and forms to be screwed to the floor. No messing about with the desks, at least, in the classrooms of the Inst! Also to be ordered were: a pair of globes, a set of 'Keith Johnston maps' with rollers and stand, a large black slate in a frame, to move on pivots at the side and to be used with chalk, for each classroom, and a Master's desk or table.

In the Boarding department, the dormitories should be divided into compartments capable of holding three beds, and a washing stand for each boy. The beds were to be of iron (as indeed some still were up to the 1980s!) with *"hair and seaweed mattresses"*, pillows and quilts. Each boarder should bring a silver spoon and fork (why not a knife?), six towels, two pairs of sheets and a pair of light shoes or slippers. The Committee would provide fuel for the dormitories and schoolrooms, but the Principal would provide the fuel for his own residence and kitchen.

Regarding the Principal's role in managing the financial affairs of the new school, the Committee agreed to guarantee him the board and salary of an Assistant, say £30 for board and at least £60 for salary. Mr Young was to select and pay his Assistants, subject to the ever-watchful Committee's approval. On the matter of giving notice, the contract between the Committee and the Principal could be terminated at any time, providing either party gave six months notice from the commencement of a school term.

The secretary of the Committee was instructed to advertise immediately for Masters in French, German and Drawing and to obtain copies of the prospectuses of various schools in Ireland, for Mr Young's information in preparing a prospectus for the Institution. This prospectus was to be issued not later than February 1860, so that the School could advertise for pupils in several provincial newspapers.

The general Committee was very busy at this time, in order to meet the deadline for the opening of the school, later in the year. In January, the Committee met five times. Amongst other items, they finally agreed on school holidays, which would be *"5 weeks at Midsummer and 3 weeks at Christmas"*. The Boarding fee was revised from £40 to 40 guineas, this figure to *"include washing"* and any boys under twelve were to be charged 39 guineas. A Mr V.H. Rylski of Belfast was appointed as teacher of French and German but the Committee would not pay any part of his travelling expenses.

Various members of the Committee made visits to the school to arrange the number and size of the desks, the furnishing of dormitories, dining hall, etc, and Mr Kilpatrick was asked for an estimate for the provision of school desks, Form Master's desk, cap rack, slate and stand, two kitchen tables, a laundry table, a long dining table with forms to match, and a side table. After some preliminary skirmishing with the Committee, Mr Kilpatrick agreed to do all this for £66.

The commitment of some Committee members and subscribers was still giving cause for concern and there were meetings, *"to consider the propriety and best mode of purging the Committee of members who would neither attend meetings nor bear any share of the liabilities."* Accordingly, D. Gailey and A. McElwaine were confronted by Hugh Bellas and Joseph McCarter about their outstanding subscriptions, if Mr Gailey wished to remain on the Committee and Mr McElwaine as a Trustee. The results of this 'confrontation' were favourable, because both gentlemen appear on the final list of subscribers to the fund.

There was a suggestion from the Principal at this stage that the Junior English class should be abolished in favour of one English class, at £1-10s-0d per quarter. This was due to a misapprehension on Mr Young's part, that a much younger age group would be admitted. The Committee firmly pointed out that, *"the School was not intended for pupils under 8 or 9 years who may not have learned the elements of English and are unable to read or write a little."* Obviously, the Principal did not have everything his own way and his suggestions, quite rightly, were subject to the approval of the Committee. On 23 January 1860, the Committee considered an application for the post of Drawing Master from a Mr Croome of Belfast, who boldly proposed one lesson daily at the rate of £1 and travelling expenses. He was told that the Committee would not give any guarantees and that he would have to take his chances, based on the fees of the pupils admitted.

Also at that meeting, Dr Cavin said he intended to propose that, *"the sanitary condition of the Institution and the intended arrangement of the grounds be taken into consideration."* This matter was discussed at the next meeting, on Thursday 26 January, when the committee decided not to alter the present arrangements for water closets and drains. At a later meeting of 9 February 1860, when the architect produced his plans for the laying out of the grounds, flushing water closets, privies, urinals and the carrying away of sewage into a tank or large cesspool for the collection of 'night soil', these plans were approved despite an amendment proposed by Dr Cavin and Mr Rowan.

At this stage the construction of the school building was complete and the time had come for the final settlement of outstanding bills. The architect, Mr Isaac Farrell, had already certified that the builder, Mr Kilpatrick, had completed his contract satisfactorily. At a meeting on 16 February 1860, the Committee found that the final account worked out as follows:

Amount of contract	£2,652-14s-6d
For extra items	£229-9s-0d
Total	£2,873-3s-6d

(Incorrect! Should be £2,882-3s-6d.)

Already received	£2,180-15s-3d
Balance due	£694-8s-3d

(Again, incorrect! £692 not £694)

Less credit for iron bars on basement windows omitted	£24-0s-0d
Final Balance	£670-8s-3d

Obviously, the sooner the school started teaching the young people of Coleraine some basic Mathematics the better!

In addition there was Mr Farrell's account, which amounted to £58-6s-4d. Although there was no quibbling over the amount due to the builder, the Committee had some concern about the architect's bill and the secretary was instructed to refer to previous correspondence and the subject of superintendence and fees. This resulted in a letter to Mr Farrell to the effect that the Committee, *"did not consider his claim tenable, inasmuch as the second plans etc, for which he charged, were prepared in consequence of his first plans, for which he was paid, so far exceeding the sum of £2000, for which expenditure he assured the Committee, his plans could be built."* In August 1860, Mr Farrell's account was finally settled for £19. As always, the Committee drove a hard bargain. As for the builder, he received £500 in February and the outstanding balance in the middle of April 1860. At last, the building was completed and paid for, it had a Headmaster, and would soon receive its first pupils.

A few more practical matters remained, with finance still to the fore. In late February, the treasurer reported that £400 had been procured from Mr Sam W. Knox at 5% on a promissory note signed by Messrs. Hugh and Thomas Bellas, Dr Cavin, Joseph McCarter and Rev. Joseph McDonnell. Another £500 came from Mr H. Bellas of Portstewart, formerly of Liswatty, at 5%, this on a note to be signed by eleven or more of the Committee. The Provincial Bank had been paid the £489-8s-9d plus the £2-2s-10d owed and the Committee was now in credit with the Bank to the extent of £550-18s-11d. Once again, it is remarkable how many men on the Committee were prepared to take risks with their own money to ensure that the Institution was a success.

It was decided to have the school grounds drained and on 15 March arrangements were made with Mr William Bamford for the fencing of the site at 2s-9d per statute perch. The ditch, on Mr Bamford's suggestion, was to be four feet six inches high by five feet at the base, with the 'quicks' (hawthorn seedlings) to be *"laid on the sheer sod with a sod on top"*, the ditch to be altogether clay without stones. At the last minute, a clock was ordered for the Entrance Hall of the school. More importantly, on 13 March, the all-important Lease on the site, if only in draft form, arrived from the Clothworkers' Company, so the Committee could afford to breathe a sigh of relief. The Clothworkers eventually granted a lease of 999 years and founded a Scholarship of £50 a year for the benefit of the school. (This Scholarship, the top prize for academic achievement in the school, was replaced in 2007 by The Irish Society's Prize, already referred to.)

A month later, on 12 April, the Chairman of the day, Hugh Bellas, led the Committee members up the New Line to meet Mr Kilpatrick at the splendid new building, there to formally receive from him the key of the Institution. This was handed over to the secretary, Dr J.J. McCaldin, and a well-earned vote of thanks was passed to Mr Kilpatrick for the very satisfactory way in which he had completed his contract and in every way met the wishes of the Committee. Having been asked previously to estimate for the cess tank, stone steps, a weather vane and compass points, Mr Kilpatrick offered to make these and not to ask for payment for two years. This offer was eagerly accepted. The entrance roads and terraces were already contracted for with Mr David Kennedy, to Mr Kilpatrick's specifications. It was decided that the building should be insured for £2,000 and estimates were sought from The Sun Globe, Atlas and Liverpool and London insurance companies.

On Thursday 27 April 1860, the General or Managing Committee met for the first time in the Academical Institution itself. Present were: Rev. William Richey in the Chair, Rev. George Vance, Rev. James A. Canning, Rev. Joseph McDonnell, Messrs. Archie McElwaine, Hugh Bellas, Joseph McCarter, Dr William Cavin and Dr McCaldin, the secretary. There were few matters on the agenda; it was decided to advertise for a Porter, salary ten shillings weekly and a 'suit of livery', and to pay an outstanding account for advertising from the *Derry Sentinel*. Most importantly, all members of the Committee who could possibly attend were urged to meet on 1 May 1860, to open the new school for business.

Earlier, a notice in the *Coleraine Chronicle*, informing the public of this occasion, had stated, *"The Institution has been founded for the purpose of furnishing a thorough Classical and English Education in all their respective branches, or for competition for appointments in the Civil Service at home or abroad. The locality is very healthy; and the building, with an extensive playground, is beautifully situated on an eminence convenient to the town, and within 4 miles of the most picturesque part of the northern coast. The internal accommodation and the domestic arrangements are on the newest and most approved plan, and have been made with a view to secure the health and comfort of the pupils. Their religious and moral education will be carefully attended to, though the committee are strongly of opinion that the deepest religious feeling is the result of home influence."*

Opening The New School

On that long-awaited day, formal proceedings opened with a scripture reading by Rev. William Richey and a prayer by Rev. J. Canning. They were listened to by Rev. Mooney, Rev. John Kydd, Messrs. Hugh and Thomas Bellas, Dr William Cavin and Dr J.J. McCaldin, along with the Headmaster, Mr Alex. Waugh Young, Mr Taylor, the resident English Assistant Master, Mr Rylski, the French and German Master, and fourteen pupils. The *Chronicle* report of the event commented that, *"The appearance of the airy and admirably-lighted schoolrooms, with well arranged desks* (screwed to the floor, of course!) *and pupils in their neat clothes, was very cheering."* It was a low-key event for such a momentous occasion but a much more glittering ceremony was planned for the official opening of Coleraine Academical Institution later in the year. The secretary stated that the 'ceremonial inauguration' would take place at the end of the summer vacation and that the committee intended to 'make this as impressive as possible.' The secretary also stated, *"In reply to many enquiries, as there will be now only two months until the summer vacation, the Committee has determined not to charge for a full quarter."*

Perhaps the most important people attending that initial opening, although perhaps feeling rather shy in the presence of all the reverend gentlemen and the Headmaster himself, were the fourteen pupils present. They were the privileged first of many thousands of pupils to receive their education at 'the school on the hill'; the school had been built for them and succeeding generations, and no doubt they were aware of the importance of the occasion which they were attending. Rather than allow those first pupils to remain anonymous, it is important to try to identify them. Thirteen pupils had been formally enrolled in the new school on 26 March 1860, so it is reasonable to assume that they were all present at the official opening, plus one other. From the sources at hand, those pupils included:

George Bellas, Cronbannagh Cottage
Hugh Bellas, Cronbannagh Cottage
Thomas H. Bellas, Cronbannagh Cottage
Fr. Wilson Kilpatrick, Meetinghouse Place
Andrew McCaldin
Thomas McCaldin
George McCarter
John McCarter
Robert Moore, Priestland
Bobbie Neill
Thomas Craig Smith, Castlerock
Bennett Thompson, the Diamond
James A. Young, Meetinghouse Street

It is interesting to note the surnames here for another reason: in the cases of more than half of them, their fathers or uncles were long-serving members of the Committee. For those hard-working, generous and public-spirited Committee members, there was also a private incentive in ensuring that the new school was finally completed and in operation – their own sons or nephews were to be amongst the first pupils.

Contributions To The Building Fund

Before bringing the first chapter of this history to a conclusion, it might be important, for the record, to see exactly how the funds for the Institution were raised. This is a list of all the subscribers, whose generosity made the creation of C.A.I. possible:

£1,000 – The Honourable The Irish Society of London, with an endowment of £100 annually.

£910 – The Worshipful Company of Clothworkers of London, with a grant of Five Acres of land, rent free in perpetuity.

£150 – Thomas Bennett; Messrs. H. & T. Bellas.

£100 – The Worshipful Company of Ironmongers; William Wilson Campbell; William Cavin, M.D.; James Moore.

£75 – Joseph McCarter.

£60 – Archibald McElwaine.

£50 – Henry Kyle; J.J. McCaldin, M.D.; H.B. Mackey; Charles James Knox; R.B. Touse; Rev. James Canning; Daniel Gailey; S.W. Knox; Curtis Hemphill; Rev. John Martin; William Warke; Alexander Barklie; Miss Cochrane; Alexander Cuthbert; Rev. William Richey; John Adams; Mrs F. Bennett; Joseph Cuthbert; Sir H.H. Bruce, Bart, M.P.; A.W. Young; William Robb; Mrs McNaghten.

£30 – David R. Taylor; John Lusk; J.C.L Carson, M.D.

£25 – The Worshipful Company of Fishmongers; Messrs. D. & R. Taylor; John Cromie, M.P., D.L.

£20 – Robert Thompson; Lord Naas.

£15 – James Lyle; Robert Nevin.

£12-10s-0d – Rev. John Kydd.

£10 – Alexander Anderson; Rev.
John Alexander; Dr Clarke; John Getty;
Rev. Joseph McDonnell; James Robinson;
Edward Gribben; William Galt (Gault??);
Hugh Bellas, Liswatty;
Messrs. S. & R. Given; John McCurdy;
Messrs. J. & R. Wilson, Londonderry;
James Boyce; John Huey;
Sir F.W. Heygate, Bart, M.P.

£5-5s-0d – Timothy Tyrrel, London;
George Virtue, London.

£5 – Robert Small; Thomas Hyndman;
Thomas Gordon; Messrs. J. & J. Matthews,
John Horner; David Kennedy;
Martin Cathcart; A.J.H. Moody;
James Low, London; James Thomas;
John Taggart; William Moore;
John Canning; 'A Friend to Education';
Rev. Hugh Hamill; Samuel Kilpatrick;
Baron Martin.

£4 – Arthur Curry.

£2-10s-0d – Thomas Henry.

£2 – Adam Lyons; John McAfee;
Samuel Wallace; J.T. Byron.

£1 – Alex Maddison.

This list shows that the Irish Society and
several other London Companies contributed
£2,035 of the total subscribed and the local
people some £2,306.

The Academical Institution, Coleraine, had
been a difficult fourteen years in the making
but it was now complete, appropriately
furnished, officially opened, and it had its
first Headmaster, Assistant Masters and
scholars. In those very early days, with just
fourteen pupils, the pupil/teacher ratio was
pleasantly low; the next chapters will reveal
how the school rapidly expanded and became
the highly successful academic establishment
which it remains today.

Chapter 2

The First Decade 1860 - 1870

Alexander Waugh Young, B.A., Headmaster

As was seen in the previous chapter, Coleraine Academical Institution was opened for business on 1 May 1860 and lessons continued during May and June of that year. The promised 'ceremonial inauguration' was to be at 'the end of the summer vacation' and it duly took place on 23 July 1860. It proved to be the most glittering occasion on the Coleraine social scene for many years and the accounts of it in the local press give an interesting insight into not only perceptions of the new school but also the 'high society' of Coleraine (and further afield) in the mid Victorian period.

The proceedings of 23 July were reported in considerable detail in the *Coleraine Chronicle* issue of that week:

"After almost unparalleled exertions and many disappointments, the labours of the Committee of this educational establishment have been crowned with success. On Monday last, the inaugural ceremony took place in an apartment of the Institution, which, as the day was exceedingly favourable, was crowded with visitors. The building itself, as stated in the secretary's report, is rather more useful than ornamental, though its commanding situation and graceful proportions present some features of the picturesque.
At all events, the lack of external architectural beauty and finish is amply compensated for by appropriate internal accommodation. The Institution is intended to accommodate about 40 boarders and as many as 150 day-pupils, and we can testify that the schoolrooms are exactly suited to the purpose for which they are intended. The Principal of the Institution has apartments in the southern wing of the building, which also contains the kitchen, pantries etc., required for boarders. The middle and northern portions are devoted to the educational uses of the Institution. This is surrounded with five acres of the best land – the gift of the Worshipful Company of Clothworkers – which it is intended to lay out in ornamental patches and shrubs etc. This, of course, has not yet been accomplished, but will add greatly to the rare beauty of the location when completed."

The report also added that *"the National Model School of the district, which is an admirably conducted establishment and well attended – the site for which was also the gift of the Clothworkers' Company – is within a short distance of the Institution, both buildings constituting a very interesting group."* The old Model School was, as most readers will know, just across the New Line (the present Castlerock Road) from the Institution and, as described in a later chapter, it was eventually incorporated into the Institution campus, providing much-needed classrooms and dormitories for later generations of pupils.

The Inauguration Of The School

The great day of the inauguration began with an inspection of the *"spacious schoolrooms, dormitories and other parts of the building."* When the formal part of the ceremony commenced, the large room on the second floor *"was crowded by a highly respected assemblage."* Amongst those worthies present, the *Coleraine Chronicle* report noted: "Charles J. Bloxam, Master of the Worshipful Company of Clothworkers; Sir John Musgave, Bart., Chairman of the Clothworkers' Company; Mr Chattres, Master of the Merchant Tailors' Company; Mr Allen; Mr Davis; Mr Porter, Surveyor; Mr Towse, Clerk of the Clothworkers' Company; John Alexander, High Sheriff for Co. Derry; John Boyd, J.P., M.P. for Coleraine; Edmond Stronge, J.P., Agent to the Worshipful Company of Clothworkers; Henry Anderson, J.P., Agent to the Worshipful Company of Ironmongers; William Green, Agent to The Honourable The Irish Society; S.M. Greer, ex-M.P.; Henry Kyle, J.P and Master Kyle; William Warke, J.P.; Counsellor Gibson, Belfast; Rev. James Smith, Archdeacon of Connor; Rev. Dr Brown, Aghadowey; Rev. Mr Dill, Ballymena, Moderator of the General Assembly; Rev. Dr Denham, Derry; Rev. Dr Boaz, Missionary from India; Rev. J.A. Canning and Masters John, Alfred and the Misses Canning, Coleraine; Rev. R. Parke, A.M., Ballymoney; Rev. Richard Smith,

A.M., Derry; Rev. Joseph McDonnell, Coleraine; Rev. John Martin, Camus; Rev. William McClure, Derry; Rev. George Vance, Wesleyan minister, Coleraine; Rev. T.P. Mooney, curate, Coleraine; Rev. Dr W. Young and Miss Young, London; Rev. John Kydd and Mrs Kydd, Coleraine; Rev. John Stewart, Portstewart; Rev. Wm. Stewart, Whins; Rev. John Hart, Ballylagan; Rev. L.A. Lyle, Dunboe; Miss Bloxam, London: John Givin and Mrs Givin; John McFarland and Mrs McFarland, Coleraine; Miss Jeffries, Dublin; Daniel Taylor, Coleraine; J.H. Macaulay and Mrs Macaulay; Hugh Bellas, Tom Bellas, Mrs Bellas and family, Coleraine; W. Alexander, Derry; Captain McBride, Portstewart; Mr Green, Derry; A. McElwaine, Mrs McElwaine and Miss McElwaine; Joseph McCarter and Masters McCarter; P.D. Grant and Mrs Grant; Mr and Mrs McCombie, Coleraine; Miss Gilmour, Liverpool; James McCardie, Birmingham; Hamie Smith, the Lodge; James Moore, Coleraine; James Thompson, Edward Thompson and Miss Thompson, Coleraine; Miss Leath, London; Miss McCaldin; Wm. Young, John Young, Mrs Young and family; Joseph Cuthbert and Mrs Cuthbert; Mrs Hyndman; James McCurdy; John Matthews; the Misses Caldwell; Hugh Lyle; Mrs Horner; Miss Carson; Charles Morris, Model School, Coleraine; Thomas Forsythe, Macosquin; Thomas Nevin; Wm. Kirkpatrick, Coleraine, etc."

Presumably the others present on that occasion, lumped together anonymously under the dismissive term 'etc.', were considered as unworthy of individual mention. Such was the nature of Victorian society!

On the motion of Rev. J.A. Canning, Charles J. Bloxam, no doubt resplendent in his robes and regalia of office as Master of the Worshipful Company of Clothworkers, took the chair for the occasion. He requested the Reverend T.P. Mooney, in the absence of the Archdeacon of Connor, who was late in arriving (tut,tut!), to read a portion of Scripture, which he did, from the *Book of Proverbs*, third chapter. Rev. Mr Dill, Moderator of the General Assembly, then *"engaged in prayer"*, following which the secretary of the Committee, Dr J.J.

McCaldin, read a detailed report of how the new Institution had come about.

Disregarding The Irish Society's earlier concerns about, as they saw it, the 'sectarian nature' of some parts of the Constitution, Dr McCaldin outlined how in 1846 *"a committee was appointed, composed of the leading men of every Protestant sect, with the clergymen of every evangelical denomination officiating in the borough as ex-officio members, to establish, on a permanent footing, a first-class school."* The precise nature of the term *"evangelical denomination"* was spelled out very clearly in the original 'Constitution' of the school, presented in full very shortly. To those of the more liberal and secular views typical of the 21st century, such clauses no doubt do seem 'sectarian'; however, in 1860, attitudes in a small town in a remote corner of the north of Ireland were different.

In his report, Dr McCaldin next mentioned how, just as the original Committee was commencing its business, *"progress was arrested by famine and pestilence"* – the 'Great Hunger', or Irish Famine, of the 1840s. Dr McCaldin continued: *"We have sometimes been criticised for want of architectural taste in the external features of the building. To this we can only reply that our means would not afford both internal accommodation and external ornamentation. We preferred the former as infinitely the more important, leaving the latter to be carried out at some future time; and the style of the building, arrangement of cornices and projections will render this an easy matter, whenever the liberality of the public or the generosity of our patrons enable us to do so."*

Dr McCaldin, on behalf of the Committee, was not making any apology for the functional and practical nature of the external appearance of the building (the lack of 'external ornamentation'), although the 1860 woodcut (referred to in the previous chapter and shown elsewhere in this book) reflects a building of pleasingly clean lines and sound architectural balance. At present, the '1860s building' as it is now known, still the central core of the school campus, is actually a Listed Building, under Department of the Environment regulations, giving it the status of a building of special architectural interest. The architectural

20

experts of today obviously do not agree with Dr McCaldin's modest appraisal of that original building at the official inauguration in 1860.

Dr McCaldin, in his report, also referred to the curriculum which would be taught in the new Institution. *"The course of education,"* he said, *"as will be seen by the prospectus in your hands, is very extended, embracing from junior English, or that which a boy of eight years is fitted to learn, to the higher branches of classics and science. We are expected to fit a boy to take his place at the highest competitive examinations; also, for the business of the counting house, or for entering college with honours; and we trust the expectations formed by us will not be disappointed."* It is interesting to note here that one of the expectations of the Committee, comprised mainly of leading businessmen in the town, was that some of the pupils, including no doubt their own sons, would become qualified for *"the business of the counting house"*, in other words to be accountants or business managers, often in a family firm.

With a touch of envy of the already established schools in the northern province, Dr McCaldin went on to explain that: *"To enable us to compete with our rivals of Portora, Dungannon and Armagh, basking in the sunshine of royal endowments, we will require aid in the shape of scholarships; these will at once test the proficiency of the pupil and attract numbers to compete. While the Institution, to succeed, must be self-supporting, yet, at the same time, aid in the form of bursaries and scholarships affords the very highest stimulus to exertion, and rewards the meritorious pupil in the way most gratifying to his feelings and most conducive to the success of his future career."* Sadly, Coleraine Academical Institution has not as yet received a 'royal endowment' to elevate it to the envied status of the 'rivals' quoted here; but over the last 150 years many organisations and philanthropic individuals have responded to Dr McCaldin's appeal here, and have provided bursaries or annual prizes as stimuli to the 'exertion' of pupils.

In concluding, Dr McCaldin presented the new school as very much a pace-setter for educational advancement throughout the rest of Ireland. He thanked The Irish Society and the Clothworkers' Company for their generous financial support for *"this first attempt to provide for the neighbourhood of Coleraine a seminary which, we trust, under the Divine blessing and direction, will be eminently distinguished for the amount of benefit it will confer on the community, and whose example thus set for the advance of intermediate education it is hoped other districts in Ireland may be induced to follow."*

The Original "Constitution"

Note here Dr McCaldin's description of the new school as a 'seminary', which implied that it was to be an establishment where religious, moral and spiritual guidance was viewed as important. This aspect of the school's ethos is reflected in the third clause of the original Constitution of the new school, quoted in full below. To those who might be curious about the amount of detail spelled out in this Clause, it is worth remembering that the school was officially opened in 1860, just a few months after the great religious Revival of 1859, when no doubt many of the ex-officio clergymen on the Committee, and at least some of the other members, might still be fuelled by the evangelical fervour of those times.

The Constitution and Rules of the Coleraine Academical Institution (1860)

1st – All the property of the Institution to be vested in not fewer than six, nor more than eight, trustees.

2nd – The general management of the whole establishment to be under the control of the committee appointed at the town meeting, held in the year 1846.

3rd – All members of the Committee of Management, all trustees, and all teachers in the Institution to be persons holding the principles set forth in outline of Christian truth, adopted by the Evangelical Alliance, which are:

1. *The Divine inspiration, authority, and sufficiency of the Holy Scriptures.*
2. *The right and duty of private judgement in the interpretation of the Holy Scriptures.*
3. *The Unity of the Godhead, and the Trinity of Persons therein.*
4. *The utter depravity of human nature in consequence of the fall.*
5. *The incarnation of the Son of God, His work*

of atonement for sinners of mankind, and His mediatorial intercession and reign.

6. The justification of the sinner by faith alone.

7. The work of the Holy Spirit in the conversion and sanctification of the sinner.

8. The immortality of the soul, the resurrection of the body, the judgement of the world by our Lord Jesus Christ, with the eternal blessedness of the righteous and the eternal punishment of the wicked.

9. The Divine Institution of the Christian ministry, and the obligation and perpetuity of the ordinances of Baptism and the Lord's Supper.

4th – In the erection of the buildings: in the filling up of vacancies occurring from time to time in the Committee: in the appointment of Trustees, and in the election of teachers, subscribers of £50 and upwards (or their representatives) towards the original fund of £1500, required to be raised by The Honourable The Irish Society, shall have, subject to all other regulations, the right of one vote and other privilege or right enjoyed by them in connection with the Institution.

5th – The teachers to consist of a Principal having a degree in Arts, and qualified to superintend all the branches of education imparted in the Institution, and at least two assistants – one in the classical, and one in the English and mercantile department; and, in addition, the necessary masters for foreign languages, music, drawing etc.

6th – The course of education to embrace classics, mathematics and algebra, arithmetic, the elements of natural philosophy, and natural history, ancient and modern history, geography, and use of the globes, writing, and everything included in the general designation of a complete English and mercantile education; and, at the same time, provision made for acquiring a knowledge of modern continental languages, music, drawing and gymnastics. Such an education, in short, as will prepare the pupil either for entering any of the Protestant Universities, or Queen's Colleges, or the merchant's or banker's office.

7th – Each contributor of £50 to the funds of the Institution to have the privilege of presenting one free day pupil for seven years (the average length of the whole course of instruction), and so on in the same proportion up to £400, which sum to give the right of one free day pupil in perpetuo.

8th – The School to be opened and closed each day with reading of portion of Scriptures, and with Prayer.

9th – Whilst details are still open for consideration, the above are the principles upon which the Committee have determined that the Institution shall be based, and from which there shall in future be no departure.

William Cavin, Chairman; J.J. McCaldin, Secretary

There are many interesting features of this first Constitution, not least the third clause, which required *"all members of the Committee of Management, all trustees, and all teachers in the Institution"* to hold the nine precisely detailed principles of the 'Evangelical Alliance'. One wonders how closely those first Assistant Masters were questioned at their interviews regarding their religious affiliation or principles. Earlier, as seen in the previous chapter, the members of The Irish Society had been troubled by this clause which they saw as 'sectarian', but Dr McCaldin in his report at the Inauguration seemed to go out of his way to play down the significance of the clause. He publicly explained that, *"those who framed the Constitution had no intention of making the Institution in the slightest degree sectarian, as none of those who exercised control in it would be allowed to interfere with the religious scruples of any pupil taking advantage of the education it was intended to provide."* He did not make clear exactly who would not allow such interference!

Another interesting aspect of the Constitution is the stipulation that each subscriber of £50 would have the right to present *"one free day pupil for seven years."* Those long-serving, patient, and hard-working Committee members who had young sons in their families had a further incentive for their efforts. Sound businessmen, in 1860s Coleraine or elsewhere, of course had an eye out for a bargain!

The conclusion of the Constitution solemnly states that *"there shall in future be no departure"* from the principles laid down in its clauses. The school's Constitution has in fact developed considerably over the years and the current 'Scheme of Management,' as it is now called, is a much lengthier and more detailed document than this first attempt. However, in line with the general 'principles' laid down in the original Constitution, the school still maintains (as do most other schools) its own distinct moral and spiritual ethos – although no member of the school community is now expected to subscribe to the requirements of the Evangelical Alliance!

Following Dr McCaldin's report, Dr William Cavin, honorary treasurer of the building fund, presented a brief statement of accounts showing that the cost of building and equipping the Institution was £3,895. Many speeches followed, including one by Sir John Musgrave, Bart., chairman of the Clothworkers' Company.

Social Events On Inauguration Day

The newspaper report of the day's proceedings also gave details of the 'Dejeuner' which followed the inauguration ceremony. This event took place at 3 p.m. in The Clothworkers' Arms, where about fifty invited guests, *"sat down to one of the most recherché banquets we have ever seen provided in this establishment, famous for the quality of its cuisine, and the mode in which public entertainments are got up."* For those who are unfamiliar with the jargon of Victorian social occasions, 'recherché' means that the menu at this banquet was specially selected, indeed exotic. Presiding at the Dejeuner was Mr John Boyd, M.P. for Coleraine.

Further celebrations, in the form of a 'Conversazione', (a meeting for conversation, especially on learned subjects) took place at eight o'clock that evening in the Town Hall. The *Chronicle* report states that this part of the day's proceedings was *"most anxiously looked forward to by the more youthful portion of the community."* This Conversazione was again a glittering occasion on the Coleraine social scene, and it was described in glowing terms in the newspaper report: *"The magnificent hall of the building presented an array of beauty, fashion, and real enjoyment which we can never hope to see surpassed in Coleraine. For several days previously, all who had anything in the departments of art and science worthy of inspection in the town, or within the circle of the indefatigable secretary's acquaintance,*

were laid under contribution, until the hall, on the night of the entertainment, presented the appearance of a modern museum, or an exhibition of painting, statuary, and recent inventions in scientific studies."

At the end of the summer vacation of 1860, with the high excitement of Inauguration, Dejeuner and Conversazione now all over, the school re-opened and Mr Young and his Assistants continued with the task of educating the boys of Coleraine, and of course the boarders, who came from further afield. An interesting development at this time was the retirement of Mr Gowdy, principal of the old Coleraine Academy ('Gowdy's Academy'), and the closure of his school, which resulted in an increase in the number of pupils attending the new Institution. Two new teachers were appointed to help cope with this influx.

In the advertisements which appeared in the *Coleraine Chronicle* after the official inauguration of the school in July 1860, the scale of fees quoted for day boys ranged from £4 a year in the junior school, to £8 in the upper school. The fees in the junior school covered the teaching of reading, writing and arithmetic; in the senior school, where the fees were £6 a year, the course consisted of reading, grammar, composition, writing, book-keeping, arithmetic, geography and history, with elementary classics or mathematics. In the upper school, the course embraced Latin and Greek, geometry, algebra, natural philosophy, ancient and modern history, logic etc. Boarders paid fees of forty guineas and thirty-five guineas (for those under twelve) per annum for board, tuition, laundry and stationery, and all pupils paid one guinea extra for each of the subjects French, German, music, drawing and gymnastics, each year. One guinea a year was also charged to each boarder in respect of medical services.

The first annual distribution of prizes took place on 24 January 1861. Mr Young reported that the number of pupils was now thirty-two, of whom nine were boarders. He mentioned Edward Thompson as the first pupil to bring distinction to the School by passing, with great credit, the Blackstone Examination at Glasgow University. In his speech, Mr Young also referred to the *"great progress in*

Classics at the Institution", expressed his opinion that he *"had found Irish boys to possess little aptitude for Mathematics"*, but declared that he *"had no intention of allowing Classics to exclude Mathematics."* In a moment of wildly wishful thinking he also said he was glad to report that, *"the old-fashioned idea of masters and boys forming opposing parties had disappeared."*

By 3 April 1861, the end of the first school year, the number of pupils enrolled had increased to fifty-one. For the benefit of readers who may be searching for a mention of their ancestors, these pupils were: Hugh Bellas, Thomas Bellas, James Canning, Thomas Carson, Thomas Curry, William Eccles, John C. Hall, John Heyney, John Huey, John A. Hyndman, Thomas Hyndman, James Kerr, James Kennedy, William Kilpatrick, William Lynn, James Lawrence, Robert Lyons, Peter McArthur, Robert McAfee, William McGowan, Robert Moore, Henry McAuley, Carey McClennan, Sam McCurdy, Charles McKay, William McIlroy, Robert Nevin, John Patrick, William Sharpe, Bennett Thompson, William Torrence, Henry Welsh, James Young, Thomas Smyth, Thomas McCaldin, Torrens Boyd, Robert Hunter, George Eaton, Thomas Richardson, William Richardson, John Scott, George McCarter, William McCarter, Archibald McCorkell, George McCorkell, John Munn, William Patterson, Halford Smyth, Joseph Martin, Jonathan McIlroy, Gustavius Pirrie. This list does not identify which were boarders and which were day-boys.

Boarding School Life

What was life like for the first boarders in the school in those days? Part of the answer is revealed in an inventory of the furnishings of the boarding department, taken in January 1861:

Dormitories: *12 Iron Bedsteads, 9 Mattresses, 9 Palliasses, 9 Feather Pillows, 12 Cane-bottomed Chairs, 12 Galvanised Basins, 6 Water Cans, 6 Looking Glasses.*

Mr Taylor's Bedroom: *1 Iron Bedstead, 1 Mattress, 1 Palliasse, 1 Pillow and Bolster, 2 Cane-bottomed Chairs, 1 Chest of Drawers, 1 Dressing Table and Towel Rack, 1 Looking Glass, 1 Basin Stand, Basin*

and Jug, Soap and Brush Drainer, 1 Fender & 1 Set of Fire Irons.

Sitting Room: *1 Dining Table, 4 Hair-bottomed chairs, 1 Book Rack, Crumb Cloth, 1 Fender, 1 Set of Fire Irons.*

Committee Room: *Coconut Matting, 12 Hair-bottomed Chairs, 1 Long Table, 1 Screen, 1 Piano Forte.*

Hall: *2 Hall Chairs, 1 Hall Table, Umbrella Stand, Inner and Outer Halls covered with Matting.*

Housekeeper's Closet: *41 Pairs Blankets, 20 Counterpanes.*

Laundry: *1 Table*

Dining Room: *1 Long Table, 1 Side Table, 2 Long Forms, Fender & Fire Irons, Floor covered with coconut matting.*

Kitchen: *2 Tables, 2 Chairs, 1 Plate Rack.*

By today's standards, this inventory reveals the bare minimum of furnishings (with the possible exception of the relative luxury of the Assistant Master's bedroom!) Conditions in the boarding department remained, for many years, Spartan to say the least – very much in keeping with the Victorian idea that healthy living meant simple living. By the way, the 'Piano Forte' in the Committee Room was probably for the singing of the National Anthem at the conclusion of Committee meetings! Also, boarders of more recent years will remember vividly those 'Long Forms' on which they sat at their 'Long Tables', even in the more modern Dining Hall!

The financial well-being of the Institution continued to give cause for concern in these early years. The total income for the year ending 3 April 1861 amounted to £229-19s-6d while expenditure was £309-10s-6d. Such a deficit was clearly viewed as unacceptable and as a result the Classical and English assistant masters had their salaries cut and the Porter's wage was reduced from ten shillings to eight shillings a week. Even the headmaster did not escape these stringent cuts, for the Committee decided that he should no longer receive a percentage of school fees.

A 'Bazaar' to raise funds for laying out, planting and ornamenting the school grounds was held in the Town Hall, from 14 – 16 August 1861. This was described as the most magnificent sight ever seen in Coleraine. The ever-faithful and energetic Committee secretary, Dr McCaldin, was responsible for arranging the bazaar, which concluded with yet another 'Conversazione'. Lavishly organized bazaars were to become a most successful form of fund-raising for the school over the next four decades, as described later in this book.

At the Distribution of Prizes on 22 January 1862, it was reported that the number of pupils had increased to sixty-five, of whom nineteen were boarders. Drawing had been added to the school curriculum and a teacher of that subject had been appointed. Two learned gentlemen from Queen's College, Belfast, Rev. James McCosh, Professor of Logic, and Mr Charles McDouall, Professor of Greek, had been asked to 'examine' the school and their report, which mentioned that fifty-four pupils were studying Classics, was very satisfactory. In a list of the places from which boarders had come to study at the school, India was mentioned. Throughout the days of the Empire, many army officers or civil servants posted abroad to run the Colonies, as they were then called, sent their sons to be educated at Coleraine Academical Institution. At this prize distribution, one of the pupils read an address, *"couched in most chaste and appropriate terms"* to Mr Young, and another, on behalf of the pupils, made a presentation of *"a beautiful and valuable timepiece as a token of friendship to their teacher."*

Secretary's Resignation

The year 1862 saw a sad development, in the resignation from the Committee and from his role as secretary of Dr James Jasper McCaldin, who was moving to take up a new position in London. Dr McCaldin had for sixteen years been the pivotal figure in the quest for an Institution in Coleraine; he had stood firm, in the face of pessimism, frustration and the resignations of some of his colleagues when the going became tough, and it was very fitting that he had seen the project through to the triumphant inauguration of the school and its first two years in business. His record speaks for itself: of the 106 meetings of full Committee and sub-committees which took place between

16 September 1846 and 15 May 1862, he had missed only two, in each case to make urgent medical visits. As well as having a key role in the foundation of the school, Dr McCaldin had been a very well known figure in the Coleraine community, holding the position of Medical Officer of the Coleraine and Killowen Dispensary. He had a particular interest in improving the poorer streets and houses of the town. He was a persistent advocate of proper sewers and the daily sweeping of the streets.

The Committee ordered that an Address in praise of Dr McCaldin should be recorded in the Minutes. There was also a public meeting in the Town Hall, with William Warke Esq., J.P. in the Chair, at which the citizens of Coleraine not only presented him with a formal 'address', but also a purse containing 100 guineas, in appreciation of his devoted care of his patients. At his final meeting, Dr McCaldin said to the Committee: *"I worked hard, it is true, and often under much discouragement, but in you I had all the support that sacrifices of time, business habits, earnestness for the common good and pecuniary responsibility could afford. Had I spent my years in Coleraine to accomplish no other work than helping forward the development of the Institution, which you now represent, and which this day, although only two years in operation, numbers in its halls and on its benches upwards of seventy pupils - sixteen of whom are boarders - I had not laboured in vain."* Indeed, without Dr McCaldin's constant 'labours' over those years, the Institution as we know it might never have come into existence.

However, the Institution had to continue into the future without its leading torch-bearer. With the school population doubling between 1861 and 1862, and with the consequent increase in income, Mr Young now felt he could challenge the Committee regarding the cuts in salaries mentioned above. In a long memorandum to the Committee in August 1862, he threatened his resignation unless the Committee agreed to twelve points which he set out within it. As a result, the Committee reached an agreement with Mr Young whereby he would have the £100 annual endowment from The Irish Society paid directly to him, along with 15% of all school fees of both day pupils and boarders. His assistant resident Classical and

English masters would receive £60 per annum and a writing master £30 per annum. Also, the agreement provided the principal with clear lines of authority, stating that: *"the arrangement and management of the educational department in all its branches, be in the hands of the Principal – who is entrusted also with the selection of all masters, subject to the sanction of the Committee."*

Despite appearances, this agreement was not entirely a climb-down on the part of the Committee, when faced with the wrath of Mr Young. At times they did make clear their overall authority and responsibility for the new Institution. Thus, in January 1863, the Committee noted that *"considerable damage had been done to the property of the Committee"* and instructed Mr Young to record *"all damage done to furniture and other property of the Institution"* and to *"endeavour in every case to make the pupils responsible for the cost of any repairs done to property injured by them."* Obviously, vandalism by pupils in schools is not a feature of the 21st century only! Also, in April 1863, Mr Young was summoned to *"converse with the Committee*

as to the amount of work given by the masters to the pupils to be done at home." Around this time, the Committee agreed that Mr Young could *"use all the grass growing on the school grounds"* but firmly refused to allow him to graze a cow on the premises, stating that *"the keeping of a cow within the grounds would be incompatible with that neatness of appearance which it is desirable to secure."*

In 1863, the number of pupils had increased to seventy, eighteen of these being boarders. The outstanding event of the year was the foundation of the Clothworkers' Scholarship by the Worshipful Company of Clothworkers. This was of the value of £50 per annum, tenable for two years at a University or College. It was awarded to a pupil who was placed first at a special examination for which the papers were set by external examiners. The examination consisted of three branches: Mathematics (500 marks), Classics (500 marks) and History (250 marks). The first winner of this valuable and prestigious Scholarship was John Carey Hall (mentioned in the list above of the fifty-one pupils on the rolls in 1861).

The earliest extant photograph of the school community, sometime in the late 1860s. The Headmaster, Alex. Waugh Young, B.A., with top hat, is seated centre rear. Cricket was obviously the favourite past-time, though, rather alarmingly, the young man standing at the front is casually sporting a shotgun.

In 1864 the number of pupils on the roll was fifty-seven, of whom nine were boarders. The Clothworkers' Scholarship was won that year by John Huey.

In August 1865, the sum of £572 was raised by public subscription, and this was augmented by gifts of £500 from The Irish Society and a similar sum from the Clothworkers' Company, resulting in the reduction of the outstanding debt on the school to £500. This new income was very welcome indeed, but the school was obviously not out of the financial woods just yet. Signs were promising though, especially the fact that the school population continued to grow, reaching ninety-nine, including twenty-one boarders. Neil Forsythe won the Clothworkers' Scholarship in 1865.

From 1866 to 1869 the School progressed steadily, although this period was not marked by any outstanding event. The numbers of pupils on the rolls were: 1866, eighty-five (nineteen boarders); 1867, 110 (thirty boarders); 1868, 100 (thirty boarders); 1869, ninety-one (twenty-eight boarders). The Clothworkers' Scholars in these years were: Thomas Lyle, James McMaster, Thomas M. Greer and Alfred H. Rentoul. At the annual Distribution of Prizes in 1868, Mr Young stated that the total number of boys passing through the school since its opening was 370, and of these eighty had progressed to College.

Academic successes at University or College during the Young era included: John Campbell (Engineering Scholarship, Q.C.B., 1862 and 1863); William McGowan (Science Scholarship, Q.C.B., 1863 and 1865, B.A. and M.D. degrees); John C. Hall (Literary Scholarship, Q.C.B., 1863-64, First Class B.A., Gold Medal Classics, Senior Scholar in Classics 1866); Neil Forsythe (Literary Scholarship, Q.C.B., 1866-67 B.A. Honours); James McMaster (Literary Scholarship, Q.C.B., 1868, Senior Scholarship B.A., Gold Medal in Classics, M.A. with First Class Honours and Gold Medal, Hughes Scholarship). Coleraine Academical Institution was obviously supplying Queen's College, Belfast, with some of its most gifted students.

At his interview for the post of Principal, back in 1859, Mr Young had been asked how he would occupy the boarders when they were not in lessons. There is no record of what his response to this question was, but sporting activity was clearly encouraged in these early years. The principal outdoor sport was cricket, with the season extending into October in some years. The earliest extant photograph of the school, shows several pupils confidently holding cricket bats. (More alarmingly, one holds a shotgun!). Cricket matches were played, with varying results, against Foyle College, Dunboe, Ballymoney, Articlave, Grangemore, Gracehill School (Ballymena), Banagher and Coleraine Town sides. In 1868, a professional cricket coach was employed. Prizes for 'Athletic Sports' were awarded at the Prize Distribution of 1868, but football, though mentioned, does not seem to have developed beyond the practice stage, and it is not stated which variety – rugby or soccer – was played.

Tributes To The First Headmaster

In April 1869, the first Principal of Coleraine Academical Institution, Mr Young, resigned his post to take up the Principalship of Tettenhall College, Wolverhampton, a position he held until 1891. Young's successor, T.G. Houston, later said that, *"Mr Young's career at Tettenhall was a repetition of his successes in Coleraine. He raised that school to a high position among secondary schools in England."* The present school historian at Tettenhall College confirms that Mr Young's tenure at Tettenhall did coincide with the years often referred to as that school's 'golden age'. Along with Mr Young went Mr James Shaw, who had been Resident Classical and Mathematical Master at the school since 1863; Mr Shaw was later to become Vice-Principal of Belfast Royal Academy. Addresses and Presentations were made to them by the staff and pupils, Mr Young being presented with a 'Massive Silver Epergne' (a branched ornamental centrepiece for the table) and Mr Shaw with a Gold Watch. The addresses were signed on behalf of the pupils by Robert J. Craig and George McCarter, on behalf of the staff by Mr James Donaldson.

There are, unfortunately, no copies of those Addresses in school archives. However, at a much later date, in 1911 in fact, an Address was sent to Mr Young from the Committee of Management of Coleraine Academical Institution on the occasion of the presentation to him of a portrait of himself as Headmaster of the school. Eleven years earlier, in 1900, the Committee had presented a portrait to Mr Houston, to mark his thirty years as Headmaster, and it was now felt, rather belatedly, that Mr Young should also have his portrait presented. In 1911, Mr Houston and his Committee were of the opinion that this would be the start of an excellent tradition, of having the portraits of successive headmasters displayed prominently in the school.

Speaking in 1911, Mr Houston said, *"It is now eleven years since my kind friends presented me with my portrait, which will ultimately, if desired, become the property of the School. Ever since then I have felt, and many have felt with me, that that portrait should not be placed in the Institution until Mr Young's had preceded it. I was therefore delighted to find in the beginning of this year that a movement was in progress to remedy a very obvious defect in the equipment of the School."* Mr Young was at last to have artistic recognition of his service to the school.

A framed copy of the 1911 Address to Mr Young by the Committee of Management, is on display in the school museum, but is reproduced in full below. This Address is rather curious, in that it is merely typed on a fairly nondescript sheet of paper; whereas in those times such addresses were usually much more ornately presented, often in beautifully illuminated script. It may well be that a much more attractive original version was given to Mr Young.

Dear Mr Young,
Though many years have passed since you left Coleraine, your former pupils and other friends desire to assure you that you are still regarded with affectionate esteem amongst them. Your good work first as the honoured Principal of the Academical Institution is remembered with high appreciation by all who had the advantage of your teaching and it would be difficult to express the obligation which this community owes to you for the high ideals in education which you constantly set forth. It is not too much to say that the success of the school has been in no small measure due to the maintenance of the high traditions established under your wise guidance as its first Head Master.

A number of your friends have deemed it fitting that your great services to the cause of education in this district should be recognised in some way, and accordingly as a slight token of personal esteem and affection and as a memento of your connection with the School we beg to present you with your portrait in oils.

It is a gratification to us to know that your desire is that this portrait should be hung on the walls of your old School where it will serve to remind us all of your genial personality and to recall the fine example of true gentlemanliness which you ever set before your pupils.

Assuring you of our deep regard and admiration and most heartily wishing you a long and happy eventide of life.

We are, dear Mr Young,

Yours Very Sincerely

(Signed on behalf of the Subscribers)

There had been much correspondence between Mr Young and his successor, Mr Houston, around this time, on the matter of the portrait and the Address. Two items from this correspondence are still in existence. The first letter shows Mr Young very courteously giving permission for his portrait to be permanently displayed in the Institution.

19 Cluny Drive
Edinburgh
September 1, 1911

Dear Mr Houston,
Your telegram just received.
Kindly add to my letter, which has been posted –
"In accepting very gratefully from the Committee the portrait which they have given me, I desire to say that I would like it to have its home in the place where my work was done, and, with their permission, I present it

to them, that they may make what arrangements are necessary for its permanent abode in the Institution." This should come in, I think, just before the last paragraph. I hope this will be sufficient.

Yours very sincerely
Alex. Waugh Young

The second letter shows that Mr Young had very much returned to his Scottish roots and obviously enjoyed relaxing visits to his little Highland retreat. The reference to Mr Houston's *"trouble"* reflects the amount of correspondence arising from the decision to present the portrait and Address to Mr Young.

19 Cluny Drive
Edinburgh

September 2, 1911

Dear Mr Houston,
Your letter has been received by me in explanation of the telegram. You will have my letter in reply, in which I suggested an addendum to my former communication.

If you think further change necessary, it will save time if you communicate with me at Dunedin, Newtonmore, Inverness-shire, our little Highland home, for which Mrs Young and I are leaving in an hour or two, for a rest. I ought to receive the Committee's address on Monday at Newtonmore, for the p.o. people have instructions to forward letters.

I am sorry you are having so much trouble.

Yours very sincerely
Alex. Waugh Young

Records for this period of the school's history are scarce and there are few indications as to the nature of Alex. Waugh Young, the man. However, he had played a crucial role in firmly establishing the new Institution and in making it a success, with the pupil numbers increasing from the original intake of fourteen to over 100 during his tenure as principal. In September 1870, at the annual Distribution of Prizes, his successor paid a tribute to *"the efficiency of Mr Young and his staff"* and commented in particular on *"the healthy spirit which he found among the boys and the good relations between teachers and pupils."*

At the school Prize Distribution of 1911, over forty years after Mr Young had left the school, Mr Houston spoke at length about his predecessor, first of all giving details of what he was doing at that time. *"On leaving Tettenhall he retired from the scholastic profession, and since then has been living a life of varied activities in Edinburgh. He has been engaged in editing Greek and Latin authors and writing important educational work of his own, in acting as examiner for the London University and to the Civil Service Commission, and as inspector of higher schools under the Scottish Education Board."* Going on to give his personal estimation of Alex. Waugh Young, Houston said that he had been, *"brought up in a refined and cultured Christian home, as a result of which he gave early evidence of those endowments of head and heart which afterwards brought so much honour to himself and to those among whom his lot was cast."* Paying tribute to him, Houston said that Mr Young, *"laboured in Coleraine with an ability and an assiduity rarely equalled in the scholastic profession. Under his care the Institution soon rose to the very first rank among Irish secondary schools. He was possessed of very remarkable mental powers, very wide culture, and unusual versatility. When I came to Coleraine there were current among his pupils many traditions of the wonderful intellectual feats he could perform."*

Mr Houston said that in his educational aims Alex. Waugh Young was much in advance of his time. In public schools in the mid-19th century, the classical subjects such as Latin and Greek were the main focus for learning, while a vital subject such as English was often shamefully neglected. Mr Young is credited with bringing subjects such as English, English History, Geography and Modern Languages into a much more prominent place in the school curriculum, both in Coleraine Academical Institution and, later, in Tettenhall. However, according to Mr Houston, Mr Young did not view the intellectual training of his pupils as his sole aim; he was also concerned with the *"moral and spiritual influences he brought to bear on them. His constant aim was not merely to make his pupils good scholars, but to make them Christian gentlemen."*

Houston continued his eulogy, becoming ever more eloquent in his praise, telling his audience both what Mr Young brought to

Mr A.W. Young

the Institution and what he did not bring. *"He brought some of the best things from Eton and Rugby into Coleraine. He did not bring everything, nor was it possible or desirable that he should do so; he did not bring noble birth, wealth, high social position, or historical privilege. He did not bring a vulgar desire to imitate the possessors of these advantages by affected speech, by expensive clothing, and by contempt for the homely surroundings in which most of us Northern Irish are brought up. What lessons did he bring from the English public school and university? He brought the lessons of public spirit, esprit de corps, power to subordinate personal claims to those of the community, self-abnegation, indomitable courage, regard for the rights and feelings of others, and zeal for the glory of the body to which we belong."* At the conclusion of Mr Houston's speech, Lady Bruce unveiled

the portrait of Mr Young, referred to above. It is said that the likeness is a faithful one in every respect of Mr Young at the time he resigned as Headmaster of the Institution, and depicts him seated as if in deep meditation.

A scholarly, highly principled, but essentially modest man, Alexander Waugh Young had left his mark on the school community and it was now up to others to continue his good works.

A. W. Young died in Edinburgh on 2 January 1915. Three years later, the youngest of his three sons, Captain Alexander Waugh Young, F.R.C.S.E., Royal Army Medical Corps, was awarded the Military Cross for conspicuous gallantry in the Great War.

Thomas Galway Houston, M.A., a graduate of Queen's College, Belfast, was selected by the Institution's Managing Committee to succeed Mr Young, and he assumed control of the school in May 1870. In July of the same year, he married Miss Maud Millar, a daughter of Rev. Thomas Millar, of Cookstown. Mrs Houston very quickly took upon herself the task of looking after the boarders and *"by her capacity for administration and her sympathetic and affectionate interest in the boarders, was largely responsible for the Institution becoming one of the leading boarding schools in Ireland."* Mr Houston was to remain Headmaster of the school for the remarkable term of 45 years and he proved to be a hugely talented administrator who seems to have been highly respected by everyone who knew him, indeed almost worshipped by some. For example, R.H. Gilmour (1886 –

89), writing in the 1950 Jubilee edition of the school magazine, says, *"The school took its character from the Principal, whom the boys looked up to with the deepest respect and even awe. No college president or professor ever impressed one half so much as our revered Headmaster, as I remember his stately and handsome figure clad in cap and gown, entering the classroom for the daily mental drill in the classics."* The copious records of his long reign are regularly punctuated by eulogies in praise of his skills as the great leader of the Institution.

T.G. Houston had been a brilliant and promising student, teacher and Principal in the years before his arrival at the Inst. He was born on 13 September 1843, educated first at a private school in Cookstown and then prepared for college at the Belfast Academy (B.R.A.) under Dr Bryce. He entered Queen's College, Belfast, in 1860, was President of the College Literary and Scientific Society in his

The Academical Institution in November 1883. The Headmaster's Wing is on the left. At the extreme right, the new "Covered Playground", or gymnasium, can be seen under construction.

final year, and graduated B.A. Honours in 1863. He went on to Queen's College, Cork, on a Senior Scholarship and there completed his M.A. with Honours in 1864. Wishing to widen his experience, he entered London University, obtaining a high place in the Honours Division, then attended Trinity College, Dublin, where he *"kept several terms by examination."*

He began his professional work in Belfast as *"visiting tutor in schools and private families, in which capacity he was employed during the greater part of his college course."* Dr Bryce then offered him the post of Classical and English Master at the Belfast Academy. In fact, his post was much more important than this, as revealed in A.T.Q. Stewart's history of B.R.A. *"By 1860, Bryce had lost some of his earlier energy and enthusiasm. . . . In 1864 there were only thirteen pupils at the school and four of these had given notice they were leaving. . . At this juncture Bryce appointed a former pupil, T.G. Houston, as head of both the Classical and English departments. Houston was for three years virtually the acting Principal, and through hard work, shrewdness and diplomacy he weathered the storm. The numbers rose to fifty and the school survived. . . . Bryce retired in 1865 and the Classical and English schools were united under the capable headship of T.G. Houston."* In 1868, Houston was approached by a deputation of the principal inhabitants of the town of Cookstown, in connection with the Principalship of 'The Academy' there. He stayed in Cookstown for eighteen months, until his appointment at C.A.I., during which short time the size of The Academy at Cookstown trebled.

The Irish 'Arnold'

In contrast to the lack of detailed information about his predecessor, much is known about T.G. Houston the man. One personal estimation of him is in the Reverend Dr D. Frazer-Hurst's book *The Bridge of Life* (Rev. Dr Frazer-Hurst was an old boy of Coleraine Academical Institution, having gone there as a boarder, in the footsteps of his elder brother, Livy, in the 1890s). He writes:
"The headmaster, known to us as 'The Chief', was a truly remarkable man. To his M.A. degree, Queen's University later added an honorary doctorate, recognising in him one of the foremost educationalists

in the North of Ireland. His high ideals and constant care for the moral welfare of the pupils in his charge caused him often to be styled the 'Irish Arnold*', and he well deserved the name. He was tall and exceedingly handsome with keen bright eyes and a voice of authority. He took himself very seriously, for he was rather deficient in a sense of humour. This defect may not have been a disadvantage to one in his position, for a keen sense of the ludicrous is apt to blunt the edge of authority. His influence in the school and on the lives of the pupils was deep and enduring, for those who had been in his care bore, throughout their lives, the impress of his teaching and personality. Few human institutions are more deeply affected by the quality of the person in charge than a school. It is the headmaster who gives it character and prestige, for it is largely a reflection of his own personality and outlook on life. This was particularly true in the case of Mr T.G. Houston. Under his leadership the school advanced steadily to a foremost place amongst the public schools of Ireland, and Irishmen, like my father, thought it worthwhile to send their sons from distant places to be educated under this renowned headmaster."

(* Thomas Arnold was headmaster of Rugby School from 1828 – 1841 and he had a profound effect on the development of public school education in England. The system he introduced in Rugby School is vividly described in the famous novel *Tom Brown's Schooldays*, written by Thomas Hughes, a former pupil of Rugby.)

Frazer-Hurst's comments are a fine tribute to the serious-minded *"renowned headmaster"* who was to have such a *"deep and enduring"* effect on C.A.I. pupils for forty-five years. It is true that, to a great extent, the school in those days was imbued with Mr Houston's *"own personality and outlook on life."* Amongst other writings, Mr Houston was the author of a book entitled *School and Home*, published in 1895, which presents in detail his thoughts and theories - many of them quite modern and enlightened for the time - about the education of boys, especially those in boarding schools. He also dares to offer advice to parents as to how best to bring up their children in the family home! Above all, in this quaint little book Mr Houston firmly believed that, *"the moral tone which should pervade a school . . . is a matter of still greater importance to the boys than even their intellectual triumphs."*

There will be more references to Mr Houston, the man, and his educational ideals, as this chapter progresses. The details of the first ten years or so of his time in charge show a school that was successful and steadily progressing, no doubt fulfilling the aims and aspirations of its original founders and its current Managing Committee.

At his first distribution of prizes, in September 1870, Mr Houston said that his short acquaintance with the school prevented him from giving a full report of the year's work. The number of pupils that year was given as *"upwards of 100"* and the Clothworkers' Scholarship was won by A.J. McElwaine.

COLERAINE ACADEMICAL INSTITUTION.

THE PARENTS or GUARDIANS of PUPILS about to enter the INSTITUTION are requested to fill up the Subjoined Form with as much accuracy as possible.

Christian and Surname of Boy in full, ...

Age, _____ Years on _____ day of _____ 188

Date of Entrance, _____

Name and Address of Father or Guardian, _____

Religious Persuasion, _____

For what Profession or Calling intended, .. _____

Day Pupil or Boarder, _____

Any Special Instructions with regard to supplying Pocket Money, Books, &c., ... _____

Particulars of Previous Education, Health, &c.*

I have read the foregoing Prospectus and agree to its terms.

Signed _____

Date _____

N.B.—A certificate of good conduct is required before a boy can be admitted as a pupil of the Institution.

* Under this head, please state whether the boy has had any or all of the ordinary diseases of children.

Admission Form from a school prospectus of the 1880s.

In 1871, for unknown reasons, The Irish Society let it be known that only half the usual grant would be given to the school, but the Reverends Martin and Fleming went to London and persuaded the Society to continue the grant. Also in this year, the Clothworkers' Company set aside a sufficient sum of money to ensure that the valuable Clothworkers' Scholarship would be continued in perpetuity. An interesting innovation at this time was the imposition of small fines for minor offences, presumably as an alternative to a more painful form of punishment! There must have been a considerable number of minor offences because, before long, a School Library was founded as a result. A link with the past was lost when Mr Henry Taylor, who had been Resident English Master since the opening of the school, left Coleraine after more than ten years' valuable service. (The 'Henry Taylor Shakespeare Prize' is still awarded annually.) The winner of the Clothworkers' Scholarship in 1871 was John Clarke.

In 1872, Mr Houston reported that the number of pupils had remained steady, *"at from 95 to 100"*, and that the boarders included pupils from India, Russia, U.S.A., Belgium and Australia. J.C. Hall, the first winner of the Clothworkers' Scholarship, was appointed Vice-Consul to Japan by the British government. Thomas Brookes won the Clothworkers' Scholarship, the course for which had been *"made longer and more difficult."* Apparently, little of note occurred in 1873, although Mr Houston described it as the most successful year since he had come to Coleraine. There was a slight increase in the number of pupils and John A. Wallace won the Clothworkers' prize.

The year 1874 was described as a most unfavourable year for schools in general, but Coleraine escaped the general depression and numbers remained steady at about 100. Mr Houston announced that the *"dormitories were completely filled"* and that increased accommodation was urgently required. To improve the standard of Arithmetic in the school, a prize of £5, provided by the small fines system, was awarded. The conditions were that: *"All sums worked on a slate should be copied neatly into an exercise book, and the quantity and quality of this work, together with an Arithmetic examination at the end of the year, should determine the winner."* These conditions show that in those days most of the rough-work done in schools was with chalk, on slates. The winner of this prize was H. Hunter. Mr J. Cochrane, of Australia, provided a sum of £200 to found a Scholarship of £10 per annum, with the aim of *"encouraging commercial education in the school."* This scholarship, much changed over the years, is still awarded annually, as the 'Cochrane Modern Language Prize'. The Clothworkers' Scholarship of 1874 was won by M. Steen.

In 1875, the number of pupils increased to 140, of whom sixty-seven were boarders, and accommodation was now *"taxed to the uttermost."* This was a traumatic year for the entire school community because of a drowning accident in which two pupils lost their lives. A holiday, following the annual Prize Distribution, was spent at Downhill beach and at one stage H.S. McMullan got into difficulty while bathing. Thomas Milton Gallaher went to his assistance, but found the current too strong. Gallaher, who was a strong swimmer, refused to abandon McMullan and sacrificed his life in a heroic effort to save his fellow pupil. In happier events that year, James McMaster, a former Clothworkers' Scholar, was appointed Professor of Ancient Classics at Magee College, Derry, James V. Young won the Clothworkers' Scholarship and John I. Brown was the first winner of the Cochrane Scholarship.

New Extension Built

In 1876, the number of pupils was 145, including seventy boarders, and several rooms, including a portion of the Headmaster's Residence, had to be converted into sleeping apartments. Mr Houston announced that a new wing was being built and hoped that it would be completed by the beginning of the following year. He thanked the Irish Society for a grant of £200 towards the cost of the scheme, and a further £50 for current expenses. John Moody won the Clothworkers' Scholarship and William Brown the Cochrane Scholarship.

The outstanding event of 1877 was the completion of the new wing, which comprised two classrooms, a large dormitory ('the New') and, on the ground floor, a cloakroom and *"large bath room, with twelve bathing boxes and a plunge bath large enough for boys to learn swimming."*

The 'plunge' as it was known ever afterwards became a familiar (if not fond!) feature of the daily lives of generations of boarders. With the 'Chief's' belief in the old maxim that cleanliness is next to godliness, and that proper, healthy cleanliness could only be achieved through the stoically masculine habit of cold water washing, the sleepy-eyed youngsters lined up about 7.00 a.m., in the shivery basement, for their morning plunge. Any who felt reluctant about literally 'taking the plunge' were firmly assisted by the school's 'Drill Sergeant', as he was known.

The construction of the new wing was not without its problems and delays. Mr Houston made reference to these in his report at the Distribution of Prizes on Monday 27 August 1877. *"Another misfortune, which, though it did not involve much pecuniary loss to the Institution, caused a great deal of inconvenience and delay, was the fall of a large portion of this wing when it had been raised almost to the roof. Although this occurrence was rather trying at the time, it may be looked upon by all as a benefit. The fallen wall was re-built in a much stronger way, and with much better material than had been used at first, so that the recurrence of such an accident is, humanly speaking, an impossibility."*

Lessons were no doubt learnt by all involved, as a result of this 'fall'! Thankfully, although not entirely an 'impossibility', there has been no similar 'accident' since then and the 'new wing' still stands strongly today.

As part of this 1877 extension, a new furnace was included in the equipment and the total expenditure amounted to about £1,400. There was a decrease in the number of pupils on the rolls for this year, to 112 (fifty boarders). Again in his Prize Distribution speech, Mr Houston explained the reason for this unexpected drop.

"In the beginning of last autumn we were visited by the great scourge of schools – scarlatina. As soon as the disease made its appearance, intimation of the fact was promptly sent to parents of all our pupils. The malady was of so mild a type, and confined to so small a number of cases, and the isolation of the sick boys from the rest of the pupils was so complete, that our medical officer thought it quite unnecessary to break up the school. A great number of boarders,

however, and some day-pupils were withdrawn. A good many of these came back in about a month, when the disease had been entirely banished from the premises, but a considerable number did not return, while in all probability many others who would have joined the school were deterred from doing so by the fear of infection. The attack lasted, as I have said, for a very short time, and the alarm caused by it soon subsided. Our numbers are at present large, but not equal to what they were before the occurrence of the disease."

Drastic Measures To Prevent Infection

Throughout those early years of the Institution, in the boarding department in particular, the 'fear of infection' was a dominant concern of the headmaster and his Committee. Those were the days before modern cures or mass vaccinations, and diseases such as 'scarlatina' (scarlet fever), diphtheria and the dreaded consumption were rife. Even influenza could often be a killer disease in those, and later, days. (During the First World War, for example, it is claimed that more soldiers died of influenza than as a result of enemy action.) Hence it is understandable that much attention was paid to hygiene and sanitation at the school, with regular checks being made on water supply and sewerage systems. Indeed, the lengthy first chapter of Mr Houston's book *School and Home* is entitled 'School Hygiene'. (This chapter was originally a 'Paper read before the Schoolmasters' Association, December, 1885', just a few years after the scarlatina outbreak in the Institution.) Houston stated that the *"chief requisites of a healthy life could be included under four headings: proper food, proper clothing, proper exercise, and proper house accommodation."* For the boarders at the Institution, all of these, and especially the fourth, were very important. This constant concern, at times amounting almost to paranoia, about health led to the construction a few years later of a 'Sanatorium' for sick boys, deliberately set well apart from the main building.

In his book *Home and School*, Houston revealed the terrible fear of disease prevalent in boarding schools at the time and the drastic measures which those in charge should take to ensure further infection was prevented. His instructions are nothing if not dramatic, but

would hardly meet with the approval of Health and Safety experts today!

"If one or two boys in a large dormitory have had scarlet fever, the dormitory must be disinfected. The first step is aerial disinfection. All the air in the dormitory must be displaced by say chloride of lime, or at least enough of this gas must be evolved to displace all the air of the room. This will take (in the case of a room say 40 feet by 20, with a high ceiling), not a saucerful of the chloride, but from 20 to 30 lbs. — say the full of a large pail. After hermetically sealing the room, place this amount of chloride of lime in a large earthenware vessel, pour into it an almost equal weight of sulphuric acid, stir it once or twice holding your breath, and then literally run for your life. Close and plaster the door. In twenty-four hours it may be possible to enter the room and open the windows. Then set to work on the walls, floor and solid furniture. All paper must be torn off and burnt; all paint had better be burnt off with the lamp and then renewed. The walls and ceilings must first be washed with a strong solution of chloride of lime and then whitewashed or papered, the floors very carefully washed with some strong liquid disinfectant."

Another important item in Houston's report to that 1877 Prize Distribution was his concern that many parents were leaving it too late to send their sons to the Institution, if they hoped to gain admission to College.

"With regard to the time in which boys are expected to be ready to leave school, we may take for an example of this the way in which those reading for entrance into College are obliged to hurry over their preparation. Boys of this class are often the sons of respectable farmers, who live too far away from town to send their children to school there from the first. The boys are sent to a National School in the country where they learn with more or less accuracy the primary elements of education. At the age of 16 or 17 they are brought to the Institution, or some other school of the same kind, to finish their education, with a view to entering College. This they are expected to do in two or at the most three years, sometimes even in one. Let me assure all who may hear or read these words, that it is a very serious mistake for a boy who is intended for College to leave off the principal part of his preparation till he is 16 or even 15 years of age. He should begin his Classics and Mathematics at 11 or 12 at the latest; then, if he has ability and

35

perseverance, he will be ready to enter College at 17 or 18, and to reap some benefit from the more advanced studies pursued by him there."

No doubt, what Mr Houston was saying here was true in most cases; but at the same time it was also a fine piece of marketing for the school, encouraging parents to send their sons to the Academical Institution at an earlier age.

At the end of his 1877 report, Mr Houston proudly proclaimed that since he had come to the school he and his Committee had never pestered the public of Coleraine for help with funding. However, he now proceeded to do just that!

"Since I became connected with the School, the Committee has never appealed to the public, although the Institution is more strictly the property and care of the public than perhaps any other place in Coleraine. We have never begged from our friends. But all the while we would be nothing the worse for their help. It may be no harm to remind my hearers now that though much has been done for the improvement of the Institution, more remains to be done. We have satisfied pretty well the demands of utility; but surely in looking round the old school-rooms, with their well-worn furniture; looking at the weather-beaten front of

the building, you will agree with me that it is time for us to sacrifice a little more to the graces – to look a little more to the beauty of the place where the youth of Coleraine are to receive their earliest culture."

Moving on to 1878, the number on the roll was 117. The Clothworkers' Scholarship was withheld, and two boys – John Ramsay and J.R. McNeill – tied for the Cochrane Scholarship. To meet this situation, an extra £10 was provided, to give each a prize. A published list for this year shows the staff at the Institution as follows:

Coleraine Academical Institution
1878

Principal:
THOMAS G. HOUSTON, M.A.

Resident Mathematical Master:
WILLIAM STOOPS, B.A., Q.U.I.. Sen. Sch. in Pure Mathematics.
Sen. Sch. in Mixed Mathematics and Experimental Physics.
Peel Prizeman in Geometry, &c., Q.C.C.

Resident Classical Master:
ROBERT M. MOLLAN, B.A., T.C.D., First Honorman and Prizeman.

The Boarders in November 1883, elegantly turned out in their silk hats and Eton jackets, possibly before setting out for church.

The Boarders in November 1883, in more relaxed pose, wearing their school caps.

English Master:
WILLIAM GILLESPIE, Lond. Univ., and Sch.
M.C.D.

Writing and Assistant English Master:
JAMES ANDERSON, Lond. Univ.

French and Drawing Master:
M. CH. F. MASTRALE

Music Master:
MR. COONEY

Dancing:
MADAME SKINNER de LENGLEE

Drill Sergeant:
MR. ATKINSON

Medical Adviser:
JAMES C. L. CARSON, M.D., J.P., F.R.C.S.,
&c

In relation to the above list, Mr Houston, in his book *Home and Abroad*, bemoaned the *"slouching carriage of the body, which is almost a disease among our boys"*, but added that this problem could be at least partly rectified through *"a seasoning of drill and gymnastics"* or *"a few months in the hands of the fencing master and dancing master."* He obviously put his ideas into practice because in 1878, although the Institution did not have a 'fencing master', it did have a 'Drill Sergeant' and the gloriously-named Madame Skinner de Lenglee as dancing mistress! Those readers who might want to see a fine example of someone who does not have a 'slouching' posture should look at the photograph of Mr Houston himself, most elegantly attired and magnificently posed on the steps of the headmaster's house.

Thomas Galway Houston, M.A., in the later stages of his 45-year reign. Here he is, as always elegantly attired and splendidly posed, on the steps of the Headmaster's Wing.

The same 1878 document also shows the Trustees and the members of the Managing Committee for that year. Many of these names are already familiar, some of them having been on the original Committee of 1846 and others on the Committee of 1860, when the school opened.

Trustees.
Henry Kyle. Esq., J.P., Joseph McCarter, Esq., Thomas Bellas, Esq., Daniel Gailey, Esq., James Lyle, Esq.

Managing Committee for 1878.
Henry Kyle, Esq., J.P., President.
Thomas Bellas, Esq., Treasurer.   Wm. Young, Esq., Secretary.
Sir H.H. Bruce, Bart., J.C.L. Carson, Esq., M.D., J.P., Joseph Cuthbert, Esq., Daniel Gailey, Esq., Drummond Grant, Esq., John Huey, Esq., James Bellas, Esq., James Lyle, Esq., Joseph McCarter, Esq., William Robb, Esq., William Warke, Esq.

Ex-officio members
The Reverends W.M. Crawford, M.A., R.W. Fleming, T.A.P. Hackett, B.A., T.W. McClenaghan, D. McCrory, Henry S. O'Hara, M.A., James Stewart, M.A., R. Wallace, R.B. Wylie, M.A., LLD.

In 1879, after the setback arising from the scarlatina outbreak, the number of pupils had risen to 125, sixty-three of them boarders. This was the first year of the Intermediate Examinations, created by the new Intermediate Education Act of Ireland, and the school emerged successfully from this new test. Forty-six pupils entered for the examination and forty-three passed. Senior Grade Exhibitions of £50 each were won by John McNeill (3rd in Ireland), Thomas R. Lyle (6th), and W.C. Steele (12th), while Junior Grade Exhibitions of £20 a year for three years were gained by W.J.McK. Hardy and R.J. Duffin. Such outstanding successes were proof of the success of the teaching methods of Mr Houston and his staff; Mr Houston had indeed made the school *"amongst the foremost in the island."* Also in this year, Dr McCaldin, whose role in the foundation of the school was so vital, was a guest at the Distribution of Prizes, and declared he was astounded at the growth of the school, which the original Committee had never expected to house even 100 pupils. Two Clothworkers' Scholarships were awarded in 1879, the winners being Thomas R. Lyle and John McNeill. W.C. Steele won the Cochrane Scholarship.

The 1st Form 1883, looking rather uncertain, surrounded by so many stern-looking Masters. The names appended below the photograph do not include all of the nine boys shown and the positions are not identified. (Bruce, C. Beresford, Geo. Woodside, L. Frazer-Hurst, Cyril Proctor-Sims, J. Woodside).

The 2nd Form, November 1883. Individuals identified are:

G. Strahan, J.B. Huston, ___, R. Nevin, ___, ___, H. Smith

___, C. Major, W. Ogilvy, ___, ___, ___, ___, J.G. Brown.

In 1880, the number on rolls reached the record figure of 157, including sixty-one boarders. With the increase in numbers, the *"old methods of ventilation"* were deemed inadequate and a new system was installed at a cost of £250. Work was also started on a new separate building to serve as a school hospital or 'Sanatorium', at an estimated cost of £500. This building, now demolished, later became the school Sergeant's house. Towards these improvements, the ever-helpful Irish Society gave a grant of £300. Forty-eight candidates succeeded in passing the Intermediate Examinations, three Exhibitions and six Prizes being obtained. W.J. Hardy won an Exhibition of £30 for two years in Middle Grade, while S.J. Hunter (of whom much more later), and R.W. Haslett secured Junior Exhibitions at £20 a year for three years. Prize-winners in Middle Grade were R. Hunter, R.J. Duffin and W.A. Martin, and in Junior Grade, S. Dunlop, W. Dawson and H.H. Macready. The Clothworkers' Scholar was H.A. Irvine and H. Hughes won the Cochrane Scholarship. During this period, cricket was still the main outdoor sport, with matches played regularly against Foyle College, Londonderry Academy, Gracehill

Academy and teams from neighbouring districts. An 'Athletic Sports Meeting' was held at the school annually and competitors from Belfast and Derry entered for the open events on the programme. There is no trace of organised football in the existing records.

The year 1881 was a lean year for most Irish schools and C.A.I. suffered from the prevailing depression. Numbers fell to 125 and the completion of the sanatorium and the new ventilation system at a total cost of almost £900 left the School with a debt of £450. On the academic side, results were very satisfactory and forty-six pupils were successful in passing the Intermediate examination. In Senior Grade, W.J.McK. Hardy won an Exhibition of £50, with Gold Medal in Greek. In a later Prize Distribution speech, Mr Houston commented that in addition to *"the best answering in Greek in all Ireland"* Hardy's marks were: *"96 ahead of those of the candidate who came next to him. This is one of the highest honours that has ever fallen to the lot of the School, and it must be most gratifying to Hardy, and to his friends, that after his seven years' residence at the Institution, he leaves behind him such an honourable memorial of*

his ability and industry." R.J. Duffin retained an Exhibition won in Middle Grade. S.J. Hunter, in Middle, retained his Junior Exhibition, and W.J. Dawson secured one in Junior Grade. Prizes in Middle Grade were awarded to S.J. Hunter, S. Dunlop and S.G. Connor, and in Junior to G.M. Irvine and R.H. Drennan. The Clothworkers' Scholarship was won by C.W. Steele and the Cochrane Scholarship by R. Duffin. In this year, French, German and Drawing were removed from the list of 'extra subjects' and added to the ordinary curriculum.

The year 1882 was a year of steady progress. At the Intermediate Examinations, S.J. Hunter in Senior Grade and W.J. Dawson in Middle Grade, retained their Exhibitions, while J. Johnston, A.E. Crawford and W.G. Connolly secured Exhibitions in Junior Grade. Amongst the various prizes awarded, S. Dunlop in Senior Grade won the Gold Medal in English. W.J. Hardy won the Clothworkers' Scholarship and J. Johnstone the Cochrane Scholarship.

Grand Fund-raising Bazaar

However, the outstanding event of 1882 was a magnificent three-day 'Bazaar' held in the Town Hall, Coleraine, on Wednesday 23, Thursday 24 and Friday 25 August. The object of this event was to raise funds, firstly for the erection of a new gymnasium (sometimes referred to as the 'covered playground') and to liquidate the existing debt on the school account. Much planning and preparation went into this event, it involved a large number of people of all classes who had an interest in the success of the Institution, and the detailed and amusing 'Whimsical Programme' for it is a marvellous piece of Victoriana. If any original copies of this programme, in good condition, are still in existence they are possibly worth some money on the antiques market. Some photocopies can be viewed in the School Museum and are well worth detailed perusal, giving as they do a glimpse into Coleraine society of the day and of Victorian culture in general. Here are some of extracts from the programme to whet readers' appetites.

The opening page of the programme described the event as a 'Bazaar and Fancy Fair' and

The opening page of the "whimsical" programme for the "Bazaar and Fancy Fair" 1882.

featured an introductory stanza, apparently specially written for the event, by the famous American poet Oliver Wendell Holmes, at Beverly Farms, Massachussetts, on July 11th 1881:

"Build thee more stately mansions, O my soul,
As the swift seasons roll;
Leave thy unvaulted past:
Let each new temple, nobler than the last,
Shut thee from Heaven, with a dome more vast,
Till thou at length art free,
Leaving thine outgrown shell by life's unresting sea."

The Bazaar was open on each of the three days from '12 o'clock noon till 4.30 o'clock, p.m. and each evening from 7 o'clock, p.m., till 10 o'clock, p.m.', with the Coleraine Brass Band, under its conductor, Mr Kerr, in attendance On the afternoon sessions on Wednesday and Thursday the admission fee was one shilling, but on Friday afternoon, and on the evening sessions of all three days, admission was

PROCLAMATION.

V. R.

WHEREAS.—The Coleraine Academical Institution has recently undergone many improvements, including an enlargement of the School-rooms and Dormitories, a complete system of ventilation and the erection of a detached sanatorium.

WHEREAS.—There still remaineth a portion of the cost of these improvements unpaid, as a debt against the Institution.

WHEREAS.—There are still some improvements to be made, viz., a covered Play-ground, and the formation of a School Library, as suggested by Professor Mahaffey, in his Parliamentary Report on Public Schools in Ireland.

WHEREAS.—It is purposed to hold, in the Town Hall of the Borough of Coleraine, in the County of Londonderry, Ireland, a Public Bazaar and Fancy Fair, the proceeds of which it is purposed to apply to the clearance of the aforesaid debt, and for the carrying out of the aforesaid further improvements. The said Bazaar will be opened at 12 o'clock noon, on the 23rd day of August, in the year of our Lord, 1882, and shall continue for that day and the two days immediately succeeding, at certain hours, to be hereafter specified.

KNOW YE THEREFORE, all men and women, by these presents that we command all true and loyal citizens *not* to refrain from taking part in said Bazaar and Fancy Fair, but to go, they and their neighbours, and all that is of their households, and all that they can influence or persuade, and assist by every means in their power to the full securing of success for this undertaking, and thereby further the good cause of Education and Enlightenment in this our beloved land.

Issued by Order of the Bazaar Committee.
GOD SAVE THE QUEEN.

The mock-serious "Proclamation" at the start of the programme for the "Bazaar and Fancy Fair" 1882.

sixpence. Children under twelve were admitted at half-price, at all times, with the additional comment: *"Children in arms not admitted, if the arms are loaded. This rule will be strictly enforced, to comply with the provisions of the Prevention of Crime (Ireland) Act."* A disclaimer on the inside page advised readers that, *"The Editor and Compiler of this Programme is not responsible for anything contained herein, and he does not know anyone else who is."* The *"Invitation"* to the great event (poet not known, but presumably local) reads:

"Ye ladies and ye gentlemen,
Come hasten to the fair,
To see the many wondrous things
That are collected there:
There are smoking caps and slippers,
There are splendid Irish 'buhls'
There are brigantines and needles,
There are scrapscreens, there are spools,
There are albums, there are foot-stools,
There are cushions, there are dolls,

There are lovely things for ladies
To wear at morning calls.
There are pretty children's dresses
For waking and for sleep;
There are dogs of every species,
There are horses, cows and sheep:
There are rugs and quilts and laces,
There are tables, there are toys,
There are lots of pretty faces
To interest the boys.
There are things grotesque and luminous,
Things so unique and queer,
And things so very numerous,
They can't be mentioned here –
Things wrought by dext'rous fingers,
Things ladies fair have made –
All must be sold, because the folk
Are going out of trade.
There are all the latest wonders
Of science to be shewn:
'Tis a liberal education
To see these things alone.
So fill your purse with money,
And hasten to the Fair
Lest all the strange and lovely things
Are sold ere you get there."

Obviously, the organisers of this great 'Bazaar' had experienced a lot of fun in preparing for the event, as well as much hard work in collecting *"all the strange and lovely things"*! It is particularly interesting to note that, although the Bazaar was largely run by the prim and proper ladies of Coleraine and further afield, there was at least some attempt to attract Institution pupils to the event, with the promise that:

"There are lots of pretty faces
To interest the boys."

It is indeed also interesting to note that the various stalls, run by the same sedate matrons, had numerous younger, and so far unattached, female assistants! How many romances, of whatever length, began in Coleraine Town Hall over those three days of the Bazaar?

For those readers who may not have the opportunity to visit the present school museum to see the programme in its entirety, the following extracts give examples of some of the items to be purchased or raffled at the various stalls. No. 1 Stall, presided over of course by Lady Bruce, the wife of the President of the Managing Committee, offered in a Raffle, tickets 2s-6d each, 'An Autograph Screen', featuring the *"genuine autographs of many leading Men and Women of the Age"*. These autographs comprised those of: The Queen, The Late Prince Consort, The Dowager Queen Adelaide, The President of the U.S. America, the King and Queen of the Sandwich Islands, Archbishops of York and Canterbury, Sir F. Leighton, Colonel Burnaby, Noel Paton, Alma Tadema, J. Bright, W.E. Forster, Parnell, Dillon, Tennyson, Chas. Keane, the Bishop of Derry, Mrs Alexander, Mr & Mrs Gladstone. Is this 'autograph screen' mouldering in someone's attic at the moment?

No. 2 Stall, presided over by Mrs Taylor and Mrs Warke offered for sale, for example, 'Antimacassors' and for raffle 'A Beautiful 4-Panelled Scrap Screen'. No. 3 Stall, presided over by Mrs Woodside but ably assisted by

two Miss Woodsides and two Miss Martins, offered for raffle, amongst other items, 'A Fine Leicester Sheep (presented by Messrs. M. McGrath)' and 'A thorough-bred Irish Terrier, 6 months old (presented by James Hunter Esq., J.P.).' No. 4 Stall was presided over by no less a person than Mrs Houston, the Headmaster's wife, assisted by, amongst others, The Misses Dysart, The Misses Leslie and The Misses McCormick. The items on offer included 'A Magnificent Collection of Japanese Pottery (Presented by the Masters of the Institution)' and for Raffle 'A Mare and Foal', presented by her husband, the Headmaster himself, tickets selling at 2s-6d each.

No. 5 Stall, the 'Old Boarders' Stall' offered for raffle 'A Table, in Macrame Lace', presented by R. O'Conor, and 'A Bicycle', presented by J. Stewart-Moore, Esq., J.P. One item for sale at No. 6 Stall, the 'Old Day Boys' Stall', presided over by some twenty ladies, was 'A Case of Indian Butterflies', presented by

---

10

No. 4 STALL.

PRESIDED OVER BY

MRS. HOUSTON,

ASSISTED BY

Mrs. Browne.	The Misses Dysart.	Miss M‘Millan.
Mrs. Charles.	Miss Gaussen.	Miss M. Millar.
Mrs. Sharpe.	The Misses Leslie.	Miss Wilson.
Miss Browne	The Misses M‘Cormick	

At this Stall will be shewn: Paintings on Terra-Cotta, wood and satin; Hand-painted Tables; Hand Screens. A Magnificent collection of

JAPANESE POTTERY,

(Presented by the Masters of the Institution.)

Sofa Blankets, Couvrettes, Antelopes' Heads, Xmas Card Tables, Articles of Vertu, exquisite Fret-work, presented by Miss N. Dysart, &c., &c.

AMONG THE ARTICLES TO BE RAFFLED FOR AT THIS STALL ARE

A Mare and Foal, presented by T. G. Houston, Esq., M.A., ...		tickets	2/6 ea.
A Heifer, presented by Messrs Hughes Bros., ...		,,	1/- ,,
A Tennis Set, ,, ,, T. Millar, Esq., ...		,,	6d ,,
A Cheval Screen, ...		,,	6d ,,
A Bicycle, presented by Mr D. M‘Collum, ...		,,	6d ,,
A Pair Exquisite Girandoles, presented by A. Millar, Esq., London, ..		,,	1/- ,,
A Fine Art Needle-work Chair, ...		,,	1/- ,,
A Silver Biscuit Box, presented by S. Rogers, Esq., ...		,,	6d ,,
A Case Preserved Ginger, presented by James Moore, Esq., ...		,,	6d ,,
A Cricket Bat, presented by J. Fyvie, Esq., ...		,,	6d ,,
A Sofa Blanket, ...		,,	6d ,,
A Hand-painted Cushion, ...		,,	6d ,,
A Fender Stool, ...		,,	6d ,,
A Group Exquisite Wax Flowers, ...		,,	6d ,,
A Leather Bracket, ...		,,	1/- ,,

12

Little drops of water,
Little grains of sand,
Make the mighty ocean
And the bounteous land.
Little bits of cotton,
Coloured, red and white,
Make a beauteous covering
To keep one warm at night.

——:o:——

See the Autograph Quilt,

AT "OLD BOARDERS'" Stall,

A SPLENDID STUDY, IN RED & WHITE,

CAN BE USED IN SUMMER AS A CHESS BOARD.

Reform ! Reform ! Reform !

GREAT REDUCTION OF THE FRANCHISE!

WOMAN'S RIGHTS TRIUMPHANT!

A VOTE FOR A SIXPENCE!

AN ELECTION IMPENDING.

"We are informed by one behind the scenes that an election, on the basis of the new franchise, will take place to elect the Clergyman most worthy to become possessor of a BEAUTIFUL CARRIAGE RUG."—vide *Daily Paper*.

To enable every voter to poll, the polling will extend over three days—Wednesday, Thursday, and Friday, the 23rd, 24th and 25th August.

Payment of Sixpence entitles to one Vote. Polling Booth at the "Old Boarders'" Stall, Town Hall.

COME IN YOUR THOUSANDS!

BRING LOTS OF SIXPENCES.

Poll early, and poll often. Hurrah for Reform !

(Let us therefore turn over a new leaf)

Extracts from the programme for the "Bazaar and Fancy Fair" 1882.

COALS! COALS!!

PORTRUSH IRON ORE AND COAL
⊹ COMPANY. ⊹

Always on hand

Scotch, Cumberland, Wigan, & Smith
⇥ COALS. ⊹⇤

The above Company having the advantage of an Outward Cargo are able to supply a good quality of Coal at greatly reduced prices, either at

PORTRUSH or COLERAINE.

A Coal Yard has lately been opened at Lime Market Street, COLERAINE.

The Working Classes supplied by the Tub.

Captain T. Simmons, Manager.

An advertisement in the programme for the "Bazaar and Fancy Fair" 1882, not entirely politically correct by today's standards.

J. Cuthbert, Esq., while the items for raffle included 'A Drontheim Boat', presented by E. McLaughlin, Esq., and, believe it or not, 'A Donkey', presented by T. Wray Esquire. The advertisement for this stall finished with a reference to the donkey raffle (sixpence per ticket): *"There once was a donkey that would not go,"* but this one <u>will go</u> to the holder of the winning ticket.

For sale at No. 7, the 'Present Day Boys' Stall', were *"some heads of chin-raras and antelopes"*, a 'Model of a Yacht', presented by Charles Lynn, Esq., and 'French Articles of Vertu' (brought home by Mrs Andrews). To be raffled at No. 8, the 'Present Boarders' Stall', were *"A Pair of Chinese Panels, brought home in the Sunbeam by Lady Brassey, and presented by W. Dawson, Esq."* The Flower Stall, presided over by Lady Macnaghten, assisted by the Misses Macnaghten, was, like some of the others, advertised poetically, though Oliver Wendell Holmes might not have approved of the metre:

"Come and see the flowers we're showing;
Some are budding, some are blowing –
We have specimens of all the sorts that grow.
We have all the fruits in season,
Every taste we would be pleasing:
So come and see our treasures ere you go."

At Mrs Stronge's 'Utility Stall', *"among the many articles to be disposed of, the following two will be raffled: A Sack of Flour, presented by Mr J. Barbour and A Handsome Knitted Counterpane, presented by Mrs Stewart"*. The Refreshment Stall was presided over by Mrs O'Hara and Mrs Lyle and offered a fairly simple *"Bill of Fare"*, with a 2-course Lunch for 2 shillings, Tea or Coffee at 6d per cup, Ices at 6d each, Mineral and Aerated waters at 3d per bottle, and, surprisingly, knowing Mr Houston's strong views about alcohol, *"Claret cup"* at 6d per glass. There was a *"Het Vivjer"*, presided over by Miss Goulding, which featured, for example, a 'Fishing Pond', with Line Fishing at 3d per cast and Net Fishing at 6d per cast, and various scientific wonders to be observed,

Doherty & Son's
CABINET, PIANOFORTE, & CARPET WAREROOMS.

(Established A.D. 1799.)

A Large Stock of
⊹ FIRST-CLASS FURNITURE, ⊹
ALWAYS ON HAND.

Pianofortes, Harmoniums by best makers,
ON SALE AND HIRE.

CARPETS made to Order—A Fit Guaranteed.

Undertaking attended to in all its Branches on the shortest notice

AUCTION SALES AND VALUATIONS ATTENDED TO.

Bridge Street, Coleraine.

GENERAL HOUSE-FURNISHING, IRONMONGERY,
AND
FANCY WAREHOUSE,
DIAMOND, COLERAINE.

CRAWFORD & CO.
Would Respectfully call the attention of intending Purchasers to their Present Stock of FIRST-CLASS GOODS in
GENERAL HARDWARE & HOUSE-FURNISHING,
INCLUDING —

Close and open Kitchen Ranges, Stoves, Register Grates and Chimney Pieces, Brass and Iron Bedsteads, Hair and flock Mattresses, Children's Cots, Dressing, Pier, and Chimney Glasses, Ladies' and Gentlemen's Travelling Trunks, in wood and Iron; Hand Bags, Leather Portmanteaus, and Gladstone Travelling Bags ; Brushes all kinds.

ELECTRO-PLATE in Spoons, Forks, Tea and Coffee Services, Cruets, &c.

JOSEPH RODGERS & SON'S CELEBRATED CUTLERY.

A Large stock of Perambulators and Bassinettes.

JAPANNED BATHS and Fancy Toilet Ware in great variety.

A Large Assortment of Fishing Tackle, Lawn Tennis, Croquet, and Cricket Goods, all by Best Makers.

Another advertisement in the programme for the "Bazaar and Fancy Fair" 1882.

such as 'A Sympalmograph' and a 'Luminous Chamber' which you could *"enter and see in the dark"*.

This entertaining and definitely 'whimsical' programme for the Bazaar also included many advertisements by local businesses, which give a further insight into the social and commercial life of the town of Coleraine in the early 1880s. In the end, the Bazaar was a resounding success and fulfilled its objectives. A published list the following year gave a breakdown of the amounts raised at the various 'Stalls' referred to above.

Stall No. 1 – Lady Bruce £42 18s 3d
Stall No. 2 – Mrs Taylor
and Miss Warke £145 11s 7d
Stall No.3 – Mrs Woodside £234   0s 0d
Stall No. 4 – Mrs Houston £203 5s 1d
Stall No. 5 – Old Boarders £149 13s 4d
Stall No. 6 – Old Day-boys £157 17s 6d
Stall No. 7 – Present Day-boys £76 18s 5d
Stall No. 8 – Present Boarders £80   2s 9d
Stall No. 9 – Flower Stall
– Lady Macnaghten £17   1s 0d
Stall No. 10 – Utility Stall –
Mrs Stronge £20   1s 3d
Refreshment Stall
– Mrs O'Hara............................... £23   5s 8d
Cash at door, programmes,
phonograph, fish-pond &c............£83   6s 3d

                                    £1,234 1s 1d
Expenses,
as in published Statement £172 0s 5d

                                    £1,062   0s 8d

Of the total sum realised by the Bazaar, £600 was allocated to the 'Covered Playground' and the remainder to clearance of debt. Mr Houston later paid tribute to the friends of the school for organising the event and to the citizens of Coleraine and district for supporting it so well: *"As far as my experience goes, no more spirited, energetic, and generous effort has ever been made by the people of Coleraine."* The financial well-being of the Institution was secured, but only in the short term; as the school prospered and expanded in the not-too-distant future, further funds would soon be needed.

Moving on to 1883, the number of pupils was 150, of whom exactly half were boarders. During the year about £500 was spent on drainage, sewerage and similar improvements. The President of the Managing Committee, Sir Hervey Bruce, gave a long-term lease of a field of about six acres, to be used for 'Cricket and Football'. Forty-one candidates were successful at the Intermediate Examinations. A.G. Crawford and W.G. Connolly (Middle Grade) retained their Exhibitions, while H.E. Rutherford (6th place in Ireland) and H.A. Anderson obtained Exhibitions in Junior Grade. S.J. Hunter won the Clothworkers' Scholarship and Basil Ewing the Cochrane Scholarship. S.J. Hunter, Clothworkers' Scholar 1883, will feature frequently in the later pages of this history, eventually becoming a Master, Vice-Principal, and acting Headmaster of the school for a time.

It was around this time that Mr Houston had instituted the publication of an annual Coleraine Academical Institution *Calendar*. This interesting archive, some copies of which are still extant and can be viewed in the present School Museum, was much more than a calendar. It was packed with all sorts of detailed information about the school, including a list of the original and later benefactors of the school, a list of the Clothworkers' Scholars, a prospectus, the school curriculum or *"Course of Instruction"*, the Headmaster's Report at the annual Distribution of Prizes, Examination Papers for the Clothworkers' Scholarship, and even the results, by subject, for every pupil in the school, in all school examinations. A perusal of the 1883 Calendar, as with all the others, gives an often vivid glimpse into the life of the school at the time and also a further insight into Mr Houston's running of the school and his ideals for its pupils.

The 1883 Calendar begins with the following emphatic statement:
THE PRINCIPAL *of the Institution will be happy to receive Visitors from* 12 TILL 1 O'CLOCK, P.M., *on all weekdays except Saturdays.*
During the remainder of the time, FROM 9 A.M. TILL 3 P.M., *he is constantly engaged at his professional duties, which cannot be interrupted without great inconvenience, and injury to the working of the School.*

While modern headmasters might initially feel somewhat envious of Mr Houston in this matter, it must be remembered that he probably had a full timetable to teach, as well as seeing to the administration of the school and 'receiving Visitors'. And exactly when did he have his lunch?

THE PRINCIPAL *of the Institution will be happy to receive* Visitors FROM 1 TILL 2 O'CLOCK, P.M., *on all week days except Saturdays.*

During the remainder of the time, FROM 9 A.M. TILL 3 P.M., *he is constantly engaged at his professional duties, which cannot be interrupted without great inconvenience and injury to the working of the School.*

Headmaster T.G. Houston's restrictions on visitors, from the 1883 "School Calendar".

The school "Prospectus" for 1883 states that the Institution is: *"provided with every accommodation for an educational establishment. The School Rooms and Common Hall are large, well-lighted and airy. The Building has been specially designed for the reception of boarders, and contains dining-hall, lavatory, bath-room, with bathing compartments, and swimming bath, cloak-room, drying-room, trunk-room, and spacious dormitories, in which each boy has a separate bed. The establishment is efficiently heated by means of hot-water pipes, and has recently been provided with a complete and thorough system of ventilation, on the most approved scientific principles."* To reassure those parents who might have worries about the health of their sons attending the school, especially as boarders, they are told: *"The whole Establishment is under the care of a medical man of acknowledged eminence, to whose unremitting attention the excellent sanitary condition of the Institution is largely attributable. At a considerable distance from the main building, there is a detached hospital, furnished with every appliance for the treatment of sick boys. This building is also thoroughly warmed and ventilated."*

Mr Houston firmly believed in an all-round education for his pupils – moral, spiritual and physical, as well as intellectual. Hence, prospective parents are told that: *"Careful attention is paid to the Physical culture of the boys. The class for drill is in a high state of efficiency, and all boarders are required to attend it."* Church attendance was also important: *"The School*

is conducted on non-sectarian principles, the basis adopted for religious instruction being the outline of Christian faith agreed upon by the Evangelical Alliance. Every facility is afforded for pupils to attend their own places of worship. The Episcopalian and Presbyterian boarders are accompanied to their respective churches by the Resident Masters." (This custom of 'Church Lines', as it became known, continued almost until the closure of the boarding school in 1998, with the authors of this book, as young Resident Masters in the early 1970s, accompanying long, straggling lines of neatly-dressed, if not always spiritually enthusiastic, boarders to St Patrick's, Terrace Row, First Coleraine or New Row churches on a Sunday morning.) Also, in line with the original Constitution, *"The school is opened and closed each day with the reading of a portion of Scripture and with prayer."*

Regarding the fees charged in 1883, the terms for day pupils, including instruction in English, Latin, Greek, Mathematics, French and Drawing, were: one-and-a-half guineas per quarter in the Lower School, two guineas in the Middle School and two-and-a-half guineas in the Upper School. For boarders, the quarterly fee, including instruction in the above subjects and full board, was nine guineas, with boys over twelve years of age paying ten-and-a-half guineas. Optional lessons at additional quarterly fees were: Elocution and Calisthenics 10s-6d and Music £1-1s-0d, with 5s-0d for Use of Piano. A small charge of one shilling per quarter was made for Singing Lessons, and *"both Boarders and Day pupils are expected to attend the Singing-class."*

Rules And Regulations

A boarder in the early 1880s was required to bring with him, *"two pair of sheets, three pillowcases, six towels, bath sheet, a pair of bathing drawers, three dinner napkins, and a dessert spoon and fork, which will be returned on his leaving school."* It was also felt desirable that, *"all Boarders should be provided with flannel suits, jerseys, and cricketing shoes for outdoor games."* Although a school uniform as known today did not exist then, Mr Houston was precise in some of the details he gave regarding what his pupils should wear. *"All Boarders are expected to bring with them a Silk Hat*

Each Boarder will be required to bring with him two pair of sheets, three pillow cases, six towels, bath sheet, a pair of bathing drawers, three dinner napkins, and a dessert spoon and fork, which will be returned on his leaving school.

☞ *It is also necessary that all articles be distinctly marked.* The particular attention of parents is respectfully requested to this rule of the school. Owing to the large numbers in attendance, it is found very difficult to prevent unmarked articles from being lost—boys being frequently unable to identify their own property. It is even more necessary that boots, hats, overcoats, umbrellas, &c., should be marked than underclothing. The name should be in full and indelible. It is also desirable that all Boarders should be provided with flannel suits, jerseys, and cricketing shoes for out-door games.

In addition to the above, all Boarders are expected to bring with them a Silk Hat for Sundays, and other dress occasions.

Boys under five feet four inches in height are required to wear for dress the Eton Jacket. Taller boys may, if they prefer it, wear a black cloth coat instead.

Trousers may be black or grey, and of any material. They must, in all cases, be without pockets, as nothing is more calculated to produce a vulgar and slouching carriage, than the habit, almost universal among boys, of constantly walking and sitting with their hands in the pockets of their trousers.

The ordinary wearing Cap, which is part of the School uniform, can be had at the Institution.

No pupil will be admitted to the School without a satisfactory certificate of good conduct. This should, if possible, be obtained from a boy's last teacher. No boy whose character does not bear such scrutiny will be received in the Institution either as Day Pupil or Boarder.

Boarders will also be required both on entering School for the first time, and returning to it after vacations, to bring with them a certificate stating that for at least two months previous to date of certificate they have not resided in a house where there was infectious disease, or been in contact with any one likely to communicate infection. A declaration to this effect by a boy's parent will be accepted.

The Principal feels that in the two last Rules he has the hearty sympathy of the parents of his pupils, in whose interests such regulations are made. It is his wish that the school under his care, whether large or small in point of numbers, should be *select in a moral point of view*, and protected by every available means against anything that might prove injurious to the health of the boys.

PAYMENT IN ALL CASES QUARTERLY, AND IN ADVANCE.*

First Quarter,	...	15th August till 1st November.
Second Quarter,	...	1st November till 1st February.
Third Quarter,	...	1st February till 15th April.
Fourth Quarter,	...	15th April till 1st July.

Pupils entering the School after the commencement of the Quarter are charged only from date of entrance. No allowance is made for occasional absence, or for fractions of a week at entrance.

All applications for further information to be made to the Principal.

* Compliance with this rule can in no case be dispensed with.

Extract from School Regulations of the 1880s.
Of particular interest is the Headmaster's ban on pockets!

for Sundays, and other dress occasions. Boys under five feet four inches in height are required to wear for dress the Eton Jacket. Taller boys may, if they prefer, wear a black cloth coat instead." Moving on to one of his pet hates, as described earlier, he begins by saying that trousers, "may be black or grey, and of any material," but absolutely must, in all cases, "be without pockets, as nothing is more calculated to produce a vulgar and slouching carriage, than the habit, almost universal among boys, of constantly walking and sitting with their hands in the pockets of their trousers." The reactions of schoolboys of 2010 to this 1883 regulation can be guessed fairly accurately!

In his report at the Annual Distribution of Prizes in 1883, Mr Houston elaborated at length one of his concerns about the education system which had developed in the wake of the Intermediate Act of 1878, which required pupils at schools such as the Institution to prepare for, and sit, the Intermediate Examinations. The school's success rate in the annual Intermediate Examinations understandably became a very important feature of the results published at

Prize Distributions. However, Mr Houston quite rightly felt that such a system led to what he called 'examination fever', with the school's curriculum being skewed by external forces to 'cram' for the new government examinations. Mr Houston very strongly felt that education was about much, much more than cramming for examinations. Modern school principals, whose pupils are required to prepare for externally-set GCSEs, AS levels and A-Levels, for example, would probably agree with him. Houston outlines very clearly the unpleasant consequences of such an educational system: "*The high pressure under which teacher and taught must labour, the constant unrest, the eager ambition, the often vulgar rivalry, the desire after the rewards of knowledge rather than after knowledge itself, the 'auri sacra fames', the haste with which, owing to the limits of age, pupils must be prepared for their yearly trial – all these are evils which have followed in the train of the Act of 1878, and which cannot but have a most deleterious effect upon the physical, the intellectual, and the moral health of many of the youth of Ireland.*"

Here, Houston was not merely making a token Prize Distribution protest for the ears of those politicians who exercised powers over schools; he was genuinely convinced of the *"injurious effects which the present system of examinations exercises on the health of the pupils who are obliged to prepare for them"*, and he had already taken some action to relieve this pressure on the pupils of his Institution. He told the audience on that Prize Day in September 1883: *"I have thought it my duty to make a stand against the pressure which urges teachers to overwork the intellects of their young charges. For more than a year I have thought it right to shorten the hours of study for our boarders, and to lengthen their time for recreation. Instead of studying an hour before breakfast, all our resident pupils begin the day with a good invigorating bath to their entire person (in 'the plunge', mentioned earlier), and a short but energetic drill afterwards. No doubt this abolition of morning study may shorten a little our list of honours at the end of the year; but it will, I feel confident, tend to lengthen the lives of the boys, and I am sure that in this aim, I shall have approbation of all parents whose love for their children is greater than their ambition for them."* Mr Houston's earnestness here, in unashamedly putting the health of his pupils before the academic honours which the school might gain, is to be much admired, and no doubt his bold move did meet with the 'approbation' of most parents. The pupils themselves, however, might not all have voted for 'an invigorating bath' followed by some 'energetic drill' instead of a sleepy study hour, had they been given the opportunity to do so!

As well as his concern for their physical well-being, Mr Houston had other ideals which he believed were just as important as intellectual achievement. He did not think that he and his teaching staff should focus entirely on *"the heavier and more utilitarian work of teaching Greek, Latin, Mathematics and English"*; indeed he stated that *"much of these could be learnt, and the learner still go out into the world little better than an intellectual barbarian"*. He had noticed in his pupils an increase in *"the desire for culture as distinguished from mere knowledge"* and he praised his Managing Committee for their new regulations, which made *"drawing and vocal music branches of the ordinary school education"*. In regard to this, he appealed to parents to

The Masters, November 1883.
Rear: G.W. Hawker, M.A., J. Adams, B.A., L. Coulter, B.A.
Front: R. Walker, B.A., T.G. Houston, M.A., Headmaster, G. Wefers (Berlin),
R. Collingwood, Cantab.

support *"the effort we are making to cultivate the higher side of their children's intellectual nature."*

Finally, in that 1883 speech, he went on to identify what he thought was the most important feature of all in the condition of a school, *"the moral welfare of the boys."* His strong contention was that, *"If this is not right, then all is wrong."* He was delighted to report that, *"the moral tone of the School is excellent"* and praised the boys in this respect. *"We have many boys of the highest principles and the truest honour, while, so far as my knowledge goes, there is not a distinctly bad or vicious boy amongst us. I have never been so well satisfied with the conduct of the boys as during the past session. There has never been so little punishment of any kind in the School."* He attributed much of the credit for this happy state of affairs to his assistant teachers – at that time, Messrs. Hunter, Walker, Collingwood, Wefers and Macey – who had *"managed the boys in a patient and gentle manner."*

Mr Houston's comments in this Annual Report of 1883 reveal him to be a Headmaster with strong, distinct views about education and a clear vision of the sort of pupils he would like to see graduating from the Institution. They would be accomplished, intelligent and personable young men, who had been thoroughly imbued with his particular brand of all-round education - physical, cultural, and moral, as well as intellectual. Houston obviously was one of the greatest headmasters of his time and it is clear from this Annual Report, and others, that the members of his Managing Committee were very satisfied with the man and his regime.

In 1884, the number of pupils on the roll was 147 and seventy-four of these were boarders. The annual Distribution of Prizes was held in the new Gymnasium ('Covered Playground'), which had been built with the funds raised by the Bazaar of 1882. Past pupils continued to bring honour to themselves and to the school: Thomas R. Lyle, Clothworkers' Scholar of 1879, won the Mathematical Studentship (value £700) and the McCullagh Prize in Dublin University, while James Tate won a similar honour (value £500) at the Royal University. The results of the Intermediate Examinations were again excellent, with one Gold Medal, seven Exhibitions, three Retained

School Prefects and Monitors, November 1883
Prefect: S. Connor, Senior Prefect: W.J. Davison, Prefect: G.M. Irvine
Monitors: R.J. Bell, A.J. Irwin, W.J. Millar, W.W. Boyd, B.G. Ewing, W. Couser, J.T. Wiggins, A.B. Cassidy, R.P. Wilson, Geo. Woodburn.

Exhibitions, and nine Prizes coming to the school. A Senior Exhibition (£40) was won by A.E. Crawford; Exhibitions in Middle Grade (£25) were won by H. E. Rutherford and W.M. Henry, and in Junior Grade (£15) by T.H. Taylor, Thomas Houston, James Beatty and J. Cochrane. W.J. Dawson, W.G. Connolly and H.E. Rutherford retained their previous Exhibitions. H.E. Rutherford obtained the Gold Medal in English, while Prizes were won by J.A. Workman and W.G. Connolly (Senior), James Millar and H.A. Anderson (Middle), and R. Dunlop and W.C. Macann (Junior) J. Johnstone won the Clothworkers' Scholarship and R. Dunlop the Cochrane Scholarship.

The Start Of A Proud Sporting Tradition

However, the academic year 1883/1884 was much more important for another reason, and indeed some aficionados of a particular sport (which involves much vigorous but, in most cases, fairly gentlemanly pushing and shoving around an oval-shaped ball) would say that the Institution's glorious history only began in that year. Rugby football had arrived in the school on the hill – and in this very first year of entering the competition, the school carried off the coveted Schools' Cup.

On display in the present School Museum is a meticulously-kept, hand-written 'Football Record' of the school's performance in rugby, during the years 1884 – 1920. The first entry states:

"The game of football may be said to have begun in this School in the year 1883. Before that time, indeed, there was some attempt made to play it, but its real beginning may be rightly assigned to that date. During the season 1883 – 84, after severe and hard-contested matches, including several draws, the Ulster Schools' Challenge Cup fell to the lot of this Institution.
The honourable post of Captain of our first Cup Team was attained by G.M. Irvine, whose ability for the post was amply proved by the result of the season's play.
The Cup Team was constituted as follows: Back. R. Fall; Half Backs. J.T Wiggins, B.G. Ewing, T. Smith; Quarter Backs. S. Young, W. Boyd; Forwards. K. Boyd, G.M. Irvine, F. McCay, A.J. Irwin, R. Moore, W. McIntyre, J. Johnston, W.J. Millar, T. Gardiner; Substitutes. J.R. Rankin, W.A. Clugston."

THE FIRST C.A.I. CUP TEAM, 1883-1884.

B. G. E. Wing.   K. Boyd.   R. Walker, Esq.   W. M'Intyre.   R. Moore.   F. M'Kay.   J. R. Rankin.   J. T. Wiggins.
W. W. Boyd.   A. J. Irwin.   J. Johnston.   S. Young.   R. A. Fall.   W. Millar.
T. Gardiner.   G. M Irvine.   T. Smith.

The Cup Final took place in Coleraine, against Foyle College, on Thursday 10 April 1884, these schools having met three times previously, the result on each occasion being a draw. The result on this occasion was a goal to nil, courtesy of *"Basil Ewing dropping a goal from the field of play."* The C.A.I. XV had an unbeaten record that season, winning three games and drawing four.

The year 1885, however, was a very different year for the school rugby team, which played only three matches, winning one of the two friendlies and drawing the other, before losing to Armagh Royal School in the first round of the Cup competition, by one goal to nil. The despondency and bitter frustration felt by all can be sensed in the club secretary's report for that year. *"Mr Irvine's successor in the office of Captain was A.J. Irwin. During his term of office, the reaction set in strong, and the play became lax and destitute of energy and vitality. This state of matters led to the loss of the Cup in the first round of ties."*

This frustration turned to real desperation later in the season when (heresy of heresies!) the club had a go at Association Football. This time there is a tone of grim satisfaction in the secretary's account of what happened. *"After the loss of the Cup it was found almost impossible to continue practice, so an attempt was made to introduce the Association game, and the school entered the competition for the Schools' Association Cup, but happily for the Rugby game, was beaten by St. Malachy's College by three goals to two."*

However, the popularity of the new competitive sport of rugby is reflected in the fact that the number of members in the school club in 1885 was 130 (fifty boarders and thirty day-boys) - out of a total school population of 143.

In 1885, the results of the Intermediate examinations were again very satisfactory. Senior Exhibitions were won by W.G. Connolly, H.A. Anderson and W.M. Henry, while Thomas Houston obtained an Exhibition in Middle Grade, as did R. McElderry, T.H. Stevenson, W.H. Boyle and W.A. Houston in Junior Grade. W.A. Houston won the Gold Medal in Mathematics and a special prize of £10 in the same subject was awarded to E.J. Esdale. Prizes were won by H. Rutherford and R.D. Megaw (Senior), J.K. Bresland, D. Megaw, J. Gibson, T.H. Taylor, J. Beatty and A.S. Young (Middle), and J.D. Mullan, J. Marshall, and E.J. Esdale (Junior). Clothworkers' Scholar for the year was A.E. Crawford and the Cochrane Scholarship was won by J. Bresland.

In 1886, the number on the roll had fallen slightly to 132, with fifty-three of these being boarders. It was another glory year for the rugby 1st XV, with the Schools' Challenge Cup returning to Coleraine. The writer of the "Football Record" for that year describes the improved season generally and presents the Cup Final, against R.B.A.I., as an almost titanic struggle.

> After the loss of the Cup it was found almost impossible to continue practice, so an attempt was made to introduce the association game, and the School entered the competition for the Schools' Association Cup, but happily for the Rugby game, was beaten by St. Malachy's College by three goals to two.

Extract from the rugby "Football Record" for 1885. Frustration at not winning the Schools' Cup led to a brief flirtation with soccer!

The Schools' Cup Team 1885 - 1886. Back row: E.W.P. Sims, J. Barkley, J.K. Bresland, D. Lyle, T. Houston, W. McKay, J. Cochrane, S.W. Ogilvy. Front, seated: R. Dunlop, W. Huston, R.K. Thistle, W. Henry, R.S. Young, H.A. Anderson.

"The succeeding Captain, R. Dunlop, made a determined effort to rally the fallen fortunes of the game and, ably backed by many comrades, succeeded in winning back the coveted trophy after one of the closest and most determined struggles ever witnessed in almost any school match. The final tie with Belfast Institution will never be forgotten by those who played in it. The Belfast team, though far superior in individual weight and strength, was outmatched by the superior combination and training of their opponents, and after a most exciting game, Coleraine came off victorious by a goal to nil. Dunlop scored the try and Wm. McCay kicked the goal. After playing two forties, neither side had scored, so the referee ordered the match to be continued for an equal time (15min) each way. In the middle of the second half, amidst great applause, Dunlop scored the decisive point."

The heroes who played in that 1886 Cup Final are listed as: Back, E. Sims; Half Backs, Dunlop, Anderson, Henry; Quarter Backs, F. Ogilvy, T. Houston; Forwards, W. McCay, S. McCay, R.S. Young, W.B. Huston, J.K.

Bresland, J. Cochrane, J. Barklie, R.K. Thistle, D. Lyle (sub).

Looking at the school 'Calendar' for 1886, some items are perhaps worth noting. The list of staff shows that Sergeant Wotton had replaced Sergeant Atkinson as 'Drill Sergeant' and that the school now employed a 'Dancing Professor', a Madame Iff, of Glasgow. The school Prospectus, in the matter of the educational fees payable, states that, *"A reduction of 25 per cent of above fees will be made in favour of Clergymen's sons, whether Day pupils or boarders."* An addition to the lessons available is described as follows:

"On two evenings in the week an Elocution class meets, at which a limited number of pupils are received under the immediate superintendence of the Principal. The business of this class includes:
1ˢᵗ, Instruction and practice in the art of extemporaneous speaking and in the management of the business of public meetings.

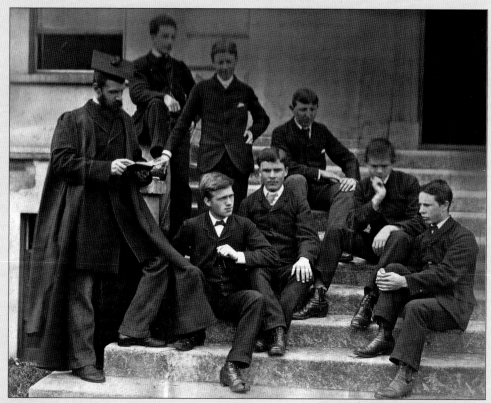

At the feet of the master! The Senior VI Form, November 1883, in a somewhat pensive pose, with Mr Houston, the Headmaster. From left, the pupils are: R.J. Duffin, T. McC. Williamson, H.V. Taylor, S.J. Hunter, W.H. Wray, S. Dunlop, W.J. Girvan. (S.J. Hunter, exact centre, went on to become a Master and eventually Vice-Principal at the school.)

2nd, *Readings and recitations in prose and poetry.*
3rd, *Calisthenic exercises for the improvement of carriage and deportment.*
The charge for this class is 10s 6d per quarter."

Mr Houston had recently gained a qualification in elocution and was keen to impart his knowledge to his pupils. In the *"calisthenic exercises"*, he was of course continuing his personal crusade against what he saw as the *"slouching carriage"* prevalent amongst modern boys. In addition to gaining a sound academic education at his Institution, Houston wanted his pupils to be well-spoken and to be physically, as well as morally, upright!

The Prospectus, as in past years, reminded parents of two important requirements, if they wished their sons to be educated at the school.

1. *"No pupil will be admitted to the School without a satisfactory certificate of good conduct. This should if possible, be obtained from the boy's last teacher. No boy whose character does not bear such scrutiny will be received in the Institution either as Day pupil or Boarder."* In a Prize Distribution speech, Mr Houston had claimed that this requirement was at least partly responsible for the excellent behaviour of pupils in the school. He claimed to be a fore-runner in this matter, stating that because of this certificate of character: *"we have been preserved from much of that moral contagion which is more to be dreaded than the most virulent disease. In accordance with a resolution of the Schoolmasters' Association, a similar rule has been adopted by most of the leading Schools in Ireland; and indeed I cannot understand the position of any respectable School which does not require some guarantee from all its pupils."*

2. *"Every Boarder will also be required both on entering School for the first time, and on returning to it after vacations, to bring with him a certificate stating that for at least two months previous to date of certificate he has not resided in a house where there was any infectious disease, or been in contact with anyone likely to communicate infection."* This clause again reflects the great fear of 'virulent diseases' prevalent in boarding schools at the time.

Praise For The School

The school Prospectus 1886 also contained a wide range of recommendations by influential people, testifying to the excellence of the Institution. Sir Charles A. Cameron, Kt., 'President of the Royal College of Surgeons, City Analyst of Dublin, &c, &c,' has pleasure in reporting a most favourable inspection of the 'Sanitary condition' of the school and adds: *"I think I could adduce no better proof of the estimation in which I hold this School, than the fact of one of my sons being educated in it."* J.C.L. Carson, M.D., 'Physician to the Coleraine Academical Institution and Consulting Sanitary Officer for the Borough of Coleraine' is certainly fulsome in his praise of the Headmaster and his wife: *"It would be quite impossible to imagine any parties more anxious than Mr and Mrs Houston are for the health and comfort of the boys committed to their care. They get an abundance of wholesome food; and the attention bestowed on them is unremitting."*

Rev. F. Stuart Gardner, M.A., Minister of First Presbyterian Church, Coleraine, testifies to the excellence of the moral and religious education which the Institution pupils receive: *"I have never known any School where the moral tone is so high. This is due to Mr Houston's personal influence, and to his unwearied care in regard to this matter. I do not know of any school to which parents could send their boys with more perfect confidence that their moral and religious training would be in excellent hands."* Anthony Traill, Esq., 'LL.D., M.D., Fellow and Tutor, Trinity College, Dublin, &c, &c, &c', writing from Ballylough House, Bushmills, on September 24, 1885, pays tribute to the quality of the young men coming to him from the Institution:

"I have much pleasure in stating that a great many of Mr Houston's pupils from the Academical Institution, Coleraine, have entered Trinity College, Dublin, under me as their College Tutor. They have all shown very careful training and a high standard of education, and several of them have been remarkably successful – one in particular, Mr Thomas R. Lyle, has gained all the highest honours in Mathematics and in the Experimental Sciences, which it was possible for him to obtain. . . . . From the report of the results of the Intermediate Examination for 1885, it appears that the Academical Institution stood 2ⁿᵈ upon the list of Protestant Schools of Ireland, having secured 21 Honor places and 45 places on the Pass List. I cannot speak too highly of the good characters and moral qualities of the young men, without exception, who have come to Trinity College, Dublin, from the Academical Institution."

Mr T.G. Houston had opinions on all matters educational and was seldom afraid to express them. In his Prize Distribution report in 1886, with most of his school governors present, he praised the excellent working relationship which had developed between himself and his Managing Committee:

"I think very few Head Masters are so fortunate in their governors. Our Committee seem to have formed an unusually correct idea of the duties of their position. They have avoided the two extremes of indifference to the concerns of the School under their care, and undue interference with its internal discipline. Whilst they have given a great deal of valuable time and thought to the general interests of the Institution, they have steadily and constantly acted on the principle that in all purely scholastic matters, the Head Master should be left perfectly free to act as his judgement might dictate. This policy has been, I believe, as wise as it was courteous and kind. It has preserved the School from those endless disputes and heart-burnings among governing boards, head masters, assistant masters, and even pupils, which have proved disastrous to many important and flourishing Schools."

It may well have been the case that at least a few of the members of the Managing Committee felt a little uncomfortable, listening to this rather patronising lecture as to how wise school governors should allow the Headmaster they had chosen to be *"perfectly free to act as his judgement might dictate."* However, Mr Houston obviously enjoyed the complete trust and confidence of his governors, as Sir Hervey Bruce, still the President of the Committee, commented that he and his fellow Committee members, *"had always felt that it was their duty to leave the educational part of the School in the Principal's hands, well knowing how well qualified Mr Houston was to perform the duties of a great and flourishing School."*

Taking a final look at the Institution 'Calendar' for 1886, it is worth noting a few further items.

The Examination Papers for the Clothworkers' Scholarship of the previous year showed how demanding was the competition for this most valuable annual prize of £50. There were papers in Greek; Greek Composition, Grammar and History; Latin; Latin Grammar, Composition and History; Algebra; Arithmetic; Geometry; Trigonometry; English History; Geography; English Grammar, Parsing and Analysis; Philology and English Literature; French Translation; French Grammar and Composition; and Chemistry. All of these papers featured very demanding questions, far beyond the reach of most modern school pupils. As mentioned earlier, the school 'Calendar' printed the results, in every subject, for all pupils, in all examinations in the school, throughout the academic year. Thus it was possible for the entire public of Coleraine and further afield to see how well, or how badly, each pupil had performed. All was revealed! For example, in the Monthly Examinations of May 1886, in the Fourth Form, five boys in the class of twenty-five pupils achieved the maximum mark of forty in Arithmetic, but a further four boys (and their names will certainly not be published in this volume) registered zero on the score sheet!

Another important event of 1886 was a 'Visitation' (dreaded word!) by the Commissioners appointed under the Education Endowment (Ireland) Act of 1885 to *"make an enquiry"* into the affairs of the School. As a result they offered to constitute the Board of Management into a Corporation and to give it corporate powers. This offer was accepted and a new scheme was drawn up for the administration of the school. The new scheme provided for three Classes of members of the Institution, each class summarised as follows:
Class 1: subscribers of £50. Members in this class had *"the privilege of transferring their rights as hereinafter provided, and each of whom shall be entitled to membership for his life, or until he shall transfer his rights."*
Class 2: subscribers of £10; those who had spent £20 on school fees and in addition had subscribed £5; all past pupils who had been at the school for at least three years and subscribed £5. Members in this class did not have the privilege of transferring their rights.

Illustrious past pupil in the 1880s Dr T.T. McKendry, who generously founded the Dr T.T. McKendry Prize, still awarded at Prize Distributions today for the best overall performances in Year 11.

Class 3: subscribers of £2 and all past pupils who had been at school for at least three years and subscribed annually £1. Members in this Class were described as 'Annual Members.'

The Governing Body of the School was elected from these members and by them. The General Agent of The Honourable The Irish Society in Coleraine and the Protestant clergymen of the town were appointed ex-officio members of the Board.

Academic successes continued in 1886. Among the many distinctions gained by former pupils of the school (an extensive list of these was published each year in the 'Calendar') the most noteworthy was that of A. Boyd, who finished a brilliant career at the Royal University by winning a Studentship value £500. In the Intermediate Examinations forty candidates were successful. J. Beatty took 5th place in Ireland and R.K. McElderry and J.K. Bresland won Exhibitions in Middle Grade, while J.A. McClelland and W.C. Marshall won Exhibitions in Junior Grade. J. Beatty won the Gold Medal in English (Middle), and Silver Medals were awarded to D. Megaw (Senior Drawing) and W.F. Todd (Middle Music). W.M. Henry won the

Clothworkers' Scholarship and E.J. Esdale the Cochrane Scholarship.

In 1887, the number of pupils increased to 147, seventy-one of these being boarders. It was another hugely successful year for the rugby 1st XV, with the Ulster Schools' Cup coming to Coleraine for the third time in four years. In his report for the year, the club secretary writes: *"Mr Dunlop retained his position as Captain during the season, also the most victorious the school ever enjoyed, not a single match being lost. The Cup was easily won."* The confident tone apparent here is repeated in comments on various matches during the season. A match against Foyle College, which the school won by two goals and five tries to one try, was described as, *"very dull and one-sided throughout, the first try being scored within two minutes of kick-off."* A cup-tie against Derry Academy (result C.A.I. two goals and three tries, Academy nil) is again described as, *"a rather one-sided match."* Another confrontation with Foyle College, which the school won by two goals and five tries to nil, is described as *"a very uninteresting match, the Foyle team being compelled to touch down five times in defence."*

The Cup Final, played in Belfast, was against Galway Grammar School *"and resulted in a win for Coleraine by two goals and a try to nil. The ground was in a very bad way, being frozen quite hard, and covered with snow. Dunlop scored two tries and W. McCay one. The latter also brought off both goals."*

At the close of the rugby season for the year, the club, *"unanimously decided to give Dunlop a presentation Cup, both for the excellence of play and for the ability he displayed in managing the affairs of the club."* Robert Dunlop, the captain of the school team in the glory years of 1886 and 1887, went on to be an outstanding player for Trinity College, Dublin, and eventually an Irish international, with eleven caps between 1889 and 1894. A B.A. and LL.B of Trinity, he was appointed Divisional Commissioner for Cork and Kerry with the Royal Irish Constabulary, in the days before Partition.

Away from the snowy fields of physical conflict, 1887 saw the usual academic successes in the Intermediate Examinations. Forty pupils were successful, with the star performer being R.K. McElderry, described as 'a brilliant student.' He obtained a Senior Exhibition (value £40), Gold Medal in Classics, and Silver Medals in Greek and Latin. Senior Exhibitions were also won by J. Beatty and D. Megaw, and Exhibitions were also gained by D. Lyle (Middle Grade) and M.M. Houston (Junior Grade). The Clothworkers' Scholar was T. Houston and R. Burns won the Cochrane Scholarship.

In the year 1888, the number on the school roll comprised seventy-seven day-pupils and sixty-seven boarders, total 144. The rugby team played five games, winning three, losing one and drawing one. The one game lost was the final of the Schools' Cup, against R.B.A.I., and the try which ended the hope of a third consecutive triumph was the only one scored against the side during the season. It is noted in the football report for the season that, *"owing to an epidemic of small-pox in Derry, no matches were played before Xmas"*, justifying the fear of infectious diseases in schools at the time. Another interesting decision taken by the school rugby club that year initiated a tradition that was to continue until the present day: *"As an inducement to good play, it was resolved to present the best and most regular players with 'colours'."* On 7 April 1888, a Schools' Inter-Provincial match took place between Ulster and Leinster and on the Ulster side were the following Institution pupils: T. Dunlop, D. Lyle and J. Finnigan, with J. Clarke, and W.B. Huston as substitutes. At the end of the season it was decided that the surplus balance in the club account should be spent in purchasing and framing the photographs of all the football teams, from 1883-84 until the present time, and these photos put on display in the school Committee Room.

In the Intermediate Examinations the school had another excellent year. W.A. Houston was the outstanding pupil, with a Senior Exhibition, Gold Medal in Mathematics and Gold Medal in English. Junior Exhibitions were obtained by D. Mair and M.G. Houston. Prizes were won by D. Lyle, J. Cassidy, J. McClelland (Senior), R.McCutcheon, T Bresland, R. Burns, J. Craig (Middle), and R.H. Gilmour

(Junior). The Clothworkers' Scholarship was won by R.K. McElderry and the Cochrane Scholarship by A.J. Irwin.

New Rules For The Governing Body

It was in 1888 that the new Scheme of Management for the Institution, referred to above, was finally approved by the government in Dublin and published. For historians who might be interested in official government-speak of that time, the opening proclamation reads as follows:

Whereas the Right Honourable Gerald Fitzgibbon and the Right Honourable John Naish, the Judicial Commissioners constituted by the Educational Endowments (Ireland) Act, 1885, have, in virtue of the powers conferred upon them by the said Act, and of every other power enabling them in that behalf, framed and signed under their hands a Scheme relating to the Educational Endowments of and belonging to the Coleraine Academical Institution, which Scheme is annexed to this Order:

And whereas all the conditions in regard to the said Scheme which are required by the said Act to be fulfilled to enable the said Scheme to be finally approved, have been fulfilled:

Now, therefore, We, the Lord Lieutenant-General and General Governor of Ireland, by and with the consent of Her Majesty's Privy Council in Ireland, do, by this order, pursuant to the 27th section of the said Act, declare our approbation of the aforesaid Scheme, and the same is hereby finally approved.

Given at the Council Chamber, Dublin Castle, this 18th day of May, 1888.

HEDGES EYRE CHATTERTON
P.J. KEENAN
PETER O'BRIEN

In noting the main endowments of the school in the opening paragraph of the Scheme, the writers refer to donations from *"The Master Wardens and Commonalty of Freemen of the Art or Mystery of Clothworkers, London"*, presumably the full title of the Clothworkers' Company.

The new Scheme stated that the Governing Body should consist of ex-officio Governors and Representative Governors. The ex-officio Governors were, namely: *The General Agent of The Honourable The Irish Society, being a Protestant, and the Clergyman or Minister, or, if there be more than one, the Senior or Principal Officiating Clergyman or Minister of each Protestant Congregation having a Church or other place of worship within the limits of the parishes of Coleraine and Killowen, all for the time being."* The Scheme of Management has undergone various changes since then, one of them being the removal of the term *"being a Protestant"*, from the reference to the Irish Society's representative on the Board.

The 1888 Scheme also stated that any member of the Institution who, *"being a Protestant, shall reside in or within nine miles of the town of Coleraine, shall be eligible to be elected or co-opted"* a Governor. Again, this clause no longer features in the 2010 Scheme of Management.

The Representative Governors should be fifteen in number, initially the fifteen persons who were the existing Trustees or members of the Committee of Management:

1. Sir H.H. Bruce, Bart., Downhill
2. Daniel Taylor, Millburn, Coleraine
3. Joseph Cuthbert, Coleraine
4. Drummond Grant, Coleraine
5. John Huey, Cloonavin, Coleraine
6. James Bellas, Cronbannagh, Coleraine
7. James A. Lyle, Portstewart
8. William Robb, Coleraine
9. Hugh Anderson, Tiev-Tara, Coleraine
10. Stewart Hunter, Breezemount, Coleraine
11. J.S. Anderson, Coleraine
12. C. Forsythe, M.D., Coleraine
13. Thomas G. Carson, Bannfield House, Coleraine
14. J.J.C. Canning, Coleraine
15. William Woodside, Dundooan House, Coleraine

The current (2010) Board of Governors is considerably larger than fifteen, and includes representatives appointed by the Department of Education and the North Eastern Education and Library Board and also elected representatives of the parents and the teaching staff.

Some other points in the 1888 Scheme are perhaps worth mentioning.

- The Governors could, if they wished, *"maintain an evening school or evening classes for the education of the boys who are engaged during the day at trade or business, and who are desirous of carrying on their education in the evening."*

- The Governors could, upon such terms as they saw fit, appoint a Headmaster, *"provided he be a graduate of one of the Universities of Ireland, England, or Scotland."* Were there no universities in Wales in those days? (Actually, University College South Wales and University College North Wales were both set up after the Aberdare Report of 1881, but Houston and his Governors might not at that time have taken them seriously. The University of Wales did not come into existence as a federal university until 1893.)

- An Annual Meeting of *"Members of the Institution"* should be held, at which the Governors should *"submit to the Members, a report upon the workings of the Institution during the current year."* This custom still continues today.

- As always, religion could be a thorny issue in this part of the island and so the Scheme made it clear that, while the Governors could provide for the pupils whatever form of religious instruction they thought fit, *"no pupil shall at any time be permitted to receive or be present at any religious instruction to which his parents or guardians shall object."*

- While the original Constitution for the school was claimed to be 'unalterable', this new Scheme could *"be altered from time to time by the Commissioners of Charitable Donations and Bequests for Ireland, in any matter whatsoever upon the application of the Governors."*

This Scheme for the management of the Institution was a very important and useful document in that it laid down very clearly, and in detail, the powers and duties of Governors, and the procedures which they should follow. A further, very brief, *"Supplemental Scheme"* was added in 1894, the Principal (No. 20) and the Supplemental (No. 140) Schemes *"to be read and to take effect as one Scheme."*

Returning now to the year 1889, the number of pupils was 138, of whom seventy-eight were boarders. The 1st XV again reached the Final of the Schools' Cup, but lost by one try to nil against Methodist College, Belfast. D. Ogilvy was Captain, and the side played six matches, winning three, losing two and drawing one. Ogilvy, J.G. Brown and J.A. Wilson played for Ulster Schools versus Leinster Schools, Ogilvy captaining the Ulster side.

At the Prize Distribution that year, Mr Houston announced that the boarding department was full to capacity and appealed for funds to build a new wing. On the educational side, he mentioned, among the many successes of former pupils, the achievements of R.K. McElderry, who, after a brilliant school career, had won the First Classical Scholarship of £150 at the Royal University and the First Literary Scholarship in Queen's College, Belfast. At the Intermediate Examinations, twenty-nine candidates were successful. Exhibitions were won by J.F. Cox (Middle,) and W. Houston and A.M. Bulloch (Junior). Silver Medals were awarded to M.M. Houston (Middle Greek) and J.L. Frazer-Hurst (Junior German). Prizes were won by D. Mair and M.G. Houston (Middle), J.L. Frazer-Hurst (three) and H.M. Thompson (Junior). W.A. Houston won the Clothworkers' Scholarship and R. Johnstone the Cochrane Scholarship.

In 1890, the pupils at the Institution numbered 140, including a record eighty-six boarders. At the Prize Distribution, Mr Houston again emphasised the pressure on accommodation in the boarding department, pointing out that the steady increase in the number of boarders had made it necessary to obtain temporary accommodation outside the school. This year brought to an end the fortunate immunity from illness which the school had experienced for such a long time, and a serious illness suffered by Mrs Houston, together with a virulent influenza epidemic, which only a few of the 100 people living in the Institution escaped, made the year a particularly difficult one.

Football and examination results both suffered from the trouble experienced during the year. The 1st XV, *"with colours changed from Bismark and*

Sir H.H. Bruce

Chairman, Board of Governors 1880-1907

Cardinal to plain Cardinal", once more contested the Final of the Schools' Cup, but were beaten by R.B.A.I., the score being two goals and two tries to nil. The account of the match in the Football Report is very gracious. *"The match came off in fine weather in Belfast on the ground of N.I.F.C. and after a fast match, which was all in favour of Belfast after the first 20 minutes, resulted in an easy victory for R.B.A.I. The combination and passing of the Belfast team was splendid and indeed won them the match. After the match, Coleraine were splendidly entertained to dinner by the winning team."* D. Ogilvy again captained the side, which played five matches, winning one, losing two and drawing two. Hughes and D. McCay were selected to play for Ulster versus Leinster in the annual School' Inter-Provincial match. Records also note that during this period, cricket was played regularly and *"the Cycling Club had many enthusiastic members."*

Twenty-five pupils were successful at the Intermediate Examinations. R. Hilton won a Junior Exhibition and J.C. Davidson won the First £10 Prize in Junior. The Silver Medal in Middle German was won by J.L. Frazer-Hurst. A.J. Irwin was the Clothworkers' Scholar and J.C. Davidson won the Cochrane Scholarship.

At this stage, it is perhaps useful to pause for a moment in presenting these annals of the Institution; Mr T.G. Houston had just completed twenty very successful years as Headmaster and the school was entering the last decade of the 19th century. Her Imperial Majesty Queen Victoria had been on the throne since long before the founding of Coleraine Academical Institution and had a further ten years in which to 'reign victorious'. Houston had some twenty-five years of his reign in Coleraine still remaining, and those years are dealt with in the next chapter.

In the last decade of the 19th century, the school continued to prosper, the main problem at first being accommodation for the boarders. In 1891, the number on the roll was 142, of whom well over half (eighty-five) were boarders. So great was the congestion in the boarding department that the Sanatorium had to be requisitioned for sleeping accommodation and a house rented in the town to serve as a hospital, at times when it might be needed.

In this year Mr Henry Taylor, a former English Master at the Institution, (mentioned earlier in Chapter 2) died and bequeathed to the school a sum of money which was allocated by the Governors to the establishment of the annual Henry Taylor Shakespeare Prize. The results of the Intermediate Examinations in 1891 were not up to their usual standard, only twenty-one pupils being successful in the three grades. In Middle Grade, J.C. Davidson was awarded an Exhibition and R. Hilton a Prize. W. Macafee and A. Barr qualified for Prizes in Junior Grade, while A.M. Bulloch (Senior) and R. Hilton (Middle) retained their Exhibitions from the previous year. David Mair won the Clothworkers' Scholarship and William Macafee the Cochrane Scholarship.

There was some bitter disappointment on the football field as well, for, although the 1st XV won four of the five games played during 1890/91, the one match lost was against Methodist College, Belfast, by one try to nil – the only point recorded against the school throughout the season. The comments on the match in the 'Football Record' are terse, and much is, perhaps rightly, left unsaid! *"We had hard lines in losing this match as our team was considered to be superior to our opponents' but the tactics resorted to by the College were too much for our team."* However, a great honour for the school rugby club that season was that a record six members of the Institution side were picked to play for Ulster Schools against Leinster. The match was played in Dublin and Ulster

won easily by two goals and three tries to a penalty goal. Unfortunately, the names of those six heroes, and whether or not any of them featured in the scoring, are not shown in school records. This record representation on an Ulster Schools' side remained unequalled until 1939, when six of H. Hegan's Cup-winning team secured Inter-Provincial caps.)

A very pleasant event involving the rugby club took place just before the mid-summer holidays in 1891, this event being a presentation to David Ogilvy, who had captained the 1st XV for a record three years (a record which was only equalled by the talented Brian Fillis in the mid-1960s). The last of three brothers to attend the school, Ogilvy is eulogised as follows in the Football Record: *"At last Midsummer holidays there left the school one who had been most closely identified with it for the last three years, one who, since Bresland left in 1888, had filled the highest offices in the gift of the boys, one who ruled as Senior Prefect with discipline rarely equalled and yet without unnecessary severity; one by whose departure a blank was left in the management of the affairs of the Institution which we feared it would be nigh impossible to fill for many a day. During the three years of his captaincy he managed the affairs of the Club to the general satisfaction of all, on one occasion being appointed Captain of the Ulster Schools – an honour he richly deserved. In return for his so great services to the School a presentation was made him, and a most enthusiastic farewell accorded to David, 'the last of the Ogilvies'."*

In 1892, the number of pupils was 140. Mr Houston again drew attention to the lack of accommodation, pointing out that his ten teachers were often all at work at the same time in the five classrooms. The results of the Intermediate Examinations were again disappointing, the total number of passes being sixteen, which included one in the new Preparatory Grade. In Senior Grade, J.C. Davidson retained his Exhibition from a previous year and won a Prize, while J. Hezlett secured a Prize in Middle Grade. The Clothworkers' Scholar for the year

The Cricket 1st XI 1893. Mr McQuillan is on the extreme right, rear row. Other legible names appended to the original photograph are: A.D. Waring, R. McCormack, T. McNeil, J.C. Davison, S. Clark, W. Millar, W. Houston, L. Young.

was A.M. Bulloch and J. Hezlett won the Cochrane Scholarship.

The 1st XV, captained by J.L. Frazer-Hurst, had a good season - despite early misgivings! The Football Report states: *"Before play commenced, the prospects of a brilliant season were not very bright and again and again was failure predicted. Nothing daunted by the croaking of these prophets the C.A.I. rose to the occasion and went in with enthusiasm for a course of hard training and practice such as had not been known in the old school for several years."* The school side yet again contested the Final of the Schools' Cup, losing to Methodist College by one goal and one try to nil. This team consisted of: Back – Gibson; Halves – Carson, Wilson W.O., Houston W.; Quarters – McNeil T., Wilson W.A.; Forwards – McCay, Hilton, Lowry G., Linton, Smith S., Ross, Davison, Wray, Frazer-Hurst (capt.). In this season, Dr S.J. Hunter, a master at the school and one-time winner of the Clothworkers' Scholarship as a pupil, became Honorary Treasurer of the Football Club, a post which he occupied until his retirement more than 40 years later, in 1934. (This remarkable man gave loyal, life-long service to the Institution, as a pupil, a teacher and Vice-Principal, at one stage acting as Headmaster during the illness of his superior.) J.L. Frazer-Hurst and D. McCay were selected for the Ulster Schools XV against Leinster. A

recurring problem in these years was finding a suitable field on which to play the matches — often the Cricket Field was used for practice sessions. In 1892 the football secretary writes of how, after considerable trouble, *"we came to terms with Mr Coleman and rented the old historical field where we won the Cup in 1884, though he took advantage of the site and charged us an exorbitant sum."*

A glimpse into social life in the school this year is revealed when Mr Houston decided to assist the football club meet the expenses involved in travelling to away matches by, first of all, giving the club half of the 'fines' (imposed for minor offences) during the season and, secondly, to give a 'Magic Lantern Entertainment.' This Entertainment, on Tuesday November 17th, consisted of, *"a Reading (Alice in Wonderland) illustrated by some forty slides, with an interval of half an hour during which several songs were given by members of the C.A.I. Glee Club, and a couple of solos by Mr Macey while Mrs Houston played the accompaniments."* To what extent the gruff-voiced, rugby-playing senior boarders were 'entertained' by the reading of 'Alice in Wonderland' is not clear, but the old saying in the boarding school always was, 'anything's better than prep' (evening study). On a more serious note, it is also recorded that the day after this event the football captain developed influenza and for the next three or four weeks the epidemic raged through the school and whole countryside.

In 1893, the number of pupils was 130, including seventy-four boarders. Mr Houston explained that the reason for this fall in the number attending the school was the deliberate increase in the fees for boarders, a desperate measure to ease congestion in the boarding department. However, his pleas in recent years for a much-needed further expansion of the school had not fallen on deaf ears. He was able to announce that the Old Boys of the school had decided to assist in a scheme for the extension of the school buildings, that £650 had been subscribed in a remarkably short time, and that it was proposed to hold another Bazaar in the following year to raise the rest of the funds required. The scheme provided for the building of a new wing which would include a large dormitory, several new classrooms, a few private bedrooms for pupils whose parents desired to pay extra for 'this luxury', new Music and Art Rooms, as well as dressing rooms and store-rooms for the various Athletic Clubs. It was also intended to enlarge and improve the Dining Hall, to cope with the greater number of boarders.

The results of the Intermediate Examinations were a little better this year, although an epidemic of measles during the examination period caused several of the best candidates to withdraw. Twenty-five pupils passed in the various Grades, and Prizes were won by J. Hezlett (Senior), J.G. Wallis (Junior), and M. Madill (Preparatory). J.C. Davidson won the Clothworkers' Scholarship and J.G. Wallis the Cochrane Scholarship.

T. M. McNeil captained the 1st XV, which played seven matches, winning two, losing three and drawing two. One of the games lost was the Schools' Cup Final against old enemies, Methodist College Belfast. It was particularly frustrating that the team was beaten by just one penalty goal, which at that time counted only as one point. The overall high standard of play in the school was reflected in selection of T.M. McNeil, W. Gibson, R. Thompson and T. McFetridge for the Ulster Schools' XV.

Another Successful Bazaar

The year 1894 was a very exciting and successful one for the school, for at least two reasons. First of all, it was 'Pandora' year, so-called because of the 'Grand Pandoric Fete and Bazaar' which was held in order to raise funds for the building of the 'Old Boys' Wing', referred to earlier. This grand event was more ambitious than the 'Bazaar' of 1882, but unfortunately no actual programmes are currently available, so the details of what was in this 'Pandora's Box' are somewhat more sketchy than its 1882 fore-runner. The 1894 Fete and Bazaar was scheduled to run for three days, but it was so successful that it continued for a further two days, and attracted visitors from all over the Province. The idea was originated by Mrs Houston, who *"had the assistance of over 200 ladies"* (a formidable team!), the teaching staff, and many other friends of the school, in her demanding project.

On 14 August, the Fete was opened with a fancy-dress parade of the helpers, headed by the Excelsior Military Band from London, after which the business of persuading visitors to part with their money in this good cause began in earnest. Numerous stalls, a refreshment department called the 'Angel Inn', an Arts and Crafts Exhibition, an Art Gallery, a Waxworks, a Shooting Gallery, 'Dancing thrice daily', Dramatic Productions, Concerts and Band Performances all combined to provide the guests with plenty of amusement and spectacle, and *"to make them poorer in the process."* At the Prize Distribution the next year, Mr Houston announced that the proceeds of 'Pandora', together with subscriptions from the Old Boys, had amounted to £2,550. A grant of £750 from the ever-helpful Irish Society brought the total to £3,300, which was still over £1,000 short of the estimated cost of the proposed improvements. However, the sum raised seemed to be enough to give the school Governors the confidence to begin construction of the much-needed extension.

In school 'Calendars' in following years, there was a printed list of the names of some 250 subscribers to the Old Boys' Wing. It is not possible to print that list in its entirety here (the full list can be viewed in the School Museum), but it is useful to select some names of Old Boys who had contributed, to illustrate how many past pupils of the school had achieved success and had embarked on illustrious careers in various parts of Queen Victoria's great Empire, and beyond. These examples are:

W.M. Cuthbert, Cape Town
A. Ogilvy, M.D., Dublin
Professor Drury, Lahore, India
R. M. Boyce, Philadelphia
Captain Reid, Hong Kong
D. Browne, Yezd, Persia.
Surgeon-Captain R. Havelock Charles, India
W.J. Hardy, D.I., Slane
S.C. Young, Sydney
R.D. Morrison, D.I., Cork
C. Armstrong, Canada
S.T. Bryan, Rio De Janeiro
W.J. Millar, New York
T. McNeill, Newfoundland
Professor T.R. Lyle, Melbourne
Arthur Irvine, Honolulu
J. Young, M.D., Cyprus
Professor MacMaster, Derry
Reverend S. Walker, Australia
Reverend J. Brown, Rotterdam
D. Anderson, London
James Smith, St Louis
Joseph Davison, Selo Velikoe

Owing to 'Pandora' it was decided not to hold a Prize Distribution in 1894, but the results of the Intermediate Examinations were made available. Twenty-two candidates passed and Exhibitions were won by J.T. Boyd (Junior) and E. Bennett (Preparatory). Prizes were obtained by R.M. Houston (Junior) and D.S. Madill (Prep.), while W. Hamilton (Junior) was awarded a Prize in Composition. J.M. Hezlett won the Clothworkers' Scholarship and R. Houston the Cochrane Scholarship.

It was another glorious year in football, for S. Smyth captained an unbeaten side and the Ulster Schools' Cup came to Coleraine for a fourth time. Simmons scored the only try in the Final, in Belfast, yet again versus Methodist College. However, Methody discovered that Coleraine had inadvertently played a boy who was over age and *"the Union*

ordered the match to be replayed at Coleraine on Saturday 21 April." The home side won this match by one goal, one penalty goal (eight pts.) to one penalty goal (three pts.). Young scored the try and Magee kicked both goals. The cup-winning side consisted of: Back – W.L. Myles; Halves – J.C. Clark, J.R. Magee, R.G. Henry; Quarters – W.P. Ringland, R. Simmons; Forwards – S. Booth, A.P. Edgar, J.M. Hezlett, J.D. Houston, W. Macafee, T. McFetridge, J.B. Murphy, S. Smyth (captain) and J.M. Young. All eight games played by the 1st XV during the season were won and Clark, Henry, Magee, McFetridge and Young secured Inter-Provincial caps.

In 1895, Mr Houston reported a slight decrease in the numbers attending the school, but the actual figures were not given. The most pleasing feature of the year was the school's success in the Intermediate Examinations. While only fifteen candidates passed, six Exhibitions, one Gold Medal, two Prizes and a Latin Composition Prize were obtained. The

Latin.— Midsummer, 1895.   ix

LATIN.

Examiner—MR. CRAWFORD.

COMPOSITION.

I. Translate into Latin Prose :—
The rapid progress of the Spaniards, whose light troops made excursions even to the gates of Rome, filled that city with consternation. Paul though inflexible and undaunted himself, was obliged to give way so far to the fears and solicitations of the cardinals as to send deputies to Alva, in order to propose a cessation of arms. He yielded the more readily as he was sensible of a double advantage which might be derived from obtaining that point. It would deliver the inhabitants of Rome from their present terror, and would afford time for the arrival of the succours which he expected from France. Nor was Alva unwilling to close with the overture, both as he knew how desirous his master was to terminate a war which he had undertaken with reluctance, and as his army was so much weakened by garrisoning the great number of towns which he had reduced, that it was hardly in a condition to keep the field without fresh recruits. A truce was accordingly concluded first for ten, and afterwards for forty days, during which various schemes of peace were proposed, and perpetual negotiations were carried on, but with no sincerity on the part of Paul.

GRAMMAR.

II. 1. Give the superlative of the following adjectives :—
nequam, frugi, egenus, pius, maturus, strenuus, vetus.

2. Explain precisely, with illustrations, what is the force of the *present subjunctive*, the *perfect indicative*, and the *imperfect subjunctive* respectively, in hypothetical and conditional sentences.

3. Illustrate the meaning of *ethic dative*, *proleptic accusative*, *oblique petition*, *iterative subjunctive*, *prolative infinitive*.

Extract from a rather daunting Latin examination paper of 1895.

The school rugby team 1895 - 1896. Back row, standing: S.J.Hunter, Esq., D. Simmons, J. Ferguson, R. Steel, A. McMath, A.C.S. Thompson, C.C. Harman, J. Hind. Middle row, seated: F. McCay, F.J. Morton, W.P. Ringland (captain), H. Ferguson, R. Richards. Front row, on ground: G. Armstrong, R. Houston. F.P. Odlum, M. Kirk.

Exhibitioners were J.G. Wallis and J.T. Boyd (Middle), R.M. Houston, J.M.M. Madill and G. Browne (Junior), and D.G. Madill (Preparatory). Houston won a Gold Medal for first place in Mathematics and J.M.M. Madill a Prize in Latin Composition. Prizes in Junior Grade were awarded to S. Pringle and E. Bennett. A. Barr was Clothworkers' Scholar for 1895 and R. Houston won the Cochrane Scholarship.

S. Smyth again captained the 1st XV, but what might have been another great year for Coleraine was ruined by a severe frost, which lasted for six or seven weeks, and the scratching of many fixtures. The mood in the football club was certainly confident, to say the least, as suggested by the following comment in the Football Record: "The Rugby Union decided that Foyle College should play us in the Semi-Final at Coleraine on the 17 December, but Foyle scratched on the 16 so we were deprived from giving them a good beating." The school side met R.B.A.I. in the Final of the Schools' Cup on Monday 18 March, without having played a match since the middle of December. The Belfast team won by two tries (six points) to one goal (five points). Only four games were played this season, three of them being won. Magee, Smyth, Booth and McFetridge were chosen to play for Ulster Schools.

Three other sports clubs are mentioned that year, 1895. The Cycling Club was "not in such a flourishing state as in former years. The annual run was to Portrush, where the members were entertained to dinner by the President (Mr Houston), at the Eglinton Hotel. After dinner, the toasts of the Queen, the Cycling Club, and our next Merry Meeting were proposed and responded to with great enthusiasm. The members then had a pleasant run along the sands to the White Rocks, after which they started on their homeward journey." The Cricket Club "was not so successful in its matches as in the former year. After midsummer a new crease was laid, and probably if the team had had the advantage of this in the earlier part of the season, they would have been more successful. Of the five matches played, two were won, two lost and one drawn. The tennis club was doing well and was able to make some improvements to the courts. "In the tournament which was held, the singles were won by J.S. Brien, but owing to a break up in the weather the doubles could not be finished."

Further Expansion -
The Old Boys' Wing

By the Distribution of Prizes for 1895, the new extension to the school, the 'Old Boys' Wing', had been completed. Mr Houston thanked all the many friends of the Institution whose efforts had made it a reality and he was confident that, *"The stately and beautiful buildings, so admirably designed by our worthy architect, Mr Given, will stand for many a long year as a testimony to the energy and public spirit of Coleraine."* This *"stately and beautiful"* extension comprised what still remains the most visibly striking section of the school buildings, the central four-storey block which, in the heyday of the boarding school, housed on its fourth storey the huge dormitory (forty-five beds) known as 'the Gods'. (There was originally a fifth storey, known not unsurprisingly as 'the Heavens', but this had to be removed in 1931.)

Houston was so delighted by this improvement to the school that he ventured to predict that the Institution could become, *"a school unsurpassed by any of its kind in the United Kingdom. We can see here a great seat of learning numbering on its staff the most distinguished scholars our Universities can produce, men who will attract by their reputation pupils from far and near. We can see rising up under the benignant influence of such a school a new generation of men, men wiser, greater, happier than their predecessors."* The great 'Chief' could certainly be inspiring and visionary in his Prize Distribution reports!

Indeed, he got so carried away with his imaginings that he went on to unfold, for the benefit of his listeners, his rather romantic dream of what the school might be like when it was 100 years old, in 1960, *"when the September of that year covers the fields with its wealth of gold. It may cheer us up a little to picture the place as we hope it will be then. The fields, the river, all the main features of the landscape are the same as now. The church tower still shows itself through the trees, old trees then, no longer shrubs – 'The many-wintered crow' still 'leads the clanging rookery home'. The bugle calls the lads in from the playing fields in which many a cup has been lost and won. From the great clock above the Old Boys' Wing chimes out the Jubilate. The sweet solemn sound is heard far down the valley*

of our beautiful river. It falls like a blessing on many an ear that has learned from childhood to listen for it and to love it. It wakens no faint echo of Pandora in any human breast. The heads that planned that great enterprise, the deft hands that worked for it have long been dust; but their work is there. That work has raised, it has cheered, it has blessed three generations of the good people of Coleraine." Sadly, the 'sweet solemn' chimes of the 'great clock' above the Old Boys' Wing were not heard in 1960, nor in 2010, as it was removed along with the upper storey of that building.

Like any good speaker, though, Houston could change the mood and tone of his speech with ease. He went on to criticise quite harshly some of the effects of the education system at the time, stating that, *"The change in tone and method which has been brought about by the sixteen years of Irish intermediate education seems to me greatly to be deplored. It is only too plain that in the majority of Irish schools a purely commercial spirit now prevails. A pupil has come to be regarded simply as an animal in a herd in which there is so much money."* He explained that a clever pupil, with the right tuition, could have the chance of winning an Exhibition worth £20, £30, even £50. Moreover, at that time headmasters and assistant teachers received substantial *"result fees"* if their pupils were successful in the Intermediate examinations, so there was much pressure to achieve good results.

In a successful school, with a valuable income from these result fees, the governors could afford to set fairly low tuition fees, so that parents had a *"pecuniary inducement"* to send their sons to such a school. The effect of the Intermediate system, Houston thought, was to create a vicious circle, in which the central focus for pupils, parents, teachers and school governors was on money. Houston was a shrewd and successful school manager, who knew how important proper funding was for the success of a school, but he had no time for mere pursuit of money as an end in itself. As he wryly observed, *"if you hold a sovereign close to the eye it shuts out the view of all the world."* An all-round education was about much more than giving his youthful pupils the skills with which to acquire wealth in their adult lives.

Houston's Philosophy

Mr Houston made it quite clear that his aim was to *"educate a whole school"*, to provide a wide and balanced curriculum for all of its pupils, rather than focus on 'cramming' a few academically gifted boys who would bring financial reward to both themselves and the school. The school was not just for high-fliers, although these were more than adequately catered for. He proudly proclaimed that every boy who came to the Institution, *"is liberally educated to the full extent of his capacity, and receives without extra charge instruction in all the branches usually included in the curriculum of a good school."* He went on to condense his philosophy of education in the following sentences: *"We try to educate a boy with a view to his ultimate success in life, his usefulness and his happiness more than with reference to the immediate pecuniary rewards which either he or his teachers may obtain for their labours. The great use of a school, the great end of education, is to turn out good men and good citizens. If in passing through a school a boy does not acquire a brave and manly character, intellectual tastes and a genuine love of knowledge, some tinge of culture and refinement of feeling, good principles and good manners – in short, if he does not in some measure attain to the standard which would entitle him to be called a scholar and a gentleman, then his life at school has been a failure. I believe it is the earnest desire of the Governors, and of all concerned in the working of the Institution, that every pupil who passes through its classrooms should in after-life bear this stamp."* Even in today's much more complex world of education, perhaps few headmasters could express more appropriate and impassioned aspirations for their pupils.

It is easy to see why T.G. Houston was such a frequent and popular speaker at meetings of the Headmasters' Association. His skills as a public speaker are reflected in some comments made by a contributor to the 'Presbyterian Churchman', a Munter Byrne, in the latter half of the 1890s: *"I cannot help referring here to the singularly beautiful address delivered by Mr T.G. Houston, the Head Master of the Coleraine Academical Institution, at the recent prize distribution in connection with his school. There is a manly Christian ring about every sentence of it, and a marked absence of the effeminate conventionalities which are often served out to boys and their parents on such occasions. Mr Houston's boys are respected now not only in the examination-room, but in the cricket and football field as well, and it will be strange if we do not soon see them in still greater numbers among the most prominent clergymen, physicians and lawyers of the province. It is pleasant to find that the Irish Arnold's powers in shaping youthful talent are being appreciated, and that the school could not possibly be in a more flourishing condition than it is at present. I sincerely hope that he will see his way to act on the recommendations of his many friends, and give this address a far wider circulation than that afforded by the local papers."* Fulsome praise indeed, if a little politically incorrect by today's standards, with its commendation of the *"manly Christian ring"* of the address and the absence of *"effeminate conventionalities"*!

The year 1896 was a generally uneventful year. The school 'Calendar' listed Mr Houston's staff as: Classical Master - S.J. Hunter, M.A., LL.D; Mathematical Master – C.A. Gaul, B.A.; English Master – J. McQuillan, B.A.; Assistant Classical and English Master – T.A. Dixon, B.A.; Writing and Assistant Master – R.C. Macey, R.U.I.; Modern Languages and Drawing Master – Herr G. Wefers, Berlin University; Music Master – E. Cooney, Mus.D.; Violin – R.C. Macey; Dancing – Miss Haines; Practical Carpentry – Mr Callaghan; Shorthand – Mr Shannon; Drill Sergeant – Sergeant Watton; Medical Officer – J. Tate Creery, M.D.

The school Prefects for 1895/96 (the posts of Head Boy and Deputy Head Boy had not yet been created) were: Senior – L.C. Stevenson and W.P. Ringland; Junior: J.G. Wallis and G. Armstrong. 'Monitors' for the year were: Primi – D. Anderson and Thompson; Secundi – J. Hind and C. Harman; Tertii – W. Carr and R. Simmons; Quarti – F. Morton and H. Thompson; Quinti – W.P. Odlum and Gillespie. The sporting club captains were: Football – W.P. Ringland; Cricket – J.R. Magee; Cycling – W.P. Ringland. The Prospectus in the 1896 Calendar states that amongst the various classrooms, dormitories and other facilities provided through the recent construction of the Old Boys' Wing was *"A Turkish Bath, which will be invaluable as a means of preventing serious illness."*

Nineteen pupils passed the Intermediate Examinations. An outstanding achievement was that of R.M. Houston, who secured an Exhibition in Middle Grade, won the Gold Medal for first place in the grade and qualified for the Gold Medal for first place in Mathematics. J.G. Wallis and J.T. Boyd obtained Prizes in Senior Grade, J.M.M. Madill and G. Browne won Prizes in Middle, while A. Barr was awarded a Prize in Junior. W. Stewart won the Clothworkers' Scholarship and A. Barr the Cochrane Scholarship.

W.P. Ringland was captain of the 1ˢᵗ XV, which won four of the six games played. An epidemic of measles prevented any matches taking place before the end of November. The school side lost in the semi-final of the Schools' Cup, against Londonderry Academy, by three points to nil. The Football Record grumpily states: *"We stopped football after we got put out for the Cup."* Simmons, Ringland and McKay played in the Ulster Schools' XV.

One small detail of the year 1896 is interesting, not least for its repercussions in the next century. In that year, the Modern Languages and Drawing Master, Herr G. Wefers, constructed a handsome brass sundial for the school. Latin wording on the sundial states *G. Wefers fecit 1896* and a Greek inscription on it comes from the Christmas story in Luke's Gospel, "Glory to God in the Highest, and on earth peace to men of goodwill". It is not clear where this sundial was originally placed but around the late 1920s it was illegally removed from the school premises, presumably by a pupil who was leaving the school at that time, as a sort of trophy of his time spent there. Much later, in the mid-1990s, after this pupil's death, his next-of-kin, an elderly lady who wished to remain anonymous, returned the sundial to the school. It can now be seen in the garden of the Headmaster's house.

In 1897, an attempt was made to wipe out the debt of £1,700 remaining from the construction of the Old Boys' Wing. Once again Mrs Houston was the driving force, and a Bazaar entitled 'Culrathain' (the Gaelic word for Coleraine) was organized on the same lines as 'Pandora' in 1894, though on a much smaller

The school sundial, made by Herr Wefers in 1896.

scale. It was held at the school and proved even more successful than anticipated. The event lasted for four days, and was followed a few days later by a 'Fancy Fair' in the Town Hall, Portrush, at which most of the attractions at 'Culrathain' were reproduced in miniature. A 'Sociable' in the Town Hall, Coleraine, completed a great effort which reduced the deficit to £300.

Another Glorious Victory

As in 'Pandora' year, 1894, the football team rose to the occasion and helped to make 1897 memorable by going through the season unbeaten and winning the Schools' Cup for a fifth time. G. Armstrong was captain, and five of the six games were won, the other being drawn. In the final, unconverted tries by F. McKay and Mark enabled the side to beat Methodist College. Although that St. Patrick's Day was very wet and the pitch, at Ballynafeigh, *"a regular marsh"*, the final triumphant comment in the Football Record was: *"This was the easiest match we played during the season and the Methodists were sadly sold, expecting easily to win."* The cup-winning side consisted of: R. Houston, Hamilton, Harman, Millar, Wallis, Cox A., Halliday, McKay F., Ferguson J., Steele, Ferguson H., Mark, Mayberry R.J., Boyd J.T., Armstrong G. (Captain), with the substitutes being Campbell and Sharpe E. F. McKay and J. Ferguson were later selected to play for Ulster Schools against Leinster.

Rev. Dr D. Frazer-Hurst, in his book *The Bridge of Life*, gives a vivid, and at times almost surreal, account of the return of the Schools' Cup to Coleraine after that match.

"In a mighty struggle with our chief and most dangerous opponent, Methodist College, Belfast, we won the cup and bore it home in triumph to Coleraine. What a night that was!
The town, which took our victory to be their own, went wild with joy. We were met at the station by a band and there followed a joyous torchlight procession through the town and up the long road to the school. There a surging crowd gathered around the headmaster's house and presently, amid frenzied cheers, the 'Chief' himself appeared at the head of the steps which led to his front door. It was a wild, tumultuous scene, the
excited faces lit up by the flare of the torches and the 'Chief', a tall commanding figure, dominating us all like some victorious general in his hour of triumph.
He held a paper in his hand and announced that, when the intimation of our success reached him, he composed a song of victory, which he begged leave to read to us. Like the crowd of Roman citizens who implored Mark Antony to read the will of Julius Caesar, we roared our assent, and the 'Chief' read out his poem in ringing triumphant tones. The opening verse remains engraved upon my memory.
'St Patrick's Day, in the evening,
Good news has reached Coleraine,
For the fight is done
And the cup is won
And the lads are home again.'
At the end he received a tremendous ovation, which probably owed more to the occasion than to any surpassing merit in the poem, although at the time we acclaimed it as the greatest ever written. I believe it was as wonderful a day for him as it was for us."

Although not destined to be a Poet Laureate, T.G. Houston could rise to any occasion and manipulating an excited crowd in a torchlight rally was certainly no problem for him.

The Cup victory was commemorated on 27 March by a dinner and a re-union of former pupils, presided over by Mr Houston, in Jury's Hotel, Dublin. After the dinner, those present were treated to a rendering by Mr Houston of the full text (with some slight re-drafting) of the above poem. He said that the poem had been written by someone with the pen-name of 'Sentimental Tommy'! Presumably, no-one but his wife would have dared to refer to him by that pen-name! Here it is, very distinctly T.G. Houston in its language, tone and sentiments!

'Tis Patrick's Day in the evening,
Good news has reached Coleraine,
For the fight is done,
And the School has won,
And the Cup is ours again

The lads by the Foyle and Lagan
May win it if they can;
But we'll try to show
As the seasons go
That its home is near the Bann.

The pater cries: "You're losing time;"
The mater: "I'll lose my son;"
But they like to hear
Our ringing cheer
When the Rugby Cup is won.

For they know that life is a battle,
With no quarter for knave or fool,
And we learn to fight
For truth and right
As we fight for the dear old School.

In the less emotionally-charged atmosphere of the Intermediate Examinations in 1897, twenty-one candidates were successful. R.M. Houston won a Senior Exhibition and D.G. Magill obtained one in Junior. Prizes were awarded to G. Browne (Senior), J.H.G. Brookes, J.G. Madill and R.D. Smyth (Prep.), while Browne and J.M.M. Madill retained their former Exhibitions. J.G. Wallis won the Clothworkers' Scholarship and J.A. Moore was Cochrane Scholar.

In 1898, Mr Houston reported that The Honourable The Irish Society had increased its grant to the school from £200 to £225 plus a capitation grant of £1 10s per pupil, which meant practically the doubling of their contribution. The results of the Intermediate Examinations showed that fifteen pupils had been successful. Prizes were won by D.G. Madill (Middle), J.W. Tomb (Junior) and W.M. Gilmore (Preparatory). The 1st XV, captained by B. Richards, had an excellent season and won seven of the eight matches played. The side contested the final tie for the Schools' Cup, yet again versus the chief enemy, Methodist College, but lost by one dropped goal and one try (seven points) to nil. Richards, H. Ferguson and R.J. Knox secured Inter-Provincial caps. R.M. Houston was Clothworkers' Scholar, and the Cochrane Scholarhip was won by J.W. Tomb.

A sad event involving a past pupil of the school took place in early 1898. On 1 January, Lieutenant Henry D. Hammond, Royal Artillery, was mortally wounded at the Battle of Lundi Kotal, on the Indian 'North-West Frontier', and died on 8 February. Henry Hammond is shown in school records as

having been in the Upper School in 1886; his father was Colonel H.A. Hammond, who was based with his regiment at Nagpore, Central Provinces, India. Lieutenant Hammond was not quite twenty-six when he died. His stern but youthful photograph, in faded sepia tones, hangs in the School Museum.

Past pupil Lieutenant Henry D. Hammond, Royal Artillery, who was mortally wounded at The Battle of Lundi Kotal, on the Indian North-West Frontier, on 1st January 1898. The inscription under his portrait, which hangs in the school museum, reads: "He was the first Coleraine boy who had the great honour of giving his life for his country."

The year 1899 was a pleasing year, financially, for the Institution. First of all, the school bank account was freed from debt as a result of the death of Mr Hugh Anderson, who had always been a very good friend of the school. In his will he bequeathed £1,000, half of which was allocated to the foundation of a scholarship and the remainder to the general funds of the school. The Governors decided that the Anderson Scholarship should be given to the boy who was second in the examination for the Clothworkers'. Second, Mr William Cuthbert, of South Africa, a former pupil, also gave a sum of money to provide an annual Scholarship of £10. Both of these scholarships are still awarded today.

The results of the Intermediate Examinations were more satisfactory this year. W.R. Browne and J.H. Brookes were awarded Exhibitions in Junior Grade, while Prizes were won by D.G. Madill (Senior), and R.F. Seddall and J.G. Madill (Junior). D.G. Madill also won a Prize in Greek Composition, while prizes in English Composition were won by Brookes and Seddall. W.J. Morrison won the Clothworkers' Scholarship and R.F. Seddall the Cochrane Scholarship.

The football team was captained by J.R. Headech and eight matches were played, four being won, three lost and one drawn. The Football Report describes, very graciously, how the side was defeated in the first round of the Schools' Cup by Campbell College: *"We were extremely misfortunate in being drawn against Campbell in the first round, as they were stronger than most senior teams. We played them on our own ground and were beaten by 4 goals and three tries to nil. Allison was the shining light of their team and was too much for our three quarters, having played in two Internationals, and supposed to be the best three quarter in Ireland. Altogether it was no disgrace being beaten by such a team."* That last school Cup side of the 19th century consisted of: Jackson G., Henry F.*, Casement F., Kirk C., Harvey G., Glover, Houston J.W., Wylie, Casement H., Jackson T., Fulton, Weir, Duncan, Barr, and Henry T. (*Henry F. played instead of Headech who was laid up with a sprained ankle.) H. Casement and Wylie played for Ulster Schools against Leinster.

Life As A Boarder, Late 1890s

Before leaving these fin-de-siecle years, it is interesting to have a glimpse into the life of a boarder at the school at that time. Even today, in 2010, it is possible to hear one Old Boy of the school say to another, perhaps at an annual dinner of the Belfast Branch of the Old Boys' Association, *"Of course, you were only a day-boy!"* Because of their total involvement in the life of the school, boarders always considered themselves to be more genuine Institution products than mere day-boys, who went home at half past three in the afternoon.

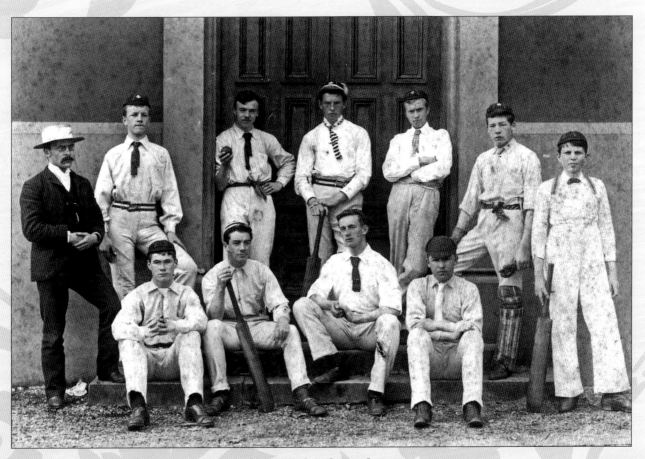

A pre 1900 school Cricket Team.

The school in the late 1890s, from a coloured postcard of the time. To the left is the recently-constructed Old Boys' Wing, complete with its fifth storey, known as "the Heavens", eventually removed in 1931. The circular aperture on the top of the fifth storey was intended for a huge clock.

Rev. Dr Frazer-Hurst, in his memoir *The Bridge of Life*, writes of the *"many bleak journeys"* which he had to make from his home near Newcastle-upon-Tyne to Coleraine. He says that, *"a number of day-boys attended the school. They came and went into the town of which we knew very little, for the boarders were a very self-contained little community. The town, so far as we were concerned, was made up of churches and tuck-shops."* He describes his first impressions of the actual buildings: *"The school consisted of a large red building containing the headmaster's house and various school-rooms and dormitories. Behind it towered a huge white concrete building which had been recently added. In my day it was still very new and beside the warm terra-cotta of the older buildings it had a rather spectral appearance, especially in the moonlight."* This new 'concrete building' was the recently constructed Old Boys' Wing, referred to earlier.

He describes some of his memories of 'church lines' on a Sunday morning. *"On Sundays we were marched solemnly to church, attired in our Eton jackets, clean collars and glossy silk hats. Before we set off to the Presbyterian church known as 'First Coleraine' there was a 'Collection Parade'.*

To the horror of the elders, and the annoyance of the treasurer, buttons had been found mingling with the other offerings on the plate. So, to avoid this affront, 'both to God and Man', as the headmaster put it, we were lined up and the 'Chief' passed along the rows of boys, glancing at the proposed offering on each extended palm. His face brightened at silver and darkened at copper, but he made no comment so long as it was a coin of the realm." On his own way to church, Mr Houston, *"invariably passed us on his private jaunting car, driving to the Covenanting church at Ballyclabber, for he was a distant relative of the famous Dr Houston of Knockbracken, and as he passed the long line of marching boys he raised his hat in a courtly salute and held it aloft until he was borne out of sight. We in turn saluted him in like fashion."* One wonders if modern schoolboys would be inclined to give such a *"courtly salute"* to their Headmaster when his back was turned!

Mr Houston's attempts to improve both the minds and the manners of his youthful charges extended even to the Dining Hall. In his book *School and Home*, he had made clear his distaste for the way modern boys gulped down their food. He called this method of eating 'stoking' and felt that it was *"almost universal among boys if they are left to their own devices."* He explained further: *"The method of dining natural to them seems to be to bolt as much solid food as will satisfy them, without the slightest attempt at mastication, for which they substitute the less tedious process of washing down, mouthful after mouthful, by copious draughts of whatever fluid is accessible. Then as soon as the stoking process is completed to their satisfaction they are inclined to start up immediately from table and rush off to some game requiring intense bodily exertion."* In this matter, modern schoolboys have perhaps changed little since Houston's day!

Regarding the *"fluids accessible"*, Mr Houston, as a Covenanter, had very clear views about liquid refreshment in schools. In *School and Home*, he stated: *"There is one article which I believe should be utterly banished from our school bills of fare, and that is alcohol in any form, beer, wine, fermented drink of any kind. I am not taking into account the moral aspect of the question. I make the suggestion solely on the grounds of health, and I am confident that on these grounds the great majority of properly educated medical men will agree with me. Quite recently I heard on good authority that the boys at a large public school in England had petitioned their head master to give them no more beer at dinner. Of course I am not prepared to say to what extent the quality of the beer previously supplied may have influenced the boys to take such a virtuous step; but whether the beer was bad or not, the petition was undoubtedly good."* This was one of the instances where Houston showed that he did have at least a little sense of humour! Going on, he dismissed even tea or coffee as little better for young people than beer or wine and recommended instead *"good milk and good water."*

Frazer-Hurst's experiences at the Institution confirmed Houston's determination not to leave boys 'to their own devices', not even in the dining hall, and he also comments on the food served there. He described the pleasure he had in watching the salmon leaping at the weir on the River Bann, but added rather wistfully, *"None of them ever landed on our dinner plates, however, for the fare in the school dining-room was of the unexciting variety which is termed 'plain and wholesome'. Whether to lift our minds above such a mundane affair as eating and drinking, or from a*

real desire to inculcate good manners, it was a settled rule that the boarders must converse with one another instead of concentrating fiercely on the consumption of their food.

'Gentlemen,' the Chief was wont to say, 'in civilised society the meal is a social function.' He himself conversed on high themes with the unfortunates seated upon his left and right. I fear that the range of subjects narrowed and the general tone declined the further the boys were removed from his immediate presence. Nevertheless, it was 'conversation' and I believe that the effect was good. It is said that to this day a Coleraine boy can be recognised by his leisurely way of eating and his frequent pauses for conversation."

The undeniable fact that 'boys will be boys', even in the hallowed classrooms, dormitories and dining hall of Houston's great Institution, is proved by another of Frazer-Hurst's recollections of his time at the school. As he was the brother of one of Mr Houston's star pupils, he was *"regarded with much favour"* but recalls an occasion when he *"nearly fell from grace."* Mr Houston hated untidiness, especially school books that were left lying about the classrooms; these were collected and, at the end of each day, held up to be claimed by the owner. *"One day as Mr Houston was looking at the books before returning them, he suddenly stood transfixed with horror at what he saw written on the front page of one of them. With a sinking heart I recognised the book as one of my own and remembered only too clearly that a boy near me in a class had scribbled on the front page"* an all-too-familiar Ulster political slogan, best unmentioned in this volume! *"The Chief, with a brow of wrath, held up the book and demanded the owner's name, but I felt no moral compulsion to acknowledge it as mine, for I had not written the offensive remark. 'Very well,' said the Chief, at the end of a long and tense silence, 'the book will go back into my desk and presently the owner will be discovered and suffer a much heavier punishment.' This was a bleak prospect for me and after consultation with a friend we decided to extract the book from the desk. Accordingly with a candle and a hairpin, which we borrowed from one of the maids, we stole down in the dead of night and while I held the flickering light my companion got to work on the lock. Even to an amateur cracksman it was an easy job, for the crazy old lock soon gave way, and I eagerly recovered the book and hastily rubbed out the words of offence. Strange to say the matter was never referred to again. I can only suppose that, the chief not seeing the book in the desk, failed to recall the incident and luckily for us he was agitated the next day by some other breach of discipline."*

Regarding games at the school in the late 1890s, Frazer-Hurst says that, *"other games were played in season, cricket, tennis and rowing on the Bann River, but football excited most interest. It was, in fact, an unending source of conversation, and the boarders' letters were so much concerned with the prospects of the football season that Mr Houston, who exercised a mild supervision over our correspondence, remarked that he would take it as a personal favour if the boys would occasionally mention in their letters to their parents that some school work was also being done. Sarcasm is a weapon used by almost all teachers and Mr Houston could employ it effectively . . . although he could also, on occasion, use the cane with deadly effect."* The custom of the headmaster, or later, housemasters, *"exercising a mild supervision"* over boarders' letters home continued until modern times, until in fact the practice of writing letters home became more or less extinct! Edward Simpson, who was a boarder in the years 1934 – 1939, recalls his father, Hugh Simpson, who was also a boarder at the school around 1900 – 1905, telling him that the pupils always brought their weekly letters home to T.G. Houston, who inspected them before they were posted. Mr Houston always ostentatiously removed his glasses

NOTE ON ENTRANCE, REMOVES, &c.

PROMOTION from one form to another is only made at Midsummer, and as the result of examination. A Pupil entering the School is examined and placed in the Form which the Principal considers most suitable for him. He must, unless for very special reasons, remain here until the Midsummer following, and cannot then be promoted unless he show sufficient merit. Classes for commencing Latin, Greek, and French are formed after each Mid-summer vacation. A Class of beginners in Latin is also generally formed after the Christmas holidays.

Suggestions are sometimes rather thoughtlessly offered to Head Masters regarding the propriety of changing a pupil from the class in which he has been placed to another either higher or lower in the School. A moment's reflection will show that all such interference with School arrangements is a mistake. No one but the Head Master can possibly be in a position to judge in what class a pupil should be placed, and it is extremely embarrassing for him to have advice on such a subject tendered to him from any quarter. Suggestions of this kind, if carried out, are almost invariably most prejudicial to the educational interests of the pupil in whose behalf they are offered.

The Headmaster knows best! An extract from School Regulations of the 1890s.

before doing so, to emphasise to the boys that he was merely checking the length and neatness of each letter, and not prying into the content.

Moving on to 1900, Mr Houston announced that the numbers had increased steadily during the last two years and that the Institution was rapidly recovering from the set-back caused by the opening of many new schools in the province. In this year the School Magazine, 'C.A.I.', appeared, the first number being published in March. It was founded by James Brookes, Robert Duncan and Daniel Johnston. Interestingly, in the editorial of that first magazine a tribute is paid to Miss Mary Houston, the Headmaster's daughter, obviously a talented artist, *"for the amount of time and trouble she has spent in designing the cover for this issue."* This was Miss Mary, not Miss Margaret, who became the unofficial matron of the school, after the sad death of her mother. A few years later, Miss Mary Houston was congratulated in the magazine for having had two miniatures exhibited by the selection and sanction of the Royal Academy. Her delicate, if somewhat curious, drawing remained the cover illustration of the school magazine until 1922.

Amongst other items, that first slim number contained a report of the annual Old Boys' Dinner, which had taken place on Friday March 16 in 'Ye Olde Castle' restaurant, Belfast. Mr W.J. Hardy, LL.D., proposed an eloquent toast to the school in which he paid tribute to Mr and Mrs Houston for being, *"mainly instrumental in raising the school to the proud position which it then deservedly held among Irish schools."* In the absence of Mr Houston, Dr S.J. Hunter responded to the toast to the school, claiming that, *"Coleraine men never forgot their Alma Mater; they were bound to her by a sympathy and goodwill which grew stronger with years, and whether they were in South Africa or India or Australia, they still felt the force of those ties which 'light as air though strong as iron' bound them to their dear old school."*

In referring to Trinity College, Dublin, in the 'University Echoes' section of that first magazine, it was reported that *"The number of*

❖ C.A.I. ❖

Vol. I.—No. 1.　　　APRIL, 1900.　　　Price 4d.

Editorial.

We hope that in placing this the first number of the School Magazine before the past and present boys of the Coleraine Academical Institution we are filling a want which, we venture to think, has been felt for some time in our school life.

An enterprise of this nature is of necessity handicapped to a great extent by the inexperience of its promoters, so that any assistance in the form either of criticism or suggestion would be most acceptable.

The Old Boys' dinner, which has now, we are happy to say, become an annual institution, was held in Belfast on St. Patrick's Eve under the presidency of Dr. Davison. As may be seen in our columns, it was characterised by all the elements which should be prominent in such a meeting, uniting as it does all those who possess in common pleasant recollections of their old school.

This is the second year in which our 1st XV. has been deprived of the valuable services of its leader when most needed; and we wish to offer our sympathy to this year's captain, who has had the misfortune to have been prevented by illness from playing in the cup matches.

It is pleasing to note that during the interval which occurs between the football and cricket seasons, the youth of the school do not find the time hanging heavily on their hands. The improvement in their gymnastic displays in the morning shows how much they have taken to heart the comparison instituted between their own performances, whilst wriggling beneath the bar, and those of the "spider perilously suspended between heaven and earth."

Our thanks are due to Miss Houston for the amount of time and trouble she has spent in designing the cover for this issue.

Editorial of the very first School Magazine, April 1900.

School Magazine Cover, 1902.

our Old Boys at present in the university of Dublin is something over thirty, and each school of learning – Divinity, Medicine, Law, and Engineering – has as one or more of its pupils old Coleraine boys." Students are of course famous for getting up to high jinks and, in the politically charged atmosphere of the time, some Coleraine old boys demonstrated their loyalty by scaling the Mansion House to remove a Nationalist flag mischievously placed there. *"On the visit of the Right Hon. Joseph Chamberlain to the University to receive the honorary degree of LL.D., and also on Ladysmith Day, the College youths made themselves famous in the capital city. The Mansion House flag was captured on both occasions, and more than one former pupil of the old School could show his treasured trophy of green. The loyalty to the Crown taught us when at school has not yet passed away, and though true and loyal sons of Erin, yet we condemn treason, which flourishes rather abundantly in Dublin, the capital of Ireland."*

At the Prize Distribution of 1900, Mr Houston was presented with an 'Address', contained in an album, and a portrait of himself in academic costume. These were the gifts of the Old Boys

School Magazine Cover, 1925.

to mark the completion of a term of thirty years as Headmaster of the school. The Address was read by Dr J.R. Davison, and the portrait, which was painted by Mr E.E. Taylor, was unveiled by Dr Anderson and Mr J.A. Irwin.

A final excerpt from Frazer-Hurst's book gives us a deeply personal memory and awestruck appraisal of T.G. Houston. Just before he was to leave Coleraine Inst. and continue his education in Newcastle-on-Tyne, this young boarder realised how important it had been for him to be a part of this *"notable school"*, presided over by its noble but caring headmaster.

"The 'Chief' was at his best in talks on behaviour, which he gave on Sundays to the boarders. When the talk was over he would continue to sit in the big armchair behind his desk, alone and plunged in thought. Presently the lights were lowered and the deserted classroom was full of shadows. Yet there the 'Chief' would sit, revolving many memories, his fine features reflecting both his innate nobility of soul and his sense of personal responsibility for all the young life surging around him in the school. Often, passing quietly through the room, I stole a look at him and wondered, with a kind of childish awe, what thoughts and memories were passing through his mind. That is how I like best to remember him, for in those moments of stillness and of reverie I saw, behind the headmaster, the man. Young as I was, I realised that it was a privilege to be under his care.
I am glad to think that this realization came to me while I was still at this notable school and that I was there long enough to be inspired by its ideals and to enter into the spirit of the place."

Mr T. G. Houston

The results of the Intermediate Examinations were very satisfactory in 1900. Exhibitions were won in Middle Grade by J.H. Brookes and W.R. Browne, and in Junior by W.M. Gilmore. Brookes was awarded a Gold Medal for first place in English and Prizes were won by T. May (Senior) and W. Dudley (Junior), May also receiving a Prize in English Composition. D.G. Madill won the Clothworkers' Scholarship and W.R. Browne the Cochrane Scholarship. R.H. Casement was captain of the 1st XV, which won two, lost three and drew one of the six matches played. Weir was the only member of the side chosen to play for Ulster Schools. During this period, cricket, tennis and cycling were the principal summer pastimes, and the cricket XI had several successful seasons from the competitive point of view. The members of the Cricket Club were particularly grateful to Mr Houston who, with typical generosity, had *"very kindly bought a large horse-mower, by means of which all the area for play can be cut, and not merely the pitch as formerly."*

Mr Houston's generosity extended also to the Cycling Club, for which he provided an annual dinner. At the 1900 dinner in the Eglinton Hotel, Portrush, toasts were drunk to the Queen, the Cycling Club, the C.A.I., the health of Mrs Houston, to Our Next Merry Meeting, and also, believe it or not, to The Masters! This toast was, *"drunk with great vigour, the boys singing vociferously 'For they're the jolly good fellows.' In reply each master present had his option of making a speech or singing a song. Needless to say most of them chose the former. Mr Wefers, however, elicited great applause by singing, 'The Old Rhine Wine'"* Knowing Mr Houston's firm views on liquid refreshment, one would assume that these vigorous toasts were of either water or milk; however, Mr Wefers, the German and Drawing master, may well have partaken of something a little stronger!

Past Pupils In Action On The World Stage

The August 1900 issue of the school magazine tells of more solemn and sombre events involving past pupils of the Institution, of adventurous young men serving in far-flung corners of the Empire and beyond, in troubled and dangerous times. The Boer War was raging in 1900 and, not surprisingly, Coleraine old boys were amongst the casualties.

"Since our last issue several old boys have distinguished themselves. Before all others we must mention captains S. Lawrence and Girley, who have both nobly laid down their lives for their country. The sad news was received soon after the Easter holidays, and a short memorial service was held at morning prayers on the 1st May.

We have also heard of several other old boys who are at present serving their Queen in South Africa. In the Imperial Yeomanry there are Cochrane, De La Poer, F. Henry, Hughes, Mackey, F. Ogilby, W. Ogilby, Todd and Wainwright. Of these, F. Henry and F. Ogilby have been in hospital; the former has quite recovered, and the latter is progressing favourably.

From Trinity College, Harman and Traill, two of our old boys, have secured commissions in the regular army; and Harman has gone to the Barbadoes to take up his duties.

The school is also represented in China. Dr L.Frazer-Hurst, a former captain of the football club, who was ten miles north of Tientsin when the Boxer Rebellion broke out, managed to escape to Chefoo with the loss of his books, instruments, and clothes; he subsequently volunteered to serve on the medical staff of the Naval Brigade.

In our last number we mentioned that Dr D. McCay was at Allahabad in the Indian Medical Service. He has since left for China, in the Indian Contingent, under the command of General Gaselee."

A great public occasion took place on 14 June 1900, when Sir George White, V.C., distinguished military hero and commander of the garrison during the recent Siege of Ladysmith, visited Coleraine. Eventually promoted to Field-Marshal in 1903, Sir George had actually been born just a few miles away from Coleraine, at Rock Castle, Portstewart. Mr Houston was determined that he, his assistant masters and his pupils would have a part in the events of this momentous day for Coleraine. Sir George was received in the Recreation Ground by the people of Coleraine and before the procession set out for Laurel Hill, as the boys were passing the grandstand, a short halt was made and Mr Houston said, *"The pupils of the Coleraine Academical Institution beg that you will do them the honour of receiving* from them a small token of their admiration of your splendid services to the British Empire, and of the noble example you have set all your countrymen, particularly to young people, who are looking forward to the battle of life. I assure you that there is no place where those services are more highly appreciated, and where the example is likely to do more, than in the public schools of Great Britain. We hope you will see your way to do us this honour." A committee of senior pupils, consisting of Wylie, Casement, Weir and Madill, then presented Sir George with a beautifully-chased silver cigar and cigarette case and match-box combined. The great man replied graciously and, in keeping with the intensely patriotic spirit of the times, offered the boys the following stirring advice: "I say to you – stand shoulder to shoulder for your Queen and country, and show that spirit of comradeship – that spirit of denying self for the sake of your country, and it will lead you in life, not only to success, but to happiness."

In 1901 the number of boarders was seventy-five, an exceptionally large increase on the previous year's total of forty-two. The consequent improvement in the financial state of the school came at a very opportune time because fresh demands had been made by the changes in the Intermediate system of education. The most important change was the formation of a *"modern side"* for boys who intended to prepare for engineering, business, agriculture etc. In addition to Modern Languages and Commercial Subjects the curriculum included Technical Education, which consisted of Physics, Chemistry and Drawing. In order to secure recognition and qualify for grants given by the newly-formed Department of Agriculture and Technical Instruction for Ireland, it was essential for a school to possess rooms equipped with suitable apparatus for the teaching of these subjects. To comply with this condition, laboratories were erected, and two rooms in the Old Boys' Wing were fitted up as Art rooms for the teaching of Drawing.

In this year, The Irish Society founded three Scholarships of £15 each, tenable for four years at C.A.I., restricted to the pupils of their own Elementary schools in Coleraine. In his Prize Distribution report, Mr Houston explained how, with these scholarships, "a clever boy, educated at the Society's schools, may thus be prepared for college here without cost to his parents." At the Institution, that boy could then, "win the Clothworkers' Scholarship on leaving Coleraine for the university, and there he may win one valuable prize after another until he reaches his profession with, perhaps, something still in hand from the honours he has gained." His whole purpose here was to encourage the creation of further scholarships: "Would not the founding of more such scholarships be a noble work for some benevolent citizen of Coleraine or its neighbourhood?"

The results of the Intermediate Examinations showed that twenty-two pupils passed, and that three Exhibitions and six Prizes had been won. W.R. Browne, J.H.G. Brookes (Senior) and J.A Tomb (Junior) were awarded Exhibitions, Special prizes were obtained by J.H.G. Brookes (English) and H.B. Dudley (Latin), while Book Prizes were awarded to H.B. Dudley (Senior), W.M. Gilmore, W.L. Dudley, and E.O. Cox (Middle). The main school Scholarships were won by T. May (Clothworkers'), J.W. Tomb (Anderson), and W. M. Gilmore (Cochrane).

Important events on the world stage usually had an impact on the life of the school community and the sad event which dominated the newspapers, nationally and internationally, in the early part of 1901 was the death of Queen Victoria, who had reigned since 1837. The Queen died on 22 January 1901 and a few days later the Headmaster had a solemn, black-edged announcement to this effect circulated within the school. This announcement expressed deep regret that, "the Victorian era is ended" and emphasised that, "in all her wide dominions," the late Queen "had no more loyal or devoted subjects than the boys and masters of the Coleraine Academical Institution."

The school magazine reported that on the morning of the Queen's funeral a most solemn and impressive special assembly was held. "The room draped in black, the portrait of Her Majesty, the sorrowful faces of all – masters and boys alike – formed a picture which will not easily be effaced from the minds of all who attended." After the opening prayers and the hymn "When our hearts are bowed with woe," the Principal delivered a short address, at the conclusion of which the masters present spoke a few words, associating themselves with the general feeling of sorrow. The Lessons were then read, after which Casement and Johnstone, on behalf of the boarders, and Brookes, Tomb and Dudley for the day boys, *"gave public expression to the sorrow of the School at the death of the greatest and best Monarch the world has ever seen."* The Principal then engaged in prayer and the service terminated with the "Dead March in Saul," played by Mr Wefers.

The Boer War was still rumbling on and it is interesting to read the following note in the April 1901 issue of the school magazine: *"W. Houston, the eldest son of the Principal, has joined the Capetown Guard, recently formed on the invasion of Cape Colony. During his distinguished career at School, there was no more popular fellow in the Institution, and we join with his many friends in wishing him all prosperity and good luck."*

In one way, 1901 was a good year for the Football Club because Mr Houston purchased, apparently at his own expense, a permanent playing pitch, adjacent to the school grounds. At a special meeting of the Club on February 12, members were told that Mr Houston had been trying for some time to buy 'Mr Coleman's farm', between the river and the Ballycairn Road, and that the deeds were about to be signed. A sum of nearly £120 was expended on this wise purchase, which provided the school with the basis of the current extensive sports grounds. R.H. Casement was the Captain of the 1st XV and the side met old rivals Methodist College in the Schools' Cup Final, the thirteenth appearance of a C.A.I. XV in the deciding tie. Unfortunately it was a case of 'unlucky thirteenth', as Methody won by a penalty goal scored during extra time, after the normal period had ended with each side having one try to its credit. R.H. Casement, J. Weir, E. Henry and W. Owens played for the Ulster Schools' XV against Leinster, Casement captaining the Ulster side. Writing about that Inter-Provincial match, the school magazine states, *"we are proud to think that Ulster succeeded in breaking a long series of defeats under the captaincy of a Coleraine boy."* The noble captain

signed off his own report of that rugby season with the comments, *"Thus ends a not unsuccessful year, in a defeat but by no means a disgrace. May all good fortune attend the team in the future is the fervent wish of – R.H Casement."* The Cricket XI was captained that year by R.F. Seddall and the side won three and lost three of the six matches played.

School Songs

One further detail from the year 1901 is perhaps worth mentioning. In the October issue of the school magazine, the editor noted a suggestion that, *"we should publish a series of original school songs."* Mr D. Frazer-Hurst (now an old boy), whose memoirs are referred to in detail earlier in this chapter, contributed the first of these songs, quoted below.

C.A.I.
Though scattered widely o'er the earth,
Our hearts their ancient warmth retain,
And oft from far across the seas
Revert to our old school again.

Before our eyes the visions rise:
The crowded rooms again we view,
Some luckless scholar, overcome,
In desperate efforts to construe.

Or fancy leads us to the ground
Where that elusive Cup is sought –
The altar of our boyish zeal,
Where well-contested fields we fought.

To work and play, 'While yet 'tis day,'
Lest 'steep destruction' on us fall,
That each may hear the glad 'well done'
When even brings the final call.

This precept taught from day to day
In dreams we seem to hear again,
And though in distant climes we rove
Yet we are true to old Coleraine.

In 1902, the number of new pupils coming into the school was the largest for many years, the increase being particularly marked in the day school, but the actual figures were not given. In spite of the expenditure incurred by the construction of the new laboratories and art rooms, Mr Houston was able to report that the school was virtually free from debt. This welcome state of affairs was due to a bequest of £250 from Sir Robert Taylor, late Vice-President of the Governing Body, and a donation of £150 from The Irish Society. When drawing up the new scheme for Intermediate Education in 1901, the Board decided that the results of the examination would be communicated privately to each school and that no public list would be issued. This change was made to stop the unhealthy competition which had been encouraged by the listing of the successes of various schools in the press. As a result of this regulation it is not possible to find out how the Institution fared at the examinations held in 1902, 1903 and 1904. Scholarship winners in 1902 were: J.H.G. Brookes (Clothworkers'), T. Jack (Anderson), and J.A. Tomb (Cochrane).

The Rugby 1st XV, captained by W. Owens, had an unusually lean season, winning one and losing five of the six matches played. W. Hall, who led the Cup team against Foyle College because Owens was over age by a few days, secured another Inter-Provincial cap. W. Owens' final comment in the football report for the year was, *"I hope we'll prove next year that 'We fall to rise, are baffled to fight better.'"* J.H.G. Brookes was captain of the Cricket XI and the side won three matches, drew two and lost one. The annual Athletic Sports competition was revived in 1902, after a lapse of several years.

An announcement in the April 1902 issue of the school magazine shows the continuing effect of the South African war on the school community. *"We deeply regret to say that another of our Old Boys has fallen for his country in South Africa. Those who knew the late Captain W. Stevenson saw in him a perfect gentleman, and an officer of very high promise. He was one of a family of five who were all educated at this school, and who were all deservedly popular with their fellows, and none more so than he. Captain Stevenson held a commission in the Canadian Scouts, and was greatly liked by all his fellow-officers. He fell a victim to enteric fever, and died in hospital in Bloemfontein. He was buried with full military honours, General Tucker and other officers of his division being present at the funeral. At prayers on March 18th a short service was held in*

memory of the late officer, and at the conclusion the Dead March in 'Saul' – with which we have become so familiar of late – was played by Mr Wefers." The playing of the "Dead March in Saul" sadly became an all-too-familiar feature of special school assemblies in later years, especially during 1914 – 1918.

At the annual dinner of the Old Boys, in the Imperial Hotel, Donegall Place, Belfast, the toast of 'The School' was given by the Rev. Dr Walker and responded to by Mr Houston, who was present at the occasion. Dr Walker said that when he looked at Mr Houston he always thought of the school motto – the Greek phrase *'Heos Hemera Estin'*, still featured in the school crest, which translates approximately as 'work while it is day.' The origins of the motto are unclear, but Dr Walker believed that, *"Mr Houston had chosen it himself; at any rate he had imprinted it deeply upon the School history and upon the characters of the boys, as their success in after-life showed."*

In that April 1902 school magazine, D. Frazer-Hurst had again been exercising his poetic talents, producing School Song No. II, this time entitled 'The Bells'. His offering on this occasion (sadly failing to match the literary quality of his first attempt, 'C.A.I.'!) was actually set to music by Mrs Houston herself. The first two verses give a flavour of life in the boarding school at the time:

In the drowsy air of morning,
How disturbing is the warning,
That discordantly is flung,
By that sleep-dispelling tongue –
By that slumber-breaking,
Anger waking,
Early morning bell.

In the plunge and out at drill
We can hear it clanging still,
But in School its joy has flown,
And we utter with a groan –
'Oh, that pain-foretelling,
Work-compelling,
Stern and cruel bell.'

But it was not all hard work and no play in the boarding school – there were fun occasions as well. In October 1902, there was a 'Halloweve

Entertainment' (something which became a tradition for a number of years) in the Committee Room at the school. The main event was a two-act comedy called 'Leave it to Me', which *"had been got up amongst the boys, and which they played with great ease and elegance, to the amusement of all present."* Any time the heroine of the play, Amelia, appeared on stage, she was, *"vociferously applauded. In this graceful and pretty young lady one could hardly recognise N. Morton, who, even by his voice, scarcely betrayed his sex."* Between acts, Mr Robertson, one of the masters, *"delighted the audience by his rich and mellow rendering of 'Out on the Deep'. Indeed he did not satisfy the audience with this song, but responded to a prolonged and persistent encore by singing the less classical but very popular 'Mush, mush', in the chorus of which the audience joined with evident relish."*

A more formal, but no less enjoyable event took place on Friday 28 November, when Coleraine was one of the few provincial towns to be honoured by a visit from the Lord Lieutenant of Ireland and his wife. The school magazine tells us that, *"the town presented a very gay and loyal aspect"* on that day and that a glance towards the hill on which the school was situated showed that, *"the Institution was not in the background as far as the display of bunting was concerned."* The magazine also notes that, *"a casual observer might have been disposed to bestow more than a passing glance on the long and ordered line that made its way steadily across the Bridge and finally halted in a conspicuous position in the Diamond with a view to welcoming their Excellencies with a round of those ringing cheers for which the School is famous."* His Excellency the Lord Lieutenant must have been impressed by the hearty reception he received from the Institution boys because he graciously agreed to grant them a holiday the next day! (Yes, Saturday morning school was a feature of those times!)

Boarding School Memories

Before leaving the year 1902, an interesting account of some unusual mayhem in the study hall, or prep room as it was sometimes called, was given in a letter from a boarder called Bob Swanson to his sister Alison. He mentions the *"larks"* the boarders were sometimes involved

in, for example an occasion when a master came into the dormitory, *"to find us all in our beds with our silk hats on."* He then writes, *"Another night when we were in study a rat came out. The boy nearest saw it but did not raise the alarm till it got well away from its hole and he then made a rush for it. Immediately the whole 80 boarders rose and ran over desks and everything, rulers, books, caps, shoes and inkpots were thrown at it and in the end it got away. The reason of this may be easily explained. You see, Mrs Houston gives small money rewards for all rats caught and then makes the boys cut off their tails so that they cannot show them twice."* This story does have a ring of truth about it, especially in the description of the chaotic pursuit of the profitable rodent, but no doubt part of young Bob's purpose was to give his more sensitive sister the shivers!

In another letter to his sister, on 11 December 1902, Bob Swanston is distinctly unimpressed by the heating system in the school and by the endless daily routine of school life. *"The whole building is very badly heated the hot water pipes are not half warm and nearly every night from 9.30 till about quarter to ten everyone is running about classrooms with chattering teeth, not to mention all the dark evenings from 5 to 6 which is as bad for we do not get dinner until half four. Besides from the day you come until the day you go that is the whole term it is one continual rush from morning till night. You get up and rush to the plunge which mind you is not heated these mornings at all. That is you wash with hot water and then dive or jump into a big tank about 4 feet deep of quite cold water which according to the prospectus is tepid in winter that is absurd. You have about quarter of an hour until drill to dress in and if you are late for drill you get more extra drill added on in the afternoon and so on from hour till another all through school but I have got so used to this that I do not feel it much."* Bob certainly is in complaining mode here - and he does make the place sound a bit like a boot-camp! Knowing his forthright opinions, we can understand the hasty P.S. added to his letter: *"I am writing under difficulties and have to stuff this under the desk every time the master comes round my way."*

In 1903, Mr Drummond Grant, formerly honorary secretary and then Vice-President of the Governing Body, founded a Science Scholarship of £30 per annum, to be awarded to the best pupil who had completed a three years' course of Science in the school laboratories. Mr Houston announced that, owing to the generosity of Mr William Cuthbert, founder of the Cuthbert Scholarship, it had been possible to re-invest the capital sums providing the Clothworkers' and Anderson Scholarships so that these would stand permanently at their full values of £50 and £25 respectively. Scholarship winners that year were W.R. Browne (Clothworkers'), W.M. Gilmore (Anderson), and J.W. Morrow (Cochrane).

J.R. Jackson was captain of football and the team had a fairly good season, but were beaten in the Cup semi-final by R.B.A.I., the eventual winners. Four matches were won and three lost during the season, and J. McIvor and W.S. McKee were selected for the Ulster Schools' XV against Leinster. At the annual Old Boys' Dinner that year, Mr Houston spoke of how provincial schools were disadvantaged in their appearances at Cup finals. *"In these final matches we believe that we were beaten several times just because we were the travelling team. Our boys were exhausted by an early start, a long railway journey, a long wait in Belfast, and a field where naturally the home teams were favourites. If the same matches had been played on our own ground, or even on neutral ground at about the same distance from either team, the results might have been very different. Why should provincial schools be placed at such a disadvantage?"* This has been a constant complaint by provincial schools down through the years, but the honour of appearing on the sacred turf of Ravenhill has perhaps outweighed the disadvantages.

W.R. Browne (Clothworkers' Scholar 1903) has been named frequently in the academic records of the school and a few words concerning him are relevant at this stage. William Rowan Browne, son of the principal at Lislea National School, Kilrea, was the second of two brothers to board at the Institution. At the end of his career at the school (1898 – 1903), he won the Clothworkers' Scholarship and brought further credit on the school by obtaining a Junior Exhibition to Trinity College, Dublin, being the first in the whole of Ireland in those examinations. However, in the autumn of 1903, when he should have

been enjoying student life in the city of Dublin, he contracted the dread disease tuberculosis. As there was no known antidote at the time, a hard choice had to be made, either to stay and suffer in Ireland close to his family, or go abroad to settle in a drier, warmer climate. He decided to go to Australia and to this end a collection by staff at the school, former pupils and well-wishers raised £45 to send him on his way. Browne went on to become one of Australia's most respected scientists in the first half of the 20th century, helping to ensure that the geology of that huge continent was properly documented. One of his most prized possessions, still in the family archives, was the letter of commendation written for him by Mr Houston, prior to his departure. The following comments are quoted from that letter: *"He was for about five years under my care in Coleraine; and during that time won the respect and affection of his teachers and schoolfellows to a degree that, in my long experience, I have rarely seen equalled and never surpassed in the case of any pupil who has come under my notice. . . . . Mr Browne possesses intellectual ability of a high order, and his diligence as a student, combined with unusual mental powers, enabled him to take a very high place all through his course at school. . . . . Of Mr Browne's moral qualities I cannot speak too highly. His sterling integrity, his strong sympathy with every good object, his unselfishness and readiness to labour for the welfare of others, and at the same time his singular modesty, have left an impression on our School that will not soon be effaced."*

1904 was a quiet year for the Institution. Mr John McCandless, Coleraine, presented to the school a beautifully bound copy of the latest edition of the Encyclopaedia Britannica, for which the boys sent him a vote of thanks. The school scholarships were won by J.A. Tomb (Clothworkers'), J.W. Morrow (Grant), H.B. Dudley (Anderson), and W. Millar (Cochrane). The First XV, captained by L. McCullough, had a frustrating year, winning only one and losing six of the seven matches played. E.R. Casement was selected to play for the Ulster Schools' XV; he also captained the school Cricket XI. The first rugby practice of the season gave the writer of the Football Report some cause for concern. *"The attendance at this first practice was very good, the day-boys turning out in great force, and play was pretty hard*

and steady, with heavy scoring on both sides; but the ignorance of some of the most rudimentary rules of the game that was displayed in some instances was simply lamentable." However, a decidedly more spirited description of Institution rugby at the time can be seen in a mock-heroic song, in the style of the immortal Percy French's 'Slattery's Mounted Fut', printed in the February edition of the school magazine. Here are the first two verses of this song, entitled 'The Coleraine First Fifteen', which celebrates their one win of the season, against Foyle College.

You've heard of Berry Richards and of Cherry
Casement too,
And how the great George Armstrong brought his
team the final through;
But here's a page of glory such as never yet has been,
And that's the football story of the
Coleraine First Fifteen.
This gallant team had matches played –
but never won - before,
For though their game was excellent
they never got a score;
And many a man was tackled, aye,
and many a fall was seen
Whilst trainin' in the football field with
Coleraine First Fifteen.

Chorus:
Down by the river such a fight has never been –
Fifteen men on either side, the referee between;
And all along the touchline were spectators
by the score.
In crowds they came to see the game –
boys, men and girls galore.

Ere yet the game was started,
says McCullough to his men,
'We have been bate before, my boys;
we won't be bate again.
Remember that your countrymen
are here to see ye play,
So don't disgrace yourselves, my boys,
when joinin' in the fray.'
And then the fight began, bedad,
and faith 'twas hard to see,
When watching how they fought,
to which the victory would be.
Bowld Alley's play was murdersome –
he never missed his man,
And Casement, like an elephant,
was fightin' in the van."

At the Old Boys' Dinner in Dublin that year, Dr Anthony Traill of Trinity College proposed the toast of 'The School' and made a point that would have greatly pleased Mr Houston. *"One of the great characteristics of the School in regard to the class of boys that came to it was that it was an essentially democratic institution. All met on a common platform, and it was a very great characteristic of this School that nothing but merit was considered and nothing but talent respected. The result was that, no matter where the student came from, he was turned out and educated a gentleman."* This feature of the school, that it provides a 'common platform' on which all can meet on terms of equality, irrespective of wealth or social status, has remained a proud tradition for 150 years.

In 1905, Coleraine in general and the school in particular suffered a huge loss in the death of Mrs Houston. Resolutions of sympathy from all the public bodies in the town and letters of condolence from old boys all over the world revealed how deeply that loss was felt. On the Sunday following her death, in a service in Terrace Row Presbyterian Church, the Rev. R.B. Wylie made reference to her remarkable qualities. *"I cannot close this morning without referring briefly to the great loss we have all sustained by the sad and sudden removal from our midst of Mrs Houston. She filled so large a place, she exercised such a refining, sweetening influence, she lived so much for others, she was, at once, so brilliant and so good, so clever and so kind, so versatile in her accomplishments, and so devoted to duty, that we feel, all the more deeply, how much she will be missed, and what a large and painful blank her death has caused."*

The Governors of the Institution, at their quarterly meeting, adopted a resolution conveying to Mr Houston, *"the intense sympathy of all the Governors in his great bereavement, by which he has lost so dear a helpmeet, and the companion of his life."* The Governors also expressed, *"their deep sense of the great benefits the Academical Institution enjoyed for so many years through Mrs Houston. By her unfailing tact and kindness and sympathy she won for herself the gratitude and affection of successive generations of pupils at the School; while by her resourcefulness and powers of administration she largely increased the funds at the disposal of the Governors, and thereby assisted them* to make extensive additions and many improvements in their buildings, so as more thoroughly to equip the School for its educational work."

Shortly after her death, a meeting of Coleraine Old Boys was held in the Town Hall, to consider the best form of memorial to commemorate the late Mrs Houston and to express the great esteem in which she was held by past pupils of the school. A committee was appointed, with three honorary secretaries (including Dr S.J. Hunter) and an honorary treasurer, and subscriptions and suggestions for a memorial were invited. Initial suggestions favoured a Scholarship within the school, but the eventual outcome will be described later in this chapter.

One can only speculate as to the extent of the grief felt by the 'Chief' himself at the loss of his beloved wife. The Prize Distribution of September 5, 1905, must have been a sensitive experience for him, but he was no doubt greatly helped by the presence at his side of his daughter, Miss Margaret Houston, who went on to take her mother's place in the running of the boarding school. Guests at the Prize Distribution remarked how, *"Miss M. Houston, with becoming grace and admirable fortitude, filled her beloved and lamented mother's place in the reception of the visitors; her presence reminding very many as they passed into the hall of 'the touch of a vanished hand, and the sound of a voice that is still.'"*
It is perhaps typical of Houston's selflessness and stoicism that he said little about his own grief on that occasion, but instead spoke most movingly about the effect of another tragedy that year on the school community, the loss at a most untimely age of Mrs Willis, the new wife of one of his masters.

In the school magazine of November 1905, a contributor and past pupil signed 'W.J.H.' presented a moving poem entitled 'A Memory', based on his attendance at that 1905 Prize Day and his memories of Mrs Houston. The last two verses are:

"Proudly the old school stands upon the hill,
The noble river to the sea winds on;
Tomorrow we return our tasks to fill,
But thou – thy task is done.

Done and well done. Thy wages thou hast ta'en,
And home art gone to join the invisible choir;
Leaving to us, thy nurslings, who remain,
A memory to inspire."

At the Intermediate Examinations of 1905, twenty-four candidates were successful. R. McCahon (Middle) and G.R. Gilmore (Junior) gained Exhibitions and W.J.K. Bell (Junior) won a Prize. R. McCahon also obtained the Medal for Latin and a Prize in Latin Composition. Scholarship winners for the year were H.J.T. Madill (Clothworkers'), E.R. Casement (Grant), J.T. Moon (Anderson), and R. McCahon (Cochrane). E.R. Casement led the First XV, which won one and lost five of the six matches played. The school side lost to Methodist College in the first round of the cup, by thirty-two points to three and comments in the football report were fairly forthright: *"When the scoring did start it came hot and heavy and the Methodists got four scores at intervals of about three minutes, the Coleraine defence being remarkable only for its absence."* The captain claimed that this unfortunate season could be attributed to a great extent to the unwillingness of the parents of day-boys to allow their sons to travel to matches, perhaps because of the expense involved, and he appealed to, *"some rich and philanthropic Old Boy to see his way to endowing the Football Club sufficiently to enable it to pay all travelling expenses."* N. Morton was captain of the Cricket First XI, which won three and lost three of the six matches played.

In 1906, Mr Houston reported that the decrease in numbers which occurred during the previous session had been counteracted by the greatest entry of new pupils experienced for many years; however, no precise figures are given. One reason for the decrease in numbers around this time was that the new Intermediate Examination system had resulted in the opening of a considerable number of new schools, thus increasing competition.

Patriotism In Action At C.A.I.

In the previous year, with the memory of how unprepared the Empire had been for lengthy combat in the South African war, and also perhaps because of the rising tide

Whole school photograph, circa 1908. The cup shown is not the Schools' Cup, but a cup presented by the staff to the winners of an internal "Rovers v. Wanderers" game. An extract from an old school magazine identifies individuals as follows, with the warning that "some of the identifications may be incorrect".

"Staff (from left to right): Mr D.A. Bruce, Mr T.G. Houston (Principal), Dr S.J. Hunter, Mr S. Willis, Mr W. Robertson, Mr J.J. Davis (Irish rugby international), Mr Joseph Thompson.

Footballers: R.F. Walker (captain), W. Lees Lynd (behind him), Witherow (on Lynd's left), behind G.W Walker and to the right of Johnston Murphy; further left R.R. Neely (U.S.A.), and in front of him H. Hamilton (late of White House, Portrush), and T.A. Speer. At the far end of the group G.H. Pinkerton, Rex Breen (S. Africa), E. Hamilton, G.R.B. Purce (specialist), R. Henry. Also in the group are Tom Wallace (future Irish international), A. Zarroga (Spain), McCleary, Dickson, Alley Shaw, Billy Curran, John McKay, N.I. Brown (now senior inspector), Lecky, Christie.

Non-footballers: On extreme right A.O. Schneider and Hamilton Barrett, R. Davison, R. M. Campbell, Dan McGonigle, near them W. Boddie, J. Davis.
Top left: T. Madill, R. Anderson, S. Leeburn, S. Lees, McRoberts. Lower: Gainsford, Donald Boddie. In centre: Witherow, Eustace Hay (died in S. Africa), H.P. Giles (bank manager), Baird, Ivan Russell, the brothers Innis (sons of British Consul in Spain), W. Scott, Shane, Joseph Bamford (killed in Great War), Claude Dudley (son of former rector), Moorhead, W. McCullough (Portrush), H. Jackson, John Anderson, T. Shaw, B. McGusty."

of militarism in Europe at that time, Field-Marshal Lord Roberts of Kandahar had made a national appeal that every schoolboy should be taught rifle-shooting and military drill. Mr Houston had spent much of his speech at the Prize Distribution of 1905 explaining to his listeners how he thought this was a noble and necessary call, inspiring *"the virtues of patriotism and self-sacrifice"*, and how he intended that the pupils of the Institution should respond to it. Accordingly, a Rifle Club was formed at C.A.I., a miniature shooting range was provided in the gymnasium, and the Club was affiliated to the National Rifle Association. It was reported

Coleraine Academical Institution Branch
of
National Rifle Association –

Club Rules. Rules approved.

C. B. Crossley.
28. Oct 1905.   Lc. WRd.

1. The name of the Club shall be "Coleraine Academical Institution Rifle Club".

2. The object of the club is to provide instruction and practice in the use of the Rifle.

3. The Club shall consist of a President, Captain, Honorary Sect?, Honorary Treasurer and ordinary members all of whom shall be either masters or Boys of the School, and a Sergeant Instructor.

4. The officers and committee, who shall be appointed by the Headmaster, shall have power to legislate upon any point that may arise for which provision is not made in these rules.

Range Rules.

1. No rifles or ammunition shall be used except such as conform to the Regulations of the N. R. A. for miniature and full Range Clubs, and are also sanctioned by the Headmaster.

2. No firing shall take place except under the superintendence of an officer of the club – the Sergeant Instructor – or other person duly authorised by the Headmaster. This superintendent shall have sole authority and responsibility on the Range.

3. No one but the shooting superintendent, or person authorised by him, shall be allowed to go in front of the firing point whilst practice is being carried on.

4. Any member pointing a rifle, loaded or unloaded, at any person under any circumstances, or being guilty of any practice which in the opinion of the Committee is dangerous will be liable to expulsion from the club.

5. Whilst the danger flag is flying at the firing point, or from the marker's mantlet, and at the word "cease fire", all rifles must be unloaded and remain so until "all clear" is given. Rifles to be loaded at the firing point under the superintendence of the officer in charge, all ammunition being supplied by

84

him alone at the time required.

6.   Club rifles and ammunition must be stored in a place provided by the club for that purpose, and no Boy will be allowed to retain even his private rifle or ammunition in his own possession.

7.   Every boy shall be passed as proficient in the Firing Exercises by the Captain or Sergeant Instructor before being allowed to use the Range.

8.   All rifles must be examined by the Shooting Superintendent after firing.

9.   In the case of a "miss fire" the rifle must be kept fixed upon the target until the attention of the Superintendent has been called to it and he has taken it into his hands.

10.   Every possible precaution is to be taken against accidents, the strictest order and discipline to be maintained.

11.   No person except the master in charge, or the marker, is to pass from the firing point to the target during practice, and if either of them do so, all guns must be unloaded, & left open until they return behind the firing line.

12.   The master in charge to call the names of firers, and the value of each hit, a record of which will be kept. He will always blow a whistle before commencing, & at conclusion of practice. Targets to be checked and cleaned or renewed, after each five rounds is fired. Rifles to be cleaned after each 30 or 40 rounds have been fired and always at the finish of the practice by the last firer, who will shew the rifle to the master in charge.

13.   No talking or noise allowed when firing is taking place, & on no account is the person firing to be spoken to, when in the firing position.

14.   Value of hits:

Bulls eye = 5 points	Ties are decided by 1st fewest misses
Inner = 4 "	2nd " outers
Magpie = 3 "	3rd " magpies
Outer = 2 "	4th " inners
	If still a tie shots to be taken in inverse order, best last shot to win.

T. G. Houston, J.P,
President

The Rules of the C.A.I. Rifle Club.

Staff 1905.
Back Row: Sam Willis, W. S. Robertson, R. J. Knox, Bywater, Unknown
Seated: Classen, S. J. Hunter, R. C. Macey.

in the school magazine of May 1906 that, *"A consignment of old service rifles has been received from the War Office. These are used in the drill every Wednesday during the latter part of recess."*

This venture was so successful that a 100-yard outdoor range was constructed in the football field. At the same time, an open-air swimming pond, measuring eighteen yards by fifteen feet, with the bottom sloping from three feet six inches to six feet six inches, was built in a corner of the football field. Both were formally declared open by Colonel Bruce in August 1906, the ceremony being followed by an 'aquatic display' in which well-known Ulster swimmers participated, and by a shooting competition for a Silver Challenge Shield, presented by Mr G.H. Moore-Browne, J.P. Rifle Clubs from Garvagh, Londonderry, Limavady, Coleraine and C.A.I. competed and the event was won by Garvagh, with the school team in third place. The local newspaper report of the event notes that, *"the popular headmaster himself formed one of the college team."* Mr Houston had been in touch personally with Lord Roberts about the school's response to his call; as a result, one of the individual prizes at this competition was provided by Lord Roberts himself.

For the next few years, rifle shooting remained a popular activity at the school and regular competitions were held, often against Portora Royal School. To encourage competition within the school club, and thereby to enhance marksmanship, the boys were formed into five 'squads', each squad having a member of staff as the 'commanding officer' and a senior pupil as 'Lieutenant.' Squad III, known as the 'Third Bucks.', had as its commanding officer Mr Houston himself with J. McIntyre as his Lieutenant, while the ubiquitous Dr S. J. Hunter (often affectionately referred to as 'the wee doctor') commanded Squad IV, the 'Death or Glory Boys', ably supported by his Lieutenant, S.J. Stronge. This all sounds like tremendous fun, but sadly, in less than a decade, the horrid realities of death and glory would await many past pupils of the Institution on the Great War battlefields in France and Belgium.

In 1906, Old Boys and other friends of the Institution bought and presented to the school a cricket field, that part of the current school grounds currently known as the 'front field', bounded by the Castlerock and Ballycairn Roads. At the entrance to the cricket field, they erected a Memorial Arch to perpetuate the

Mrs Houston,
wife of T.G. Houston, in 1870.

Mrs Houston in 1904,
not long before her death.

memory of the late Mrs Houston. This elegant sandstone arch, which is of classic Doric design, is surmounted by a pediment which bears the inscription: *"These playing fields were purchased and presented to the School by Old Boys and other friends as a memorial of Maud, wife of T.G. Houston, Principal of the Institution, who for more than 30 years devoted her many gifts of head and heart to the welfare of the School, and enriched the town and neighbourhood by a life of noble endeavour."* On each pier of the arch is a portrait of Mrs Houston, one as she was in 1870 when she came to Coleraine, and the other as she was in the year of her death. The 'Memorial Gate', as it is now known, remains a central feature of the school grounds and is often the backdrop against which photographs of school teams are taken.

At the Intermediate Examinations of 1906, twenty-four candidates passed and Exhibitions were awarded to R. McCahon (Senior) and G.R. Gilmore (Middle), while W.J.K. Bell won a Prize in Middle Grade. Scholarship winners were: J.L. McFall (Clothworkers'), G.R. Gilmore (Grant), S.J. Stronge (Anderson), and G.R. Gilmore (Cochrane). Addie Small captained the 1st XV, which won only one of the seven matches played, losing the other six. The Cricket XI won only one of the five matches played, losing the other four. These

were indeed lean times for current school sides, as far as victories were concerned. However, recent past pupils continued to win fame for themselves, some at international level, as the 'University Echoes – Trinity College, Dublin' notes in the school magazine of May 1906 show: *"F. Casement is to be congratulated on the way in which he captained the Rugger XV. He obtained his International Cap, and by his play justified his selection. H.G. Wilson, another old Coleraine man, was one of the team that defeated Wales."*

A less pleasant event during three days in October 1906 involved the visit of J. Finlay Peddie, Consulting Engineer to the Ulster Sanitary Association, to compile a report on 'The Sanitary Arrangements at the Coleraine Academical Institution'. Despite the attention paid, from the earliest days, to sanitary arrangements at the school, by 1906 the situation seemed to have deteriorated dramatically. Mr Peddie noted, with Victorian precision, that *"the latrines, urinals and privy arrangements are upon the old system, with old metal troughs, flushed by valves, in a foul and offensive condition, with three open privies alongside. The urinals consist of the slate troughs division, and cement backs with channels flushed only by stop cock with three-quarter inch weeping pipe fixed along the top."* Not content with his own observations, Mr Peddie subjected the school's sanitary

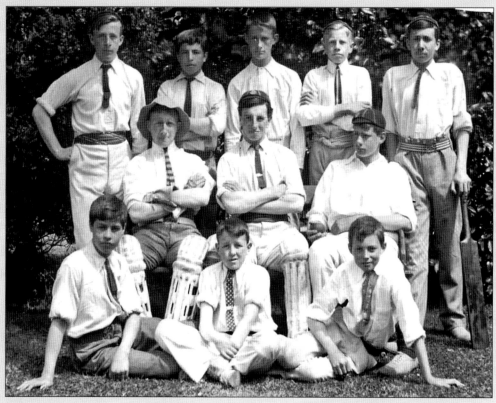

C.A.I.C.C. 1st XI 1906

R. Sproule, J.C. Shaw, Pinkerton, J. McIntyre, W.J.K. Bell
W.J.K. Moon, A. Small (Captain), R.J. Walden
F. Harris, C.D. McCommon, J. Pollock.

system to a series of tests, the precise details of which are best left to speculation. His official finding was that, *"The drains in connection with this latrine and urinal are in a highly defective condition, as proved by tests – smoke escaped in volumes into this place, and, together with the offensive emanations from the latrines, privies and urinals, besides there is a want of privacy that is certainly most desirable among better class boys in a high class school such as this, instead of having the closets exposed with passage in front."* He was of the opinion that, *"this whole arrangement should be entirely removed"* and replaced *"with enclosed closets."* To add insult to consternation, Mr Peddie mentioned that he had made a *"similar re-arrangement at Portora Royal School, which gave the Governors, and all concerned, complete satisfaction."* To be fair to Mr Houston and the school Governors, health and sanitation arrangements always had a high priority and no doubt the *"offensive emanations"* were soon prevented!

The year 1907 was a quiet one for the school, with the average number on rolls being 108, of whom forty-five were boarders. The Rifle Club prospered and a team competed for the

Irish Schools' Challenge Shield, finishing second to Portora. Thirty-one candidates were successful at the Intermediate Examinations, and J. Murphy obtained an Exhibition in Junior Grade. Prizes were won by G.R. Gilmore (Senior), J. McKay, W.D. McAfee (Middle), and G.R.B. Purce (Junior). The winners of the various scholarships were: R. McCahon (Clothworkers'), W.J.K. Bell (Grant), J. McIntyre (Anderson), and W.D. McAfee (Cochrane). G.C.V. Riddall was elected captain of football, but resigned after Christmas, and W.C. Neill led the side for the rest of the season. Two games were won and five lost. The Cricket XI was captained by J. McIntyre, the playing record being four won, four lost and one drawn. In his annual Prize Distribution report that year, Mr Houston stated that 'minor sports' such as tennis, badminton and hockey *"have had their proper place among our School sports,"* and mentioned in more detail the success following the opening of the Swimming Pond the previous year. *"A team representing the Institution took part in a great swimming display at Foyle College, Derry. The first place among the seniors fell to Robert Sproule; the*

first and second places among the juniors to R. Walker and S. Neill. A silver cup offered by Foyle College for competition was won by the Coleraine squadron."

The now annual 'Hallowe'en Entertainment' took place as usual. The main item was a play entitled 'Done on Both Sides', which *"provided an hour's capital enjoyment."* The first part of the evening's programme, featuring some long-forgotten popular songs of the Edwardian period, is described in the magazine as follows: *"The concert part of the programme opened with a pianoforte duet by Miss Lynn and Miss Woodburn, which was well received. Mr MacD. Campbell was encored for his rendering of 'Lanagan's Log,' and responded with 'The Veteran's Song.' The Misses Lynn and Miss Woodburn next delighted the audience with their graceful rendering of 'Oft in the Stilly Night.' The next item, a hornpipe by four of the boys - Shaw T., Davison, Schneider, and Ross - was given a well-deserved encore. Mr D. McLaughlin sang 'Rabbits' in his own style, and responded to an imperative encore with 'Awfully Good at Algebra.'"* It is not made clear whether the four boys played or danced the hornpipe!

In 1908, the school lost the services of Sir H.H. Bruce, for many years President of the Institution, and Mr James Bellas, honorary treasurer. In a tribute to the valuable work done by these gentlemen, Mr Houston mentioned that the financial affairs of the school had been in the hands of only two honorary treasurers since its foundation in 1860 – Mr Thomas Bellas, who died in 1883, and his son James, who had held the post ever since. The school owed a great debt of gratitude to this family for their long-standing, public spirited and unselfish service. In 1908, thirty-four candidates passed at the Intermediate Examinations and J. Murphy won an Exhibition in Middle Grade. Prizes were obtained by J. McKay, W.D. McAfee (Senior), and W.B. Shane and J.T. Witherow (Junior). G.R. Gilmore won the Clothworkers' Scholarship, G.H. Pinkerton the Grant, W.C. Neill the Anderson and J. Murphy the Cochrane. The total number of pupils in the school that year was 110, fifty of these being boarders.

The 1st XV, led by W.C. Neill, was a powerful combination and in any other year would

have won the Schools' Cup. Unfortunately for C.A.I., Portora produced their wonder team, captained by R.A. Lloyd, and the school's fourteenth Cup final was lost by eight goals and four tries (fifty-two points) to nil. Portora also won a friendly match against the Institution in Derry, by three goals and two tries to nil, but was the only school that year to score against Neill's side, which won its other eight games with an aggregate of 181 points to nil. Neill, Lees and Walker secured Inter-Provincial Caps. The Cricket XI, led by R.F. Walker, won six matches, lost one, and drew two.

Girls Not Allowed!

An interesting Special Meeting of the Governors took place on Tuesday 31 March 1908, in the Town Hall. The second item on the agenda was *"To receive Report from the Principal re admission of girls to School."* Minute Books of Governors' meetings previous to 1907 are not available, and it is unclear when or by whom this suggestion was made. The Principal's report was decidedly terse: *"Mr Houston made a statement on the subject, giving it as his opinion that a mixed school would not be a success, considering that the admission of girls to the school would be undesirable."* Despite the Headmaster's negative attitude on this matter, further discussion took place and it was proposed by Mr Whiteside, seconded by Rev. Freeman, and passed, *"that a Committee of the Governors and others be formed to take into consideration the feasibility of establishing a first class Girls' School in Coleraine, all the Governors with Mr Houston to form the Committee with power to add to their number, Revd. Davis to act as Convenor."* However, this part of the minute is stroked out in red ink and a note added, in different handwriting: *"That the matter be left in the hands of an outside Committee."* There seems to be no further reference to this matter – it remains, certainly to today's Inst. boys, a case of 'what might have been'!

In his Prize Distribution report that year, Mr Houston remarked on a new and interesting departure in the teaching of modern languages in the school – the teaching of dictation by means of the new-fangled phonograph. Houston confessed that, *"Until I procured a phonograph for the teaching of French I knew little* or nothing about the invention. In fact I had rather a prejudice against it, associating it with vulgar songs and a host of squeaking abominations provided at seaside resorts and elsewhere for the entertainment of the masses." However, he was now pleased to report that the phonograph had become a distinct feature of school life, especially as it was also useful for playing hymns and sacred music. Houston would not be the first old-style Headmaster of the school to eventually welcome the latest advances in technology.

A charming annual event in school life around that time was the custom of presenting a formal 'Address' and making a presentation to a respected senior pupil who was moving on (or had recently moved on) to higher things; usually, this person was the football captain, the unofficial head boy of the school. On Thursday 11 September 1908, at the conclusion of evening prayers, Mr Houston called on F. Harris to read the address to W. Neill, Senior Prefect and Captain of the Football Team.

"Dear Neill, [*]
*We take advantage of this brief visit to your old school to attempt some expression of our indebtedness to you. The occasion is auspicious. You have just been the recipient of the Anderson Scholarship and Henry Taylor Shakespeare Prize – two of the most important prizes your School offers. The presentation of the Football Inter-Provincial Caps has reminded us of the fitting consummation of your career as an expert player of school football. These are happy auguries of your future literary and athletic success. But it is not for your successes that we most honour you. It is for all you have done to maintain the esprit de corps of your school, for all you have done to stiffen the spirit of others less hardy than yourself; for all you have done is to encourage us to play the man. On the four-and-a-half years you have been our school-fellow you can look back with just pride on none more than the last. No Senior Prefect, no Captain in the Football Field has enjoyed more complete command of those under his control.
We believe that, in the qualities which have assured wise generalship, and have called out what is best in others, you have a priceless asset for the battle of life. Our gift is small; but we know that, far more than it, you will value the affection and respect you have so deservedly won. You may rest assured that nowhere will your future career be watched with more interest,*

nowhere will you find heartier well-wishers than in the C.A.I."

Neill responded with appropriate modesty and gratitude for the presentation, which consisted of two handsomely-bound editions of Wordsworth and Tennyson, and ended with the hope that his school-fellows would, *"all have useful and happy lives."* That sense of the importance of having 'useful' as well as happy lives probably originated in the teachings of their noble headmaster, T.G. Houston.

([*] Tradition in the school has always been that pupils referred to each other solely by surnames, except in cases where there were two or more brothers, when the distinguishing initial of the first name would often be used. If boys on occasions wished to be more informal, the boy's nickname - usually affectionate! - would be used. It is strange sometimes today, when teachers at the school refer to their pupils by their Christian names, the boys themselves still use only the surname.)

An unusual event in October 1908 involved the official visit of the armoured cruiser *H.M.S. Drake* to the north coast of Ireland; the vessel 'lay off Portrush' from 17 to 27 October. The school 1st XV played the officers of the ship on 24 October (defeating them by twenty-five points to ten) and a few days later the schoolboys were given a half day holiday and invited to tour the ship. The school magazine describes the pupils' awe at the might of this great warship, built in 1901:
"Few of us but were impressed by the immense capacity of the vessel – the number of compartments and passages and ladders seemed to be endless. Special interest was taken in the guns, and our guides were untiring in their efforts to satisfy our curiosity about their mechanism. While we were aboard a display of torpedo firing took place, which was eagerly watched by a number of us who were lucky enough to be in the vicinity. At four o'clock we were entertained to tea by the officers, a repast to which we did ample justice after our dose of sea air."

Sadly, the *H.M.S. Drake* was herself torpedoed, by U-Boat 79 in October 1917, and sank, with considerable loss of life, in Rathlin Sound, just over twenty miles from the school.

90

The year 1909 was an uneventful one. Mr Houston reported that the numbers on the school roll had been well maintained and mentioned that during only one quarter in the last forty years had the attendance fallen below 100. That year, there were sixty-seven day pupils and forty-three boarders, making a total of 110. Twenty-six candidates were successful at the Intermediate Examinations and J. Murphy was awarded an Exhibition in Senior Grade. The Scholarship winners were: J.McCay (Clothworkers'), G.R.B. Purce (Grant), W.D. McAfee (Anderson), and W.B. Shane (Cochrane). R.F. Walker led the 1st XV, which was a very strong side, but Portora had retained most of the members of their famous team of the previous year and C.A.I. lost the Cup final by forty-two points to nil. The ten school matches played resulted in seven wins and three defeats. Walker and R.I. Henry played for Ulster Schools versus Leinster. W.R.G. Breen was captain of cricket and the 1st XI played eleven matches, winning four, losing four, and drawing three. A comment in the February edition of the school magazine refers to how reading was a pastime encouraged amongst the boarders: *"The Reading Room, under the curatorship of A. Dickson, now beguiles the dark winter evenings, and in this connection we wish to thank Schneider for presenting to the library 3 volumes of 'Young England'. With the volumes of 'The Captain' presented by Mr R.E.O. Chipp there should be no dearth of good wholesome reading."* No 'penny dreadfuls' for Mr Houston's boys in the school Reading Room!

The year 1910 was important and memorable for the school: the Institution was fifty years old and its current Headmaster, Thomas Galway Houston, had been at the helm for forty years. To mark this double event, the Governors organised a presentation to Mr Houston and his daughter, Miss Margaret, who had taken the place formerly occupied by her mother in the life of the school. In the space of three months, governors, past pupils and friends of the school contributed to a gift for Mr Houston, the total amount subscribed being £1,200, a remarkable sum in those days. The testimonial to Mr Houston consisted of an illuminated address in album form, illustrated with water-colour views of the Institution,

the Mrs Houston Memorial Arch and places of interest in the town and neighbourhood, accompanied by a cheque. Miss Houston was presented with gold watch-bracelet. Mr A.G. Crawford, honorary secretary of the governing body, read the address and handed over the album, while Mr J.J.C. Canning, honorary treasurer, handed a cheque for over £1,100 to Mr Houston. R. Davison, one of the youngest boarders, presented Miss Houston, with the bracelet.

This event took place on 2 June and, *"glorious weather prevailing, the visitors were provided with seats in front of the south entrance, while the speakers used the terrace as platform."* Amongst other expressions of appreciation and congratulation, the address contained the following words: *"We welcome this opportunity of assuring you of our warm appreciation of your high character, generous spirit, and unselfish life. You have lived and laboured for others with a single-minded purpose and a self-sacrificing zeal, which we have all wondered at and admired. Your lofty ideals of education and of life you have persistently maintained. While your educational standards have been uniformly high your moral standards have always been supreme, and the moral tone of the school under your personal influence, wise discipline, and exemplary manner of life has always been its chief attraction and distinguished feature."* In his reply, Mr Houston displayed his firm Christian convictions, acknowledging, *"our obligations to Almighty God, whose blessing was invoked when the foundation stone of the School was laid, and Whose help has been sought at the beginning and the end of every day's work that has ever been done in our class-rooms. To God all that has been really successful in the School is due."* He also paid a charming tribute to his current pupils: *"I hope that they know how highly I think of them. I have found them, with few exceptions, young gentlemen of the highest principles and kindest hearts to be met with in any country in the world."*

In contrast to the above celebrations, the mood at the start of a quarterly meeting of the Governors on 1 June 1910 had been a little more sombre, reflected in the following resolution: *"The Governors of the Coleraine Academical Institution, in meeting assembled, place on record their sense of the great loss the United Kingdom and the Empire have sustained by the*

Mr Drummond Grant

Chairman, Board of Governors 1908-1909

death of His Most Gracious Majesty, King Edward VII, and they desire most respectfully to convey to Her Majesty Queen Alexandra, His Majesty King George, and the members of the Royal family, this expression of sincere sympathy and condolence in their great affliction." As always, the life of Coleraine Academical Institution was set against the wider events of world history, and that old-fashioned loyalty and patriotism of the school was never in doubt.

First Boy Scout Troop

At the Distribution of Prizes later that year, Houston told his audience of his latest innovation in the school – the formation of a troop of Boy Scouts, some of whom were in attendance, dressed in their Scout uniforms.

The Scout movement, started just two years earlier by General Sir Robert Baden-Powell, was commended by Mr Houston, as always ready to respond to a national call to service, as *"one of the finest things ever started for the improvement of the race."* Its aim was, he said, *"to enrol in a new order of chivalry all the generous, ardent lads of the country who are willing to pledge themselves to a life of purity, unselfishness, and service to humanity;"* waxing ever more eloquent as his speech progressed, he claimed that the Scouts formed, *"an order of Knighthood; they are training themselves in all knightly pursuits."* The school Scout troop remained popular until 1992, especially amongst the boarders, who were excused first prep on Friday evenings to attend meetings.

Another topic dealt with by Mr Houston at that 1910 Prize Distribution was in connection with the effect of a *"mischievous rumour."* Houston had recently been appointed a Senator of the Queen's University of Belfast and some people had put about the rumour that this position *"brought in a large salary"* and required him to live in Belfast. The rumour that he would be resigning from his position at the Institution had grown to such an extent that Houston had even received a circular from a Belfast firm offering to remove his furniture. However, this matter was far from a joke and had actually done serious damage to the school; the headmaster reported that, *"quite a number of people who intended to send their sons to us as boarders have been prevented from doing so by this utterly false report."* He went on to issue an emphatic denial that he intended to leave the school and that he wished to continue his work there. This matter reflects very clearly how the success of the school in those times was closely intertwined with the reputation of the great 'Chief' himself.

To illustrate the continuing successes of past pupils, in the 'Old Boys' Column' of the school magazine for September 1910, it was noted, amongst other announcements, that George W. Connor was the President of the Irish Dental Association, C.K. Cox had passed his final for solicitor in the English Courts and had gone to manage a Rubber Plantation in North Singapore, and that Sir Richard Havelock Charles had been *"with the King at Balmoral."* This last-named old boy was one of the most talented students ever to pass through Coleraine Inst. After a brilliant and distinguished career in the Indian Medical Service, he had obviously been appointed a royal physician. King George, on his accession to the throne in 1910, appointed him 'serjeant-surgeon' to the King, an ancient post which required the holder to attend the King when he went on official tours. Hence, we read in the November 1911 edition of the school magazine that, *"Sir Richard Havelock Charles is accompanying the King to the Indian Durbar."*

The Intermediate Examination results of 1910 were less satisfactory than usual, twenty-six candidates being successful but without obtaining any Exhibitions or Prizes. The football team, captained by R.R. Neely, was a very powerful one and had an undefeated eleven-match record until the Schools' Cup final, which Campbell College won by seven points to nil. Neely, T. Henry and J. Murphy secured Inter-Provincial Caps. The captain of the Cricket XI was W.R.G. Breen until mid-summer, and R. Henry after the holidays. The team won six matches, lost three, and drew one during the season. The Rifle Club notes for that year show that Mr Houston, at the age of sixty-eight, was still a regular member of the C.A.I. shooting team. Scholarship winners for the year were: J. Murphy (Clothworkers'), W.B. Shane (Grant), J. McFall (Anderson) and B. McGusty (Cochrane).

In schools today, there is quite rightly much focus on anti-bullying policies and anti-bullying strategies. An anonymous contributor to a school magazine of 1910 recalls being taken to the school for the first time, as a boarder, in 1872, and describes his initial trepidation as he approached the main entrance, but then explains how he was befriended immediately by another boy who showed him around the school and helped him settle in. He concludes his article: *"So began my years as a boarder at school. I had read before going there fearsome tales of the bullying of small boys by big boys, but I found next to nothing of that sort. I had also read of the sad fate of the new boy, and of his treatment by those who had been at school before him, but so far as my own experience went, I was led to the conclusion that any youngster who behaves with ordinary common sense and gives himself no airs will find almost all his companions gentlemen by nature – at least, so they were at Coleraine."*

Moving on to 1911, as described earlier in this book, Mr A.W. Young, headmaster from 1860 until 1870, presented his recently painted portrait to the school. Mr Houston thanked Mr Young in his absence and said that the portrait would be hung with his own (presented to him in 1900) in an appropriate place in the school. He explained how he felt that the constant presence of Mr Young's portrait would be a powerful stimulus to succeeding headmasters in their efforts for the welfare of the school: *"If they should ever grow indolent or careless about their*

work it will sternly rebuke them, if they are doing well it will encourage them, if they are struggling their best against difficulties it will cheer their drooping spirits." Today, in 2010, portraits of eight past headmasters of the school can now be seen in the school Library.

In 1911, the Board of Governors announced that five scholarships would be given annually to day-pupils under thirteen years, the main aim being to encourage boys to enter the school at an earlier age. The results of the Intermediate Examinations were not very satisfactory, the number of successful candidates being seventeen, of whom six passed with honours. R.I. Henry captained the 1st XV, which won five, lost one, and drew one of the school matches played. The side reached the semi-final of the Schools' Cup, but a dispute with the Rugby Union about venues for the matches caused the provincial schools – C.A.I. and Portora – to withdraw from the competition. T. Henry, J.T. Johnston and T. Wallace secured Inter-Provincial Caps. W.McC. Sharpe was captain of Cricket. J.T. Anderson won the Clothworkers' Scholarship, T. Wallace the Grant and Anderson Scholarships, and T. Madill the Cochrane Scholarship. That year the number on the school roll was 102, of whom thirty-six were boarders.

In 1912, Mr Houston reported that the number of boarders had been maintained and that the day school was the largest for many years. Day-boys numbered seventy-five and boarders thirty-six, making a total of 111. He announced that the Governors had decided to open a Preparatory Section for boys between seven and ten years of age, the number of pupils to be limited to twenty. At the Intermediate Examinations, thirty candidates were successful, five passing with honours, and H.B. Barrett (Middle Grade) won Prizes of £3 in Modern Languages and £2 in Science. The rugby season was again spoiled by the failure to settle the dispute with the Union about venues for the Cup semi-finals. An attempt by the provincial schools to compete for their own Cup ended in failure, as described in the words of the school captain. "The Provincial Schools purchased a Cup of their own, but unfortunately the coal strike made train arrangements impossible and

the affair had to be abandoned. I trust that before another season comes there may be some settlement, as the loss of the enthusiasm which the cup promotes is injurious to us now, and is likely to prove hurtful to all football in the future."

W.McC. Sharpe was football captain and the side won two and lost four of the six school fixtures. J.T. Johnston played for Ulster Schools against Leinster. The 'Football Notes' in the school magazine state that, "We are handicapped this season by the fact that so many of our players live at long distances from the School, which makes it difficult for them to turn out often during the short winter afternoons." This difficulty is perfectly understandable, taking into account the very limited transport facilities for school pupils in those days. W.McC. Sharpe again captained the Cricket XI that year. The 1912 Scholarship winners were: S. Fullerton (Clothworkers'), T. Madill (Grant), S. Lees (Anderson), and H.B. Barrett (Cochrane). The 'Old Boys' Column' of the magazine in 1912, as always, listed the continuing successes and achievements of past pupils. Examples this year were:

- "We congratulate Mr William A. Houston, M.A., Professor of Mathematics at University College, Galway, on his appointment to be Assistant Commissioner of Intermediate Education in Ireland. Mr Houston was Clothworkers' Scholar in 1889;
- Another Old Boy has been distinguishing himself in the literary line – Dr G.M. Irvine, Mountnorris, Armagh. His latest success is entitled 'In the Valley of Vision'. Dr Irvine, it will be remembered, had the honour of captaining the first team which brought the Cup to Coleraine."

In his annual report to the Governors for 1912, Houston refers to the 'old members' of his staff, Dr Hunter, Mr Willis, Mr Bruce and Mr McKew, who "leave nothing to be desired in their teaching and the management of their classes", while new teachers Mr Dent and Mr Tackaberry "are promising well." A Miss Henson was in charge of the new Preparatory Department in the school. A Sergeant Smith had been appointed to the post of school Drill-Sergeant and Mr Houston was pleased to report that, "The entire school has two drills from him each week, and he has already effected a great improvement in the appearance and carriage of many of our Day-Pupils, who are greatly in need of proper physical training." Presumably the boarders got some extra attention from the Sergeant and their 'carriage' was deemed satisfactory!

In 1913, The Honourable The Irish Society granted a sum of £300 per annum for three years to augment the school income, which for some time had been insufficient to meet the increased expenditure. At the Intermediate Examinations, twenty-one candidates were successful, five passing with honours. H.B. Barrett (Senior) won the Bronze Medal for first place in Ireland in History and Historical Geography. In Junior Grade, F.R. Franklin obtained Prizes of £2 in Science and £1 in Mathematics, and H.K. May £1 in Science. T. Madill was captain of the 1st XV, which was quite bluntly stated to be *"not up to standard"*, winning only one and losing six of the seven matches played. J.D. Johnston was selected to play for Ulster Schools. A.O. Schneider was captain of Cricket. Scholarship winners were: T. Madill (Clothworkers'), A. Gilmore (Grant), H.B. Barrett (Anderson), and F.W. Robertson (Cochrane).

There is an interesting but rather unsettling letter, received by the Governors at their quarterly meeting of 11 June 1913, from a Mr Currie who had recently carried out some repairs at the school.

Dear Sirs,
I enclose a/c for work at the Institution as requested. With reference to the trouble with rats, if you want to do away with them, you will have to clear away the old Piggeries, as this is where they breed. Piggeries can be constructed in proper manner on some site further removed from the vicinity of the Sanatorium.

The piggery was a profitable way of disposing of left-over food from the boarders' dining hall and a piggery actually continued in operation at the school until well into the 1980s, in Mr Forsythe's time as headmaster of the school. However, this piggery (now derelict but still in existence) was located well away from the school, on the banks of the river, about 100 yards south of the current River Pavilion.

In his report to the Governors for the year 1913, Mr Houston refers to an epidemic of chicken-pox which, *"affected a large number both of our Boarders and Day-Pupils. As many as twenty-seven of our boys were absent from School on the day when Professor McMaster, Inspector under the Endowed Schools Commission, called. No serious result has followed in any case; but the work of the school has suffered a good deal from the lengthened absence of so many pupils."* He also stated, *"The moral tone of the school is excellent, and the conduct of the boys, as a rule, exemplary."*

For those few whose conduct was far from 'exemplary' at times, Houston could be a stern disciplinarian, as was expected in schoolmasters at the time. A. McCurdy, who came to the school as a boarder in 1913, writing of his memories in the school magazine of 1960, said that when Mr Houston had to deliver corporal punishment, *"the delinquent was taken up four flights of stairs, to the Head's study. There he pointed out the gravity of the offence, while he chose a suitable cane from a bundle of 2 or 3 dozen, which he kept behind a row of books. The lecture was much harder to bear than the caning, which was usually three of the best on the palm of each hand."* Another old boy, N. Morton, who came to the school in 1898, writing in the same school magazine of 1960, confirms that corporal punishment usually involved, *"six stingers on the tips of the fingers with a wobbly cane."* He added that before following the offender upstairs to administer the punishment, the Chief would often mutter to the other boys in study room, *"Thank goodness, gentlemen, the resources of civilization are not yet exhausted."* The bundle of '2 or 3 dozen' canes was no doubt regularly re-stocked!

In 1914, the scholarship founded by Mr Drummond Grant expired, consisting as it did of a capital sum, payable in ten annual instalments, but Mr Houston announced that its place would be taken by the Joseph Cuthbert Science Scholarship. This happy solution was made possible by the generosity of the Reverend A. Cuthbert and his brother, Mr W. Cuthbert, who provided £500 to found the scholarship in memory of their late father. This was in addition to the Cuthbert Commercial Scholarship, founded some years previously by Mr W. Cuthbert. Cuthbert

Scholarship prizes are still awarded annually at Prize Distributions.

There were several deaths around that time, of people who had been very much part of the Institution family. On 19 November 1913, a memorial service was held after morning roll in the school, in honour of Mr J.J.C. Canning, who had been a Governor of the school for over thirty years. His funeral, on the same day, was attended by the whole school, both masters and boys. At the annual meeting of members of the Institution on 27 January 1914, the Governing members put on record their deep sense of sorrow and loss at the death of, *"their old friend and honoured townsman, Mr Joseph Cuthbert. For forty years he had been a leading Governor, and throughout that time his guiding hand, his courage, and his generosity never failed."*

The school magazine of February 1914 expressed great regret at the death, on Christmas Day, of *"one of our schoolfellows, E. Archibald."* He had been at the school since 1910 and had, *"distinguished himself both by his scholarship and his proficiency in sports, being our full-back on the 1ˢᵗ XV."* On November 26 1913, there was a short service in school in memory of a past pupil, J.M. Davis, whose early death had taken place two days previously. He had, as Mr Houston said in his address, *"hardly entered on the battle of life,"* having left the school only a year before. He had been a scholar there for eight years and had proved himself, *"a diligent student, a loyal son of the School, and a leader in its sports."* At his funeral, *"Mr Houston, Dr Hunter, Mr Willis, Mr Bruce, Barrett and Schneider bore the coffin from the hearse to the graveside."*

Later in 1914, reference was made after morning prayers to the death of one of Mr Houston's personal heroes, Field-Marshal Lord Roberts, and to the recent death of Mr Traill, late Provost of Trinity College, Dublin. Houston paid tribute to, *"his wise and kindly guidance to those of our number who had enjoyed the great advantage of having him for their college tutor at the University."* He also mentioned the honour Mr Traill had done to the school, *"in sending four of his sons to it as pupils."*

Response To The Call To Arms

At the Prize Distribution of 1914, Mr Houston spoke of the manner in which Old Boys of the School were already answering the call of King and Country, following the outbreak of the Great War, a month or so before. Later, the report of the Governors for the year stated that a 'Roll of Honour' was being prepared, recording the names of all the past pupils who were serving their country in the armed forces. It was believed that by the time Lord Kitchener's new armies took the field in the following spring, *"not less than 100 old boys from the school will be found in the ranks of the defenders of the Empire."*

The noble response to the call of duty was made more personal to the school in an event which took place on Friday 20 November. The masters and boys had come together to say a formal farewell to Mr Samuel Willis, B.A., a long-serving and highly esteemed member of the teaching staff, who had been commissioned as a captain in the 14ᵗʰ Battalion, Royal Irish Rifles. This was the same Mr Willis who had suffered a terrible tragedy, in the loss of his young wife of just a few months, referred to so movingly by Mr Houston at the Prize Distribution of 1905.

Mr Willis was no longer in the first flush of youth, having taught Mathematics for eighteen years at the Institution, but as Dr S.J. Hunter said to the boys on that occasion, he, *"had heard the call to arms"* and, *"like a true patriot, he felt that the needs of his country were greater than theirs."* Mr Willis had previously, Mr Houston said, *"done work of the highest value for the local Ulster Volunteer Force"* and, not surprisingly, *"in the Rifle Club he was perhaps the best shot we have ever had."* Mr Willis was presented with a pair of valuable field glasses as a token of the honour and affection in which he was held by the masters and pupils.

In his formal response, Mr Willis thanked them all from the bottom of his heart for the beautiful and useful present, and even more sincerely for the kind thoughts which had prompted it. He felt that the experience he had gained amongst them, and the discipline he had learnt at the school, would be of some use to his country. He hoped he was only leaving them for a short time and concluded by saying, *"I wish you all the best of luck, and may God bless you all till we meet again."* Sadly, the brave Mr Willis did not return to his teaching post at the Institution. He was declared killed in action on the first day of the Battle of the Somme; Mr Robert Thompson, in his book *The Coleraine Heroes*, writes: *"it is believed that Captain Willis was taken prisoner on the 1st of July and that Private Cochrane made an attempt with bombs to rescue him, only to be driven back when reinforcements arrived."*

There is no known grave, but Captain Willis is commemorated on the Thiepval Memorial, on the school Roll of Honour, and in St Patrick's Church, Coleraine, where he had worshipped. In the school magazine of December 1918 there is the following touching poetic tribute to him, signed simply by 'D.W.McG.', presumably one of his former pupils. The poem deserves to be quoted in full.

Samuel Willis, Esq., B.A.

Captain 14th Battalion Royal Irish Rifles, late Mathematical and Science Master at the Academical Institution, Coleraine, and who was killed at the Battle of the Somme on the 1 July 1916.

You proved yourself a tried and trusted friend
To those you taught, in by-gone days, at School,
Who could not grasp some algebraic sign
Nor understand a tricky Euclid rule;
They came to you, and did not come in vain,
To get the help that you would freely give –
To them, through all the years that lie ahead,
Your memory, enriched by Death, shall live.

You took a helpful interest in our sport;
You taught us how to keep our courage up;
You cheered, upon the touch-line, like a boy,
Whenever we were playing for the Cup.
You helped us in our love for C.A.I.,
To hold it up to honour and to fame;
You taught us life's best lesson from the start
By showing us the way you 'played the game.'

You heard your country crying in distress;
You answered, in the way that Britons can;
And with you were the wishes and the hopes
Of every boy you helped to be a man.
You won the love of 'Tommy' by your grit;
You proved that truth was better than a lie;
You showed him how to fight for England's cause,
And, later on, you showed him how to die.

Amid the strife and carnage round the Somme,
Your gentlemanly soul returned to God –
You joined the gallant army of the dead
In peace and love, where Angel feet have trod.
No honours here, on earth, were your reward,
No ribbons – signs of bronze and silver stars –
But, better still, you won the Golden Crown,
The Cross of Love, from Higher Hands than ours.

The years to come will run their fitful course,
And each will give unto the world its men;
But through the ages, till the last farewell,
We will not look upon your like again.
The boys you taught, Sir, never will forget,
Your name will ever float across the Bann,
Carried, by memory, to the good old School,
With this, your epitaph, 'You were a man.'

In 1914, three new masters were appointed: Mr Ronald R. Whitcombe as English Master in place of Mr J.B. Tackaberry, resigned; Mr W.H. Moore as Assistant Classical and English master in place of Mr McKew, resigned; and Mr Archd. Lloyd, Commercial and Drawing Master, in place of Mr Coulter, resigned. An item on the agenda at a special Governors' meeting on 26 August 1914 was, *"to consider pension scheme for teachers in connection with recent Treasury Grant."* Arising from their discussions on pensions for assistant masters, it seemed there was already a realisation that the 'Chief' himself would require a pension soon. Accordingly, it was agreed at that meting that, *"in the event of Mr Houston retiring from the Principalship of the School, the Governors undertake to grant him a pension not less than £150 per year, to be a first charge on the School funds, and that Memorial be drawn up asking The Honourable The Irish Society for a similar amount for this object."* Later, the Finance sub-committee of the Governors learnt that The Irish Society was willing to provide £200 for this pension and, as Mr Houston had generously declined to accept more than £300 as a pension, the sub-committee agreed to provide £100 from school funds.

In 1914, twenty-seven candidates were successful at the Intermediate Examinations, seven of them passing with honours. R.N. Henry (Junior) won Exhibitions in the Mathematical and Science Groups and a prize of £1 in Modern Languages. F.R. Franklin (Junior) obtained an Exhibition in the Science Group and prizes of £2 in Maths and £1 in Modern Languages. T.J. McKee (Junior) won prizes of £3 in Maths and £1 in Science. R. Davison was football captain, and the side was described as *"rather weak"*, winning three and losing seven of the ten games played. A.O. Schneider again led the Cricket XI. The various scholarships were won by A. Gilmore (Clothworkers'), W.G. Boggs (Grant), A.O. Schneider (Anderson), and W.G. Boggs (Cochrane).

The End Of A Long Reign

On 1 March 1915, Mr Houston informed the Governors that he wished to retire at the end of the summer term that year. In his courteous letter asking for his resignation to be accepted he said, *"I am now in my seventy-second year, and therefore long past the usual age for superannuation. My health is still very good and I am not conscious of any serious failings in my powers, except that of hearing, which is of essential importance to a schoolmaster; but I feel that it is best for me to resign before my powers begin to fail me and while the School is in a thoroughly efficient condition as it is at present. . . . In this condition I wish to hand over the Institution to you and to the man you may appoint as my successor."* At a subsequent meeting, the Chairman, Rev. R.B. Wylie, and members of the Governing Body accepted the resignation with profound regret, and many striking tributes were paid by them to the inspiring personality of Mr Houston and the immeasurable services he had rendered to the school, not only by himself but also by the late Mrs Houston and Miss Margaret Houston. An appreciation of these services was entered in the minute book.

An extract from that appreciation in the minute book shows the high esteem in which Mr Houston was held by the Governors. *"The*

Governors cannot find language adequately to express their appreciation of Mr Houston's life, influence, and labours during his entire term of office. His life has always been lived on such an elevated plane; his influence has been so potent, not only in moulding the characters, in forming the tastes, manners and ideals of his pupils, and in giving an upward bent to their lives, but in leavening and uplifting the whole community; his work has been so single-minded, so wholehearted, so unweariedly and conscientiously devoted to promoting the best interests of the School throughout his long and honoured Principalship, that the Governors feel they owe him a debt of gratitude which can never be re-paid."

The last medal awarded for academic achievement in the school, presented by T.G. Houston to pupil J.H.R. Patterson, in 1915. Such medals were highly prized by recipients and the hallmarking would suggest that the medal was quite valuable.

The Prize Distribution that year was held before the summer vacation, and the people of Coleraine and friends of the school from much further afield took the opportunity to say farewell to Mr and Miss Houston. The ceremony, not surprisingly, attracted a record attendance. Mr Houston, in a memorable speech, thanked the Board of Governors, The Irish Society, Dr S.J. Hunter, his faithful senior master, and the other members of staff for the loyal help which they had given him in his work. He paid a tribute to his predecessor, Mr Young, whose death had taken place that year, and welcomed the appointment of his successor (of whom much more later). In appreciation of his many Old Boys, and the service which many of them were giving to their country at this dangerous time, he mentioned that 152 names were already listed on the School Roll of Honour, and the number was increasing daily.

J.E. McLarnon then read an address to Miss Margaret Houston and G.M. Walker handed to her a purse of sovereigns. Both were farewell gifts from the boys of the school. After the Distribution of Prizes, Mr Houston presented to the school the portrait given to him fifteen years earlier. This was accepted by Mr A.G. Crawford, honorary secretary, on behalf of the Board of Governors, and was hung in the school alongside that of Mr Young, presented in 1911.

Before moving on to a final comment on Mr Houston and his forty-five-year reign, and looking at the comparatively more mundane details of the year 1915, at the Intermediate Examinations seventeen candidates were successful, three passing with honours. F.R. Franklin (Middle) won an Exhibition in the Modern Language Group and won prizes of £3 in Classics, £3 in English Composition and £2 in Science. R.N. Henry (Middle) was awarded a prize of £1 in Science. The school Scholarship winners were: F.W. Walker (Clothworkers'), R.N. Henry (Joseph Cuthbert), and F.R. Franklin (Cochrane). J.E. McLarnon was captain of football, and the First XV won three and lost four of the seven matches played. The school side was defeated in the first round of the Schools' Cup by Foyle College, the score being twenty-one points to nil. McLarnon played for the Ulster Schools' XV versus Leinster. The writer of the 'Football Record' for that year commented philosophically, *"Another football season has come to an end and though we had not a very successful season, still we console ourselves with the thought that we were an improvement on the four previous seasons."*

In that summer of 1915 the great 'Chief' was leaving his life's work. For forty-five years, this remarkable man had been unswerving in his mission not just to educate in an academic sense, but above all to build sound moral character, to send out into the world young men who would not just be successes in the eyes of themselves and their parents, but useful pillars of society as a whole, young men inspired with a sense of duty. The vital roles which some of those Institution pupils played in later life, in those last decades of Empire and beyond, are testament to the sound training they received from Thomas Galway Houston. Throughout his career, he had not only represented but had painstakingly shaped everything that was good in the school. Yes, he most certainly was the 'Irish Arnold' of his time.

The last comments on T.G. Houston are from his past pupils, first an anonymous Old Boy, writing in the school magazine of May 1915. *"There was one lesson which by precept and example was always being impressed on one at Coleraine – that in this world the one necessity was to play fair. Results didn't matter so much as the manner of playing; and the loser might be a better man than the winner. You didn't realise this all at once; it was only when you were out in the world for a while and saw the tricks and the sham of it all; when men won unfairly, and the temptation came to do likewise, that you suddenly realised that this conclusion was fully formed in your mind. That wouldn't have been done in Coleraine. The Chief wouldn't like it. And close on the heels of the first came the second thought: it was from him I learned that. . . . To spend his life for the school; to labour unceasingly to fit men to face the world as gentlemen; to consider nothing but the welfare of his boys; to forget self in serving others – these were his ideals, and he attained them."*

The second is found in the memoirs of W.E. Wylie, who left the school in 1899. *"The Coleraine Academical Institution with T.G. Houston as Headmaster was an absolutely first-class school. It was not a school where you had to learn but you could learn if you wanted to. One thing however you did have to do. You had to behave yourself and you were taught that far above scholarship were honour and truth and decency. . . . He had one verse of poetry printed in large letters and hanging behind his desk.*

> *'One who never turned his back but marched breast forward,*
>   *Never doubted clouds would break,*
>   *Never dreamed, though right were worsted, wrong would triumph,*
>   *Held we fall to rise, are baffled to fight better,*
>   *Sleep to wake.'*

I have often quoted that to myself; in fact I think I have taken it as a sort of text or motto in life. It has often helped me out and I thank the Coleraine Institution for it, if for nothing else."

The verse is from Robert Browning's 'Epilogue to Asolando' and the language and sentiments are very much Victorian, but what a wonderful motto to instil into young minds by teaching and example: to be brave, to march resolutely 'breast forward' in pursuit of an honourable goal, and to be undaunted by setbacks. It is no surprise that when Houston moved to his new home after retirement he called it 'Avanti' – meaning 'Forward'!

Coleraine Academical Institution,
Co. Londonderry,

March 1st, 1915.

To the Governors of the Coleraine
Academical Institution.

Gentlemen,

In answer to your question as to whether I should like to have your arrangement with me continued for another year I thank you very sincerely for your kindness in allowing me a choice in the matter; but I have with great regret to beg from you another favour, and that is — that at the end of the half year beginning today you will kindly release me from the duties of my post and allow me to pass into the retirement that suits my years and that your generous kindness has placed within my reach.

I am now in my seventy-second year, and therefore long past the usual age for superannuation. My health is still very good; and I am not conscious of any serious failure in my powers except that of hearing which is of essential importance to a schoolmaster; but I feel that it is best for me to resign before my powers begin to fail me,

T.G. Houston's letter of resignation.

and while the school is in a thoroughly efficient condition as it is at present. Our
numbers are quite up to the standard of recent years, we have an excellent staff of
assistant masters and all departments
of our school life are in thoroughly efficient
working order. In this condition I wish to
hand over the Institution by you and to the man
whom you may appoint as my successor.

If spared till next month I shall have
completed forty-five years in your service. After
such a long ~~period of service~~ tenure of office by one person I feel that a
change would be in the interests of the school;
and I am very glad to know that you can
offer to my successor much higher induce-
ments to accept the Principalship than were
held out to me. With the assured position
of the school; its extensive and fine equipment, and greatly increased financial assistance from the Irish Society, the Intermediate Board, and the Department of Technical Instruction you will be able to command
the services of the very best men from the Universities of the United-Kingdom; and I hope
and pray that you may find a man who will
raise the position of the Institution far above
that which it has held under either my predecessor or myself.

I may add that in taking what is to me

a momentous and ~~too one~~ a very painful
step. I have to consider other interests besides
my own, and for family reasons I feel that I
must ask you to release me now.

When I think of the way in which you
have treated me during all the time I have
had the privilege of serving under you;
when I remember your generous kindness
to me, culminating in the liberal retiring allowance you have granted me, when
I think of the many tokens of friendship
I have received from you personally as
well as in your corporate capacity,
of your trust in me (however poorly deserved), of your hearty support of me in
my administration of the school, and of your
patience with me in my many short-
comings, I feel at a loss for words in
which to express my gratitude. I shall
never forget what you have been to me, and
what you have done for me; and I shall
always earnestly pray that God's blessing
may rest upon you and on the School —
which has the advantage of your wise and faithful guidance.

I remain, Gentlemen,
Gratefully and sincerely yours,
T. G. Houston.

Chapter 5

Thomas James Beare, M.A., 1915 – 1927

On Monday 8 March 1915, a special meeting of the Governing Body of Coleraine Academical Institution was held in the Town Hall, the one item on the agenda being to advertise for a new Principal. It was agreed that the advertisement should be placed in the following papers: *Athenaeum, Spectator, Education, The Times, Scotsman, Glasgow Herald, Whig (Belfast), News Letter* and *Irish Times*. The wording of the advertisement read, *"Wanted after Midsummer Holidays, a Headmaster for the above Institution, which is one of the most successful and best equipped Protestant Public Schools in Ireland. Accommodation for over 70 boarders and a large Day School. For a properly qualified candidate, the opening is a most attractive one. Full particulars of the Duties & Emoluments of the post may be obtained from the Honorary Secretary, to whom applications, with copies of Testimonials, should be addressed."*

The 'Duties' listed were fairly brief and condensed, but included the following:

3. *Pupils to be prepared for Entrance and Honours in the Universities, for the Irish Intermediate Examinations, for Banking and Commercial pursuits, and to be trained in Experimental Science and Drawing under the Department of Agriculture and Technical Instruction.*
4. *An interest in Athletic Sports is required.*
5. *The Pupils of the School belong chiefly to the Presbyterian and Episcopalian Denominations. The Head Master is required to be a member of a Protestant Church, and to be in sympathy with Evangelical Protestantism.*

The 'Emoluments' or rewards which an aspiring Headmaster might hope to obtain from the position of Headmaster of C.A.I. were listed very clearly:

1. *The use of the House, Grounds and Gardens, and any profits resulting therefrom.*
2. *The profits derived from the fees of Boarders.*

The educational fees for Boarders are paid by the Head Master to the Governors on the same scale as fees for Day Pupils.

3. *An endowment of £200 a year from The Honourable The Irish Society.*
4. *One half of the Result Fees paid by the Intermediate Board. Last year these fees amounted to £254, and might be greatly increased.*
5. *£15 per annum towards Porter's salary.*
6. *£35 towards Advertising and Printing.*
7. *Ten Tons of Coal for School Heating.*
8. *15 shillings Capitation Fee, per annum, on all Pupils attending the Institution.*
9. *The Governors pay the salaries of Assistant Masters, and spend a reasonable sum on the upkeep of the Premises. £25 per annum paid to the Head Master for Board of each Resident Master.*

In comparison with today, when all teachers, including Headmasters or Principals, are paid by the government, the financial remuneration of the post of Headmaster at C.A.I. in 1915 seems rather complex, but at the time must have indeed been 'most attractive'; there was certainly much incentive for the new Headmaster to maintain and increase the number of pupils on the roll, especially boarders, and to achieve excellent results at the Intermediate Examinations.

However, before the transfer to a new 'Chief', there were many matters of a practical and financial nature to be sorted out. Two 'valuators' were to be appointed, one by Mr Houston and one by the incoming Headmaster, to estimate the value of the furniture in the Boarding School, the Roller and the Lawn Mower, all of which had been purchased by Mr Houston. The agreed amount would be paid by the new Headmaster, through the Governors, to Mr Houston, with the assurance that, *"the new Principal shall have the benefit of the same privilege on his resignation."* In the matter of the 18-acre farm which Mr Houston had purchased (part of which was used by the Football Club) and the rent on which had been paid till now by the Governors, it was decided that this land should be transferred to the Governing Body, and not

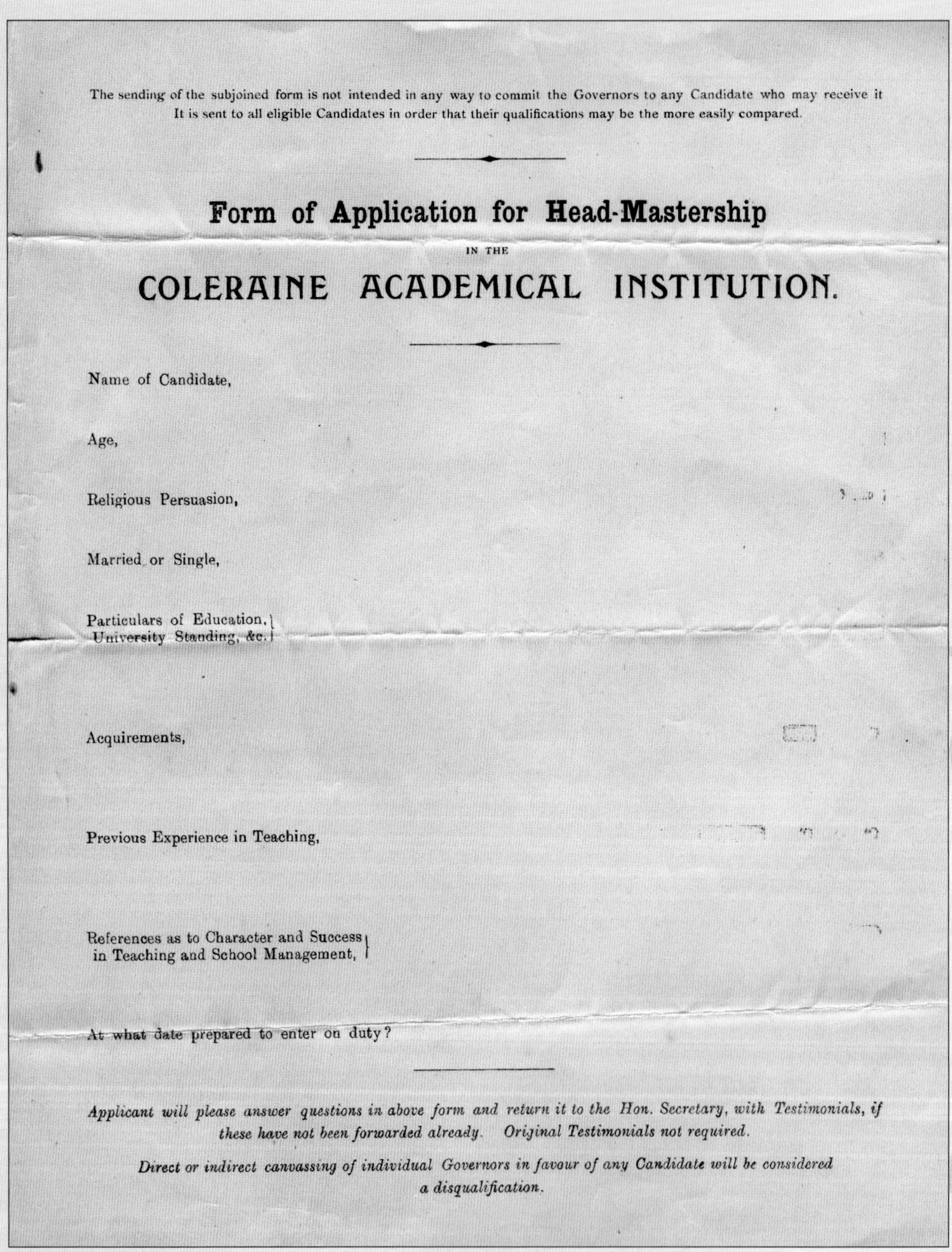

The sending of the subjoined form is not intended in any way to commit the Governors to any Candidate who may receive it
It is sent to all eligible Candidates in order that their qualifications may be the more easily compared.

Form of Application for Head-Mastership

IN THE

COLERAINE ACADEMICAL INSTITUTION.

Name of Candidate,

Age,

Religious Persuasion,

Married or Single,

Particulars of Education,
University Standing, &c.

Acquirements,

Previous Experience in Teaching,

References as to Character and Success
in Teaching and School Management,

At what date prepared to enter on duty?

*Applicant will please answer questions in above form and return it to the Hon. Secretary, with Testimonials, if
these have not been forwarded already. Original Testimonials not required.*

*Direct or indirect canvassing of individual Governors in favour of any Candidate will be considered
a disqualification.*

The Form of Application for Head-Mastership, 1915.

to the new Headmaster. The Governors also agreed to refund to Mr Houston the sum of £39 – 7s – 8d, being the balance of his out-of-pocket expenses in connection with the construction of the Swimming Pond and the Rifle Range.

On 7 April 1915, the governors appointed a seven-strong sub-committee to *"look into applications for Headmastership"* and report to the full Board. On 26 April, the sub-committee met to consider no less than fifty-five applications and, as a result of their deliberations, they struck off thirty-six names, leaving nineteen. The surviving nineteen were then divided into A and B lists, those on the A list being considered by the sub-committee the *"most likely candidates"*. The five names on the A list were: Dr James Clark, Kilmarnock; Reginald J. Castley, Worcester; T.J. Beare, Derry; E.V. Watkins, Taunton; James McQuillan, Larne. The last named was a former teacher at the Institution. Some members of the sub-committee agreed to *"write privately"* regarding the names on the A list and report at a subsequent meeting. On 7 May, the sub-committee met again and transferred E.V. Watkins from the A list to the B list, leaving a final short-list of four, which they recommended to the full Board. On 26 May 1915, nineteen members of the Governing Body met to interview the short-listed applicants and in the end appointed Mr T.J. Beare, by a very large majority.

For the record, the school Governors attending that important meeting were: Rev. R.B. Wylie, LLD., Vice-President, in the Chair; Mr A.G. Crawford, J.P., Honorary Secretary; Sir W.J. Baxter, D.L., J.P., Honorary Treasurer; Rev. Canon Dudley, M.A.; Rev. M.A. Wilson, M.A.; Rev. M.H. Giles, B.A.; Rev. G.N.D. Rea, B.A.; Rev. J.M. Freeman; Rev. M.H. Massey; Rev. J.A. Wright; Mr H.A. Anderson, LL.D.; Mr Robert Moore; Mr John McCandless; Mr W. Abraham, J.P.; Dr Forsythe, J.P.; Mr J.M. Crawford; Mr Richard Hunter; Mr Chas. R. Anderson; Mr B.H. Lane. Apologies were received from Sir Hervey Bruce, Hugh T. Barrie Esq., M.P., and Rev. M.G. Davis.

There was a great flurry of activity in the form of special Governors' meetings over the next few months, with the Educational sub-committee and the Finance sub-committee coming to agreements with Mr Beare as to certain aspects of his terms of employment. Contractors were employed to carry out re-decoration in the Headmaster's house and in some of the school-rooms. Mr Beare himself was authorised to purchase thirty-five oak desks at an auction in Derry and his expenditure on this matter was reimbursed. An interesting detail of a meeting of the Governors on 2 July 1915 reads, *"It was arranged to forward a telegram of congratulation to Mr Beare on 8th July, the day of his marriage."* A final settlement was reached with Mr Houston regarding the following items he had purchased for the school: Typewriter £10, Picture £1, Laboratory Balance £2, Portfolio of Model Drawings ten shillings, Pair Garden Vases ten shillings, Lawn Mower (Horse) £15, Horse Roller £4, Stable & Outhouses £25, Greenhouse in Garden £20, Fencing & Hoarding £5, Books in Study £25 – coming to a total of £108.

Thomas James Beare - The Man

Mr Thomas James Beare, M.A., took up duty as Headmaster of the Institution on 1 September 1915. The report of the governors for that year states that Mr Beare had not only an unusually brilliant record of distinctions in the Royal University and in Trinity College, but he also brought with him the experience gained during the fourteen years in which he acted with remarkable success as principal assistant master at Foyle College, Londonderry. He had a daunting task in taking up the reins at C.A.I. as there were no doubt expectations that he would manage and guide the school in the same way as his great predecessor. However, the new 'Chief' had his own firm views about the running of the school and was not afraid to experiment with new systems. A. McCurdy, who was a boarder in the school at that time, writing in the school magazine of 1960, said that, *"until Mr Houston's retirement, there were Prefects and Monitors and Junior Prefects, but new Kings making new laws, these were abolished. After about two years however, Mr Beare decided that the original arrangement worked very well and the Prefects were re-instated. Among the first of these were Dixon, Fred Shaw, Hugh McVicker, Chuck Wolseley,*

Moss, Anderson and McCurdy." Mr Beare was obviously keen to put his own distinctive stamp on the school, but at the same time was prepared to rescind his new directives if they proved inappropriate. It is also interesting that, for whatever reason, there were no Annual Prize Distributions during Mr Beare's tenure, with, instead, the Headmaster presenting a brief report to the Governors at each quarterly meeting. Possibly, Mr Beare had no great taste for the magnificent public occasion which the annual Distribution of Prizes had been in Mr Houston's time; at any rate, he certainly saved himself from the bane of all school Principals' lives nowadays, the preparation of a Prize Distribution speech!

Mr Houston had always been known affectionately as 'the Chief', by his colleagues and, amongst each other of course, by the boys. There seems to have been some confusion regarding how to refer to the new Headmaster informally. Some still favoured the traditional term 'the Chief' – one pupil, writing home to his parents said, *"I did not see the (head) chief yet; even the masters hardly know Mr Beare as the Head, it is always the chief."* In time, his colleagues and others referred to him informally as 'Tommy John', but another of his one-time pupils, Ernest Sandford, speaking at an Old Boys' dinner in 1984, said, not unsurprisingly, that, *"Tommy John was known as The Bear, his room was The Bear's Den and the School, with its 120 pupils, was a sort of Bear's Garden!"* What fun school pupils have always had with teachers' nicknames!

Like his predecessor, Mr Beare could be, if necessary, a thorough investigator and a stern disciplinarian, illustrated in an amusing account of some misbehaviour in the dining hall, given by Willie Crawford, a boarder, in a letter to his father. *"There was a row last night here, down at supper. A fellow threw porridge at another and missed him, the porridge stuck to the wall and the chief asked who threw the porridge and he made every person get into the way they were sitting at the supper table. At last the boy owned up and was told to come to the Chief's after roll call next morning to be caned and got Detention for Saturday (not to go out of the school door)."* As always, boys will be boys, even the young gentlemen at C.A.I., but

throwing 'plain and wholesome food' around just could not be tolerated! One suspects that not being allowed *"to go out of the school door"* all day Saturday was just as painful a punishment as the caning!

Up until this time, annual inspections of the school, under the Educational Endowments scheme had always been very favourable. These inspections usually lasted just one day, seemed to be fairly perfunctory affairs, and the inspector's report, a copy of which had to be sent to the Government in Dublin Castle, was not particularly detailed. Mr Beare got a hearty vote of confidence from F.J. Paul, the inspector who visited the school in December 1915. *"I cannot but speak in high terms of the general condition and efficiency of Coleraine Academical Institution. The classrooms, dormitories etc., are roomy, airy, and well-heated. The sanitation is good; the play ground is ample. Under the new Head Master the Institution seems to have taken a new lease of life. I was unable during my visit to come upon anything that deserved to be found fault with."* How wonderful it would be if today's teams of inspectors, descending upon the schools they have selected for thorough, week-long investigations, would say at the end that they were 'unable to come upon anything' to find fault with!

The number on the school roll when Mr Beare took up his duties was 108, the highest figure for several years. The year 1915-16 was an uneventful one at C.A.I., but many former pupils were winning fame in the great conflict which was taking place in Europe. In a letter from an 'Old Boy Serving with the Colours', published in the school magazine of May 1915, Captain Casement, R.A.M.C., aboard a transport ship with the British Mediterranean Expeditionary Force, described the excitement and danger of those times. *"We had quite a little excitement last week, when an attempt was made, within 15 miles of us, to torpedo one of our other transports by an enemy torpedo boat. One of our destroyers gave chase, and ran the torpedo boat ashore and smashed her up. She had fired three torpedoes at the transport, and missed each time."* By the end of 1915, over 200 Old Boys had responded to the call to service.

In 1916, thirty candidates were successful at the Intermediate Examinations, six passing with honours. F.R. Franklin secured an Exhibition in the Senior Grade, while prizes were won by F.R. Franklin and R.N. Henry (Senior), A. Gilmore (Middle), and R. McAuley, C. Murphy, and J.F. Alexander (Junior). C.L. Crawford was Football Captain during the Christmas term and the side was undefeated during this period. After the holidays, Crawford and several other members of the 1st XV *"answered the call of Country"*, and a very much weakened team, led by A.F. Henry, lost the remaining matches. The season's record for school matches was: two won, five lost and one drawn. A.F. Henry played for Ulster Schools and also captained the Cricket XI. In their annual report for the year 1916, the Governors expressed their confidence in their new Headmaster and their pleasure at the excellent examination results for the year. *"The brilliant record that Mr Beare enjoyed as an exceptionally successful teacher prior to accepting his present position has been evinced again by the magnificent results of his pupils at the various examinations of the Intermediate Board. In these achievements no less than in the conduct of the Institution generally, the Governors recognise not only the lustre that the Head Master has shed upon his office, but the wisdom they themselves displayed in asking him to fill it."*

A change in the Scholarship regulations resulted in the Clothworkers' and Anderson Scholarships being awarded on the results of the Senior Grade Examinations. The most successful Senior candidate secured the Clothworkers', while the next best was awarded the Anderson, provided a satisfactory standard was attained in each case. These changes, were enshrined in a little publication, setting out the *"Regulations with regard to the various Scholarships and Prizes"*, endorsed by the Governors at their meeting on 8 November 1915. It is interesting to note point three of the introductory 'General Regulations', which states that Candidates for all Scholarships competed for within the school, *"must produce a certificate of satisfactory conduct from the Head Master."* Scholarship winners in 1916 were: F.R. Franklin (Clothworkers'), R.N. Henry (Anderson), A.F. Henry (Joseph Cuthbert), and R.R Hunter (Cuthbert). The Cochrane Scholarship was withheld that year, as none of the candidates had reached the qualifying

standard. In 1916, these were still very valuable scholarships in monetary terms, and they were not handed out without careful examination of academic performances.

Wars And Rebellions

As always, the experiences of pupils and past pupils of the school reflect the wider, dramatic, and often tragic events of the times, and this was very much the case in 1916. For example, at Christmas 1916, the now-retired T.G. Houston wrote to Sloane Bolton, a past pupil, then recovering from serious wounds sustained in a raid on enemy trenches at Messines. As well as giving him details of other old boys who had been killed or injured in the Great War and of the distinctions for bravery won by many, he told him about a dramatic event in Dublin at the time of the Rising. *"You may perhaps have heard that in the recent disastrous Rebellion in Dublin some of our old boys rendered services that were not mentioned in despatches or rewarded with any Distinctions but that were of very great value. One of the great objectives of the rebels was College Green with the buildings around it, particularly the Bank of Ireland and Trinity College. The attack was so sudden that no military force was at first available for the defence of this all important part of the city; but a few students – nine in all, I understand – emulated the famous exploit of the Apprentice Boys of Derry, and by a well directed fire kept the enemy back until reinforcements arrived. Four of these students were old Coleraine boys. Their names, which should never be forgotten, were Lyn Wylie, K.C., W. Shannon, F. Robertson, and Tom Madill."*

William Evelyn (Lyn) Wylie, King's Counsel, and his fellow students were members of the Trinity College Officers' Training Corps. Lyn Wylie was the son of the Rev. R.B. Wylie, who was minister of Terrace Row Presbyterian Church, Coleraine, from 1871 until his retirement in 1913. Rev. Wylie was also Chairman of the C.A.I. Board of Governors from 1919 until 1924. In the aftermath of the Easter Rising, Lyn Wylie was Crown Prosecutor at the courts martial of the leaders of the rebellion, and it is claimed that he was instrumental in saving Eamon De Valera from execution. He later became Law Adviser to the British Government, a High Court Judge and a Judicial Commissioner of the Irish Land Commission. Always a keen horseman, he was President of the Royal Dublin Society 1939 – 1941.

Another example of Institution pupils being involved in dramatic events on the world stage can be seen in the May 1916 edition of the school magazine. An article, signed 'F.R.F.', a boarder at the school, gives a vivid account of the author's 'Experiences in Dublin during the Sinn Fein Rising', during his Easter vacation. He recalls how, at night, during the worst of the sniping along Northumberland Road, he took care to pull his bed into the corner of the room, well away from the window. He describes the destruction in Sackville (now O'Connell) Street afterwards. *As one left Grafton Street and passed over O'Connell Bridge what a scene of desolation met the eye! Sackville Street, one of the finest streets in Europe, was a mass of smoking ruins. Nelson Pillar stood alone in the midst of a scene of devastation, marked here and there by chimneys and gaunt iron girders standing among the ruins.* F.R.F. managed to reach Amiens Street Station (now Connolly Station) and was relieved to get out of Dublin, on his way back to Coleraine after a longer than expected holiday.

This 'F.R.F.' was none other than F.R. Franklin who, just a few weeks later, was awarded the Clothworkers' Scholarship for 1916. Obviously a talented student, with his valuable 'Exhibition', he entered Trinity College, Dublin, in October 1916, where he quickly joined the Officer Training Corps. He was sent to an Officers' Training Cadet Battalion in Cambridge and obtained a commission in the Royal Irish Rifles in September 1917. Sadly, nineteen-year-old Second Lieutenant Fred R. Franklin was killed in action in France on 9 December 1917. There is no known grave, but his name is commemorated on the Thiepval Memorial and on the school Roll of Honour. Freddy Franklin was typical of many of the young men who were leaving C.A.I. at that time; their bravery and their sense of duty are to be applauded, indeed marvelled at, but with the more jaundiced view of war prevalent today, we may well say, 'What a waste of youth and talent!'

In that same school magazine of May 1916, following the article written by 'F.R.F.', some items in the 'Old Boys' Notes' reflect the grimness of the situation on the Western Front at the time, and the involvement of C.A.I. lads there.

- *"It is with deep regret we record the death of Second Lieutenant Lloyd Rogers, who was killed in France by a shell while he was engaged in getting his men under cover. At the time of his death he was serving his country with the Royal Field Artillery."*

- *"It has been a great sorrow to us to learn that yet another 'Old Boy' has fallen in the battlefield. Private Herbert Curran of the Royal Fusiliers was killed in action on 7 May."*

- *"We are sorry to hear that Second Lieutenant J.B. Getty, 17th Battalion Royal Irish Rifles, has been somewhat severely wounded in France. Second Lieutenant Getty is the son of Mr Robert Getty, Carrycroey, Mosside, Ballycastle. He was standing at the entrance to a dug-out when a German shell exploded almost at his feet."*

After morning prayers on Friday 10 November 1916, a brief formal event illustrated in another way the impact which the war was having on the school community. A member of the teaching staff, Mr D.W. Lloyd, B.Sc., *"had been suddenly called to Government work at Woolwich Arsenal"*, the main munitions depot at the time. As a scientist, his services were urgently needed in support of the war effort. Mr Beare spoke of the debt which the school owed to Mr Lloyd and called upon Henry A.F. to read the address. This 'address', part of which is quoted below, is, like others which were traditionally read to School captains when they were leaving, most charmingly worded:

"In the class-room you have performed your duties zealously and well, and it was a pleasure for all of us to work under you. Your indefatigable zeal and self-sacrifice in all branches of our sports have placed us under a great debt of gratitude to you. How great your services have been will only be realised when you are no longer here; when we miss your enthusiasm in the sports, and when your good influence in the School is no longer felt. Now you have heard the call of King and country, and, like many a one who has passed from

these walls, have nobly responded to it." Mr Lloyd was presented with a handsome leather suitcase and fittings and made a suitable reply. The following Monday afternoon, in a follow-up which illustrates the close family spirit which existed within the school at the time, *"quite a number of masters and boys assembled at the station to give him a hearty send-off, and to assure him of our sincere good wishes for his joy and prosperity in the future."*

A name in the meticulously kept 'Results Register' for 1916 is of interest, that name being *Adams, John Bodkin*, who is shown as having achieved a fairly unspectacular pass in the Senior Grade of the Intermediate Examinations. All schools produce many pupils who go on to achieve fame, success and celebrity status in later life; but it is inevitable that a few may gain notoriety rather than fame. Dr John Bodkin Adams was later to become probably the only old boy of the school to narrowly escape the hangman's noose! He was born in Randalstown in 1899 and attended C.A.I. around the years 1914 – 1916, eventually going on to Queen's University, Belfast, where he graduated with a degree in medicine in 1921. In 1922, he became a general practitioner in a Christian practice in Eastbourne.

Later, between the years 1946 – 1956, more than 160 of Dr Adams' patients died under suspicious circumstances. Of these, no less than 132 left him money or items in their wills. In 1957, he was tried for the murder of one patient, but acquitted, while another count of murder was eventually withdrawn by the prosecution. The John Bodkin Adams trial featured in newspaper headlines around the world and was described as 'the murder trial of the century'. The trial was important also because of its legal ramifications, not least its establishment of the principle of 'double effect', whereby a doctor giving treatment with the aim of relieving pain, may, as an unintentional result, shorten life.

Adams was found guilty in a subsequent trial of thirteen offences of prescription fraud, lying on cremation forms, obstructing a police search and failing to keep a dangerous drugs register. He was removed from the Medical Register in 1957, but was re-instated in 1961, after two failed applications.

Moving on to 1917, the number of pupils in the school was 110. In this year, the school suffered a considerable loss by the death of Mr William M. Cuthbert, of South Africa, whose generous gifts indicated the great interest which he had always taken in the welfare of the Institution. A.F. Henry led the 1st XV, which lost to Campbell College in the Schools' Cup semi-final by fourteen points to nil. Of seven school games played, three were won, two lost and two drawn. A.F. Henry and J.W. Stewart played in the Schools' Inter-Provincial match. A.F. Henry was also captain of cricket.

The school magazine notes that the annual general meeting of the Cricket Club was followed by a meeting of the Tennis Club, at which Lowry was chosen Captain and a committee to assist him was nominated. The Scholarship winners in 1917 were: R.N.D. Wilson (Clothworkers'), R.A. Reid (Joseph Cuthbert) and J. Hunter (Cochrane). The Anderson and Cuthbert Commercial Scholarships were withheld that year, owing to the failure of candidates to reach the qualifying standard, again proof of how stringent were the conditions for the award of school scholarships.

At the Intermediate Examinations, thirty-seven candidates passed in the various Grades, with R.D. Wilson being awarded an Exhibition in the Senior Grade. In the Junior Grade, Prizes were won by J.C. McMaster (two), R.J.C. Maxwell, J. Bullick, H. McDermott, and A.L. Wilson, who also secured first place in English Composition. In the Headmaster's report at a meeting of the Governors on 7 June 1917, Mr Beare expressed his pleasure at the results of the recent Intermediate Examinations and outlined precisely how these good results were adding to the income of the school.

"The sum earned by the school in grants from the Department and Intermediate Board was £650; of this £270 was divided among the staff by agreement, and £380 or thereabouts goes into the school funds. I doubt if the school ever before benefited from this source to the extent of £150."

Happier Times

In contrast to the horrors of war which were taking place elsewhere, there was a most pleasant event for the boarders in late May of 1917. On Thursday 24, the pupils enjoyed the traditional half-holiday for the celebration of Empire Day and on the following Saturday a large number of boarders spent a very pleasant afternoon on the river. *"We rowed upstream to the Loughan Island, where we enjoyed the delights of picnicing on the green-sward. The weather was ideal, and the row homeward with the current was over all too soon. We have to thank Dr Hunter for his kindness in making the arrangements for one of the most enjoyable outings we have ever had."* Incidentally, there had been a school Boat Club in the early days, before it folded in the early 1890s, but it had been for leisure and pleasure, rather than competition. A contributor to an early school magazine, referring to the year 1893, wrote:

"The School Boat Club is, I understand, extinct, and it is well, perhaps, that it should be so, for undoubtedly it interfered largely with cricket. Still, some of my most delightful recollections of School life are associated with afternoons spent on the river, when with the sergeant in charge we made our way up to the Cutts and rested in the shade of Mountsandel, or explored the lower reaches of the river. We had two boats built for comfort rather than speed, and to pull them on a hot summer day against wind and tide was no joke." The current school Rowing Club was not founded until 1928.

Another pleasant event that year took place at Hallowe'en when, *"Mr Beare, instead of giving a holiday, let us off preparation for the next day, and provided a splendid supper for the boarders, with all kinds of Hallowe'en fare. The comic element was provided by several of the boys coming to supper in fancy dress. After supper, all the boarders adjourned to the Gym, where, owing to Mr Whitcombe's assistance (not to speak of Mr Wray's hat), a very enjoyable time was spent."*

Throughout the Institution's history, the Governors were always most attentive to the maintenance, repair and, if necessary, re-development or extension of the school premises. These matters were mainly seen to by the Building and the Finance sub-committees, which met frequently to decide on the work required, to seek tenders, and to pay bills. Their decisions were always approved by the full Board at its quarterly meetings. Mundane but necessary matters such as re-plastering, repairs to boilers, whitening of ceilings or re-painting of railings were all dealt with most methodically. An interesting item in the minutes of the Building Committee meeting of 27 November 1917 shows how better facilities for the boarders were to be provided. The Headmaster was instructed to, *"get estimates for converting Masters' Study into a sitting room for the pupils, by putting upholstered benches round the walls and Cork Linoleum on floor, walls to be papered, all woodwork painted and ceiling whitened."* As testament to the Governors' care of the school, Mr F.J. Paul, the Endowed Schools' inspector, visited the school on 24 October 1917 and commented that, *"The buildings are in an even better state of repair than they were a year ago"*, and he had *"no adverse criticism whatever to make."*

In 1918, the number of pupils had increased to 130. The provision of a new laboratory and the construction of a greatly enlarged swimming bath were welcome additions to the school. The Board of Governors suffered another loss in the death of Sir William Baxter, D.L., who had been the Board's honorary treasurer for many years. The effect of the increase in the number of boys attending the school is seen in a decision of the governors at a meeting of 30 April 1918, *"That the Principal be requested to get tenders for making new classroom and the Building Committee to decide tender."* At that same meeting, it was decided that part of a supplementary grant from the Department of Agriculture and Technical Instruction for Ireland should be distributed amongst the assistant staff as follows: Dr Hunter £55, Mr Parker £50, Mr Bruce £40, Mr Whitcombe £40, Mr Blaine £15, Miss Bradbury £9. A past pupil, R.J. Getty, writing in the centenary school magazine of 1960, recalls some of those teachers. There was, he says, *"the unobtrusively firm personality of Dr Hunter, the wee Doctor, who continued to symbolize for the school the stability, permanence, and high purpose for which he will be gratefully and affectionately remembered. The staff had its other personalities with more or less descriptive soubriquets. Why so good a Scot as 'Paddy' Bruce was so designated*

I never knew. 'Chilly' Blaine's conduct of classes in Physics and Chemistry was not so frigid and austere as to conceal a benevolent and helpful personality, and 'P.C.' Whitcombe did more for boarders and some day boys too than encourage a love for English literature in a classroom which he had transformed into a place of beauty and taste." Mr Whitcombe had indeed renovated and re-decorated his classroom at his own expense, refusing to accept any money from the Governors for his efforts. Mr Beare commended his generosity at a Board meeting and the Governors wrote to Mr Whitcombe, thanking him.

At the Intermediate Examinations, thirty-four candidates were successful, twelve of them passing with honours. Middle Grade Prizes were won by J.C. McMaster (two) and H.G. Lamont (two), the latter also securing first place and medal in Chemistry. W. Kelly won two prizes in Junior Grade. F.C. Shaw was Football Captain, and the 1st XV played eleven school matches, winning four, losing four, and drawing three. One of the games lost was the Cup semi-final, which R.B.A.I. won by the narrow margin of eight points to five. F.C. Shaw, H. McVicker and J.A. Campbell played for the Ulster Schools' XV against Leinster. The Cricket XI was also led by F.C. Shaw.

The 'Cricket Review' in the school magazine of September 1918 is less than inspiring, describing the season as, *"not a very remarkable one, for we only had two fixtures with Foyle College, one of which, unfortunately, had to be declared off owing to rain. Thus little need be said about the first eleven."* However, the report does go on to praise some of those eleven in less dismissive terms: McKee, who developed into quite a *"stylish player"*, with a good straight bat; Wolseley, the left-hander, also *"batted freely"*, putting plenty of power into his strokes; and Henry B. and Stewart were *"splendid hitters"*.

The school magazine of December 1918 gives details of another sport which had always been popular at the school - swimming. The report states that, *"At the annual swimming competitions, held at the Foyle College Baths, on Friday 4th November, C.A.I. had the most successful entry yet on our records, no competitions entered for by our team being lost."* The team consisted of Ben Henry (captain), H. McKee, E. Slade, and J.E.F. Anderson. The principal event was the winning of the Ulster Schools' Challenge Cup, which was brought to Coleraine for the first time. Scholarship winners that year were: J.F. Alexander (Clothworkers'), R. McAuley (Anderson), J.C. McMaster (Joseph Cuthbert) and W.C. Rawle (Cochrane). None of the candidates for the Cuthbert Commercial Scholarship secured the qualifying marks.

An interesting feature of the early years of the 20th century was that the girls at Coleraine High School (with its own long and distinguished history, having been founded in 1875) came to the Institution to sit the Intermediate Examinations there. An anonymous ex-High School girl, writing in the Institution magazine of September 1918, describes her memories of coming to the school for those exams. *"I well remember the thrills I experienced as we walked in 'croc' up the shady avenue and round to the Examination Hall."* She notes that *"the boys had a separate centre"* somewhere else in the building, a very wise decision, knowing the mutual distraction there might have been if the Inst. boys and the High School girls were sitting the exams in the same room. The annual arrival of the High School girls is also mentioned by A. McCurdy, a past pupil of the Institution, writing in the school magazine of 1960. He recalls how, *"The usual exam fever was rife towards the end of the summer term, but it had its lighter side too, when the High School girls came up to do their Intermediate Exams in the gym. i.e. letting the air out of the girls' bicycles, the mistake being made when the teachers' bicycles were let down as well. After that – retribution!"* One assumes that the purpose of letting the air out of the girls' bicycles was to prolong the stay of those delightful young ladies from the other side of the Bann in the *"shady"* environs of the Academical Institution! The young lady who contributed the article in the magazine also recalled how, *"every Hallows' Eve the boys gave a grand concert, and we were always lucky enough to obtain tickets of admission. The programme was full of variety. I can recall a group of boys with sleek heads and Eton suits singing in part, 'O, who will come o'er the Downs with me?"* And what romantic young girl's heart could resist such an invitation!

A photograph of the boarding school taken about 1918-19.

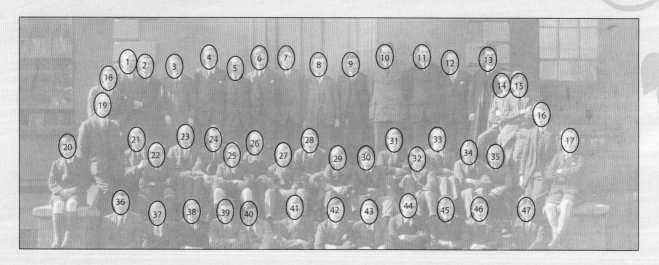

A past pupil s' comments on the 1918-19 photogaph.

1. **S.J. Hunter** — *Too well known to comment*

2. **R.R. Whitcombe** — *English Master. Good amateur gymnast. Furnished the gym himself and taught the sport. Moralist, radical and an agnostic which in those days was almost criminal. Left about 1924, committed suicide about 1930.*

3. **Morgan** — *"Taffy" Morgan. Was good rugby threequarter and coached the teams in back play.*

4. **Hugh Maxwell** — *Came from Co. Down.*

5. **McMillan** — *Came from Tyrone or Fermanagh.*

6. **McFadden** — *Came from Co. Down.*

7. **Chas McVicker** — *Youngest of famous rugby family. Was capped a number of times for Ireland. I believe he is now deceased.*

8. Johnston — *Came from Upperlands. Was rather stout and a Plymouth Brother, got the nickname of "Praise God Barebones".*

9. Unknown.

10. James McVicker — *Left school young to look after father's farm when his father died. Came back at the age of 22 to complete education. Also great rugby player, may have been capped for Ireland.*

11. Kelly — *Became Medical Practitioner. Practised in England, my brother was his partner for a time.*

12. Calwell — *Became Bank Official. Known as "Twatty".*

13. J. Beare — *Headmaster. Then known as the "Chief". Classical scholar. Left about 1925.*

14. Bamford — *One of the well known catering family of Portrush. Known as "Curly".*

15. Peter Maxwell — *Brother of Hugh (No.4). Always called "Pete".*

16. Unknown.

17. Megahey — *Known as "Towzer" at school. I think he died in his twenties.*

18. J.E.F. Anderson — *Qualified as engineer, is at present Belfast's City Surveyor.*

19. Unknown.

20. Kenneth Brew — *I think he became a Bank Official.*

21. R.A. Cunningham — *Came from India. Father in Indian Army. Was a sort of "Mad Carew" at school.*

22. John Patton — *At present he is chief pilot in Belfast Harbour.*

23. Small — *I do not know if he was related to the famous Captain Small, The President of the Old Boys.*

24. Unknown.

25. Guy Fisher — *Came from India. Father very well known Medical Practitioner. After qualifying as Medical Practitioner he went to India and became equally famous in that country, now deceased.*

26. Carson — *Belfast boy.*

27. T.D. Raphael — *Came from England. Went to Cambridge and I think afterwards emigrated.*

28. J.C. Nicholl — *Became well known Medical Practitioner in Bangor. Now deceased.*

29. Unknown.

30. Hunter — *Went into shirt business I think. May be deceased.*

31. McMillan — *Known as "Iky"*

32. Douglas Boyd — *Medical Radiologist was President B.M.A. Belfast 1966.*

33. Pinkerton — *Parents lived abroad.*

34. Cahoon — *Came from well known family in shirt business in Derry.*

35. J.P. Thompson — *Came from Mid Antrim. I think he is a Medical Practitioner.*

36. Rice — *Was a first rate boxer and I believe took part in amateur contests at Aldershot.*

37. Rew Fisher — *Brother of Guy Fisher (No. 25). Interested in the Arts and I think is now with a film company in London.*

38. G.T.L. Lowry — *Came from Kells Co. Meath. Went to Trinity. Killed by Japs in Hong Kong.*

39. Geo Kane — *Became well known Medical Practitioner practising in Mid Antrim.*

40. Allen — *I think he became a Bank Official.*

41. McMurray — *Known as "Monkey" came from Portstewart.*

42. A.T. Hardy — *Pharmaceutical Chemist, was President Pharmaceutical Society N.I. 1966/67.*

43. Unknown.

44. Dinsmore

45. J.R. Thompson — *Brother of J.P. Thompson (No.35). I think he became a Medical Practitioner.*

46. Monteith

47. Moffett

War Service Of Past Pupils

The December 1918 school magazine is most interesting, firstly because of the relief expressed in the editorial that, *"the terrible carnage which has lasted for over four years is now at an end"*, and secondly because it contains a lengthy 'C.A.I. Roll of Honour', including those who served, those who were killed or wounded, those who were prisoners of war, and those who were decorated for bravery. The editor noted that at that early stage the list was probably not complete and asked for anyone with information about other Old Boys who served to send it to the school. There are well over 300 names on this 1918 Roll of Honour. The complete Roll of Honour can, as mentioned earlier, be seen on a brass plaque in the rear foyer of the school assembly hall, but it is interesting to note how Institution Old Boys of the Great War served in a wide variety of armed units from all over the world, as well as with local regiments. A few examples are shown below.

- Abraham, J.J., M.D., F.R.C.S. Eng., - Lieutenant-Colonel, 24th Stationary Hospital, Egyptian Expeditionary Force.
- Armstrong, W. – Sergeant, Inland Water Transport, Mesopotamia.
- Barrie, F. – Second Lieutenant, Royal Flying Corps.
- Benson, J.C.H. – Lieutenant, 7th Battalion Canadians.
- Beresford, H.B. – Lieutenant, H.M.S *Lowestoft*.
- Booth, D. – Private, Rand Rifles, South Africa.
- Bolton, S. – Australian Light Horse.
- Casement, E.R. –Lieutenant, Railway Corps, British East Africa.
- Curran, W. – Private, Royal Dublin Fusiliers (Sportsman's Battalion).
- Dudley, H.B. – Volunteer, Malay States.
- French, W. – Midshipman, S.S. *Dunaff Head*.
- Gillespie, D. – Second Lieutenant, 17th Pallaniscotta Infantry, India.

- Glover, W.S.C. – Captain, 34th Sikhs' Pioneers.
- Hall, N. – Trench Mortar Battery.
- Hay, E. – Second Lieutenant, Pretoria Volunteers.
- Howard, J.W. – Lance-Corporal, Westmoreland and Cumberland Yeomanry.
- Frazer-Hurst, L. – Captain, R.A.M.C., New Zealand Expeditionary Force.
- Kennedy, H. - Corporal, Motor Despatch Rider.
- Knox, F.C. – Lieutenant, Royal Irish Rifles.
- Kyle, J.B. – Gunner, Royal Marine Artillery.
- Lowry, J. – P.W.D., Gambia Volunteer Force.
- Morton, N. – Captain, 6th Reserve Regiment of Cavalry.
- McGusty, B. – Second Lieutenant, Connaught Rangers.
- McIlhatton, J. – Private, Black Watch.
- MacLaughlin, G. – Princess Patricia's Canadian Light Infantry.
- McLaughlin, T.D. – Private, American Forces.
- Riddell, E. – North Irish Horse.
- Plissard, Roger – French Army.
- Schneider, A.O. – 38th Dugras, Indian Army.
- Smith, J. (Drill Sergeant) – Serbian Army.
- Stewart, H.A. – Major, Royal Veterinary Corps.
- Thompson, R. – Surgeon, Royal Navy.
- Wilkinson, S. – Lieutenant, Cameron Highlanders.

It may be of interest to quote the list of decorations won by C.A.I. Old Boys in World War 1, as this may well not be in existence elsewhere. Again, the list is possibly incomplete and some of these men won further honours or promotion in their military careers. It is of particular interest that the list includes several sets of brothers.

Distinguished Conduct Medal

Bolton, S. – 4th Australian Light Horse. Won by going out alone and capturing a field-gun and ten Turks.

Casement, R.J. – Lieutenant, 3rd Field Company Canadian Engineers.

Hamilton, H. – Sergeant-Major, King's Own Rifles.

Distinguished Service Order

Casement, Frank – Lieutenant-Colonel, Royal Army Medical Corps.

Harman, C. – Lieutenant-Colonel, 2nd Leinster Regiment.

Houston, J.W. – Captain, Royal Army Medical Corps (mentioned in despatches).

Hezlet, C.O. – Major R.G.A. (mentioned in despatches twice).

Martin, James – R.A.M.C.

Parr, V. - Captain, Royal Irish Fusiliers.

Parr, J. – Second Lieutenant, 1st Royal Dragoons.

Traill, E.F.T. – Lieutenant-Colonel, Army Service Corps.

Traill, Henry O. – Lieutenant-Colonel, R.F.A.

Traill, W.S. – Lieutenant-Colonel, Royal Engineers.

Woodside, W.A. – Lieutenant-Colonel, R.A.M.C.

Distinguished Service Cross

Wainwright, Alfred – Lieutenant, R.N.V.R.

Mentioned in Despatches

Casement, E.R. – Lieutenant, Railway Corps, British East Africa.

Hezlet, C.O. D.S.O. – Major, R.G.A. (twice).

Houston, J.W. – D.S.O. Captain, R.A.M.C.

Houston, T., M.D., O.B.E., S.J.A.B.

McAlery, J.M. – Captain, R.F.C.

Sharpe, W.McC. – Major, R.G.A.

Croix de Guerre

Bamford, J. – Second-Lieutenant, R.F.C.

Plissard, Roger – French Army.

Military Cross

Bell, W.J.K. – Second Lieutenant, 9th Siege Battery.

Boyle, R.M. – Captain, 12th Royal Inniskilling Fusiliers.

Barklie, R. – Second Lieutenant, King's Own Regiment.

Carson, G.W. – Second Lieutenant, King's Own Regiment.

Davison, Robert – Lieutenant, 12th Battalion Liverpool Regiment.

Frazer, G. – Sergeant, 58th Field Ambulance R.A.M.C.

Elwood, F.B. – Lieutenant, King's Own Lancashire Regiment.

Harris, Fred – Captain, R.A.M.C.

Mitchell, Blayney O. – Second Lieutenant, Royal Flying Corps.

May, Harold K. – Second Lieutenant, Royal Berkshire Regiment.

McGonigal, Robert – Captain, R.G.A.

McCarter, F.B. – Captain, R.A.M.C.

McKay, J. – Captain, R.A.M.C.

McKew, Rev. J.H. (Master) – Captain, Chaplain, Duke of Cornwall's Light Infantry.

Purce, J.R.B. – Captain, R.A.M.C.

Parr, Victor – Captain, Royal Irish Fusiliers.

Parr, J. – Second Lieutenant, 1st Royal Dragoons.

Tottenham, E. – Second Lieutenant, Royal North Lancashire Regiment.

Traill, A.

Walker, F.W. – Second Lieutenant, R.F.A.

Walker, R.F. – Captain, R.A.M.C.

Other Distinctions

Benson, G.W. – Sub-Lieutenant, Russian Squadron Armoured Cars. Two decorations from the Czar, his No. 3 squad being first in the advance in the Caucasus.

Casement, Frank – Croix de Chevalier of the Legion of Honour, Lieutenant Colonel, R.A.M.C.

Houston, T., M.D. – Order of St John of Jerusalem.

McAlery, J.M. – Captain, R.F.C. Italian Silver Medal for military valour.

Houston, T. – O.B.E.

Moving on from the First World War years, in 1919 the number of pupils had increased to 146, of whom forty-six were boarders. For the third year in succession the school lost a very great friend and supporter in the death of the President of the Board of Governors, Sir Hervey J. Ll. Bruce, Bart. His father, Sir Hervey H. Bruce, had been President of the governing body in the early days of the school. Rev. R.B. Wylie, who had been Vice-President for a number of years, was now elected president.

Thirty-six candidates were successful at the Intermediate Examinations, eight of them passing with honours. H. McKee was captain of Football and the side was a good one. An influenza epidemic, which caused the boarding school to be closed from 1 November until after Christmas, deprived the team of much-needed practice. In spite of this and the further handicap of having to do without several key players in the Cup semi-final versus R.B.A.I., the side only lost to the eventual Cup winners by eight points to nil. This was the only game lost, four of the six matches played being won and one drawn. J.W. Stewart, H. McVicker and B. Henry played for the Ulster Schools' XV that year. B. Henry was also captain of cricket. The Scholarship winners were: J.C. McMaster (Clothworkers'), H. McVicker (Joseph Cuthbert) and H.C. Caldwell (Cochrane). The other scholarships were not awarded.

The school magazine for March 1919 describes in detail a very successful 'Gymnastic Competition' which took place that month. Gymnastic classes had been popular some years previously, under the direction of Sergeant Smith, the one-time drill sergeant. Under the coaching of Mr Whitcombe, *"himself an excellent gymnast"*, regular gymnastics classes had been continuing and this competition was an important event. It was judged by a Mr James E. Bell of Belfast and marking was based on the following events: vaulting horse, rope, clubs, travelling rings, parallel bars, rings, bridge-ladder and horizontal bar. The Challenge Shield and Gold Medal (Open) was won by J. Longwell, the Silver Medal (under sixteen) by J. Caldwell, the Silver

Medal (under fourteen) by T. Raphael and the Silver Medal (under twelve) was shared by R. O'Neill and J. Brew. The medal for best in the Indian club exercises was won by A. Hardy and it is noted that, *"the pianoforte accompaniment to these exercises was played by J. Longwell"*, the Open champion himself, whose talents were obviously not restricted to gymnastics. A fun event, 'Pillow-fighting on the pole', created much merriment and was won by George Beamish, one of the three Beamish boys to pass through C.A.I. and to achieve fame later, in the Second World War. (The chief guest at the school's centenary celebrations in 1960 was none other than the hero of that very pillow-fight in 1919, but now Air Marshal Sir George R. Beamish, K.C.B., C.B.E., President of the Old Boys' Association.) As a matter of interest, Miss Margaret Houston, daughter of the former Headmaster, presented the prizes at the conclusion of the Gymnastic Competition, which became a popular annual event for the next few years.

In 1919, thoughts were turning to a permanent memorial in the school to those who had served and those who had made the supreme sacrifice in the Great War. At a meeting on 11 June, it was agreed that *"Messrs. A.G. Crawford, Moore, Davis and Huston be appointed as a committee to make enquiries regarding a War Memorial Tablet, and report to the Governors."* At that same meeting it was agreed that all former motions regarding Assistant Masters' salaries be rescinded, and that their salaries be as follows from 1 September 1919, *"without any claim to participate in Results Fees or any other Grant or Grants."*

Mr Parker - £250 per annum
Dr Hunter - £220
Mr Blaine - £200
Mr Wray - £160
Mr Bruce - £160
Mr Whitcombe - £140 per annum, Resident
Mr Stewart - £130 per annum , Resident
Mrs Parker - £60
Miss Bell - £60

Until now, the payment of Assistant Masters had been a complex matter. Their salaries were paid primarily by the Headmaster, from a grant made to him by the Governors, supported by The Irish Society, but each year other sums were added, first of all from the so-called 'Birrell Grant' from the government, and secondly from a dividing up of Result Fees, gained by the school following publication of the Intermediate Examination results. It was a messy business and each year the Governors had to decide on the allocation to individual members of staff of these additional monies. The purpose of the decision of the Board on 11 June 1919 was to set masters' salaries at a fixed amount for at least the next few years. This issue, however, rumbled on and continued to cause some problems for the Governors in the short term.

In July 1919, the Governors, always with a mind towards basic economics, updated the fees chargeable within the school as follows:

ACADEMICAL INSTITUTION COLERAINE

Owing to the continued high prices of all commodities, and increase in salaries, the Governors have been obliged to advance Fees to the following rates:

DAY BOYS

For Pupils in Lower School,	£1 5 0 *per term*
For Pupils in Middle School,	£2 10 0 *per term*
For Pupils in Upper School,	£3 0 0 *per term*

A reduction of 25 per cent is made in the case of the sons of Clergymen and School Teachers, and a reduction of 10 per cent in case of two or more brothers.

An Incidental Fee of 4/- per term is made for Stationery, School Library, and Athletics.

All Pupils taking Experimental Science pay a Laboratory Fee of 2/6 per term

FEES FOR BOARDERS

Boys under 12,
£10 per term in addition to the School Fees.

Boys over 12,
£11 per term in addition to the School Fees.

Weekly Boarders under 12,
£8 per term in addition to the School Fees.

Weekly Boarders over 12,
£9 per term in addition to the School Fees.

In case of sons of Clergymen, School Teachers, or two or more brothers, a reduction of 10 per cent from above Fees is made.

In addition to the above Fees, Boarders pay:

For School Sports	*5/6 per term*
Library	*1/0 per term*
Medical Attendance	*5/3 per term*
Pew Rent	*2/6 per term*
Laundry	*£1 per term*

18ᵗʰ July 1919   *A.G. Crawford, Hon. Secretary*

Incidentally, in his visit to the school in 1919, which lasted all of two hours, the inspector of schools under the Educational Endowments Scheme, noted that, *"The Governors perform their duties not only conscientiously but zealously."* He also comments that, *" The Headmaster and his assistants continue to give the most earnest service in furthering the educational interests and the general welfare of the pupils attending the school."*

In 1920, the total number of pupils was 166, including fifty-eight boarders. The financial position of the school was made more secure by the decision of The Honourable The Irish Society to make grant of £200 per annum towards the maintenance of the premises. This was in addition to a special grant of £375, payable in five equal instalments, made in 1916, to compensate the Governing Body for the expense incurred when Mr Houston retired. At the Intermediate Examinations, thirty-one candidates were successful, seven of them obtaining honours. Four Prizes, including a special one in English Composition, were won. At a Governors' meeting in June, Mr Beare got permission to appoint two new assistant masters, starting in September, a Mr Doak to teach Classics and English (salary £250 non-resident) and a Mr Doyle to teach French, English and Mathematics (salary £220 resident). Throughout the history of the school there were men like Mr Macey or Dr Hunter who taught in the school for all or most of their careers, providing much-needed continuity and stability, but there were others who stayed for only limited periods.

The most glorious event of the year was the return of the Schools' Cup to Coleraine, after an interval of twenty-three years. The 1ˢᵗ XV, brilliantly led by B. Henry, defeated Campbell College in the final, by one try, scored by H. McVicker, to nil. This famous side played

Taken some time after the game is the victorious Cup Team with the Schools' Cup. Most of the staff and boys are included in this picture, including the Headmaster, T.J. Beare.

ten school matches, winning eight, losing one and drawing one. To mark the occasion the Old Boys' Association presented medals to the members of the winning team. That Cup-winning team of 1920, from a photograph of the time, consisted of: J.E.F. Anderson, R.J. Cunningham, W.W. McKinney, W.D. Black, A.E. Martin, J.A. McFadden, W. Warnock, L.F. Martin, T.A. Martin, C. McVicker, F.V. Beamish, Ben Henry (Captain), H. McVicker, G.R. Beamish, W. Crawford, J.W. Rice. B. Henry, H. McVicker, C. McVicker, F.V. Beamish and G.R. Beamish secured Inter-Provincial Caps. In that year, two Old Boys of the school contested the Irish Golf Championship Final, in which Major C.O. Hezlet defeated C.L. Crawford. F.V. Beamish was Cricket Captain and the Scholarship winners were: W. Crawford (Clothworkers'), W. Kelly (Joseph Cuthbert), T.C. Small (Cuthbert), and W.E. Fullerton (Cochrane). The Anderson Scholarship was not awarded.

In 1921, the number of pupils was 171 and sixty of these were boarders. At the Intermediate Examinations forty-one candidates were successful, but the best educational achievement of the year was that of F.V. Beamish, who obtained a Cadetship in the Flying Corps and a Scholarship of £150.

He also captained a very strong rugby XV which lost to old rivals Campbell College in the Schools' Cup final by eight points to nil, after a game which was almost entirely fought out in the winners' twenty-five. Eight of the ten school games played were won and two lost. F.V. Beamish, G.R. Beamish and C. McVicker were awarded Inter-Provincial Caps. Scholarship winners for the year 1921 were: D. Black (Cuthbert) and G. Morrow (Cochrane). The other scholarships were not awarded.

The Headmaster's Report to the quarterly meeting of the Governors on 3 June 1921 revealed varied problems in retaining teaching staff and the even greater problem of finding replacements. *"Three members of the staff are leaving at the end of the present term: Miss C., who does not find herself quite equal to the work; Mr D., who has got a more highly paid post in Dublin; and Mr W., who finds he cannot agree with my methods of managing and maintaining discipline. Unfortunately, the class of applicants who have answered my advertisements is not very high, the truth being there are very few good teachers left in Ireland."* The political unrest throughout the country at that time was possibly a factor in the shortage of good teachers, as was dissatisfaction at the current system of paying teachers' salaries.

Each member of the victorious Schools' Cup Team of 1920 was given a personal gold medal by the school: this one was presented to Harry McVicker.

In 1921, the problem experienced in administering a scholarship which had been offered more than three years earlier, reflected the changing political situation in the country. In September 1917, a Mr Robert Kerr of Newry had written to the school proposing to award an annual scholarship in memory of his son, sadly one of the past pupils of the school to lose his life in the Great War. In his letter, Mr Kerr said that he, *"could never be too grateful for the intellectual and moral training"* which his son had received at the Institution and he enclosed a precisely worded 'memorandum', outlining the nature of the annual prize. It begins as follows:

The Charles Ewen Kerr Memorial Prize
For King and Country

This Prize is founded in the Coleraine Academical Institution as a memorial of Corporal Charles Ewen Kerr, 6th Black Watch, a former pupil of the School who was killed in action at Armentieres, on the 18th September 1916.

It is intended to encourage the development of those qualities, and the pursuit of those branches of education, which tend to make boys good and patriotic citizens of their native land.

In particular it is founded for the purpose of stimulating the interest of pupils in their Military Training, and in the use of the Rifle, so that they may be fitted to play a manly part in the defence of their country, if it should be attacked by an enemy.

The 'memorandum' continues, outlining the conditions under which the prize should be awarded annually. However, times had changed and the government, with memories of gun-running and the threat of civil war in the years immediately before 1914, and fears arising from the violence and unrest throughout Ireland after the war, had banned Rifle Clubs such as the one that had existed in C.A.I. in Mr Houston's time. Correspondence continued between Mr Kerr and the secretary to the Board of Governors on this matter until 16 March 1921, when Mr Kerr wrote that, *"Until the Government give you permission to allow Rifle Shooting and Military Drill, I am quite willing to allow the Prize, say 5% on £200 - - £10, to be applied to some other branch of sport in the school, that may be agreed by you and the Headmaster, and I* will continue to send this yearly, until you are able to comply with the conditions, which may not be long." He continued: "When we get our Northern Parliament established, I hope the restrictions will be removed." As a minute of the Governors' meeting 3 June 1921 reveals, Mr Kerr had enclosed a cheque for £10 for that year, but sadly he had recently died and the secretary was instructed to write to his widow, conveying the condolences of the Board.

The Headmaster's Report at the quarterly meeting of the board on 7 December 1921 showed that health problems, in the form of epidemics of serious illness, could still have a major impact on the school. There had been two, apparently unconnected, outbreaks of scarlatina during the term. In the first, four boys and a master were affected and in the second, which occurred after an interval of four weeks, six boys were affected. Mr Beare said, "As I saw no possibility of stopping it, on the advice of the doctors, I sent the boarders home. Meantime, I conferred with the Building Committee and, supported by their authority, I got the painters to scrape, wash and re-paint the walls of the dormitories. Without taking some such step I could hardly have expected parents to send their boys back." There must have been some dissension around this time, because a minute of that meeting recorded a letter being received from the Rt. Hon. H.J. Barrie, M.P. for the area, "objecting to the Sanatorium not being used during the recent scarlatina outbreak and tendering his resignation" from the Board.

In 1922, the number of pupils in the school had risen to a record 175, including sixty-eight boarders. The School War Memorial (Roll of Honour), subscribed for by past and present pupils, was completed during this year. This brass Memorial Tablet, containing the 376 names of Old Boys who had served their country in the Great War, including sixty-four who made the supreme sacrifice, was unveiled by Major-General the Right Reverend J.M. Simms, C.B., C.M.G., D.D., a former pupil, at a public meeting in Room 3, on Tuesday 2 May. The chairman on that solemn occasion was Mr T.G. Houston who made "a very appropriate and affecting speech." He described the ceremony as the most important that had ever happened within the walls of C.A.I. and it was "at once the proudest and the saddest that had ever happened in the history of the school." He and all of those assembled there had come to, "pay the highest honour to the gallant men who had once been boys or masters at C.A.I., and who went out to face the foe in the Great War; they had come to bid a sad but proud farewell to 'the brave that are no more'." He went on to pay tribute in particular to, "the sixty-four who had not come back", quoted from John McCrae's famous poem 'In Flanders Fields', and spoke of the "harvest of tears for the goodly flower of young manhood cut down by the remorseless scythe of death before it could turn to fruit." Before the formal unveiling by Major-General Simms, "Amidst profound silence Mr Beare read the names of those who made the supreme sacrifice", and afterwards the 'Last Post' was sounded, "while the large assemblage stood." At the end of the article describing this event, the writer says that the Memorial Tablet is, "an everlasting remembrance to those who died, and a call to us all to follow in their footsteps and uphold the honour of our School", and finishes with the following verse:

"Today, and here the fight's begun.
Of that great fellowship you're free;
Henceforth the School and you are one,
And what you are the race shall be."

Several renovations and improvements were made in the school buildings that year, the most important being the fitting up of the Sanatorium for the fulfilment of its proper function, the installation of a new heating apparatus for the New Wing, and the modernising of the Plunge and Dressing Room. Thirty-five candidates were successful at the Intermediate Examinations, eight of this number obtaining Honours. R. Wilson gained the Adams Bursary of £15 at Magee College entrance and G.R. Beamish a Cadetship in the Royal Air Force. George Beamish also captained the 1st XV and the cricket XI. The football team "was weaker than in the previous years" and lost to Campbell College in the Cup semi-final. Of the school matches played, three were won, six lost and one drawn. G.R. Beamish and T.A. Martin were selected to play for the Ulster Schools' XV. The various Scholarships were won by: G.R. Beamish (Anderson), T. Purce (Cuthbert Science), R. Haldane (Cuthbert) and A.E.D. Allen (Cochrane). The Clothworkers' Scholarship was not awarded.

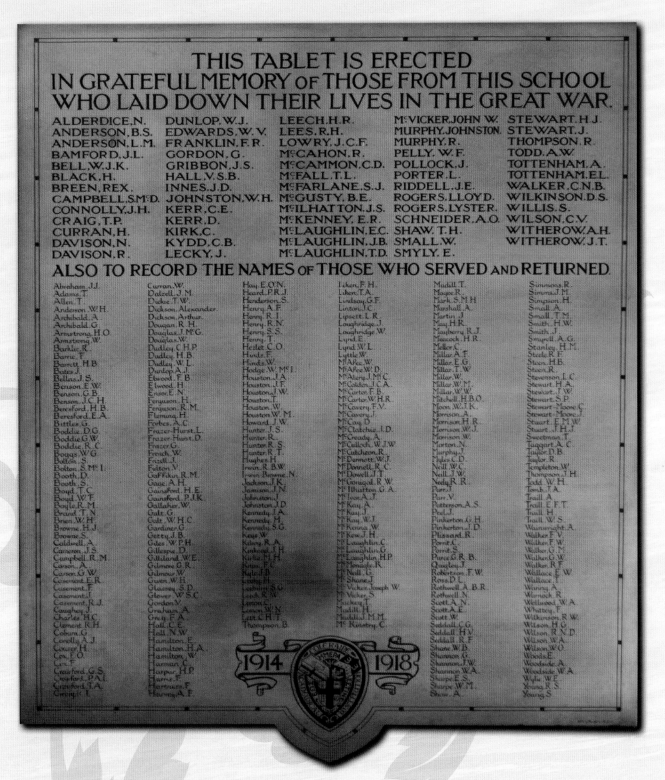

World War 1 Memorial Tablet.

It was in this year that the Preparatory department of the school, for boys between seven and ten years of age, which had been instituted in Houston's time, ran into difficulty. At a meeting on 7 March 1922, it was agreed on the motion of Mr Richard Hunter seconded by Mr C.C. Huston, that, *"on account of the small number of pupils, the Preparatory School be closed next term and that Mr Beare give Miss McKay, the teacher, the necessary notice."* A rather alarming event that year was reported to the Governors by Mr Beare – the ceiling of his dining room had *"fallen in"* and urgent repairs and restoration were ordered.

It seems that there had not been a Drill Sergeant at the school for a few years (Sergeant Smith having gone off to the War) but this matter was remedied in 1922. At a meeting on 7 September, the secretary reported that,

121

"The sub-committee in charge of the appointment of a Caretaker to take charge of the Sanatorium and act as Drill Sergeant, advertised in several papers, and out of a large number of applicants selected Sergeant Boyce, who was engaged at the weekly wage of £1 – 15 – 0, with free house, his wife to do the necessary cooking when the Sanatorium is occupied by patients. The sub-committee took the liberty of ordering uniform for Mr Boyce to be used when he is acting as Sergeant." It was something of a tradition that the school 'Sergeant' should be a general handyman as well; this is illustrated in a later suggestion in the headmaster's report of 6 December 1922. "With regard to the question of New Desks, I think it would be best to purchase the timber and let the Sergeant make them." The Board, cautious as ever, authorised Mr Beare to have a sample desk made at the school, and submit to the Governors details of the cost. A few months later, in March 1923, the Sergeant had produced a sample desk of pitch pine at a cost of twenty-five shillings, and he was instructed to produce another nineteen of these. He was also instructed to erect a corrugated iron fence, with barbed wire along the top, around the Sanatorium. This would have made the Sanatorium more secure, certainly in times of epidemics, but would have lacked something in the matter of visual appeal!

Recreational Activities

There was now a Camera Club in the school and an article in the magazine of May 1922 urges more pupils to join. For a "very moderate sum" members had the use of a dark-room, the necessary chemicals, and free entry to numerous competitions with the chance of winning substantial prizes. The writer of the article adopts a distinctly jolly tone, commenting that the members are, "a decent lot of fellows, who are always ready to assist a new hand in the spirit of 'cameraderie.' The entries for the competitions have reached a high rank as regards technique but it is evident that the competitors place truth higher than beauty." J. Heron, a thirteen-year-old boarder, writing in the same magazine, describes the heady excitement of the unofficial 'ping-pong' tournaments which were very popular in the school at the time. He says it was, "the rage of the School. If you wanted a game at all, you had to have it 'cogged' about a

dozen games in advance." He finishes by saying that, "ping-pong passed the wet afternoons and wet Saturdays very pleasantly for us." Boarders were of course always most proficient in finding ways of avoiding boredom. Something else which helped to fend off boredom was the Debating Society; the secretary that year said that the Society was, "a great boon to boarders; and besides being enjoyable, it is also useful". It is interesting to note that topics in recent debates included 'The Irish Question', 'The Irish Treaty' and 'National Education'. Continuing on the theme of finding something to do, one of the 'School Notes' at the end of the magazine says, "We wish to thank Mr Whitcombe for being so kind as to play the gramophone on wet evenings or at such times as there was nothing doing." Handball tournaments were another feature of the boarders' recreation at the time.

The annual Gymnastics Competition, now known more informally as 'The Gym. Comp.', was still continuing, under the guidance of Mr Whitcombe, and the magazine report of the event that year makes delightful reading. The 'Open' section, "started first on the horse with a vault. This exercise was very well done by all the class, Hardy, however, being unfortunate in not keeping his legs together." The fun event this year was a boxing match. "The boxing contest arranged between two well-known pugilists attracted much attention and amusement. The capabilities of these men being known, it was decided that they should box blindfolded, consequently the referee was often in considerable danger and had several narrow escapes." Those were the days long before strict 'Health and Safety' regulations! At the end, the Open Challenge Shield was won by J.G. Colhoun, the Under Sixteen Medal by G. Wilson, the Under Fourteen Medal by A. Mooney, and the Club Swinging Medal by L. Wood. Understandably, the "unfortunate" Hardy did not feature amongst the winners! The whole event was summed up as, "A very successful School competition, characterised by good sportsmanship and manliness on every side." The prizes were distributed by the guest of honour on the occasion, the Right Reverend Bishop O'Hara. In his address, he praised the competitors, thanked the adjudicator, a Mr Cousins, and commented that, "character is not built in the classrooms alone, but also in the gymnasium and *playgrounds – courage and straightness being the two great essentials of character."*

The editorial of the school magazine of September 1922 was still concerned with events taking place in the world outside the school. *"The world at present is troubled and disturbed, and nowhere more so than in Ireland, but we hope that no outside disturbances will affect the School."* In the midst of all the political turmoil, life could at times be very pleasant in the enclosed world of the school community. The Cricket Report tells us that on Empire Day, May 24, traditionally a half-holiday, *"some of the day-boys organised a party and took cricket apparatus with them to the long strand at Portstewart, and those of the boarders who were able to obtain bicycles joined them, and enjoyed a most interesting game of cricket on ideal ground. This ground is kept in splendid condition; it is rolled twice a day by the Atlantic Ocean!"* Another wildly energetic, fun event, but long-banned because of modern concerns about litter, was a Paper Chase (or 'Hares and Hounds') which took place on the first Saturday afternoon of the autumn term. *"The 'hares', Cromie and Corken, set off at 2 o'clock, and were followed in three minutes by the slow pack. Two minutes later the fast pack left, and the chase began in real earnest."* Several hours later, on a 'hot, sweltering' afternoon, having overcome many daunting obstacles such as a barbed wire fence, thick hedges, fierce dogs, mischievous onlookers, a 'local brickworks', and a 'marsh well overgrown with reeds', the weary replacement hares, Patrick W. and McFadden, *"got on to the long, steep descent from Ballycairn. Here one unlucky hare was overcome by the strain and fell a victim to the hounds. The other hare made grand running, and got in by about fifty yards from the first hound."*

Boarding School High Jinks

On 5 September 1922, W.H. Crawford, a new boy at the school, gives an insight into life in the boarding department at that time, in a letter to his father at home in Limavady. *"The hours are, up at 7 go to the plunge study at 8, breakfast at 8.30 morning school at 9, dinner at 12.30 afternoon school at 1.30, clear from 3.30 to 5.30 tea 5.30. Study 6.30 to 9 prayers bed."* He seemed reasonably happy with the food on offer, unlike many modern school pupils! *"The grub is better than I thought,*

especially the dinner, for breakfast we get porridge and plenty of milk, then 3 slices of loaf bread and butter, and a fried egg. For dinner four good slices of meat and green peas, and rice and rhubarb. Tea. Four slices of white bread and butter, for supper, porridge." Perhaps the diet was better if you liked porridge and rhubarb! Or perhaps the duty master was looking over Master Crawford's shoulder as he wrote his mandatory letter home!

Willie Crawford (later to become manager of the Northern Bank in Antrim), like all boys of his age, had a sweet tooth, as revealed by the frequent postscripts to his letters home, asking for additional 'tuck' to be sent to him. *"Send 2 pound Jam Straw or Rasp or Jelly"*, *"Tell Mother to send Jam on quick"*, *"I am the only boy in the place without jam"*, *"Jam. As fast as possible"*, *"I got a pass to Baxter's for jam today"*. He also shared with his father exciting stories of high jinks in the dormitories. *"On Sunday we (the juniors, about 15 of us) were sitting in the big school room when someone said something about wrecking the New Wing (the New Wing is composed of the biggest lads in the place). We agreed, and our first attempt was a failure. Jago caught us all and toed our - - - -s. After a time we tried again, this time our luck was in, we tossed all the beds, threw the slippers all in a bunch and mixed them up, then we opened all the windows wide & put out the fire, we then knotted all the towels and pyjamas and departed. Nearly everybody was caught except myself and two others."* 'Dorm raids' were of course popular throughout the history of the boarding school, but not always as daring as this raid by the juniors, (despite having been firmly *"toed"* by the prefect Jago) on *"the biggest lads in the place"*!

Other stories told by the redoubtable Willie Crawford are perhaps worth mentioning, the first a typical wide-eyed youngster's account of a quite frightening event. *"The youngest of the Dawsons was at the plunge this morning. He never goes in. He washes himself at the basins just. This morning he slipped and fell into the plunge. The plunge was very full and he could not bottom it. He went down once, and came up and yelled, then he went down again, and came up again, just as he was going down the third time, a boy called Gallagher jumped in, and pulled him to the side, then Jago lifted him out. He could not stand, so his brother dried him, and he soon got alright again. He looked very blue*

all morning." Jago obviously did not restrict his care of the younger pupils to *"toeing"* posteriors when required. A more pleasant memory, typically for Willie, concerns food. *"One day at the beginning of the term Willie Wood and I went into the café and had a great dinner at half fare (school boys). We had kidney soup, then shepherd's pie, and finished up with farola and prunes. It was the best feed I had this long while and the cheapest."* How many modern kids would be so delighted at being able to dine on *"farola and prunes"*?

In 1923, the number of pupils was 165, of whom sixty-three were boarders. Mr Beare commented in a quarterly report to the Governors that the slight fall-off in numbers was due to, *"the hard times farmers are at present experiencing."* The Ministry of Education at the new 'Northern Parliament' had just produced an Education Bill to replace the old all-Ireland procedures and, while there was some anxiety about changes, it was felt that there would be no serious interference with the Scheme of Management of the Academical Institution. In his report to the Governors on 12 October 1923, Mr Beare stated, *"Under the new Education Bill our position will not be much affected. We will have somewhat larger grants – I count on about £1400 for current year as compared with about £1000 for past year. In return we will have some additional obligations i.e to pay each Assistant Master a minimum salary of £210, provide further instruction in Drawing, and provide instruction in Carpentry and Choral Music. The Ministry expects us to have made full provision for these subjects by the end of the present school year."* Accordingly, Mr Beare suggested to the Governors that the ever-useful Sergeant be authorised to construct,

Rev. Dr. R.B. Wylie
Chairman, Board of Governors 1919-1924

"a brick Carpenter's Shop with corrugated iron roof and capacity to accommodate 20 pupils at once", and this was approved.

An unpleasant but presumably necessary matter was raised by the Headmaster at that meeting of 12 October – the unsatisfactory performance of one of his assistant masters. Mr Beare certainly did not mince his words, telling the Governors of the inefficiency of this man's work in the school. *"He is no longer able for it, and is rather a harm and hindrance than any benefit to the School at present"*. The Governors were similarly unsympathetic in their attitude, instructing Mr Beare to present the unfortunate master with two alternatives:

1. *Retire at end of three months, when the Governors would give him a Donation of £100.*
2. *Retire at end of year – June 1924.*

Meantime, Mr Beare is authorised to appoint a new teacher, thoroughly competent.

Employment laws and workers' rights were obviously much simpler in those days! However, the Governors were not quite as hard-hearted as the above decision might suggest. In December, the master in question wrote to the Governors asking for further 'consideration', in view of his long service to the school, and at a quarterly meeting of the Board on 12 March 1924 the previous resolution offering him the two alternatives outlined above was rescinded.

The Intermediate Examination results in 1923 were very satisfactory, forty-one pupils being successful, sixteen with Honours. Altogether seven Exhibitions, two Medals and seven Prizes were won, and this fine record was due almost entirely to three boys – T.E. Reade, T.R. Wright and R.J. Getty. The first two secured first and second Exhibitions in the Mathematics and Science Groups, Medals for first place in English and Special prizes in French Composition, while Getty won three Exhibitions, securing third place in each of the Mathematics and Science Groups and an award in the Modern Language Group. Prizes were won by E.A. Dalzell (Senior), J.G. Donaghy, H.A. Hezlett, G.A. Kane and T.McD. Stewart (Junior). The Scholarship winners were: A.E. Dalzell (Clothworkers'), G.T. Lowry (Anderson), D.R. Michael (Cuthbert Science), A.E.D. Allen (Cuthbert) and P.G. Johnston (Cochrane).

During the course of 1923, the school community was saddened by the death of the Right Reverend Dr. O'Hara, late Bishop of Cashel and Waterford, who had been associated with the school for upwards of fifty years. In their letter of condolence to his widow, the Governors paid the following tribute to him: *"By his wise counsel, faithful attention to duty and loving spirit, he endeared himself to his fellow Governors, and leaves a blank which will be difficult to fill. He was associated with the school almost since its foundation and took a justifiable pride in its good work and steady progress."* The Board also lost the services of Mr A.G. Crawford, J.P., who retired from the post of Honorary Secretary, which he had held for many years. At the conclusion of the meeting of the Board on 10 October, Mr Crawford was presented with the Encyclopaedia Britannica in a mahogany book-case, by his fellow Governors and past and present Principals. The address to Mr Crawford was read by Mr T.G. Houston, who was still taking a great interest in the affairs of the school. Mr Clarke C. Huston was appointed Honorary Secretary in Mr Crawford's place.

W.M.W. Patrick was the Football Captain that year, but the 1st XV was *"below standard"* and lost to Portora Royal School in the Cup semi-final. Three school games were won and seven lost. Only G.S. Jago was selected to play for Ulster Schools against Leinster.

In 1924, the number of pupils attending the school was 152, including fifty-seven boarders. In this year the new Northern Ireland Education Act came into force, making sweeping changes in primary and secondary education. The most significant change was the ending of the Intermediate Examinations, which for forty-five years had been the outstanding feature of the Irish Secondary Education system. In this, the last year of the Intermediate, the school maintained the fine record set the previous year. Forty-two pupils were successful, sixteen with Honours, and four Exhibitions and two Prizes were won. R.J. Getty, T.E. Reade and

T.R. Wright were awarded Exhibitions in Middle Grade, while H. Wright secured one in Junior. Getty also won First Prize in Latin Composition and T.McD. Stewart secured a Prize in Middle Grade.

At the beginning of the year, the Finance Committee decided that the old system for remuneration of the Headmaster of the school should be simplified and brought into line with the requirements of the new Education Act. They recommended to the Governors, *"That the former financial arrangement with Mr Beare be discontinued, owing to the change in the payment of Government grants; and that his salary be £700 as from 1st August 1923, irrespective of Increment Grants to the Principal from the Government; with a Bonus of £50 for this year."* This recommendation was later approved.

The Governors were very pleased with Mr Beare's management of the school and expressed most vividly their confidence in him in their report for the previous year, which they approved for release at their meeting on 30 January 1924. *"The magnificent results obtained at the recent examinations are an eloquent tribute to the superlative gifts, and brilliant attainments, and unsurpassed statesmanship of the Head Master, and of his genial and scholarly colleagues. The Governors have watched with the keenest interest, and with the profoundest gratification, the exceptionally able way in which Mr Beare has handled every department of the School, and they gladly and unhesitatingly affirm that he has brought dignity, and lustre, and success to everything he has touched relative to the physical development, and moral training, and intellectual welfare of the boys."*

Another matter which had to be dealt with as a result of the new Education Act was the matter of Assistant Masters' salaries and increments, which had to be brought into line with the new requirements. A special committee was set up to deal with this complex matter, which took quite a long time to resolve. In the end, it required the masters to be given formal notice of the ending of their employment under the old conditions and agreement to the signing of new contracts. It was only towards the end of 1925, after much discussion at Board meetings and much consultation with the teachers themselves (one refused to sign the new contract and left, while another was not offered the opportunity of signing!), that the matter was finally settled. The Ministry of Education also required some minor changes to be made to the management of the boarding school at this time. A 'Scheme Committee' of the Board had also been working at this time to bring the school Scheme of Management to a state where it could be approved by the Northern Ireland Ministry of Education. At a meeting of the Governors on 10 October 1924, the Scheme Committee reported that, *"a set of Byelaws had been sent by the Ministry which if the Governors would adopt, would in conjunction with the School Schemes Nos. 20 and 140 be approved by the Ministry."* These byelaws were scrutinised, approved, and the Seal of the Institution was attached to the three copies, one of which was returned to the Ministry.

Looking at the June 1924 edition of the school magazine, the editor hoped that readers would be pleased with the new cover design, which, *"was due to Mr T. McKaig."* This new design replaced the original cover illustration, now rather outdated, which had been drawn by Miss Mary Houston. Regarding sports and recreations at the school, the editor noted that as well as the main games, rugby, cricket, or tennis, there was always, *"some general favourite on a lesser scale"* amongst the boarders. That particular term the general favourite was 'Rounders', and *"each evening a crowd can be seen in the cricket field, where a 'den' and four 'homes' have been specially marked out in the grass."* Another interesting item in the editorial, reflecting the progress of technology at the time, said that, *"It is proposed to install a wireless set in the School, and we hope it will be ready for use at the beginning of next term."*

J.D. McClelland was Football Captain in 1924 and the side played eleven school games, winning four, losing two, and drawing five. McClelland was awarded an Inter-Provincial cap. W.E. Henry was Cricket Captain, and the Scholarship winners that year were: D.R. Michael (Clothworker's), W.M. Macaulay (Anderson), T.R. Wright (Cuthbert Science), G.W. Millar (Cuthbert) and W. Maxwell (Cochrane).

Writing in the Old Boys' Magazine of 1989, Cecil Finlay, who was a boarder in the school during the years 1921 – 24, said that his years at C.A.I. were very happy ones. He recalled various memories of school life, most of them in connection with boarding school food. *"Breakfast could be augmented by a fried egg or bacon at a cost to our parents of 6d and 1/- (I think) respectively. The Matron, Miss Lloyd, for economy used to crock eggs in waterglass in June. One year the kitchen staff got their act wrong and for a period we got greenish eggs until we went on strike one morning and when the Chief ('Tommy John') Beare joined us and saw the centre of the table lined with the untouched eggs, appropriate action was immediately taken. A sequel to that was the impact upon Jimmy Owens of Ballymena, who after eating eight of the bad eggs had two or three uncomfortable days in bed until laxatives restored his bodily functions to normality."* Those readers who wish may conduct research into the old practice of *"crocking eggs in waterglass"*! Cecil Finlay also paid tribute to the kindness of Mr Beare towards the ever-hungry boarders. *"It was the practice of the Chief and Mrs Beare and the Matron to invite two or three boys at a time up to their respective apartments occasionally for very welcome tea, usually very acceptable hot buttered scones and other goodies."* A final story from Finlay's memories (which should not be read by animal lovers) involves a pig which met its sure and certain end somewhat prematurely. *"A section of the out-offices below the Sanatorium and Sergeant Boyce's residence included the piggery where the school swill was conveniently and profitably disposed of. Invariably the pigs were in the open section and one day young Fisher threw an empty Nuggett tin into the pen. This was quickly devoured, with disastrous consequences, and there was a most unholy row about the inevitable fatality. It was not long until Masters and boys were thoroughly tired of the sight of pork in any form."*

Headmaster's Illness

Towards the end of the year 1924, Mr Beare developed a serious illness; at their meeting of 10 October, the Governors instructed the secretary to send a letter of sympathy to Mr Beare, expressing a hope for his speedy recovery. On that occasion, the Governors also appointed a 'House Committee', consisting of Mr A.G. Crawford, Dr Anderson, Mr C.C.

Huston and Mr Hugh Eccles, with powers to sign and issue cheques in payment of accounts in connection with the boarding department of the school. This was mainly because the Ministry of Education had recently required the transfer of the running of the Boarding School from the Headmaster to the Governors, Number 2 of the new 'Bye-laws' stating that, *"The Institution shall not be managed for private gain or farmed out to the Head Master or any other person."* At a meeting of the House Committee on 5 December 1924, the following accounts were settled, and they give some indication of the diet on which boarders existed at the time.

J. & W. McLeese	Groceries	2 - 12 - 5
Moore & Moore	Do.	9 - 7 - 0
Andrew Reid & Son	Bread	14 - 14 - 6
Hughes Bros.	Beef	28 - 1 - 2
Wilson & Neill	Eggs	8 - 4 - 6
John Blair	Vegetables	5 - 6
Mrs Woodburn	Meal	7 - 6
Ballyrashane Co-op	Butter	10 - 5 - 0
James Paul	Milk & Potatoes	16 - 7 - 6
Miss Cosbie (Matron), for Servants' Wages		13 - 4 - 8

The accounts suggest that the diet was certainly adequate, if 'plain and wholesome', but by today's recommended standards for healthy eating, the boys were not getting their 'daily five' of fruit and vegetables!

The Governors' Report for the year 1924 states that the Rev. G. Wilson, who was home on holiday from India, acted as Principal from 4 November until the Christmas vacation. However, Rev. Wilson then had to return to India and so, at a meeting of the Governors on 10 December, it was decided, *"to appoint Dr Hunter to act as Head Master and live on the School premises until Mr Beare is able to resume work."* The 'wee Doctor' was summoned to the meeting and with his usual unswerving commitment to the general good of the school he *"consented to undertake the duties."* At the end of their Report for 1924, the Governors stated clearly their vision of the main objective of the school, despite changes of government and educational focus in recent years. *"The Governors submit that the thing that is of importance above all else in a School is to turn out boys with a*

proper conception of the things that matter in life and who will pursue them earnestly. Thus the moulding of the boys' characters has been the aim of the School in the years that have passed. Whatever changes may be involved in the new educational system the Governors desire to say that in this hope there will be no change."

In 1925, the number on the school roll fell to 145, thirty-two of these being boarders. Dr Hunter acted as Principal of the school from January until September, when Mr Beare resumed his responsibilities. The new grouping of the old Intermediate Examination grades into Senior and Junior divisions only had the effect of reducing the number of candidates presented. Sixteen were successful, eight passing with 'distinction'. R.J. Getty and T.E. Reade won Exhibitions in Senior and R.B. Hunter was awarded a Prize in Junior. At Queen's Matriculation, R.J. Getty obtained the Pakenham Scholarship of £40 and R.J. Frizzell secured a Regional Scholarship of £120. The new workshop for Instruction in Woodwork was completed and made a valuable addition to the school buildings. As the Clothworkers' Scholarship had not been awarded in 1921 or 1922, it was decided to award three scholarships this year, and these were won by R.J. Getty, T.E. Reade and T.R. Wright, three boys who had outstanding records in all their examination years. The winners of the other scholarships were: J.G. Donaghy (Anderson) and T.E. Reade (Cuthbert Science). The Cuthbert and Cochrane Scholarships were not awarded.

The great event of the year 1925 was the return of the Schools' Cup to the banks of the Bann and the school on the hill above the river. J.D. McClelland led the 1st XV, which had an exceptionally fine pack of forwards – generally agreed to be the best the school had ever produced – and the Cup was won for the seventh time when the Methodist College XV was beaten at Ravenhill, by thirteen points to three. S.H. Martin scored two tries, J.W. Patrick one, and J.L. Baxter converted two of these to make the total thirteen points. The Old Boys of the school gave replicas of the Cup to all members of the winning team, and these were presented by Judge H.M. Thompson, K.C., the Recorder of Belfast,

at a function held in the school gymnasium, after the Athletic Sports meeting. Of the nine school matches played that year, seven were won and two lost. No less than five members of this famous school side played for Ulster Schools that season: J.D. McClelland, T.McD. Stewart, S.H. Martin, J.W. Patrick and J.L. Baxter.

The editorial of the school magazine of May 1925, states that at the beginning of the rugby season, *"when two of our old boys – McVicker and Beamish – began to shine in International rugger, C.A.I. was described as 'that nursery for forwards.' That does not seem to have been mere flattery, for it has been said, since the final, by several newspapers, that our forwards this year are the best school pack seen for some time."* The 'Old Boys' Column' of the same magazine comments, *"Coleraine is glad to see that we have another international rugger player taken from the ranks of our Old Boys in the person of George Beamish. Next year we hope to see others."*

Mr Beare was unable to attend the Ravenhill final, but sent a telegram wishing the team success. *"I hope that you will have a grand match on St. Patrick's Day, and that my boys, whether they win or lose, will play a straight, vigorous game from start to finish."* At the end of the match, the captain was presented with the Cup by Miss Gibbon, sister of the headmaster of Campbell College, and Mr J.W. Henderson, headmaster of Methodist College, heartily congratulated the Coleraine boys on *"their meritorious win."* Dr Hunter replied appropriately on behalf of Institution, conveying Mr Beare's apology for being unable to attend, and adding that he was sure *"the news of the victory would be a tonic more potent than any his medical advisers had been able to administer during his trying illness."* After the formal presentation ceremony there remained the triumphant journey back to Coleraine, which is vividly described in the school magazine. The team arrived at the Northern Counties station, Belfast, at seven o'clock, in a *"large charabanc with the school colours prominently displayed,"* and were cheered repeatedly as they were escorted to the train. They reached Coleraine just before nine o'clock, where *"a great crowd assembled at the railway station greeted the young victors."* Following the tradition set in Mr Houston's time, a triumphal procession was formed, and the Coleraine Fife and Drum Band, *"playing their liveliest airs"*, led the boys to the Academical Institution. The members of the team were carried shoulder high practically all the way. The band played several selections at the school. Dr Hunter then made a speech thanking the crowd for the great reception they had given the team and commented that it indicated the *"excellent relations existing between the town and gown."*

More mundane matters of 1925 included the decision of the Governors in September to increase Sergeant Boyce's salary from £2 to £2 – 5 – 0 per week. A little later, tenders for a new uniform for the Sergeant were invited and Messrs. Dixon & Co. (tender £1 – 17 – 6) were instructed to proceed with the work. Mr Beare told the Board that the £30 currently contributed by the Governors towards the payment of the School Porter, Mr Hugh Murdock, was insufficient, and that he was willing to pay £1 per week if the Governors would pay £1 – 5 – 0 per week. This suggestion was approved.

In 1926, the number of pupils at the school was 140, thirty of them boarders. As Mr Beare had not fully recovered from his illness, Dr Hunter was appointed Vice-Principal of the school and took over the management of the boarding department. The Certificate Examination results were below standard, only nine candidates being successful, but fifteen pupils matriculated at Queen's University, Trinity College, Dublin, or Magee College. J.N.M. Legate won an Exhibition at the Junior Certificate examination. H.O'H. O'Neill secured a Scholarship of £400 at Queen's University, Belfast, T.R. Wright won First Sizarship in Science at Trinity College, Dublin, and a Regional Scholarship, while H. Wright obtained First Scholarship at Magee College. The school Scholarship winners were: G. Wilson (Clothworkers') and H. Wright (Anderson). The other scholarships were not awarded.

Hopes of retaining the Schools' Cup at the Institution were high in the 1925/26 season. J.W. Patrick was Football Captain and led a side which was very unfortunate to lose in the Schools' Cup Final versus Campbell College, after a replay. The first contest ended in a draw at fourteen points each, and most spectators agreed that C.A.I. deserved to win, but Campbell were successful in the replay by eleven points to three. Of eleven school games played, six were won, three lost, and two drawn. For a second year in succession, five of the Institution side played for Ulster Schools against Leinster – J.W. Patrick, J.L. Baxter, V.O.G. Bell, W. Gilmour and H.O'H. O'Neill. S. H. Martin was Cricket Captain that year.

The War Cry

In connection with rugby at Coleraine Academical Institution, it was in 1926 that the school's famous 'War Cry', traditionally chanted before Schools' Cup matches, was first developed by a John McCahon, who was a pupil at the school from 1924 until 1927. David Edmiston, editor of the Old Boys' Magazine in 1984, tells the story of its origin. John McCahon was born in Cleveland, Ohio, on 15 December 1908, his parents having emigrated to the United States from the Ballymoney area. After the First World War, the family moved to Australia, settling in the town of Toowoomba, Queensland, where John attended Toowoomba Grammar School. Eventually tiring of Australia, the McCahons returned to Ulster in the early 1920s, took up residence in Portrush, and John was sent to C.A.I. In 1925, the New Zealand All-Blacks toured the British Isles and were undefeated in all their matches. The All-Blacks team, at the start of each match, performed their famous war-cry and dance, now known as the 'Haka'. When C.A.I. players reached the final of the Schools' Cup in 1926, someone thought that they, too, should have a war cry and it was John McCahon who supplied it. His former school in Toowoomba had a war cry, of New Zealand derivation, as had many other Australian schools. When a rugby match was commencing, the rival teams would line up facing each other and shout their war cries, as a sort of challenge to each other. John McCahon produced for C.A.I. the Toowoomba war cry, with only a few minor alterations, mainly substituting "C.A.I." for "Toowoomba" in the

Mr A.G. Crawford

Chairman, Board of Governors 1925-1932

last line. And so, a long tradition began. For those who, unlike past and present pupils at C.A.I., have never been rehearsed and made word-perfect in the War Cry, here it is:

He Ta He Ta He Ballywanga
He Tah He Tah Ha
Hunc a Hunc a Hunc
Ballywanga
Cra Cru Cra

Rick Rick Rickety Rick
Iski Iski I
He Ballywanga
Ting Tong Tanga
C.A.I.
Coleraine!

In print, it has to be admitted, the war cry does not sound all that war-like or intimidating! As a matter of interest, over the next two or three editions of the Old Boys' Magazine in the mid-1980s, there was some correspondence from past pupils, claiming that others had been involved in the development of the war cry. However, any dispute seems to have been put to rest by a letter from none other than the then Headmaster of Toowoomba Grammar School, Mr W. M. Dent, who confirmed that the Toowoomba and C.A.I. war cries were indeed more or less the same.

In 1927, the number of pupils fell to 120, of whom twenty-four were boarders. The school community lost one of its greatest supporters, the Rev. R.B. Wylie, a long-serving Governor who had been Vice-President and then, for a few years, President of the Board. A moving tribute to him, by his old friend T.G. Houston, was printed in the May 1927 edition of the school magazine. Sixteen candidates were successful at the Certificate Examinations, seven matriculated at Queen's University, Belfast, and three passed the Bank Examination. R.B. Hunter was the outstanding pupil of the year, winning a Senior Exhibition, a Special Prize presented by the French government for first place in Northern Ireland, and a Junior Exhibition of £50 at Trinity College, Dublin, Entrance. Scholarship winners were: R.B. Hunter (Clothworkers'), H.A.C. Johnston (Anderson) and T.L.H. Houston (Cuthbert Science). R.F. Phillips was Captain of Football, but after the dizzy heights achieved in the previous two years, there was much disappointment in the 1926-27 season. Of the ten school matches played, one was won and nine lost. For the first time in many years, there were no C.A.I. representatives on the Ulster Schools' XV. R.A. Crawford was Cricket captain. The school magazine of May 1927 stated that a Swimming Club had been formed that year, with H. Dunseith as captain and the members were *"practising keenly in the plunge."* R.B. Hunter was tennis captain for the season and the annual Tournament was progressing favourably.

Still on the subject of sport, an article in the Old Boys' Corner of that magazine of 1927 noted that a book was soon to be published by a London Company about Irish Rugby Internationals. There then followed a list of ex-C.A.I. international players, with the years in which they played and the countries they played against. For the benefit of rugby aficionados the list is shown below.

T.R. Lyle – E. 1885-6-7, S. 1885-7.
D.C. Woods – S. 1889, N.Z. 1889.
R. Dunlop – E. 1890-1-2, S. 1890-1-2, W. 1889-90-1-3-4.
F.H. Casement – E. 1906, S. 1906, W. 1906.
T. Wallace – E. 1920, S. 1920, W. 1920.
S. McVicker – E. 1922, S. 1922, W. 1922, F. 1922.
J.W. Stewart – S. 1924, F. 1922.
J. McVicker – E. 1924-5-6-7, S. 1924-5-6-7,

W. 1924-5-6-7, F. 1924-5-6-7, NZ. 1925.
G.R. Beamish – E. 1925, S. 1925, W. 1925.
T.N. Brand – NZ. 1925.
H. McVicker – E. 1927, S. 1927, W. 1927.

It is worth mentioning that Mrs Ailsa Weir, a grand-daughter of one of those famous McVicker brothers, Doctor James McVicker (who also played for the British Lions in South Africa), is teaching Mathematics in C.A.I. in 2010.

In April 1927, owing to continued ill-health, Mr Beare resigned from his position as Headmaster of the school. Almost three years previously, he had suffered a very serious illness, involving an operation, and for a considerable time his condition had been critical. This entailed a long period of absence after recovery and greatly restricted activities after he resumed duty. At their meeting on 29 April 1927, the Governors accepted Mr Beare's resignation, with much regret, and instructed that an appreciation of the good work he had done be placed on the records of the Institution. Part of that appreciation reads: *"The Governors appreciate the faithful work done by Mr Beare in his own unassuming way; he did not advertise himself, but year in, year out, laboured incessantly and quietly for the upbuilding of the School. The finances of the Institution were at a low ebb when Mr Beare took office, but they are now in a healthy state, owing largely to the business ability of the Principal."* It is indeed a fine tribute to the excellent reputation of the school, which Mr Beare had helped to 'upbuild', that there were, a few weeks later, no fewer than eighty-three applications to replace him as Headmaster.

The school magazine at that time states that the news of Mr Beare's resignation *"was a surprise to most of us, as he seemed to have regained very largely his old energy and activity. But this was not the case. During the Easter holidays he found it necessary to have a special medical consultation. It was decided that rest and freedom from responsibility were imperative. And so, acting on this advice, he has been very reluctantly compelled to resign the principalship."* A very fine tribute to the man and his contribution to the school is made in that same article in the school magazine. *"It is not possible to fully appreciate Mr Beare's gifts*

and work from mere casual contact. He has not thrust himself upon the attention of the public. Self-advertisement is abhorrent to him. To know him is not merely to appreciate him and admire him, but to love him. As a teacher he stands in the front rank. His fine scholarship and experience have been used unsparingly in the interests of the School and for the benefit of his pupils. He has shown a rare conscientiousness in the discharge of his manifold duties. He has made many sacrifices, both financial and otherwise. The highest well-being of the boys and their success in life have been his chief concern."

His successor as Headmaster of the school, Major White, speaking at the centenary celebrations in the school on 11 May 1960, made the following comment: *"If a school is to be judged by its Old Boys, and some people say that is the best way to judge it, I would say that Mr Beare's time here was as rich and rewarding as any time, either before or after, in the history of the School."* Mr Beare continued to give service to the school for some time afterwards, as a member of the Building Committee of the Board of Governors.

Mr T.J. Beare

"Is everything all right?" That question, and the quiet Scottish voice of the man who asked it during his tour of the school each afternoon, is still remembered over half a century later. In truth, though, when William White was appointed Headmaster in 1927, everything was far from all right. In the difficult 1920s the school's finances were delicately balanced, and staff salaries were at one stage reduced. "Tommy John" Beare had been a rather remote figure, whose latter years as Principal were dogged by ill-health. The numbers enrolled at the school had fallen from 175 in 1920 to 120 in 1927, and more significantly the boarding school had shrunk by almost two-thirds in the same period, from sixty-eight to twenty-four boys. The examination results in 1926 were candidly described as "disappointing", and the First XV of 1927 as "one of the weakest that the school has ever produced", with no-one from Coleraine Inst capped for the Ulster Schools XV for the first time in living memory.

"Wee" Dr Hunter was virtually acting Headmaster at the time of William White's appointment. He gave solid support to William White, and on his retirement continued to serve the school as a governor. His seventy three year connection with the school as a pupil, member of staff and governor will almost certainly never be equalled!

Major W. White

For all that, the position of Headmaster of Coleraine Inst attracted an encouraging total of eighty-three applicants, from whom four were short-listed: Wilfred Hutchings of Campbell College (later to become Headmaster of The Royal School, Armagh); A. Layng of Middleton College, Co Cork; C.H.Preston of Tunbridge Wells and the thirty-seven year old William White of Methodist College, Belfast. The process of decision making was all the more delicate since "wee" Dr. Hunter had effectively been sharing the Headmaster's duties with Mr Beare at the time of his resignation, and the Governors at least discussed the possibility of making him Headmaster without advertising the position at all. (It is interesting that following Major White's appointment, Dr Hunter was not only confirmed as Vice Principal but relieved of all responsibility for duties outside school hours!)

At the Board Meeting on 22 June 1927 following the interviews, there was a palpable atmosphere of tension as the eighteen Governors tied in their votes for Messrs Preston and White. For the first and only time in the school's history, the fateful decision lay in the hands of Alex Crawford, the recently appointed Chairman of the Board. Immediately before announcing his choice "the Chairman expressed his sense of responsibility in the giving of the deciding vote, and asked the members if they were prepared to give their wholehearted support to whomsoever he voted for." Time was to show that Crawford made an inspired choice, and from the outset William White stamped his own distinctive personality on Coleraine Inst. But before we examine the record of his headmastership, what of the man himself?

William White, The Man

A native of Ayrshire, and a product of Allan Glen's School, Glasgow, William White graduated from London University in 1910 with First Class Honours in Physics. After serving two years as a Physics Demonstrator at London University he returned to his old school in 1912 to teach Physics and Maths, moving on to George Watson's College, Edinburgh, as Second Science Master, and then to Methodist College Belfast where he was head of Maths from 1922 until 1927.

Impressive as this may have been, there were other things bound to guarantee him immediate respect. On the outbreak of war in 1914 he left the classroom to join the 15th Battalion, Highland Light Infantry. His experience on the Western Front left him with a life-long racking cough – the consequence of a gas attack – and also with the Military Cross, the Distinguished Service Order and the rank of Major. This title, and that of "The Chief", were to be his surreptitious nicknames among the boys for the whole of his headmastership. Unsurprisingly, he got on particularly well with another Ulster Headmaster who was a fellow-Scot with experience of the Great War

– William Duff Gibbon of Campbell College. Although Gibbon was by far the more brutal Headmaster, Willie concluded that "he has the root of the matter." The two got to know each other even better when Campbell was evacuated to the Northern Counties Hotel in Portrush during the Second World War.

Not only was Willie White a war hero: he was an all-round sportsman as well. At London University, academic success did not prevent him from becoming President of the Students' Union and achieving the rare distinction of a triple blue in rugby football, cricket and tennis. When he came to "Methody" he was soon involved in organising inter-schools athletics and coaching rugby. He played a bit of tennis recreationally in later years, though his wry advice to his partners in mixed doubles was "don't serve double faults, and for goodness sake keep out of my way!"

From the outset, William White grasped instinctively what was necessary in his new command. The late Ernie Sandford, whose time at Inst spanned the change of leadership, recollected years later that: "Major White had a big task, and went about it firmly. It was mainly a problem of imposing rules and discipline, licking the school into shape, and forcing hard work and hard play". And indeed he crafted his initial impact carefully. Within the first month he discovered that while he was teaching Physics downstairs, the boys in the Chemistry class upstairs were amusing themselves by blowing down the gas pipes to put out the Bunsen burners. His silent entry to the lab, and his equally silent removal of the culprit for summary justice, created a useful first impression! Equally unfortunate was a boarder who declined to accept a master's punishment and lodged an appeal with the Headmaster. "Do you think you'll get off more lightly by appealing to me?" was The Major's only comment before confirming the sentence, and executing it himself! There were, however, limits beyond which even he found it difficult to go. Early in his headmastership he confided to the Governors: "the conduct of some boys away from school is not as good as we desire, particularly boys travelling in the buses with those coming from the neighbouring seaside resorts. Too many seem out of parental control." Or again: "I cannot get the boys to wear their caps away from school. In view of this I am giving them permission to dispense with caps in the summer term provided they wear a school blazer." So much for the omnipotent Headmaster in the good old days! An interview with "The Chief", though, could be a momentous and, ultimately, a painful event – and like most schoolmasters he had his unintentional mannerisms. "If your mother could see you now, and your father – a man for whom I have the highest respect..." was very often the prelude to a stern judgement!

Yet for all his strictness, William White was at heart a kindly and fair man. A trembling first year boy who broke a window was commended for his courage in owning up, and never received the threatened bill. A senior boy who triggered a rare outburst of uncontrolled wrath in class was given a public apology at the next morning's assembly when the Headmaster was in a calmer frame of mind. Another, whose punishment later turned out to have been unjust, remembered that "for the rest of that term I could have broken anything in the school and the Major would have let me off." Hugh Montgomery, appointed as a resident master towards the end of the White era, recollected a meeting with the resident staff where two boys were mentioned by the Headmaster. "They've had problems, you know. Look out for them, please. Remember, this place is their home until half term." On the other hand, one prospective parent may not have been quite so sure. She came to see him with her son, interested in a boarding place, but fearful lest her son might be beaten for committing some serious offence. "Let me set your mind at rest" smiled Willie. "In this school we only beat boys for the most trivial offences."

That wry sense of humour manifested itself in other ways, not least in relation to a school play of the 1930s when, to ill-disguised gasps from boys in the audience, Ernest Sandford, appeared on stage – smoking! During the dress rehearsal 'The Chief' had been less than impressed by the tight roll of brown paper which Sandford was holding. "That's no good, you need a real cigar", he said to the young

actor; and producing one from his pocket he taught the young actor how to cut the end and light it. "Draw on it gently", he smiled, "and as long as you just take the odd puff it'll not make you feel sick."

Although strict, he was nonetheless a compassionate realist. In the tradition of the Ulster Sunday of his time, boarders always attended Bible Class and both services in the town churches, as well as the famous Ballycairn 'walk' in the afternoons. In the summertime, though, Willie had no objection to the boys taking rugs and radios down the pitches in the afternoon. Under pressure from the stricter Governors, he chose to be rather evasive: "Nowadays," he would say philosophically, "there's nothing a decent man can be except a hypocrite!"

From the outset, William White set himself to stiffen morale, reverse the numerical decline and improve the academic status of the school to which he was to give the rest of his life. In a day when expressions of loyalty were not a matter for sarcasm, he nailed his colours to the mast in the Christmas 1927 edition of the School Magazine: "Will we who are at CAI today realise what the Old Boys hope for us? The school for them was something to be cherished, something to work for. Will we be worthy?" This was no empty rhetoric. His pride in the school never left him, and a pupil at the time of the 1939 Schools' Cup victory against Methody recalled his heartfelt outburst: " We're only a small country school, and yet we take on these Belfast giants with a courage and a skill equal to theirs". He was no less encouraging of junior boys trying to do their best on the sports field. It was apparently well known that if a cricket ball, fairly struck from the crease on the upper front field, ever hit the Headmaster's house, the batsman would be rewarded with half-a-crown from the Chief himself!

No less significant was the influence he had on his staff. Although he began by weeding out the total incompetents, he would have been totally in sympathy with the modern concept of early professional development. He interfered unobtrusively – almost apologetically – in every department and every class. The late Maurice McDevitt ("The Boss" to a generation of boys) delighted to tell a good story against himself in this respect. Not long after he began teaching, the Headmaster appeared in his classroom on his daily round. All seemed fine: each boy was working hard at his drawing board and the room was, for once, absolutely silent. As he passed Maurice on the way out, Willie smiled and dropped a pile of comics on the table. "I think you'll find the boys will work better without these," he whispered as he closed the door behind him.

In the male-dominated world of a boy's Grammar School he not only appointed "Biddy" Carmichael to teach French, but also lost no opportunity of telling the Governors how good a teacher she was. A beginner in the profession, afraid that he was going over the heads of his class, was told kindly that "You don't know the ground into which the seed will fall". An older man, for whom Willie had a soft spot, was rescued from another school after a run-in with the management, and installed in a post which was anything but economically justifiable. A young master who foolishly tried to convince "The Chief" one morning that he had the 'flu rather than a hangover was brusquely told: " It's your business if you get drunk, but I won't let other men do your work for you!" Very occasionally, too, he sent a difficult issue down the line. After the death of a man for whom Willie preferred not to write the customary magazine tribute, another teacher found himself landed with the task. To the protest that he knew nothing about his late colleague, Willie produced one of his legendary smiles as he replied: "Oh, that's much the best starting point for writing an obituary. They're for the survivors, you know – not for the dead. Yes, and just remember - his widow's going to be reading it."

In a small school, and in a world far removed from today's non-stop bureaucracy, William White was able to combine headmastering with his first love that never left him – teaching. A more astute handler of people than of papers, he would wait until the incoming mail was on the point of toppling over before locking himself away until he had at least

created equilibrium between the in and out trays on his desk. In the quiet of his study he would indulge his one addiction – tobacco. Boys remembered the forefinger of his right hand, black and hardened from many years of tamping the bowl of his pipe before slipping it into his pocket as he entered the classroom.

His abiding love was of the classroom. As a Maths and Physics teacher he was an inspiration to the scholarship boys and an encourager to the honest plodders. R.A. Eyre, whose own career ended as Vice Principal in his old school, recollected that: "If several masters happened to be absent, it was not unusual for Major White to substitute for them all. He would put all the classes into room 3, and starting from the factors of the difference of two squares, he would work right through to the Binomial Theorem before break." On his nightly tours of prep in the boarding school he would be more than helpful to any boy he spotted struggling with a maths or a science book. One particular group of boarders, indeed, used to watch for him coming, and then contrive by their innocent questions to get their homework virtually done for them! Although his love of Physics and Maths was almost an obsession, he could at times produce surprises. When an English teacher was taken ill, "The Major" appeared himself, and held the class spellbound with his knowledge of the novels of Charles Dickens.

One would have to add that his dual roles of Headmaster and devoted teacher sometimes overlapped to the benefit of his better students. One recorded this in his diary for 27 May, 1931: "Senior Physics practical. The Chief was most assiduous in assisting us all. When he saw that I had my apparatus incorrectly connected, he slipped me a small piece of cardboard with the correct diagram, and helped us all with discreet whispers." Near the end of his career another boy remembered a similar situation when White, who had called into the labs to greet the Ministry's invigilator, noticed his experiment was wrongly set up. The tail of his gown just happened to clear the whole lot on to the floor, and the Headmaster, feigning contrite embarrassment, immediately got official permission to help set it up again.

The Start Of A Long Career

As early as June 1928, the "Coleraine Chronicle" noted that: "Major White... has accomplished big things since coming to Coleraine", and the long-term evidence was the growth of the school from 120 in 1927 to 220 by 1940. Although financially desirable, this expansion was to cause accommodation and staffing problems, and White's private reports to the Board reveal that – particularly in the boarding department – he was taking in boys of questionable academic ability. At the start of the school year 1930-1 he noted: "The ability of at least half the new boarders is suspect. Six of them were previously in attendance at other schools. The fact that they have been changed is a reflection on the boys and not their schools." Things did not improve in the 1930s when unemployment was high, and parents began to keep boys at school simply because they were unlikely to get work if they left. "Were business to improve," he said in 1931, " I should feel it my duty to advise many parents to withdraw their boys at the end of a year or two. As it is, I am doing my best to advise parents to withdraw their boys and put them into the first situation that offers, no matter how poor it may seem". Not many years later, the outbreak of war was to fuel a major expansion of boarding, even though White counselled city parents not to be panicked into sending their boys to a country boarding school. Attracting good quality boarders was not easy, as a very competitive market in boarding scholarships developed during the 1930s, and larger, more affluent schools like Methodist College, Belfast were able to offer more opportunities and more lucrative scholarships than Coleraine Inst. For all that, the school gradually developed a reputation – sustained to this day – of achieving success with both the academic high-flyers and the modest plodders. White encouraged "athletic boys of good ability" to apply for army scholarships, and for those keen to pass the examinations for a 'safe' profession, the "Bank Class" became a feature of the school curriculum from the 1930s onwards.

But what of William White's immediate impact on the school he inherited in 1927? At

This is very much the school as William White would have seen it first. The headmaster's residence was still part of the main school building, and the top storey of the New Wing was still in place. Sheep graze peacefully on the front field – something about which the boys were not particularly happy when playing games!

a most basic administrative level, he almost immediately asked for a telephone to be installed in the school, and by 1929 the school had an office and a secretary, Miss Susan Eileen Blair. "Her presence" reported the Headmaster, "now permits of letters being written and records kept in a way that was not possible before." Her presence did not go unnoticed by the younger staff, and in due course Miss Blair became Mrs Jock McKenzie!

White began with a serious cleaning up of the premises, including the purchase of "six dustbins to render unnecessary the open refuse heaps alongside the gymnasium"! This was only the start, and by 1929 there was a major plan for total refurbishment, of which the school was manifestly in need. Recurrent references in the 1920s and 1930s to damp, dry rot, wet rot and structural unsoundness also raise the question of just how well-finished the school had been at the time of its opening only sixty years earlier. In the cash-strapped 'hungry thirties' the Governors did what they could. In 1931 the structurally unsound top floor of the Old Boys Wing was removed and replaced by a hipped roof (at a total cost of £807 including painting the building!), and in 1934 a new Headmaster's house was built to release more

accommodation for the expanding boarding school. By the late 1930s the Governors had decided to plan a completely new boarding block, but World War 2 and the years of post war austerity made this visionary scheme impractical. Only after economic conditions improved in the 1950s was William White's successor, George Humphreys, able to begin the expansionary programme of which his predecessor could only have dreamed.

The biggest scheme of the 1930s was the building of a Headmaster's residence in 1934: partly so that the Whites would not have to go on living 'over the shop', but mainly so that the Headmaster's former residence in the school could be turned into more boarding and office accommodation. For its time the house was quite advanced. It had, for example, electricity throughout at a time when the school was still gas-lit, and there was central heating in all the main rooms. On the other hand the incorporation of 'servants' quarters' would seem even in the 1930s to have been faintly anachronistic. The contract was awarded to Mr Hugh Taggart, whose business has had many connections with the school over the years, and the agreed price £2846.

The school in 1939. The sheep still graze on the front field, but the top floor has disappeared from The Gods, and the Headmaster's residence has been subsumed into the boarding department.

In 1936 the present main entrance to the school was created and the path through the front cricket field turned into an entrance driveway. The gates (only replaced some six decades later) were formally opened on Prize Day, December 1936, by Lord Craigavon, Prime Minister of the Government of Northern Ireland. The prize winners received something else from the hand of the great man that day. The government had begun a "Beautiful Ulster" promotion, and each boy was given a packet of flower seeds along with his prize. Even by the standards of the time, there was a considerable surge of patriotic pride at the end of the ceremony, where it is recorded that the proceedings concluded not just with the National Anthem, but also with a rendition of "Land of Hope and Glory"!

In these years part of the front field was acquired in connection with the widening of what was then known as Institution Road. The raised dyke which was agreed as a boundary can still be seen along the Castlerock Road at the front of the school. There was a charming detail in the agreement drawn up between the school and the Borough Council: the school was to be indemnified against any problems caused by straying animals while the grounds were unfenced. This was of course a reference to another source of revenue for the school – the letting of grounds for grazing at various times of the year. (There were obvious problems arising from this, and in 1938 one of a number of suggestions brought to the visiting Governors by the boys was that cattle be no longer allowed to graze on the rugby pitches!)

It is surprising to note that only from 1 September 1934 did a full uniform became compulsory. The choice was between the familiar red, white and blue striped blazer and a black jacket, with flannel trousers (shorts for junior boys). Caps were to be worn with black jackets, but were optional with blazers. Although the Sunday silk hat had by this time gone, boarders still had to wear a Sunday uniform of pinstripe trousers, a black jacket and a shirt with detachable collar. This was notoriously sharp-edged, and a new boarder could always be recognised by the ring of chafed skin around his neck! It goes without

saying that church attendance – morning and evening - was compulsory.

Equally interesting was another 1934 proposal to change the school's name, an issue which was even aired nationally in the correspondence columns of the "Belfast News Letter". Quite what fault was found with "Coleraine Inst" is unknown, but a poll of former pupils (presumably members of the newly-formed Coleraine Old Boys' Association) resulted in sixty-three voting for no change, thirty for "Coleraine School", twenty-seven for "Coleraine College" and ten for "Coleraine Academy". Although there was no unanimity on the alternative, there seems to have been an interest in re-branding the school, but the Governors in the end opted to leave things as they were.

Staff And Curriculum

White was clearly concerned about the quality of teaching, and opened his headmastership in a fairly ruthless fashion. One man was asked to leave because "he behaved in such a way to make his retention impossible by creating a public scandal". Another was summarily dismissed (despite a tearful appeal to the Governors) "following two years' observation of his results, which were unusually poor this year." In difficult times, though, White sometimes had to make do with what he could get. In December 1930 he candidly told the Governors: "The work done by some of the pupils is not what I should like, and some of this inferiority is due to the fact that the school is largely staffed by young men who are still at the lecture stage". His reports on particular staff are amusing to read, though the subjects of these comments might have been less comfortable about them - and some examples might be savoured:

"A good disciplinarian, but as a teacher he is too colourless and impersonal… A good influence with the boys, but at present too boyish in his own outlook….Though good as a teacher, he does not identify himself with the school in a manner which promises a long stay… Though having no outward troubles, he has not obtained the grip on his classes essential for success". In 1932 White interviewed a number of staff, and told them frankly that they would be sacked unless their results improved. "This seems to have been useful", he reported to his Governors, "though in some cases it has meant increased homework being thrown on the boys"!

He did, though, recognise and reward talent when he saw it. In 1929 he was particularly sad to lose the services of the Rev. W.A.S. Blaine as a Physics teacher, following his appointment as Rector of Elphin and Headmaster of Bishop Hodson's School, and of Mr W.J.Dyer who left following appointment as an Inspector of Schools in the Gold Coast, West Africa. George Wheeler and Gilbert Wilson (known to the boys as "Skip"after his habitual "skip a line" as he dictated notes) were recognised as excellent teachers. Albert Clarke was a tower of strength all through this period, as was the totally loyal Dr Samuel Hunter, who finally retired in 1934. White was glad to see talented young men making a good start – witness his

judgement that Vincent Smith had made "a very promising, if rather severe, beginning and will prove a most useful teacher." His first female appointment, Miss Carmichael, was regularly praised in White's reports to the Governors, and he was genuinely sad when she resigned in 1936 at the time of her marriage.

Some of the young men he appointed in the 1930s became legendary figures at Inst and elsewhere, among them Vincent ('Vin') Smith (1928, to teach English), Jock McKenzie (1930, to teach French), Ralph Reynolds – known variously as "Ossie" to his colleagues but "Josh" to his closer friends - (1932, to teach Classics), Dan Cunningham (appointed on a temporary basis in 1933 to teach Physics) and Jim Edwards (1935, to teach History). Although Dan, like Jock and Jim, was to spend the rest of his life teaching at The Inst, his career illustrates the difficulties of young teachers seeking work in the 'thirties. Although he was a former pupil, a brilliant scholar and a highly competent teacher, it wasn't until

A rare photograph of some young members of staff in the mid 1930s.
In the back row are Gilbert Wilson and Jim Edwards,
while in front sit Vincent Smith, George Pointer and Jock Mackenzie.

1935 that Dan Cunningham got a permanent contract. Even then, nothing was guaranteed, as he found in 1939 when he sought release from the resident staff due to his forthcoming marriage. Though sympathetic, White needed all his resident staff and felt he could not make exceptions that set precedents: "I informed him that I saw no chance of his being transferred to the day staff in the near future, and that to avoid an impossible situation he should apply for another post". The outbreak of war, and his enlistment in the R.A.F., was actually to save Dan Cunningham's job. By the time he returned at the end of hostilities, the school had markedly increased in size and competent staff were at a premium.

William Mol, later to become the formidable Principal of Ballymena Academy, was in a similar position when appointed in 1934. With a First Moderatorship in Classics from T.C.D., where he was first student of his year, Mol was one the most outstanding academics White ever employed. By 1935, though, he had been 'head hunted' by the Principal of his old school, Methodist College. Decently enough, White told Mol that he would not stand in his way, as The Inst could not offer him any better prospects. For all his youth, Mol was equally hard-nosed, telling White that he would only move if he could be guaranteed scholarship work in Belfast!

White was far from pleased with the overall disciplinary standards in the school when he arrived. But he led from the front, and within a year he was more satisfied. At Christmas 1929 he noted that it was now "possible to dispense with incessant punishment, corporal and other." A year later he was able to report: "… almost all the boys who had inherited a noisy tradition are gone, and the masters are now able to maintain adequate discipline on their own". The year after that he claimed that the need for corporal punishment had now all but disappeared in the school – but one suspects that the boys didn't necessarily see it that way!

In the matter of curriculum innovation, White was not behind the times. In 1930 he sought the Governors' permission to buy "an H.M.V. gramophone, a set of Linguaphone French

records, a dozen textbooks and a set of 'The Daily Mail' Conversational French records. This outfit is in frequent use in the French class and is a valuable aid to teachers of French." To a later generation of old boys, exhorted to "sing it, boy, sing it!" by the unforgettable Jock McKenzie, this might be something of an eye-opener. By 1931 there was a demand for Greek classes "for some of the smarter of our junior boys". Since Dr Hunter's timetable was already filled with the senior classes, the school retained the Rev. John Legate, Minister of First Coleraine Presbyterian Church, to teach some junior Greek for a few years. More interesting still was the beginning of German teaching in the mid 1930s.

The Boarding School

Although there were only 29 boarders when he took over, William White almost immediately divided them into Junior and Senior Houses under Mr Dyer and Mr Clarke: "to develop a sense of responsibility among the staff and increase the interest taken in the boys." A resident staff room was provided, along with a 'playroom' in the South Dormitory in which, visiting Governors noted, were "a bagatelle board, piano, ping-pong table and chess men to amuse the boys." Enlightened as this was, the very success of the boarding school destroyed it, and within two years the boarders' common room had to be turned into a dormitory. A common room of sorts was eventually provided in the basement in 1938, and even boarders of the 1960s and 1970s will remember the claustrophobic atmosphere of this constricted space just before mealtimes. In 1929, White reported: "In the dining hall I have cut each long table in two and provided chairs instead of forms for the boarders". Civilisation was extended further in 1931, when the Headmaster had oilcloth replaced by linen tablecloths for the boys' tables. The tradition of visiting Governors was established early in White's headmastership, and the reporting Governors in 1930 noted "the provision made for the boarders' leisure moments…and also the arrangement of roller skating in the Gymnasium"! Sergeant Boyce and his wife opened a "buffet or tuck shop" beside the old gym where at lunch time a mug of tea could

Sergeant Boyce, looking contentedly over his gate sometime in the 1930s.

be had for 2d and a bun for a penny. The tuck shop was highly popular, and was celebrated by a revealing piece of doggerel verse in the 1927 School Magazine:

There is pushing and shouting all about
And some of the little boys might get
pushed out
Then The Sergeant speaks out –
quite sharply too
For there's far too much of a hullabaloo!

Clearly, nothing changes much about boys' behaviour over the years! The Boyces also grew a considerable amount of vegetables and fruit. In 1928, for example, we find that: "the garden is cultivated to its fullest extent with vegetables. Most of these are now available for the boys. The fruit grown is made into jam which is being sold to the boys and should represent a saving of about £5". For the record, 1932, when an astounding 530lbs of jam was made by Mrs Boyce, was a peak year for production at Coleraine Inst. One wonders if the good lady had time even to sleep! Sergeant Boyce was very much a school institution in his own right, and throughout the 1930s he was busy making and repairing furniture, doing

structural repairs - it was he who partitioned the New Dormitory in 1931 - painting and decorating, and even (after quiet negotiation with the Ministry of Education) acting as a part-time physical education teacher.

A major problem for the boarding school in the 1930s was the gas supply, which was at best intermittent. Not infrequently the boarders had to be dispersed around the school to do their homework wherever there was a convenient glimmer of light. The installation of electric light was discussed inconclusively for several years, mainly on account of the price per unit of electricity quoted by various private suppliers. But in late 1936, after years of wrangling with the Council's Gas Manager, William White's patience snapped. Choosing his moment with care, he summoned a deputation of Governors to inspect the boys doing their homework huddled around paraffin lamps one October evening. The result was an immediate decision to install electric light, at first in room 3 and later in the dormitories. In October 1939, the exigencies of the blackout accelerated the process further. "The New Wing" dormitory (known to later boarders as 'The Gods') still only had gas lights with bypasses visible at night from the main road, and White reported that "a mild protest from the Police caused me to put electric light in there as well." There were problems too with the quality of water. Despite pleas to the Borough Council for "Ballyversal water for as long as possible", it was clear that the school would have to take whatever came out of the tap. Attempts to depend on the school's own well proved fruitless, despite keeping a pump going "for as long as our gas engine will hold out".

Another, less pleasant, problem - natural enough for a school so close to the river – was periodic rat infestation. In 1930 it was noted that "these have been reduced by frequent use of Virus, Rodine and traps. The damage they do to floors and doors is very considerable." It might be noted in parenthesis that this problem recurred throughout the life of the boarding school, and that as late as the early 1980s two members of the Resident Staff – one of them later to become a Headmaster in his own right — held an informal rat cull with

The 1939 cup final ended a fourteen year gap since the previous Ravenhill victory. The match programme, signed by each player, is from the collection of Brian Smyth, one of the last surviving members of the squad who died in 2009. In the Committee Box after the game is the captain, Hugh Hegan, with his parents. William White looks positively radiant – very different from the stern composure of a headmaster in an official team photograph!

airguns in room 3 at dead of night! One man whose concerns included both the health of the boarders and the hygiene of the premises was Dr William Shannon, who served as the school's Medical Officer from 1933 until 1949, and later as a Governor from 1956 until 1979. Himself a former pupil, Shannon came of a family prominently associated with rowing at Bann Rowing Club.

While this book was in preparation, the authors were delighted to make contact with Mr Edward Simpson, who boarded between 1934 and 1939. We were delighted not only to hear from one with personal memories of the school before the war, but also to receive a fascinating account of Mr Simpson's family connection with the school, and his recollections of boarding. The full account appears as an appendix to this chapter, and it makes fascinating reading.

Games And Recreation

Sports facilities in the 'twenties and early 'thirties were narrowly focussed on rugby in the winter term, and rowing or cricket in the summer. In the winter of 1927 White bought some ground for an extension to the pitches, and the record of the negotiations shows how different things were in those more relaxed days: "Mr Hill told me one Sunday morning to go ahead, as he would let me down lightly. But I want the field to be tried out before I offer to take a lease."! Rather more formal negotiations were needed in the later 1930s with the L.M.S. railway company, operators of the main Belfast – Londonderry line which still crosses the river Bann near the present boathouse. When the present railway bridge was built in 1932, the school expressed interest in buying the old track alignment from the former bridge. It took several years of hard-nosed negotiation to add

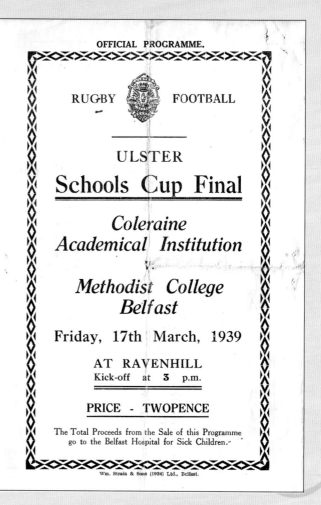
this piece of land to the school estate, not least the issue of way-leave for the GPO to maintain the telegraph wires on the old track formation.

Throughout this period there was an irritating run of years when the First XV was narrowly defeated in the later stages of the Schools' Cup after early season victories – contesting seven finals in the decade after 1933 but winning only once in 1939. The Governors tried to put a brave face on this situation. Their annual report to The Institution in 1932 said that "though the Ulster Schools' Cup eluded the grasp of the First XV last year, the Governors are glad to know that the Institution playing fields are still the training grounds for many a boy's victories in the Waterloos of life"! Quite so, but when the school was defeated by Methodist College in the semi final of 1937, White's comments were rather more wearied: "Our defeat was largely through nervousness... Even the wisdom that comes after the event could not have helped us, as we had no other boys to put in the places of the few who showed that they were not suited to the big occasion. Each year it becomes more difficult to beat the big city schools. Age, even more than numbers, tells against us." But

events proved him a bad prophet, and in 1939 the First XV captained by Hugh Hegan finally won the coveted trophy. To mark the occasion the Old Boys' Association presented engraved miniatures of the trophy to each member of the team at the annual School Sports on 27 April 1939. Appropriately, the presentation was made by Dr Gilbert Irvine, captain of the very first Schools' Cup winning team of 1884. The old man was quite carried away by the occasion: "Boys of the unconquerable Fifteen, you stand where we did, we of fifty-five years ago, and it is a pleasure for me to be in a position to regard you as A1 specimens of physical fitness. That you are here primarily with the object in view of intellectual fitness does not minimise the importance of your recent athletic triumph. In coming years you will regard these cups as emblems of something valuable in your lives." In this he was not mistaken: those little cups, two of which are now in display in the school museum, became lifelong treasures to their recipients.

Not all the Ulster Grammar schools were well disposed to this prestigious competition, though. Doubtless Old Boys of the early

TEAMS

Coleraine Academical Institution	Methodist College Belfast
FULL-BACK—	**FULL-BACK—**
J. L. PINKERTON.	J. NEILL.
THREE-QUARTERS—	**THREE-QUARTERS—**
D. S. HYNDMAN (R.W.)	W. C. LYNAS (R.W.)
P. W. J. DIMOND (R.C.)	B. W. McCREA (R.C.)
W. A. CONDY ((L.C.)	H. A. MILLAR (L.C.)
W. D. F. MARSHALL (L.W.)	A. S. GRAEME-COOK (L.W.)
HALF-BACKS—	**HALF-BACKS—**
J. D. E. MONTEITH (Out).	D. N. STEWART (Out).
F. HALLIDAY (Scrum).	S. A. JACKSON (Scrum).
FORWARDS—	**FORWARDS—**
D. B. TAYLOR.	R. McCLELLAND (Captain).
S. CRAIG.	W. M. WILKIN.
R. G. McCOLLUM.	P. W. STEWART.
H. KANE.	W. W. HOWARD.
W. A. B. THOMPSON.	J. A. MILLER.
J. W. McKAY.	E. J. McKELVEY.
B. T. SMYTH.	A. KIRKPATRICK.
H. HEGAN (Captain).	R. FORSYTHE.

REFEREE—R. R. BUTLER (Ulster Branch I.R.F.U.)

1930s looked back to that 'golden age' of 1883 to 1898 when the school contested thirteen out of fifteen finals and won the trophy five times. They were possibly forgetting that in the nineteenth century the Schools' Cup was organised in two sections – town and country – guaranteeing that a 'town' school had to meet a 'country' school in each year's final! In 1934 White reported to the Board that some Headmasters were contemplating withdrawal from the Schools' Cup, but it is as well that CAI did not go down this road. In a golden age remembered well into the 1990s by former pupils of that vintage, the school was to contest seven finals between 1935 and 1944, though a run of atrociously bad luck meant that only in 1939, under the captaincy of Hugh Hegan, did the coveted cup come to The Inst.

During the 1920s and 1930s A.A. McMath, J. McKeary, J.E. McMath, J. Cameron, A.C. Preston, T.A. Groves, J.C. Groves, J.H. Kennedy and J.A. Esler all achieved schoolboy inter-provincial selection. Additionally, Old Boys continued to achieve success after their schooldays were over. Six had achieved international caps from the foundation of the school until 1920, but during the following two decades that number was easily exceeded. T.Wallace was capped for Ireland in 1920, S. McVicker in 1922, J.W.Stewart in 1922, 1928 and 1929, J. McVicker in 1924, 1925, 1927, 1928 and 1930, George R. Beamish in 1925, 1928, 1929, 1930, 1932 and 1933, T.N. Brand in 1925, H. McVicker in 1927 and 1928, H.O'H. O'Neill in 1929 and Charles E.S. Beamish in 1933, 1934, 1935, 1936 and 1938. George Beamish and O'Hara O'Neill toured with the British Lions in 1930. The names of the three Beamish brothers – George, Charles and Victor – recur frequently in the history of the school. Here it may be noted that after the successful Lions tour, George Beamish visited the school on the occasion of the annual boxing tournament, and "there was great applause when he consented to referee two of the bouts". The 1939 Schools' Cup team included Bill McKay, who was later to represent Ireland each season from 1947 to 1950, and to be a British Lion.

Touring teams and invitation fixtures are commonplace now, but were rather more noteworthy in the 1920s and 1930s. In 1929,

One of the winners' medals presented to each member of the 1935 Medallion Shield team. Dr Ralph Reynolds, a relatively new member of staff, was a dynamic coach and the 1935 victory was not only a first for the school, but also just the second time that the Shield had left Belfast.

for example, there was an invitation game between the School and The President's XV (the President of the I.R.F.U.) which ended in a 24 – 3 defeat for the school. A similar fixture was arranged on 14 February 1934, to mark the fiftieth anniversary of the game of rugby at C.A.I. The President's XV defeated a C.A.I. "Past and Present" XV 28 – 0, although strictly speaking the CAI team included one player who was neither a pupil nor an Old Boy. Charles Beamish missed the bus that morning, and Mr George Pointer, a Geography teacher and a keen player of association football, deputised for him. Since in each game the opposition was adult club players the results were no surprise, and indeed such fixtures would not be permitted today.

In the other major Ulster Schools' competition – the Medallion Shield – there was a marked upturn in the school's fortunes in the mid 1930s. Ralph Reynolds' arrival at Coleraine Inst has already been noted, and largely due to his efforts the Medallion XV of 1935 captained by H.C. Hamilton defeated R.B.A.I. in the final. This was not only CAI's first victory in this competition, but only the second

1935 Medallion Shield winning team.

In this historic 1928 photograph of the very first C.A.I. crew are (left to right) A.N. Clarke (captain); S. Henderson (stroke); J.J. Hughes; J.F. McClenaghan; Bert Barrie (World Championship Professional Sculler – coach); E. Anderson; J.P. Patterson; E.G. Kenny; G.A.McMurray (bow).

time the Shield had left Belfast in its history. The Shield was won again in 1937, against Methodist College, and 1938, against the Royal School Dungannon.

There is a record of the inauguration of a "Goal Kicking Competition" in 1934, for a trophy presented by a Mr Alex Irwin marking the fiftieth anniversary of the first Schools Cup victory on 10 April 1884. In connection with that momentous event, Dr Gilbert Irvine of the 1884 Cup team visited the school in 1928 and spoke of the historic game.

A school Boat Club existed in the early days, though by 1893 it was described as extinct. The modern Rowing Club, described in the school magazine as a 'daring experiment' was founded in 1927, nurtured by Bann Rowing Club, and coached by the great Johnny Leonard and Mr H.A. (Bert) Barry, the world champion sculler. It was also reported that "Bann Rowing Club kindly gave us the use of one of their 'shells.'" Although no races were rowed in the inaugural year, the magazine proudly exclaimed: "truly ours is a proud distinction to be one of the two rowing schools of Ulster. It is hoped to get a

fixture with Portora". This was to happen sooner rather than later, and at the instigation of a man with a foot in both camps. Mr Samuel Wray was an Old Boy of Coleraine Inst with a son at Portora, and in 1929 he presented The Wray Cup for annual competition between the two schools. Although the Coleraine four had earlier beaten a Bann maiden four, the first of many races – which continue to the present day – went to Portora by a length. Vengeance was quick and long-lasting, for 1930 began a decade when the Wray Cup was to leave Coleraine only once, in 1935. After 1933 R.B.A.I. and Methodist College began serious competitive rowing, although in May 1932 an inter-schools race involving Methodist College, Belfast led to one of the most dramatic incidents in the history of the club. Conditions on the Bann that Saturday 25 May 1932 were so bad that the Methody boat overturned, and Terry Clarke – the CAI Captain of Rowing – dived in and rescued their cox from drowning. Clarke received the Royal Humane Society's Vellum Award – the only time a pupil of the school has been so signally honoured. During Clarke's three years in the Inst four only one race was ever lost, against R.B.A.I. in 1932 when the

The 1st XI of 1928. Back row: Major William White; F. Giffin; A.C. Preston; T.A. Groves; G.R. Crawford; M.B. Campbell; J.C. Groves; Mr Dyer.

Front: J.N.M. Legate; A.A. McMath; R.A. Crawford; M.S. Patrick; B. Heron (Captain)

enormous 'Felix' McNeill broke a slide during the race, and the crew had to stop. Disciplined preparation was rigorously observed, and Clarke's personal notes recorded: "Chocolate, confectionery and ice cream were forbidden, and the oarsmen bore the loss of those dainties without a murmur. Strict training was enforced and I even heard that Macauley had started physical jerks every morning to make himself lighter!" This reference was to Cecil "Snowball" Macauley, one of the school's best ever coxes who steered every race during the three victorious years of 1931-1933.

For the rest of the pre-war period the names of three boys were to dominate Coleraine Inst rowing — Jack Clarke, Billy Nicholson and Willie McGrath, and in 1937 victory came at Dublin Metropolitan Regatta in the Schools' Cup, recognised at the time as the unofficial championship of Ireland. These years marked a pre-war climax, in two respects. First, the generosity of the Governors and the Old Boys' Association allowed the school to acquire its first

boats, two second-hand clinker fours. Second, at the 1938 Dublin Metropolitan Regatta the school First Four entered the premier award for Fours in Ireland, producing the best-ever pre-war performance by any C.A.I. crew, to finish second to Dublin University. In what was almost an anti-climax, the Second Four, stroked by future rugby international Bill McKay, retained the Schools' Cup for a second successive year. The master largely responsible for the 1930s run of successes was Mr Gilbert "Skip" Wilson. His enthusiasm for the club included changing his Austin Seven for a more commodious Ford V8, in which he drove complete crews – with the oars tied along the side – to regattas as far afield as Enniskillen and Dublin! In retrospect this brilliant coda was tinged with pathos: of the young men responsible for the thrilling victories of the 1930s, Terry Clarke, Cecil Macauley, Willie McGrath and Alec Smyth were all to die in action during the Second World War. Alec Smyth was one of three brothers to have rowed for the school in these years. The last survivor, and also the last member of the 1939 Schools' Cup winning team, was Brian, who passed away in 2009. His personal memories, shared not long before his death with the author, have been invaluable in compiling this chapter.

Among smaller activities, a Swimming Club was active from 1935 onwards, training at the Northern Counties Hotel, and the first recorded competition was at the Foyle College Gala on 22 November 1935. The Coleraine Inst team of R.K.McNutt, N.Black, E.N.Vogan, and I.R.Hamilton won the Inter Schools Challenge Cup, defeating a Foyle College team weakened by the loss of two of its best swimmers. Lest too much be read into this victory, there is an account of the schools' race in the Queen's University Gala the following February: "Misfortune befell us. Nicholson swam into the side and lost ground thereby, and S.Clarke misjudged his timing and dived in too soon.

We were disqualified." In the light of the Swimming Club's resurgence from the late 1960s onwards, it is significant to note that this competition was won by Methodist College, with R.B.A.I. in second place. Although a later magazine report hoped that "swimming will become a more prominent activity after the successful conclusion of the war", some decades were to pass before Coleraine Inst became a force to be reckoned with in Ulster schools' swimming.

Oddly enough, cricket was not a particularly popular game in these years. In 1934 Major White told the Governors that many boys held the game "in contempt", and that year's school magazine bemoaned the fact that although rowing was making great advances, cricket in the school depended on a hard core of around seventeen boys. Two years later, the Headmaster ruefully reflected: "One cannot

The 1st XI in 1929. Back row: Mr Dyer; M.B. Campbell; T.E. Murphy; T.A. Groves; A.C. Preston; G.N. Henry.

Middle: A.A. McMath; F. Giffin; M.S. Patrick; J.C. Groves; B. Heron (captain).

Front: J.A. Mark; T.H. Tweed.

R.J.("Paddy") Getty boarded in the late 1930s, and before his death gave the school a large number of photographs taken with his own box camera. His shots of the 1938 Sports Day are particularly interesting, not least the parents' motor cars parked beside The Gods (below), the high jump event supervised by Jock McKenzie and Dan Cunningham (above), and the civilised formality of afternoon tea complete with three-decker cakestands (right). One of White's proudest boasts was that throughout his headmastership, it never rained on Sports Day!

say or do very much to a senior boy who says he does not want to play cricket, but wants to work for his examinations." For all that, cricket was by no means a negligible part of the sports curriculum. In 1935, for example, the First XI played 13 matches during the season, and in 1938 it was recorded that Foyle College was defeated for the first time since 1931. Jim Edwards, a driving force behind cricket in the 1930s and 1940s, regarded 1933, with the founding of a local Cricket League, as a turning point for the sport both in the town and the school. Surviving old boys of that vintage would not need to be reminded of the names of cricketers like Bill Henry, Andy Kelly, Walter Condy, John Esler and J.R. Pinkerton. Even after he left, Pinkerton remained a great supporter of school cricket. In addition to presenting a bat for the cricketer making best progress in the preceding season,

he did possibly even greater service by managing to procure cricket pads and balls throughout the War, when such items were as rare as hens' teeth!

As far back as 1902 there are references to occasional sports days, but Major White formally re-established sports day as an annual event in the school calendar. The "Coleraine Chronicle" of 2 June 1928 carried a fulsome report of the proceedings at the inaugural sports, which included such events as a sack race, a three-legged race, an under fourteen pillow fight and an Old Boys' race, won by a Mr Hugh Eccles JP, who had left the school in 1870! Held on the front field, it was a major social occasion for the town as well as the school. Of the 1930 sports it was recorded that "there was a large attendance of visitors, and tea was served on the front lawn. The brightness of the sunshine was especially suited to snapshotting…. and keen amateur photographers swarmed all over the field 'shooting' the exploits of their companions." From 1932 onwards, entertainment was provided during the afternoon, beginning with the band of the First Battalion, York & Lancaster Regiment. Hiring them, however, drove the sports into deficit, and in the following three years the Second Coleraine BB Old Boys Silver Band proved a cheaper option. In 1936 "a gramophone was supplied by Messrs Anderson & Co, for the entertainment of guests", and the following year "the announcing by loudspeaker of the progress of the championships was a successful innovation." In 1938 "Mr Reynolds kept the spectators informed of results and amused them frequently with remarks concerning the competitions and spectators." As ever, in those patriotic days, the function concluded with the singing of 'God Save the King'. Sports day seems to have been heavily subsidised by Old Boys, and one particular benefactor was a Mr J.K. Wilson of Ballymena who presented a Challenge Cup in 1929, and rarely let a year go by without a generous donation.

One 'previously decided' event at sports day was the annual cross-country race, held for the first time in 1928. Its predecessor was an informal 'paper chase' held as far back as 1922, described in a contemporary magazine as the idea of "some brainy youth to pass the day and open the training for the football". Dan Cunningham – who as a boy ran in the very first cross country race – recalled later that the course began at the back drive, then led along Ballycairn Road and Fisherman's Lane to the riverside, up to the Mound and back along the Castlerock Road. The course was later altered via the Irish Houses and down Castlerock Road. The first-ever race was won by Maurice Patrick, one of four brothers whose time at school spanned an unbroken 15 years from 1919 until 1934, and his name was commemorated by the Patrick Challenge Cup which the family presented in 1938. During the war part of the course was used for profitable tillage, and the event became a road race after 1940, beginning on the back drive, and then along the Ballycairn Road, past the Irish Houses, round by the Convent, along the Castlerock Road and back to the start via the front drive of the school.

The Old Boys' Association

Due largely to the efforts of Mr Norman Brand, proprietor of a well known gentlemens' outfitters in Callender Street, Belfast, an Old Boys' Association was launched in the pre-war years. The process began with the revival, after almost 25 years in limbo, of an Old Boys' dinner at the Grand Central Hotel, Belfast on St Patrick's Day 1930 under the chairmanship of Prof. Sir James Craig of Dublin. One particularly interesting Old Boy present that night was the Rev. Alexander Cuthbert, a retired Presbyterian Minister. His family presented the well-known carillon of bells to Church House Belfast, and he himself was a man of considerable private means. During a long ministry he retained a batman and visited his congregation in a chauffeur driven Rolls Royce! On 23 June 1932 a golf match was arranged at Royal Portrush, followed by a dinner at the Northern Counties Hotel which marked the formal launch of the Coleraine Old Boys' Association. On 19 November 1932 a meeting was held at the school to approve a Constitution, and the first Annual General Meeting was held, again at the school, on 28 February 1934. The first of what was to become an annual golf match was held at Royal Portrush on 20 June 1936.

Appendix: A 1930s boarder: Edward Simpson's memories

I went to the School from Ballymena, as a boarder, age eleven, in 1934. My father Hugh Simpson had been a boarder from around 1899, and his cousin Thomas Crawford Boyd a couple of years ahead of him. We were a small community of about sixty boarders: most from professional families in Belfast but we were aware that (for example) the Ford-Hutchisons were an old land-owning family in Ballycastle, and that Jack Fawcett and the Fortes represented big hotel and catering money in Portrush.

Life as a boarder was brisk but not cruel. Each day began with swimming a length of the unheated Plunge to get to the washbasins, bracing preparation for the substantial fried breakfast. If the meals were stodgy we did not mind. But at one point a group of mothers, including mine, pressed the School to include fruit in the diet. They lost, but as a compromise the Tuckshop began to stock apples, which we could buy with our pocket-money. Mondays to Fridays rolled forward on a set pattern of timetabled classes, meals and homework all together in Room Three supervised by the master on duty. There was a free-time period between end of school and tea but I do not remember it as achieving anything memorable. Saturdays could be fun. If there were home matches we watched them; if none, we could take our pocket-money down into Coleraine, to Woolworths or the pictures, unsupervised. But Sundays dragged. Sunday School and morning and evening Church services added up to a long time of sitting still, sometimes rewarded by warm and wise words from the Rev. John M. N. Legate, Minister of First Coleraine.

We walked to Sunday School and Church and back in supervised crocodiles, Presbyterians and Church of Ireland separately, each to their own. In my time there was only one Roman Catholic in the School, Dan B. Taylor, a day-boy in my year. This caused no difficulty whatever: how could it when he was First XV, First VIII, a good scholar and great fun? Later he taught Mechanical Sciences at Cambridge and was Vice-Chancellor of Victoria University in New Zealand. Between the Church services there was time for the Sunday Walk out the Ballycairn Road and for writing letters home - again all together in Room Three and supervised. One thing had changed over the generations. My Father recalled that at his compulsory letter-writing periods The Chief, T. G. Houston, ostentatiously took off his glasses before inspecting each boy's effort to demonstrate that he was not reading the content but simply checking it for length and neatness.

The Chief in my time, Major William White M.C., commanded the School overall and in detail. He was tall, always in formal suit and gown and the more daunting for speaking quietly with a gentle Scottish

edge to his voice. However the twinkle in his eye was never far away. He lived in the then newly-built house across the sports field and came into the School most evenings to walk and talk around the boarding rooms. Mrs White came to all major events, gracious and formally dressed and hatted. She knew the boarders by name and was a reminder to us that there was life beyond boarding.

It would be an exaggeration to say that rugby was the centre of the School's ethos, but it was not far off. The recent Old Boys whom we heard of were the Beamishes, who had been playing for Ireland for years, and John Esler who had just got his first cap. All these went on to the R.A.F., the Beamishes to high rank and decorations and John Esler to being lost flying over the North Sea early in 1940, the School's first war casualty. Learning the War Cry was an urgent obligation for new boys. From our heroes within the School I pick out Willie McGrath and Jackie Clark. They were outstanding in rugby and rowing, and talked to their juniors with humour and without condescension. But they were good scholars too, and stayed in School an extra year to win entrance to Woolwich Military Academy, the engineering equivalent of Sandhurst. On the outbreak of War they were commissioned at once, as The Chief had no doubt foreseen for them. Willie McGrath was killed at St Valery at the time of Dunkirk. My own contribution to School rugby was in the Medallion XV which won the Shield in 1937. Our captain was Reggie Edmiston, our match-winner David Hyndman, both younger brothers of First XV elders. I did not make Hugh Hegan's XV which won the Schools' Cup in 1939. In the 1939 summer term I initiated a Tennis Team which played (and lost) its one match against Old Boys in Coleraine.

The organisation of classes and teaching was straightforward. Each year had an A and a B form, and each subject had one specialist teacher. The Chief seized every opportunity that came his way to teach English Literature and Mathematics, giving him evident enjoyment and us some new angles. Across the board the teaching was friendly without ever straying into informality, though we were addressed always by our surnames, never by Christian name. Class discipline was almost total; I recall only one teacher with whom we felt we could take liberties. And the teaching of the main curriculum was formidably effective. Outside the main curriculum, on the other hand, the School was frankly philistine for the boarders. The nearest thing to art (and it was

nowhere near) was mechanical drawing taught by a visiting part-timer. The nearest thing to craft (also nowhere near) was carpentry taught by Sergeant Boyce, who also took us for a regimental form of gym. He was a good friend whom we could talk to, rather than to the Matron, Miss Boal. Music was not on the curriculum, and I do not remember hearing any music played except in Church and on Remembrance Day. We had no access to radio, gramophone or newspapers; we only caught up on events like Munich and the start of the abdication crisis in the holidays.

The culmination of our five years' study was the the Ministry of Education's Senior Certificate of Education. Broadly, all candidates took all ten or eleven subjects, very different from the narrower entry to A-level today. It was excruciatingly competitive. All subjects were marked out of 400. The Ministry published the results for all candidates in Northern Ireland in a big blue book in the third week of August: candidate by candidate, subject by subject, mark by mark, with all of one school's candidates grouped together. Candidates were listed by number, not by name, but the grapevine had no trouble in identifying anyone whose results were of interest. Boys were dismayed to find they had got 324 compared to a rival's 326, or only 398 in one of the three mathematics subjects where 400 was not impossible.

At the start of our final year The Chief created a Sixth Form Study for the first time, at the foot of the stairs in the New Wing, to help Jimmy Pinkerton (whose Father George was at the School with my Father), Robert T. Moore and myself to work undisturbed for the good results he expected of us. In the run-up to Senior we knew that there was a boy in Belfast, son of a Queen's Professor, whose school (it was probably Methody) confidently expected him to take top place in each of the three mathematics subjects. In the event he did not, but we did. The School secured the top individual place in Northern Ireland in both Group A (aggregate marks for English and best other literary subjects) and Group B (aggregate for English and best mathematics/science subjects) and the French Government's Prize for the top mark in French. The School awarded me the Clothworkers' Scholarship. Alongside the School's winning the Schools' Cup on St Patrick's Day, this made a triumphant finale for those of us then leaving.

To a man who had known at first hand the horrors of trench warfare, the outbreak of hostilities in 1939 would have held no illusions. World War 2 was to be of major significance both to the country and to the school, but – as in many Ulster country towns – its initial impact was limited. Indeed, as the world watched Hitler smashing the frontiers of Poland in September 1939, the Governors of Coleraine Inst were dealing with reports that their border had been violated by the D.H. Christie estate. This particular blitzkrieg involved the mobilisation of nothing more threatening than horses and carts, and the destruction of only a padlock on the gate leading to the Manor House Lane. Unlike the more serious world conflict, it was amicably resolved without recourse even to a solicitor's letter.

The first two years of the war saw the passing of two former Headmasters. T.G. Houston, Headmaster from 1870 until 1915, and President of the Old Boys' Association from its formation in 1933 until his death, passed away on 4 October 1939, aged ninety-six. T.J.Beare, Houston's successor, died on 10 May 1941. Strange as it may seem today, both men retained the status of Governors of the school until their deaths, though neither of them ever attended a Board meeting after they retired. Other deaths of the war years were Mr F.W. Crawford, a former Chairman of the Board of Governors, Mr H.A. Hamilton, still a serving member of the Board at his passing in 1942, and Mr W. Mallinson, a former music teacher, in 1943. In the same year, the boarding school was stunned by the death of a pupil, Roy Morrison, who was taken suddenly ill during term-time and died within a few days in Ratheane Hospital.

The boarding school around 1942, including Major White and Sergeant Boyce.

155

Running A School In Wartime

The most immediate result of the war was a sustained increase in the size of the school, particularly in the number of boarders. At the start of the school year 1939–40, overall numbers stood at 220, including sixty-four boarders. White at first feared that the war might actually damage the boarding school: in June 1940 he told the Board that a number of junior boarders had been withdrawn from the school, predicting that " a further falling off of numbers must be expected, and with the increased cost of living our financial position will have to be studied." Within a year he was proved wrong, partly in consequence of a rush of applications from Belfast parents after the German blitz of Easter 1941, and by the following September boarding enrolment had swollen to eighty-two. 1942 was marked by a succession of epidemics which White feared (or maybe secretly hoped?) might call a halt to the school's relentless growth: "The catalogue for this year has been scabies, chicken pox, measles, scarlet fever and three operations for appendicitis as interludes. There is no doubt that these infections have told against us." Not by much though, for in 1943 the boarding total went up again to ninety-one, and White admitted to his Governors that "I was beaten in my attempt to reduce the numbers". At the end of the war the school population totalled 262, and boarding reached a record total of ninety-three, fourteen of whom were actually accommodated by nearby householders, with a further fifty applications for boarding places being turned away.

In the winter of 1941-42 Breezemount House, which still stands on the Castlerock Road, came on to the market, and the school seriously considered its purchase as a boarding house. One private residence which did become almost a part of the boarding school for most of the war was "Holmlea", a large detached house which still stands in in its own grounds just past the school on the Castlerock Road. The house was owned by Howard Gribbon, proprietor of a mill in the town, and his sister Mrs Irwin looked after groups of boys who were accommodated there for most of the war. Among the "Holmlea" boarders were John Watt, David and Samuel Barron, Sam Leckey, John Boyd Getty, William McAllister and Rene Steele. Both the house and its owner fascinated the boys who were fortunate enough to stay there. Gribbon's study contained an eclectic range of items, from pictures of China Tea Clippers to a Boer War rifle. On some weekends Gribbon was permitted to take the boys on his own walk rather than the traditional Sunday afternoon trek around

A boarding school group in the mid 1940s. To the right of the Matron, Miss Johnston, sits Jimmy Tweed. Little did he know that one day he would be President of the Institution!

C. A. I.
School
Outfits

A comprehensive stock of Boys' and Youths' School Clothing, correct in style and in accordance with school regulations, and in keeping with the high standard of quality we have so long-maintained.

Outfitters to the leading Public Elementary & Secondary Schools in town and district.

T. D. Macready & Son

BRIDGE STREET — COLERAINE.

Phone 263.

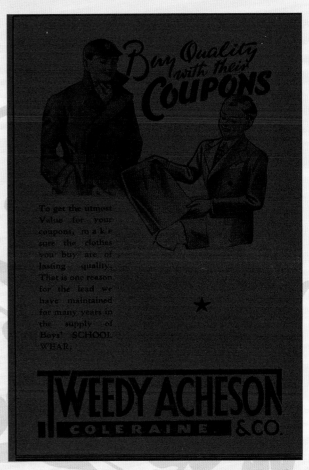

Buy Quality with their COUPONS

To get the utmost Value for your coupons, make sure the clothes you buy are of lasting quality. That is one reason for the lead we have maintained for many years in the supply of Boys' SCHOOL WEAR.

TWEEDY ACHESON & CO.
COLERAINE.

Two of the school's long-serving uniform suppliers regularly advertised in the magazine. The coupons, of course, are a reminder that rationing of clothing continued after World War 2.

the Ballycairn Road. Some of those who stayed in "Holmlea" during the war recalled being marched up to the reservoir along the Carthall Road and led down a subterranean tunnel which allegedly ran all the way to the Mountsandel Fort in ancient times. One winter of deep snow, with the connivance of Gribbon and Mrs Irwin, the "Holmlea" boys spent several enjoyable evenings on a huge sledge, long after "lights out" for their friends in the main school. Some very high speed runs were recorded, the most spectacular of which began at the top of Carthall Road. It was just as well that there was no traffic on the road that night, as the tobogganers worked up sufficient speed to take them straight over the Town Bridge, up Bridge Street and round the Town Hall to Tweedy Acheson's shop in the Diamond before they stopped! Even in those authoritarian days teachers had a human face and a touch of Nelsonian blindness. One evening they almost knocked down Jim Edwards, who was carrying a bucket of water from the spring in Captain Street to his house on the Carthall Road after his pipes had frozen. He never said a word to them about it next morning!

Inevitably in a time of shortages, the fabric of the school began to deteriorate during the war. One very practical problem was to procure enough basic furniture for an increasing number of boys. White was an inveterate bargain-hunter, and he managed to obtain nineteen desks and thirteen chairs at an auction in Belfast. In addition, cubicles in the dormitories were dismantled to provide Sergeant Boyce with the timber to make forty-five new rugby lockers. Pupils of this period also remember biscuit tins being carefully flattened and cut into squares to cover mouse holes as they appeared in the dormitory floors! Things were not helped by a storm at Christmas 1940 which brought down the ceiling of the science building, though White generated his own storm when two jobsworths from the Ministry of Education arrived to inspect the premises - and later complained about the shortage of chemical balances in the labs. "I replied to the effect that I was astounded to get such a remonstrance in these times" probably discreetly censored the gist of William White's telephone call to the Ministry in Belfast!

An even greater problem than the shortages of materials was the shortage of staff. Conscription never applied to Northern Ireland, but teachers up to the age of thirty were free to enlist by 1940, with their employer's permission, and Norman Hoey immediately joined the Royal Irish Fusiliers – all the more poignantly since his brother was reported missing after the Dunkirk Evacuation. George Wheeler also requested permission to join the Army, and in 1941 Dan Cunningham enlisted in the R.A.F. Dan was a highly competent teacher, and his temporary loss was difficult to cover. No Physics teacher could be found, but it was typical of the Headmaster's kindness that he used this opportunity to rescue a former colleague who was in need of work. Gordon Mahony – "Caesar" to a particular generation – was a man whose distinctive character made it pretty well inevitable that he and Methodist College would have to go their separate ways. White's explanation of his arrival at Coleraine Inst would make interesting reading for a twenty-first century Headmaster, trained to navigate the minefields of fair employment and equal opportunity legislation: "I have appointed Mr Mahony temporarily to replace Mr Cunningham. His subjects actually did not suit, and he did not apply for the vacancy, but he had notified me some time previously that he was disengaged." That's how things were done in a less litigious age! Two substitute teachers, Messrs R.E. Thompson and J.A. Irwin, were released for service in the spring of 1941. Joe Irwin was a former pupil who left in 1938, the Clothworkers Scholar of his year who graduated with first class honours from Queen's University. When war broke out he joined the R.A.F., and White found him a part-time job as he awaited final deployment. Tragically, within two years he was listed as missing in action.

At this point, White told the staff that the school could not for the moment release any more permanent members for military service, and warned that even if the reserved age was raised beyond thirty this policy would still apply. By the end of 1941, though, he had allowed Jock Mackenzie and "Vin" Smith to enlist. He drew the line at Jim Edwards, who twice asked permission to go, and on each occasion was firmly refused. Willie was determined to keep at least one highly experienced man during a difficult period in the staff room.

Filling staff vacancies with anyone at all, let alone competent teachers, was increasingly difficult. Three times, for example, White advertised for a Maths or Physics teacher without getting a single response. No wonder he wearily reported to the Governors in 1941 that "teachers of the desired quality are not to be found at present, and I have just had to take any man whom I could persuade to make any attempt at the work". Two were taken on, but within a month were asked to look for other situations. Another unfortunate was "not a success", yet another "steadily losing control of his classes instead of improving", and even a retired army Major described as "impossible, and after a couple of weeks I had to let him go"! By 1943, despite the loss of Gilbert Wilson to his old school, R.B.A.I., the situation was beginning to improve. Some local part-time assistance came from the Rev. John Watson of Ballyrashane Presbyterian Church, from Fergus Marshall, a member of the victorious 1939 Cup Team who by then was a student for the Presbyterian ministry, and from Roy McDowell, another former pupil awaiting call-up to the R.A.F. before beginning his post-war studies at Queens University.

The Governors also found the resources to offer starting salaries above minimum scale to attract well qualified permanent staff. In this way Moore Macauley, a former pupil who had been teaching with conspicuous success in Ballymena Academy, was attracted back to his old school, along with Dudley Magrath, later to become a vice principal in Belfast. At the end of the year White recorded "I am happier now than for some years about the teaching and disciplinary powers of the staff". The worst, it seemed, was over. Jock Mackenzie's absence caused the school a particular problem with Modern Language teaching, and it did not help that Coleraine Technical School was not only advertising classes in French and German but also running a university matriculation class. White asked the Ministry whether they approved of the Tech's tactics: unsurprisingly he received no reply! The shortage of staff presented the Governors with a moral dilemma and a serious financial problem. On the one hand, William White would have been the last man to deny anyone the right to do his patriotic duty. On the other, the Ministry of Education was recommending that schools make up the difference between the professional salaries and the army pay of men on active service: such unlimited financial liability was totally beyond the school's resources. The compromise reached by the Governors was that the full difference between the two levels of pay would be reimbursed to teachers with dependents, and a grant made to single teachers as long as funds were available. The financial burden eased as several men gained commissions, which narrowed the pay gap, and in 1943 George Wheeler was released by the army and to White's great relief immediately returned to the school. Shortages extended to ancillary staff as well. By 1944 White was sadly noting: "I am not altogether happy with the state of the grounds. Labour is the difficulty. We have the same number of men but they now have to give much attention to the field in cultivation above the science building. In addition, the men are more elderly, and slower than they were."

This comment was made all the more poignant by the sudden death of Sergeant J. W. Boyce in November 1944. As a young man Boyce had joined the Royal Inniskilling Fusiliers, and like William White saw service and suffered injury, in the trenches during World War 1. During twenty-two years of service his work included not only general supervision around the boarding school, but also building and repair work, teaching woodwork and P.E., and involving himself in rugby, cricket, boxing, rowing, athletics and in building sets for the school plays. William White described him as " a gentleman whom I was proud to call a friend". In December 1944 the Governors advertised for a new School Sergeant, and the successful candidate from a short-list of three was William Vincent – another man destined to become a Coleraine Inst legend in his lifetime. Willie, the last man to hold the title "School Sergeant", served in both a full and part-time capacity until his death in 1971. He will be mentioned again later.

The shortage of high quality teachers, and the naturally unsettling effects of the world conflict, were bound to have their effect on a school of high-spirited boys. In 1942 White confided that "the claims of the A.T.C., A.R.P. and other wartime activities have made the boys less responsive", and the following year that "the comparative lack of enthusiasm for study still remains".

Running a growing boarding school in wartime posed administrative problems, not the least of which was a raft of A.R.P. regulations. As a temporary measure, plywood shutters were placed on some study rooms, the windows of others covered with black paper, and "feeble blue" light bulbs bought for the electrically-lit dormitories. Following the conversion of the dormitories, rooms 1 and 2 were also earmarked for electric light, mainly because – due to the shortage of matches – the careless use of paper spills to light the gas mantles was leading to daily breakages both of mantles and glass globes. The threat of air attack led to the purchase of 600 sandbags to protect the windows in the basement common room. It should be added, though, that within a year the sandbags were "falling to pieces", and the windows they were shielding were bricked up. The problem was rather more suitably solved by the construction of an air-raid shelter in the basement. It should be recorded rather delicately that this brought relief of another kind to a boarding school which was rather defective in basic sanitation: one of the Headmaster's concerns in 1943 was that "it is difficult to stop the boys from using the dry closets installed in the A.R.P. scheme."!

With air raids always a possibility, parents were informed that the school could not accept liability in relation to either persons or property in the event of enemy action, but the Governors agreed to refund the full fees of any evacuated pupils to the schools whence they came. Although this situation never arose, White was warning the Governors in the spring of 1941 that: "we may be called upon to accept responsibility for secondary school pupils from Belfast." The school and the Civil Defence authorities discussed the doomsday scenario of Coleraine either being bombed or becoming a major evacuation centre. The school response was rather sniffy: "Governors are not willing for evacuees to occupy boarders' beds – but if the town is blitzed they will consider favourably all applications." There was particular consternation in May 1941, when one morning's post brought a letter from the Ministry of Defence requisitioning the school and all its effects – followed by a second letter in the afternoon countermanding the first!

On a school estate which was cultivating its own vegetables and soft fruit, rationing was not as severe as in the cities. White managed to screw a little more meat out of the Local Food Controller, and a reduction in the butter ration was balanced by the addition of more margarine. Jam was a different matter, and even the 400lbs of soft fruit which the school produced each year couldn't bridge the gap between the monthly ration of 50lbs and the pre war monthly consumption of 200lbs. Making the school more self-sufficient brought even a great Headmaster to the limits of his resources. In the spring of 1941, White told the Board that: "I have had the small field west of the school drained and I am now proposing to have it ploughed, and a corn crop sown. But I shall be grateful for any advice, as I have no experience whatever of farming."!

Corps, Cadets And Casualties: From Schoolboys To Servicemen

Attitudes to schoolwork may have deteriorated during the war, but there was considerable enthusiasm for an Air Training Corps that was set up in the school on 6 March 1941 for boys between the ages of sixteen and eighteen. The A.T.C. delivered pre-entry training which was designed to shorten the training period for eventual recruits to the R.A.F. Eighty boys joined it immediately, and Messrs Albert Clarke, Vin Smith, Gilbert Wilson and Jim Edwards applied for Commissions in the R.A.F. Volunteer Reserve in order to lead it. Soon, the campus began to resound to 'square bashing' after school, while staff who imparted History, Science and English by day were to be found teaching dynamics, navigation, armament, anti-gas instruction and aircraft recognition after school. A.T.C. camps became

Coleraine Inst Air Training Corps 808 was formed in 1941, largely under the direction of Albert Clarke and Jim Edwards. The photographs of the inspection and parade are believed to date from 1943, and those with Major White on the steps include Lord Londonderry, Pilot Officer Clarke, Squadron Leader Day and Warrant Officer Fuller.

This must have been taken very shortly before the formal disbandment of the A.C.F. in 1948. The A.T.C. and A.C.F. ran in parallel during the war, though both were disbanded shortly afterwards.

an enjoyable recreation – even though the boys had to bring their own cutlery – as were such diversions as a parade in full uniform to the Palladium Cinema to see "Target for Tonight" in October 1941. On one occasion two R.A.F. photographers took pictures of Flight 808 – these appear in this book. In 1942, 808 Flight became 802 Squadron, following amalgamation with the A.T.C. attached to Coleraine Technical School. At the end of the war it was estimated that forty-three per cent of all the boys associated with the Corps during their time at school had gone into the Armed Forces. The A.T.C. continued throughout the war, but was disbanded on 30 June 1946 following changes in the R.A.F.'s peacetime selection of air crews.

In 1943, the A.T.C. was supplemented by an Army Cadet Force, officially titled the 1st Cadet Battalion, Royal Inniskilling Fusiliers, under the command of George Wheeler following his return from active service. Its formation and early training was assisted by the N.C.O.s of Campbell College Junior Training Corps,

during the time when Campbell was evacuated to the Northern Counties Hotel in Portrush. Intended for boys too young to join the A.T.C. (for which the minimum age was sixteen), the A.C.F. became very popular both in its own right - not least since it gave boys of twelve-fifteen years the chance to handle .22 rifles and fire live ammunition! - and as a feeder for the A.T.C. In 1944 it was noted that thirteen members of that year's Medallion XV were members of the Corps, though there was also reference to a "most unfortunate delay over the issue of uniforms". The A.C.F. did not long survive the A.T.C., being disbanded in 1948.

Poignantly, signing the document authorising the winding up of the Cadets was 'Vin' Smith's last act on the final day of term, before he went off to the seashore for the swim that would result in his drowning.

In addition to the Cadets and the Corps, the summer of 1941 saw 130 boys volunteering to help on farms during the holidays. The Governors, however, declined a request from the Ministry of Education that the school should remain closed during September and October to allow all the boys to help farmers with the harvest. While readily agreeing to release any farmer's son whose father wanted him during this period, White noted that there were still plenty of unemployed men signing on, who could do with the work!

The highest price was, of course, paid by a growing number of Old boys who enlisted in the forces as soon as war broke out, or immediately after leaving school. "Many terrible things have happened since our last issue which make even us who are at school realise what our fathers have told us about the Great War and its horrors." Thus began the editorial of the summer 1940 school magazine as the enormity of a world conflict began to sink into a school and a town community where almost every family was known to each other. Successive issues of the magazine began to carry details of Old Boys serving in the forces, and soon the ominous heading "Pro Patria" introduced heartfelt obituary notices, often written by White himself, of those killed in action. The first to be so recorded in 1940 was Flight Lieutenant Terry Clarke, and by 1945 some thirty-five had paid the ultimate price. The full details of those who served and those who died are listed in a separate appendix, and behind every name was a personal story. The death of brothers Willie and Daniel McGrath, for example; Danny's death all the more tragic as it occurred near the end of the war during the famous Sixth Airborne Division's battle to establish the Rhine crossing. Or Alec Smyth, killed in Italy by an exploding shell which, by horrible coincidence, severely injured another Old boy, Captain A.F. Crook, to whom he was talking. One of the oldest, most highly decorated and most distinguished was Group Captain Victor Beamish, D.S.O., D.F.C., A.F.C., who joined the R.A.F. as far back as 1923. Illness threatened a premature end to his air force career, but with improving health he returned to uniform in 1933. Scorning a Whitehall desk job at the outbreak of war, he returned to his first love as a fearless pilot, taking part in the attack on the German battleships "Scharnhorst" and "Gneisenau" and a major assault on German installations at Le Havre. He was reported lost over enemy occupied territory in 1942. Some, like Victor Beamish, or George McFerran Clarke, killed in action over Hamburg, lacked any marked grave. Others were laid to rest far from home: like Cyril Crozier buried in the Military Cemetery in Stavanger, Norway or G.T.Lowry – a grand-nephew of T.G.Houston - killed in action in Hong Kong. Even more tragic were the cases of others who died not in action but as the result of operational accidents; like airmen Jim Bell and Norman Campbell, both killed on training exercises in England, or Bruce Douglas of the Royal Navy, whose last posting had been as a volunteer for midget submarines. Even after V.E. day the roll of honour continued to grow: Kenneth Vogan of the Fleet Air Arm lost his life in a plane crash in India at the end of May 1945.

Many of course served and returned, rapidly matured by experiences undreamed of during their days in a small and relatively remote country school. Their names are still recorded on the school's war memorial plaques, although the number of surviving old boys is now gradually decreasing. At the end of this chapter is reproduced a most valuable document – the full record of every Old Boy known to have served during World War 2, including some manuscript corrections and additions from an unknown hand. There appears also a further extract from Edward Simpson's memoirs – perhaps the only Old Boy to have been recruited for the famous code-breaking team which worked in great secrecy at Bletchley Park throughout the war.

But let the last word be a lighter one. News that Coleraine Inst had reached the Schools' Cup final in 1944 spread even to a German Prisoner of War Camp where Dick Thompson was incarcerated, having been captured at Dieppe. Miraculously, a postcard eventually reached William White from the heart of the Reich. It simply read: "Dear Sir, having heard the school has again reached the final I wish to send my congratulations. I am waiting patiently for the result, and as usual hoping. Life could be worse here, but as you know, I was never meant to be a prisoner."

Fergus Marshall in action at the 1940 Schools' Cup final.
The outcome of this controversial match is described in this chapter.

Sport During The War Years

As with everything else, wartime conditions had an impact on the school's traditional sports. The junior rugby pitch and part of the cross country course were ploughed up in 1940, and from 1940 until the end of the war, the annual sports day became a purely internal school event. Difficulties with train travel, and the rising cost of rail fares during the war, forced the Northern Ireland Grammar Schools to rationalise their fixture lists and reduce the number of away games. Cricket had something of a renaissance during the war years, although the First XI's annual fixture lists were heavily augmented by games against local cricket clubs as well as other schools.

In rugby, after the excitement of 1939, the hard-fought Schools Cup Final of 1940 ended in a draw at full time. For what I believe was the last time in the history of the competition, the referee ordered ten minutes extra time each way, and Portora won 6 – 3. Years later Fergus Marshall still recalled his exhaustion, and Willie White berating him at the end of the game: "Why did you agree with the referee when he told you he was going to play extra time?"

Ulster Schools players R.J.F. Patton and
G.R.C. McDowell pictured in 1942.
As recorded later, Roy McDowell visited
the school in 2008 and was delighted
to see this photograph displayed in
the school museum!

The 1st XV of 1941, on which Patton and McDowell played.

Back Row: H.M.C. Morrison, T.K. Given, J.C. Boyd, W.C. Millar, R.W. Kyle,
J.S.Y. Mathewson, S.G. McDowell, T.L. Wilson.

Front Row: I. McC. Todd, R.K. Beare, R.J.F. Patton, G.R.C. McDowell (Captain),
W.R. Ford-Hutchinson, F. Ferguson, M.J. Wauchob.

In those days, when the word of an adult was law whether he was a referee or a Headmaster, Fergus felt that he couldn't win! The 1st XV of 1942 were defeated in a semi-final replay, and again in the semi-final by R.B.A.I. in 1945. In the other wartime Cup Final appearances, the First XV sustained defeats against Portora in 1941, and R.B.A.I. in 1943 and 1944: it would be 1992 before the elusive trophy returned to Coleraine Inst. The Medallion had a slightly better record in these years, contesting the finals of 1940 against Ballymena Academy, and 1942 and 1943 against R.B.A.I, before winning the Shield against Methodist College in 1944. During this period a steady stream of boys won inter-provincial selection, among them A.W.L. Pollock, J.C. Boyd, H.A. Crouch, J. Boyd, A.J. Clarke, W.D.F. Marshall, P.W.J. Dimond, M.K. Wauchob, J.S.Y. Matthewson, H.M.H. Morrison, W. McGrath, A.McI. Smyth, G.B. Hyndman, H.Hegan, J.W. McKay, H. Kane, W.A. Condy, S.C. Craig, W.A.B. Thompson, G.R.C. McDowell, W.R. Ford-Hutchinson,

R.J.F. Patton, J.N. Balmer, J.D. Henry and J.B. Getty. The last pre war side had six capped players, which equalled the previous school record.

In 1942 Sam, Jim and Charles McVicker presented a Rugby honour cap in memory of their late brothers Wallace, Johnny and Hugh, awarded to the member of the 1st XV showing most promise during the season. In the following year the school received £50 from Mr William James of Portstewart to fund the James Cap for the Medallion XV player judged to have given the most unselfish service to the team. This was a mark of Mr James' appreciation of what the school had done for his son Billy during his time as a boarder, and its first recipient was Alistair Orr.

Before leaving rugby football, a word might be said about pitches during and immediately after the war. The school, wisely as it turned out, rejected a wartime offer from the Borough

Council to buy the Grove Shore Lands (the area presently occupied by the Boat House and the First XV pitch), though they did allow the military to use the area for training purposes. As a stop-gap measure to provide facilities for the increasing number of boys, a field was rented from a local farmer along the Ballycairn Road – Old Boys of a particular vintage still remember trekking along to "Paul's Fields" for their rugby – and a bulldozer was hired to level the field directly in front of the school across the Ballycairn Road. Intended to be the First XV pitch – largely due to its prominent location in front of what was then the main entrance to the school – it was, however, a major disappointment as a playing surface, and eventually disappeared in the 1970s when the running track was built.

Bann Rowing Club virtually suspended its activities during the war years, but school oarsmen continued through the war with fixtures against R.B.A.I. and M.C.B., and also the Wray Cup race against Portora. In 1939-1940, under the captaincy of W.A. Thompson, the First IV won races against Methodist College on the Bann, and R.B.A.I. on the Lagan. The one defeat of the season was in the Wray Cup competition against Portora, the only race of the season lost by a school crew in home waters. In the 1940-1941 season, Portora scratched from the Wray Cup competition, and R.B.A.I., which had lost its training facilities, decided not to compete in inter schools races. In fact the only inter-school race of the year was against Methodist College. That year's captain of rowing was Roy McDowell, who visited the school in November 2008 and met that year's captains of rowing and rugby, Jonathan Mitchell and Angus Warwicker. It is quite possible that Roy was, at the time, the oldest surviving former captain of rowing. In 1941 the school crew again sustained a Wray Cup defeat against Portora, though this defeat was handsomely avenged both in the 1942-3 and the 1943-1944 seasons. The 1943-1944 First IV, captained by Mickey Eyre - of whom much more appears later - beat Portora again at the Dublin Metropolitan Regatta, though the final race of the day was lost to a fresh Rockwell College crew. The final year of the war saw a further defeat in the Wray Cup against Portora, but a total of twelve victories since the foundation of the competition was not a bad past record.

The Wray Cup winning crew of 1944. Left to right are C.G. Eyre, T.B. Girvan, H.R. Cameron and R.A. Eyre, later to become the school's dynamic head of rowing from the 1960s until the 1980s.

Sergeant J.W. Boyce's death in 1944 was mourned throughout the school community. This photograph from the 1944 school magazine reflects the affectionate respect in which he was held.

Cricket continued despite the exigencies of the war and the competing attractions of the A.T.C. Charlie Beverland, William McVicker and Hal McGimpsey all secured First XI cricket caps in 1942, and in the same season the seniors began coaching junior cricketers, with what was described as very beneficial results for all concerned. Slightly outside the limits of this section, it might be recorded that in 1946 W.B.Morrow was capped for Ulster schools in both cricket and rugby. The postwar period was to prove a further turning point, and by 1949 the legendary Tom Ryan was in charge of a club which regularly turned out 220 rugby players of all ages every Saturday.

Athletics was mostly confined to the annual sports day, and during the war two trophies were presented to the school. In 1940 Mr John McNeill, the Chairman of the Board of Governors, presented the McNeill Challenge Cup for the Under 16 age group competition. In 1945 Mr H.P.Gilbert of Bangor presented the H.N.Gilbert Challenge Cup for the 100 yards sprint.

February 1945 saw the revival of swimming at C.A.I. In what was candidly described a "hasty scrounge for talent", a swimming team was put together under the captaincy of E.N.Vogan to compete in the Inter Schools Challenge Cup at the Foyle College gala. To the surprise of all concerned, C.A.I. won the trophy, and it was hoped that "swimming will be a more prominent activity after the successful conclusion of the war". Years were to elapse before this prediction was fulfilled.

Among the prizes still awarded at each year's Prize Distribution is the Dr T.T. McKendry prize. Its story is fascinating, and the letter which arrived at the school out of the blue is worth reproducing in full. It appears as an appendix to this chapter. The McKendry award was eventually split into three annual prizes (two for Mathematics and the Sciences, and one for Literary Subjects), and the criteria

Mr. Moore Macauley's Elementary Maths Class 1943/44

W. O'Loan, T.B. Girvan, B. Bleakley, H. Hill, _ _, W.P. Doyle, S. Hazlett, _ _,
R.W. McClure, G. Kilbride, H. Laughlin, W. Harvey, R.G. Macaulay, D. Tannahill,
W.M.H. Morrison, _ _, _ McCay, J.S. Tweed, J.B. Getty, Mr. Moore Maccauley.

Possibly taken on the same day, these photographs give a rare view of a class with their teacher, as well as a view of room 1.
As this chapter records, Moore Macauley was a capable and extremely popular teacher.

Mr John McNeill
Chairman, Board of Governors 1934-1953

for the awards were the same as those set for the Senior Exhibitions. At the same time the school benefited from a further generous bequest. A Miss Barr left the school £1000 to found the Andrew Barr Memorial Scholarship in Classics, and this was presented for the first time in 1943.

The End Of The War

V.E. Day in 1945 was celebrated with appropriate fervour. One boarder who went to Belfast on pass was congratulated by an American servicemen on the patriotic colours of his school blazer, while back in Coleraine, Howard Gribbon and the "Holmlea" boarders produced a Union Jack so big that it could be clearly seen from Portstewart Cemetery, and hoisted it on an impromptu flag pole wedged into a chimney pot at the top of the house.

In 1945, White permitted himself some philosophising on the state of the world and the school, voicing sentiments which have a strangely familiar ring today: "Boys everywhere, nowadays, seem to have too much money, and to devote this to outside amusement..... A change of outlook, a more pleasure loving outlook, on the part of the boys has contributed to a deterioration in exam results." One could not be sure, though, that White was a very accurate prophet when he predicted: " Normal peacetime conditions outside school will soon restore a more responsive and responsible attitude." !

The end of the war did not totally solve staffing problems either, particularly in the boarding school. Four of the five pre-war resident staff had either married or become engaged during the war, and the school was legally required to take them back even though they were not available for boarding duties. With a boarding school bursting at the seams but seriously short of resident staff, White could only darkly hint that "unusual measures may have to be taken to deal with abnormal circumstances in the next few years."

In the meantime, though, this situation was the means of bringing to C.A.I. one of the great

This boarding school photograph of the late 1940s includes a number of men who spent their entire careers at Coleraine Inst. Among them are Hugh Montgomery, Irwin Rainey, Tom Ryan, George Wilson and Arthur Nicholl.

characters of the post war period. Although White was still on the lookout for a Modern Language teacher, he did find a young man willing to do resident duties – and who was a rugby enthusiast as well. So began the career of Tommy Ryan, a Geography graduate who began by teaching Junior Maths and Science!

An Educational Revolution: White's Last Decade: 1946 – 1955

The last ten years of William White's headmastership were also the most challenging, and for reasons largely beyond his control. The school increased from 254 to 408 boys, and the boarding department remained at its inflated wartime level of around ninety, though without the availability of "Holmlea". Continued postwar rationing, as well as severe financial constraints, made it difficult to maintain the fabric of the school, and impossible to provide more than the bare minimum of extra teaching accommodation. Coleraine Inst, in company with most other Ulster Grammar Schools, found it very difficult to recruit well-qualified staff, particularly in Maths and the Sciences. With the introduction of Welfare State legislation, schools were required to participate in the free milk scheme and provide mid-day meals for all pupils. Further, the 1947 Education Act produced the most revolutionary changes which William White had experienced in his entire professional career. When he prophesied to the Governors in 1945 that "unusual measures may have to be taken to deal with abnormal circumstances in the next few years", he little realised how abnormal the circumstances would become, or how unusual the measures he would have to employ.

The 1947 Education Act

The Northern Ireland Education Act of 1947, based on the 1944 Butler Act in Great Britain, was part of a series of major postwar reforms which massively increased state intervention in health, education and social welfare. A detailed account of its provisions would fill a book in itself, but the basic principles are easily stated. Education was to be made available to all children up to the age of 14, and was to include primary and secondary education,

with a transfer after the age of 11. Based on the results of a new Qualifying Examination – the 'eleven plus' – primary school pupils would transfer either to a Grammar School or a Secondary Intermediate School of parents' choice. The tuition fees of qualified pupils were covered by Local Education Authority scholarships – ultimately a charge on the Northern Ireland Exchequer – which by the late 1940s accounted for three quarters of Coleraine Inst's income. At an early stage in the scheme the Government vetoed means testing and assumed full responsibility for the cost of each qualifier's education. In theory the system was meant to provide two parallel types of secondary education, equal in status and differing only in curriculum emphasis. In practice, this aim was not achieved. In Great Britain a comprehensive system of state-funded secondary education replaced the 1944 Butler Act in the 1960s. In Northern Ireland selective education lasted for a further generation, and not until 2008 was selection at eleven plus – the keystone of the system – phased out, at least in its former guise.

The immediate impact of the 1947 Act was threefold. First, transfer at eleven plus rather than twelve plus, and access to Grammar Schools for all qualified pupils, led to an immediate and sustained increase in numbers. In September 1947, Coleraine Inst had 272 pupils; twelve months later it had 333, and by William White's retirement the number stood at 408. An expanding intake brought challenges of its own, and a report to the Board in 1949 had a resonance which is still curiously familiar: "A few of the new day scholars are proving unsatisfactory. They have not the background that makes them suitable for a Grammar School, resent having homework to do, and their parents resent any compulsion on them." Such cases could easily be dealt with in those days - the Headmaster simply asked the Local Education Authority to withdraw the scholarship, and it was done! Secondly, a morning act of worship, and the teaching of R.E. became compulsory – the latter beginning with the first year intake of September 1948, and gradually spreading up the school. Finally, and much more controversially, the Government became a major provider of finance – demanding in return a proportionately greater say within the Grammar School sector. In this regard, the schools feared a serious loss of control over their funding, their existing endowments, their staffing levels and salaries, and their curriculum provision. A particular problem, as they saw it, was the Government's insistence that Grammar School fees should cover only the cost of tuition, and not the cost of new buildings, or the repair or refurbishment of existing ones. Stormont was, however, prepared to consider applications for capital expenditure schemes, and to supply 65% of the funding for those they approved. As a private memorandum by William White to the Governors in December 1949 tersely put it: "The question of the prestige of the school is involved at present."

Such eventualities had been anticipated, for as far back as April 1944 representatives of the seventy-five voluntary secondary schools met together to consider the future. From their meeting was formed The Association of Governing Bodies of Secondary Schools in Northern Ireland, renamed the Association of Governing Bodies of Grammar Schools after the passing of the 1947 Act. Better known as the G.B.A., the Association embarked on five years of hard bargaining on behalf of the Grammar School sector. The Government eventually offered a compromise on funding. Under "Scheme A", Grammar Schools were offered a more flexible formula in the fixing of fees, the right to include repair and maintenance costs in the tuition fee, the right to levy parents up to £3 annually towards the cost of new buildings, and access to sixty-five per cent state funding for approved capital expenditure schemes. This seemed a generous offer, but in the austerity years it also raised some fears. Might not a future cash-strapped government cut costs by reducing the value of Local Education Authority scholarships, or even alter the basis on which fees were calculated? For schools which had always offered a wide curriculum (Coleraine Inst's Greek, Advanced Maths and scholarship classes, for example), flexible staffing and salary arrangements (particularly in relation to boarding staff), these were more than just hypothetical questions. A small number of Grammar Schools held out for an

alternative "Scheme B" which offered their Governors greater freedom over the use of income, discretion over the number of places they allotted to qualified pupils, and the power to decide fees for non qualified pupils. There was a price, of course. Schools adopting Scheme B retained more independence, but they had to share the cost of future increases in teachers' salaries, and they lost the right to sixty-five per cent government funding towards approved capital projects. After long debate, the Governors of Coleraine Inst joined Scheme B in December 1950. Concern for the school's prestige in the local community led them to opt for the greatest possible measure of independence, but there was also a more pragmatic consideration. Schools which accepted Scheme B had the right to transfer to Scheme A in the future: schools which accepted Scheme A did not have the option of changing their minds later!

The School's more independent status was, however, of very short duration, and in retrospect it could never have afforded to be self-financing, particularly as more accommodation was urgently needed. Low-cost expedients were tried, not with any great success. Willie Vincent's workshop, for example, was turned into an additional science lab, the A.C.F. hut into a new woodwork shop and the boarders' common room into a dayboys' dining hall. In 1951 junior woodwork, which had been informally taught over the years by Sergeants Boyce and Vincent, was temporarily halted and the woodwork shop partitioned into two rooms. As the first 'bulge' in numbers began working up the school, pressure on science teaching accommodation increased, and further new laboratories became an urgent necessity. Although application for grant-aid was made to the Ministry, the building work was eventually completed at the school's expense. Accidents also proved costly, among them a major problem caused when a water main under the school burst, depriving the boarding school of water. During investigations, the original school well was opened - and found to be full of water from the town supply. When the main was repaired, the old well was refilled and used for some time as a low-level tank.

By 1951 the game was up, and the last straw was probably a general inspection in November 1951, where the Senior Inspector identified "defects, deficiencies and desirable improvements" to the fabric of the school that would cost around £100.000 to make good. With this gloomy finding, the Headmaster could only agree. Less than two years later, with numbers continuing to increase, there was an urgent need for six more classrooms and an Assembly Hall. White, whose scientific background didn't preclude a sense of the theatrical, invited a group of Governors to witness rooms 1 and 3, tightly packed for assembly one Friday morning. A few days later, at a special meeting on 12 November 1953, the Governors applied to be transferred to Scheme A, and sought government funding for the new buildings that were so sorely needed. For Coleraine Inst a new era had begun.

Coincidentally with the changes in education, the school was also required to provide dayboy meals. As noted earlier, the boarders common room was turned into a dayboy canteen, where boys could either eat their own sandwiches or purchase hot meals which at first were delivered

Mr Hoey's form 3A, 1946.

William McCloskey (second from the left on the steps) was a member of Mr Hoey's form 3 class. He recalls that Hoey enjoyed this class so much that he arranged a class photograph – though the photographer unfortunately partly decapitated the top row. Young William himself was later to marry into the school community when Joy Vincent, daughter of Sergeant Willie Vincent, became his wife! Those in the photograph are as follows: Back row: Hugh Hamill, Lewis Hannam Tony Hutchinson, Ronnie Gray.

Centre: Maurice Pepper, John Graham, Roy McCook, Derek Wheeler, David Kelly, Robert Riddell, Bobby Glenfield, J. Agnew.

Front: Eric Weir, Billy McCloskey, John McKee, Mr Hoey, J. Robertson (?), Robin English, J. McCormick(?).

to the school from a central schools cooking depot in the Strand Road. The scheme began in September 1949, and the County Education Committee was soon supplying 120 meals a day ("we could do with twice this number" thought White) at a cost of 2/6, 12 ½ pence in today's money, a week! The boys sat seven to a table, presided over by a sixth former who supervised the distribution of food and the stacking of the furniture afterwards. Reporting on the scheme in the school magazine, one anonymous pupil recorded that: "The scheme was introduced to the school by Mr Macauley, helped by Mr Hoey. Lately we have lost Mr Hoey who has been replaced by Mr Cunningham. Each day, the satisfied smiles of everybody pay a bigger tribute to Mr Macauley than could be written on paper. From the start, he has controlled all the finances and the organisation, helped by Mr Hoey who informed me privately and with typical modesty that all he did was to say Grace every other fortnight." One result of the provision of dayboy lunches was the winding-up of the tuck shop, which ceased trading in June 1949.

Other less momentous issues came before the Governors in these years. In 1948 a notable school family was commemorated in the establishment of a Rex Anderson Memorial Prize "in whatever manner, and subject to such conditions as the History master might think fit", and in 1954 the very generous bequest of £1000 established the Mary Evelyn MacNeill scholarship. In 1952 a Belfast branch of the Old Boys' Association was formed, and the first chairman was Captain Addy Small. Towards the end of White's headmastership a rather delicate issue arose when two established firms in the town, Tweedy Achesons and Dixons, each enquired about the school's policy on school uniform supply. The Board ruled that T.D.Macready were the school's official suppliers – but that practically they could not stop other shops from selling school uniform if they chose to!

Before leaving the world of high educational politics, it should be noted that the 1947 Education Act, or rather the new schools that were created by its enactment, directly affected the staff of Coleraine Inst. Moore Macauley was appointed first Principal of the newly created Kilkeel Secondary Intermediate School, while Dudley Magrath went to Belfast to become Vice Principal of Annadale Grammar School. At a time when experienced teachers were at a premium, William White was delighted at these men's success, though saddened by their loss.

School Prefects 1948-49.
Back Row: S. McK. McKillop, D. Taylor, D.G. Stewart, J.B. Jackson, D.H. McLain, A.G.H. Morrow.
Front Row: G.S.L. Wilson, W.J. McVicker, J.C. McGrath, A.M. McCurdy.

The Prefects 1950-51.

Back Row: K.F. Kyle, D.J. Wheeler, W.A. Hamilton, P.M. McKay,
A. Mencarelli, R.H. Riddell.

Seated: R.A. Smyth, R. McGrath, J.C. Graham, R.S. McElhinney, A.J. Pollock.

The Boarding School

At a time of major change in the day school organisation, the boarding school continued as an entirely free-standing unit, remaining a private undertaking until its closure in 1998. After 1947 it became an attractive proposition for parents around Northern Ireland whose boys failed to gain admission to local Grammar Schools, and boarders were not included in the school's admission quotas. The only limiting factor was space, and White candidly admitted that with numbers around the ninety mark the boarding school was beyond its limits. One of Dr Shannon's reports to the Governors sums up the dilemma: "Overcrowding is a difficult problem for Mr White, who agrees on principle but finds it impossible to refuse an applicant for whom a corner or a double-decker [i.e. a bunk bed] can be made available."! White's predictions of a peacetime slump in boarding, and his fears that the 1947 Education Act would reduce the demand for places, were not borne out. During the last decade of White's headmastership there was always a waiting list, and many prospective customers had to be turned away.

Like most postwar boarding schools, it was an austere place. Redecoration was done as finance and the availability of scarce materials permitted: but coats of paint could not conceal the postwar shabbiness of some dormitories, or ameliorate the overcrowding in others. The prewar boarders' common room had long since been turned into extra dormitory space, and the dining room was in need of redecoration and expansion. Dr Meharg, the school's new medical officer, reported in 1951 that "The plunge room would seem to warrant some attention. The front of the cupboard diagonally opposite the door is falling out. The condition of the ceiling and plastered wall is unbecoming for a bathroom." The repairs were done, but the murky waters of the plunge – iconic symbol of a spartan regime – continued to jerk junior boarders into wakefulness at the start of each day for another two decades! With his customary eye for a bargain, Willie White made do and mended. In September 1946, for example, he snapped up ten surplus beds and mattresses from the Mary Rankin Hospital for £3.10.0 each - noting that this was one third of the usual price! On the eve of his retirement in 1955 he was still enthusiastically bidding for bargains – in this case tables, chairs and a coal box from a sale at Hanover Place.

Rationing in the United Kingdom intensified after the war, but the local community's respect for 'the town school' was able to cut many a corner. In December 1946 White told the Governors: "as usual local tradespeople have been most considerate, and have done their best to help us with our rationing problems. Our baker, Mr Hezlett Reid, has never failed us, and I have been very careful not to ask any questions about the adequacy or number of BU's we give him." A year later Mr Reid was again thanked for obtaining "5 cwt of oatmeal when our supply threatened to fail. This should ensure our porridge until Easter". Broken windows were an inevitable occurrence in a boys' boarding school, and in the late 1940s glass was in short supply: "breakages have been normal, but are very vexatious at present." Accidental damage was one thing: arson was another. On 8 October 1951 "A junior boarder of 12 years of age lit a fire in the Masters' Smoke Room. Although I cannot prove that he did it deliberately… I have no doubt in my own mind about his intentions." White reimbursed the masters for their charred gowns, and the parents of the suitably chastened boy were asked to find another place of education for their offspring!

The boarders generally subsisted in rude health, succumbing only to the usual epidemics of colds and 'flu which to this day afflict schools in January and February. Occasionally there was some high drama: an outbreak of Brucilla Abortus fever in 1947, which was tracked down to a weekly boarder from Limavady, and, more worrying, a case of Poliomyelitis in 1953 which fortunately did not spread. In May 1949 Dr W.A.Shannon accepted a senior position with the Northern Ireland Hospitals Authority, and he resigned as Medical Officer after twenty years. Dr Meharg of Castlerock succeeded him, beginning an even longer period of service which ended with his own retirement in the 1970s.

Assistance from local traders may have helped to eke out rationed goods, but another shortage which proved harder to cope with was resident domestic staff. The boarding school went through a very bad patch in the early 1950s, and in January 1952 "two of the girls walked out because they were not free to stay out all night to attend dances when they chose, and another had to be dismissed". Rates of pay were another problem, and an extract from the Board minutes in the same month gives a flavour of how things were done half a century ago: "A cutting from a paper was read re-the increase of wages to hospital domestics and after consideration it was agreed to pay £8 per month to the school domestics." Just how closely the finances had to be watched can be gauged from the year 1954, when increases in the cost of the boarders' evening meal (reckoned as six old pence a head!) led to a rise in the boarding fee to prevent a deficit for the year.

The School Estate

Coleraine Inst has always been noted for the quality of its sports facilities, not least the First XV pitch beside the River Bann. What became known as the Sand Pitch was developed at the river's edge in the late 1940s, largely by voluntary labour of a kind which today would be unimaginable. The original surface was largely composed of dredged silt from the river, and Old Boys of the period still have their own painful memories of finishing a game with the skin liberally scraped from their arms and legs. A better surface was to hand, though. Kennedy's, the well-known building firm, were creating a large housing development around the school, and were only too pleased to provide hundreds of tons of topsoil excavated from the foundations of the houses. Recruiting a workforce was equally easy: Major White asked Moore Macauley and Jim Edwards ("Banjo" and "Baldy" to their students, behind their backs!) if their Fifth Formers would appreciate some manual labour as a respite from their historical and mathematical studies. The work continued into the holidays, sustained by a large number of pupils of all ages. The young labourers willingly gave up the first part of their holidays to the task, well fortified with supplies of cold milk and thick wedges of bread and jam delivered by Miss Johnston, the formidable Boarding School Matron. A six-inch thick coating of good topsoil was thus created, and on seed-sowing day a tractor was borrowed from Sammy Black's farm at Carnanee, and a grass-seed fiddle and a grass-seed harrow from Robbie Paul's nearby farm on the Ballycairn Road. Moore Macauley was the tractor driver, and he later recalled arriving home thoroughly impregnated with dust. Worse, he was due to play that night in a golf competition at Portrush, and in his haste slipped coming out of the bath and cracked two ribs!

It took more time, and thirty or forty more tons of earth, to perfect the playing surface, but the new field opened officially in December 1949 with a School & Old Boys vs President's XV match, followed by tea at the Corporation Arms Hotel. Nor did this finish the tradition. In 1951 Messrs Macauley and Edwards again mobilised volunteer labour to create a metalled road along the south side of the grounds which to this day leads down to the River Pavilion. The rubble foundation came from the Council, Sam Black lent his tractor and trailer for a fortnight without any charge other than the petrol, and Mr Howard Maxwell rolled the surface, also without cost.

The other major development of this period was the War Memorial Pavilion, still a familiar part of the school estate. The idea of a permanent memorial to those Old Boys who gave their lives in two World Wars was first suggested in 1949, and the school and the Old Boys' Association jointly financed the building. It was opened on 4 November 1953 by the Governor of Northern Ireland, Lord Wakehurst, following a service of dedication led by the Rev J.N.M. Legate, Canon L.V. Uprichard and the Rev S.W. McVicker. The pavilion was designed by one Old Boy, Mr Crofton Dalzell, and built on ground presented to the school free by another, Mr Howard Maxwell. Within a year it was supplemented by a new set of gates to the pitches, which have recently been renewed and repainted, again with the help of the Old Boys' Association.

A concurrent proposal to build houses for the teaching staff was a fascinating 'might have been' that deserves brief attention. As already

mentioned, almost every Grammar School in Northern Ireland experienced difficulty in recruiting suitably qualified teachers after the War. Coleraine Inst's practice was to offer above-scale payments to tempt men to move north, and the Headmaster and Governors felt that the availability of houses might be another way of attracting suitable teachers. At the sale of the Bruce Estate in 1949, the school bought "The Garden Field" for £300, and it was suggested that part of this land might be used to build staff houses. A few years later, as the War Memorial Pavilion took shape, the Board bought adjoining ground, and resolved to build two houses. On second thoughts, and after much debate, it was decided to use the ground to create a tennis court – possibly influenced by Dudley Magrath's success in coaching the senior tennis team which won the Schools' Cup in 1950.

The Postwar Staff

The years bridging the White and Humphreys eras were highly significant for the teaching staff. During the war it proved difficult to find suitably qualified replacements for men on war service: after the war there was a short but sharp period of similar difficulty. In the centenary edition of the school magazine Kenneth Edwards, a pupil in these years, remembered "a cloud of inexperienced or temporary teachers, often adding to the already heavy duties of the experienced men to whom the school owed so much. I can remember four French teachers in my first three years, and temporary staff ranging from an ex-boxer to an industrial chemist." Behind the scenes, William White was well aware of this. One of his characteristically frank reports to the Governors in 1953 stated: "I have been forced to patch up the staff with temporary teachers. This means a considerable financial loss to the school, and an equally serious loss of efficiency in teaching. The quality of work being done does not satisfy me at present and I am not quite sure how much this is due to weak pupils and how much to poor teaching. I have been forced to teach so much this year that I find it impossible to keep as close a watch as formerly on classes". This was not of course the full

The Staff 1950.

Back Row: Mr. M. Graham, Mr. W.I. Rainey

Middle Row: Mr. H.S. Montgomery, Mr. R.D. Macpherson, Mr. A. Nichol,
Mr. J.A.D. Magrath, Mr. T.G. Ryan, Mr. W.G. Mahony,
Dr. G.A. Wilson, Mr. M.S. MacDevitt.

Seated: Mr. N.E. Hoey, Dr. R.W. Reynolds, Mr. W.M. Macauley, Mr. A.E. Clarke,
Major W.W. White (Headmaster), Mr. G.B. Wheeler, Mr. J.A. Edwards,
Mr. J.O.H. Mackenzie, Mr. D. Cunningham.

story, for White was essentially a perfectionist who was probably being rather too hard on himself. Indeed only months later, reporting on the certificate results in June 1953, he told the Board: "Three boys won State Exhibitions in the Science group. As the great majority of the abler boys in Ulster compete in this group, having three of the twelve awards is a considerable success. No other school had as many, including the big city schools. We have appeared on the Ministry's prize lists for each of the past 27 years, a record only equalled by the largest school of all, M.C.B." As a former Head of Department at Methody, it always gave him pleasure to say something like this. For the boys, examination successes were equally welcome, but for different reasons: Kenneth Edwards recalled that White granted the occasional half-holiday to celebrate the winning of a State Exhibition!

Although there were problems with a small minority, White built up a solid core of highly competent teachers in the last years of his headship. Collectively, these men were to provide a greater degree of continuity than the school had experienced for some time. They arrived when the Inst was growing and opportunities for promotion expanding: many of them remained for almost their entire careers and a significant proportion were Old Boys. Some were characters whose mild eccentricities are remembered to this day; others were more unobtrusive practitioners. All of them answered to a description often used by White's successor George Humphreys: "real professional schoolmasters". They developed a corporate tradition which made the common room a welcoming and an entertaining place, and they communicated their vision and their standards to younger men as they joined the staff.

Dan Cunningham, Jim Edwards, Jock Mackenzie, Gordon Mahony and Albert Clarke were already established men at the end of the White era. They were joined in 1945 by Tom Ryan, in 1947 by Irwin Rainey, Maurice ("The Boss") McDevitt, and in 1948 by Dr George Wilson and Arthur Nicholl. In 1949 came R.D. McPherson (the school's first Head of P.E.) and Hugh Montgomery, as well as James Moore (organist of First Presbyterian Church, Coleraine) as a part-time music teacher. Among William White's last appointees were Jack Farrell and Donald McDonagh, who came in 1953, and R.A.(Eric) Eyre in 1954. With the exception of Moore and McPherson, all these men were still teaching in the 1970s, and the last of them retired only at the end of the following decade. On the other hand, some experienced men left in the same period. Moore Macauley and Dudley Magrath moved on to senior positions, as did Dr Ralph Reynolds, who was appointed Headmaster of Dublin High School in 1951, and Norman Hoey who joined the Schools Inspectorate in 1950. Tragically, Vincent Smith was drowned in the sea only hours after the start of the summer holidays in 1948, and in 1953 George Wheeler died after a short illness. Most poignant was the death of Dr S.J. Hunter in 1950. He came as a pupil in 1878, and after graduating from Trinity College Dublin he returned to the staff in 1886, remaining until his retirement in 1934. "The wee doctor" continued to serve as a Governor, as Vice President of the Board, and as President of the Old Boys' Association until his death in 1950. His seventy-three year connection with the school will almost certainly never be equalled, and his name is still commemorated at prize day in the award of the S.J. Hunter Memorial Prize.

As the sub-heading for this section might suggest, the Coleraine Inst tradition has always been of the school as a community embracing teachers and ancillary staff alike. The appointment of James Black of Masterabois as gardener and groundsman in 1948 began a long career which lasted into the 1970s, while one of White's last reports to the Governors mentioned the return to duty after a stroke of Hugh Murdock, at that time possibly the school's longest serving employee. Murdock

A poignant portrait of Vincent "Vin" Smith, published in the school magazine which recorded his untimely death in 1948. His death, within hours of the end of the summer term, stunned the school community.

was employed in 1913 as T.G. Houston's coachman, later becoming chauffeur to T.J. Beare as well as a gardener, handy man and general assistant around the school. He was also a self-taught mathematician, and it was recorded that Beare would often tell his senior class that: "My man Hugh" could solve geometrical problems better than they could! No less formidable in their own ways were Willie Vincent and Miss Johnston, the boarding school Matron, already mentioned, and White's last secretary Miss Eve Anderson. She was remembered as a lady of formidable presence, great charm and consummate professional skill. When she left the school in 1955 the Headmaster's testimonial recorded: "I could rely on her to take full charge of the office, indeed of the whole school. For a secretary, she had the most valuable gift of silence"!

Academical Institution,

Coleraine,

Co. Derry.

6th January, 1955.

Miss C. E. Anderson was my Secretary at this school for six years, from 1948 to 1954.

She was extremely capable in every way and most trustworthy.

She very quickly mastered all the work to be done and latterly I could rely on her to take full charge of the office, indeed of the whole school. For a Secretary, she had the most valuable gift of silence. She was even tempered, polite and courteous with the many visitors to the office and is well qualified for a post of trust and responsibility.

Wm White

HEADMASTER.

One of William White's last personal secretaries – still remembered by some old boys as a lady of great charm and competence. And "the gift of silence" too!

Sports And Games In The Early 1950s

The postwar years were a rather lean time for the major sports in the school, and White was deeply frustrated by the number of occasions in which the school's rugby sides were defeated in the semi-final of the Schools' Cup and the Medallion Shield! He was, though, delighted when two old boys, J.D.E. Monteith and J.W. (Bill) McKay, were capped for Ireland in 1947. Monteith captained the Irish team against Scotland and Wales, while McKay wore the green jersey throughout the next three seasons, achieving twenty-three caps, as well as selection for the British Lions in 1950. A fractured kneecap in 1952 put him out of action for the rest of the season, and led to his premature retirement from the game – much to the regret of the rugby fraternity in New Zealand, where he went to practice medicine. As one international career ended, another began as F.E.("Fuzzy") Anderson won four international caps in the 1951-52 season, and subsequently turned out for The Barbarians and East Midlands. Sadly, in 1954-1955, Anderson's career was cut short by an illness which led to his retirement from

the game, and his withdrawal from a place in the British Lions Touring Team, for which he had been selected. A healthy number of boys were capped for Ulster Schools in this period, among them G.A. Tanner, J.M. Foster, F.E. Anderson, W.J. McVicker, R.A. Smyth, T.B. Girvan, W.B. Morrow, N.R. Fawcett, D.N. Wallace and D.G. Stewart.

In the 1945-46 rowing season a challenge cup for an annual race involving the rowing schools of Ulster was presented by a former pupil Mr Harold Craig. Concern lest the Wray Cup should be eclipsed by the new trophy led to some disagreement about the format of the Craig Cup races. In the end a trial sequence of regattas, held in turn on the Lagan, the Erne and the Bann was agreed to, and in the first four years of its history the Cup was won by each of the four competing schools – Coleraine Inst, Methody, R.B.A.I. and Portora! Although the 1945-6 school crew lost the Wray Cup, three days later they became the first winners of the Craig Cup, beating Portora in the final. In a rather lean period for the club, it was not until 1951 that both the Wray Cup and the Craig Cup returned to Coleraine.

Dan Cunningham with the First VIII of 1950-51. The work of Dan and others provided a solid basis of rowing on which Mickey Eyre was to build so effectively in later years.

Contemporary Board minutes contain references to discussions with Bann Rowing Club about the annual payment made by the school for use of Bann's facilities. This covered the rather delicate matter of the wear and tear inflicted on Bann's oars by the boys, and the matter was resolved in 1948 when the Governors and the Old Boys' Association agreed to buy ten new oars for the school's exclusive use. Within weeks of this decision, a former pupil, Mr R.J. Kirk, offered to bear the cost himself: "as a slight acknowledgement of those happy days I spent at C.A.I.". The end of White's headmastership marked a new era for rowing, for in the 1955-56 season the decision was taken to row regularly in Eights as well as Fours, and thus fall into line with the other Irish rowing schools.

In cricket W.B. Morrow was the first boy for many years to win a provincial cap against the Leinster Schools in 1946, and also the first C.A.I. boy ever to represent Ulster in both rugby and cricket in the same year. In athletics Mr H.P. Gilbert of Bangor presented the H.N. Gilbert Challenge Cup for the 100 yards sprint at the School Sports of 1946. In the same academic year, the school community was stunned at the sudden death of Kenneth Morrison, who collapsed and died at home after a training run at Portstewart. The following year, the Kenneth Morrison Memorial cup was presented by the Morrison family for competition between dayboys and boarders in a variety of disciplines including rugby, cross country, cricket and athletics. The first winners were the boarders. The formation of a Tennis Club in 1952 has already been mentioned. Coleraine Inst were defeated finalists in that year's Schools' Cup, but won it the following year.

The sports day tradition continued unbroken throughout the 1940s and into the new decade. In 1941 and 1942 "under the present conditions" it was decided that sports day should be a purely internal school event, but so great were the numbers of parents and friends who attended that by 1943 it had again become a major social event in the town, and afternoon tea reintroduced. The austerity years at the conclusion of war saw an intensification of rationing, and in 1946 and 1947 it was regretted that the school was unable to provide refreshments for visitors! During the war, too, the award of cups and prizes was replaced by War Savings Stamps for the first three places in each event.

Form 5 Farming Team 1943, who helped with the potato harvest at
Mrs. McKee's farm at Gills, Castleroe.

**Apart from the captions, there is little that can be added to these views of Inst boys at work
on local farms during the summer holidays in the 1940s. An amusing account of one boy's
experience appears in this chapter.**

The school's expansion led to the decision in 1951 to establish a house system for internal sporting competition. White himself suggested that the houses be named Hunter, Houston and McNeill after three men who had given long service as Vice Principal, Principal and Chairman of the Governors. Although the Headmaster resisted it, a fourth house was eventually named White, though secretly he must not have been displeased. As the school continued to grow, Bill Henry and Albert Clarke, who in their own time accumulated long years of service in the boardroom and the staffroom, were honoured in the same way.

Lunch-time break at Mr. T.U. Reid's farm, Crosscandley.

Hardly a sporting activity, but certainly one of the more useful extra-curricular pursuits of the late 1940s, was the annual potato gathering in which many of the boys participated. Something of the atmosphere can be judged from this extract from the 1946 school magazine: "On arrival at Mr B.Henry's farm at Carneety, Castlerock, we set to work gathering potatoes. At first it seemed great fun, but shortly we were suffering from pains in the back. Some complaining voices were raised and each boy thought his companions were slacking, and leaving most of the work for others to do….. At the end of the day our truck arrived and whisked us back to town. The remaining days passed in much the same manner. Gradually it dawned on us that perhaps there was something to be said for schoolwork, and that there might be easier ways of earning a living than by hard unremitting toil." A remarkably honest judgement!

The End Of An Era

The Inst and The Major had become so closely intertwined, that it was with a sense of shock that a special meeting of Governors in February 1955 received a brief letter from the Headmaster intimating that since he was approaching the age of compulsory retirement he must resign on 31 July following. There was, of course, no alternative, but in the brave new world of post war educational change, one suspects that William White did not grieve at the prospect. At the start of what was to be a long and happy retirement he did some part-time examining for the Imperial Civil Service, confiding to an acquaintance: "It's the best job I've ever been paid for – I'm not allowed to fail anybody!" He also did a short spell of Maths teaching as a 'sub' in Coleraine High School, confessing to another friend – with that characteristic ghost of a smile – that although teaching girls caused him no difficulty at all, " I miss the cruelty of the boys!" In this, of course, he did himself scant justice. By the end of his career White was a mellow man, whose passing on 31 August 1976 was marked by fulsome and wholehearted tributes in the Old Boys' Assocation Magazine, and who is still remembered with great fondness by many older men in the town.

Undated boarding school group in the last years of William White's headmastership.

Appendix 1:

Coleraine Old Boys serving in the Forces 1939-45.

COLERAINE OLD BOYS

SERVING IN THE FORCES

1939-45

CHRISTMAS 1945

THIS list of Coleraine Old Boys serving in the Forces during the 1939-1945 War is very incomplete and very inadequate. But it is published with the definite purpose of eliciting more information. Many Old Boys who have served during the last six years will not find their names here. We most strenuously urge them to help us make good the deficiencies by giving us details of their service at the earliest possible moment. Others will find that their arm of service or rank is quite out of date, and we wish to hear from them too.

We request that this supplement be circulated as widely as possible among Old Boys and their parents, and that where a reader knows of an Old Boy in the Forces who may not have an immediate chance of correcting our errors and omissions, he will pass on to us the information he has.

If the response to this appeal justifies it, a revised list will be issued with the Easter edition of " C.A.I."

The list contains three hundred and forty-six names of Old Boys, and seven names of the Staff, in the Forces; thirty-five who have died or been killed on active service; one missing; six prisoners of war; eighteen who have received decorations; and four mentioned in despatches.

Please help us to make this a true record by sending additional information to The Secretary, Academical Institution, Coleraine.

Appendix 2:
Letter from Dr T.T. McKendry

> 137 Southbourne Grove
> Westcliffe on Sea, Essex
> *April 8th 1943*

Dear Sir,

You are about to read a letter from an old man whom you never saw and probably heard of. I am an old boy of the C.A.I. (1880-84.). I was contemporary with your recent Classical Master, Dr. Hunter; with W. J. M. Hardy; Sam Dunlop and his younger brother, Bob, who afterwards became a famous rugby international; G. McC. Irvine the Captain of the first Cup winning team, and many other notable boys. Irvine and I were great friends - we boarded together in both Cork and Belfast. I played rugby for the School and was considered the mainstay of the back division, but owing to a pronounced lack of pace I was very seldom in the limelight. My great regret was that I was not in the Cup winning team; but I had matriculated and was also over age and consequently ineligible. In '84 I entered U. C. Cork, taking 2nd place in the Maths Scholarships. In my 2nd and 3rd years I had first place and in my 4th year I took the Senior Scholarship. In this year I also took my B.A. I kept up my rugby football at Cork and was captain of the College team in '86-7 and '87-8. On each occasion we won the Munster Challenge Cup. Having finished with Cork I went to Belfast and began Medicine. After qualification I came to England and eventually settled down in a new district of N. E. London (Ilford). I bought a house, put up my plate and waited for my first patient. I was successful. Some years ago I retired and am now living in the residential part of Southend-on-Sea (viz Westcliff).

List of Coleraine Old Boys Serving in His Majesty's Forces, 1939–45.

Name	Years	Service	Rank
W. A. Abercrombie	(1936-42)	Recce Regiment	Lieutenant
A. E. D. Allen		Royal Artillery	Captain
C. T. Anderson	(1935-37)	Royal Air Force	
A. E. Anderson	(1932-39)	Royal Air Force	Flight Lieutenant
D. R. Anderson	(1940-44)	Royal Air Force	
E. V. Anderson	(1925-28)	Royal Air Force	
J. M. Anderson	(1932-37)	Royal Air Force	
N. A. Anderson	(1928-33)	K.S.L.I.	Private
W. G. Anderson	(1940)	Royal Air Force	
R. A. Ardill, M.C.	(1931-35)	Royal Irish Fusiliers	Lieutenant
A. J. Armstrong	(1935-36)	Royal Air Force	Sergeant
T. R. N. Balmer	(1937-41)	Royal Engineers	Captain
H. T. Barnes	(1933-38)	Army	Lieutenant
R. Barklie, O.B.E.		R.C.S.	Major
R. Barr	(1934-37)	Royal Air Force	Sergeant
S. J. Barr	(1930-34)	R.A.M.C.	
S. C. Bateman, D.F.M.	(1936-41)	Royal Air Force	Flying Officer
J. L. Baxter	(1921-26)	Royal Artillery	Major
C. E. St. J. Beamish	(1918-23)	Royal Air Force	Wing Commander
C. H. Beamish	(1930-32)	Royal Air Force	Squadron Leader
F. V. Beamish, D.S.O. (and Bar), D.F.C., A.F.C.	(1915-21)	Royal Air Force	Group Captain
G. R. Beamish, O.B.E., C.B.	(1915-22)	Royal Air Force	Air Commodore
J. H. Beare	(1937-40)	Royal Navy	Cadet
J. M. Beare	(1932-37)	R.N.V.R.	Sub-Lieutenant
R. K. Beare	(1936-41)	R.U.R.	Lieutenant
J. H. Bell	(1937-42)	Royal Air Force	Sergeant
H. M. Bennett	(1930-33)	R.A.M.C.	Captain
C. F. Beverland	(1941-43)	Royal Air Force	
John Black	(1933-38)	Royal Air Force	Flying Officer
James Black	(1938-43)	Royal Air Force	Sergeant
J. L. Blair	(1930-35)	R.A.M.C.	Captain
J. M. Blair	(1931-36)	R.A.S.C.	Lieutenant
V. Blair	(1935-40)	Royal Air Force	
W. Blair	(1933-36)	R.A.M.C.	Captain
W. B. Blair		Merchant Navy	
F. M'C. Boal	(1928)	Royal Air Force	
H. Bolton		Australian Imperial Forces	
W. R. Bond	(1937-40)	Royal Navy	Able Seaman
T. H. Boone	(1924-27)	Royal Artillery	
J. Boyd	(1932-37)	Royal Air Force	Flight Lieutenant
J. C. Boyd	(1937-42)	Royal Air Force	Pilot Officer
R. G. Boyd, M.C.	(1930-36)	R.A.M.C.	Captain
J. K. Brew		Royal Air Force	Wing Commander
J. H. Brewster	(1929-30)	Royal Air Force	Flight Lieutenant
T. H. Browne		Royal Air Force	
W. R. Bruce	(1934-39)	Army	Captain
V. P. Bryans	(1930-36)	Royal Air Force	Aircraftsman
H. C. Caldwell		Royal Navy	Sub-Lieutenant (E.)
A. N. Campbell	(1933-36)	Royal Air Force	Flying Officer
D. M. Campbell	(1925-29)	Royal Air Force	Pilot Officer
R. M. Campbell	(1908)	Pioneer Corps	Sergeant
H. F. Campbell	(1932-37)	Royal Air Force	
T. Campbell	(1936-37)	Royal Air Force	Sergt. Air Gunner
D. T. Carter	(1932-34)	Royal Air Force	Flying Officer
G. S. Carter	(1939-41)	Royal Artillery (Airborne)	Lieut.
F. Casement, D.S.O.		R.A.M.C.	Major General
R. J. Catterson	(1933-38)	Parachute Regiment	
R. Chalmers	(1936-41)	Royal Air Force	Pilot Officer
B. H. Christie	(1932-37)	Royal Air Force	Sergeant Pilot
D. E. Christie	(1927-32)	Royal Air Force	Squadron Leader
D. G. Christie	(1925-28)	Army	
D. J. Christie		Royal Artillery	Major
A. J. Clarke	(1928-38)	R.C.S.	Major
A. N. Clarke	(1923-28)	Royal Engineers	Lieut. Colonel
G. M'F. Clarke	(1930-35)	Royal Air Force	Pilot Officer
S. A. R. Clarke	(1932-37)	Royal Air Force	Pilot Officer
T. C. Clarke	(1927-32)	Royal Air Force	Flying Officer
H. Clements	(1939-41)	Royal Navy	
W. E. Clokey	(1929-34)	Royal Air Force	Sergeant
R. A. Cole	(1929-33)	Royal Air Force	Flying Officer
J. O. Y. Cole	(1926-32)	R.A.M.C.	Lieutenant
W. A. Condy	(1931-39)	Royal Air Force	Pilot Officer
C. A. Craig	(1932-38)	Royal Air Force	Cadet
H. T. M. Craig	(1935-40)	Fleet Air Arm	Sub-Lieutenant
S. C. Craig	(1935-41)	Royal Air Force	Warrant Officer
H. Crawford	(1932-36)	Royal Air Force	Sergeant
R. A. Crawford	(1922-28)	Northumberland Fusiliers	Captain
R. G. Crawford	(1924-29)	Royal Navy	Writer
A. F. Crooke	(1929-34)	R.A.M.C.	Captain
C. J. Crozier	(1922-26)	Royal Air Force	Sergeant Observer
P. L. Culver	(1942-43)	U.S. Forces	
H. A. Cummins	(1929-33)	Army	
Daniel Cunningham	(1925-33)	Royal Air Force	Flight Lieutenant
Donald Cunningham	(1926-31)	Army Admin.	Major
J. I. Cunningham	(1928-33)	Royal Navy	Lieutenant Surgeon
S. Cunningham		Merchant Navy	3rd Officer
W. I. Cunningham	(1919)	Royal Ulster Rifles	Captain
R. A. Currie	(1924-29)	A.D.C.	Captain
W. E. Currie		Royal Engineers	Sergeant
C. Dalzell		Army	Captain
P. Day	(1941-42)	Royal Air Force	Cadet
T. M. Dinsmore	(1939-42)	Royal Navy	
J. F. Doey	(1926-33)	R.E.M.E.	Warrant Officer
W. D. Doey	(1924-30)	Royal Air Force	Squadron Leader
A. J. Donaghy	(1929-33)		
A. B. Douglas	(1935-40)	Royal Navy	Ordinary Seaman
W. Douglas	(1933-39)	Infantry	Corporal
C. R. Downey	(1928-32)	Royal Air Force	Flight Sergeant
J. Dryburgh	(1939-42)	Royal Air Force	Corporal
Joseph Dryburgh	(1939-43)	Merchant Navy	
J. Duffy	(1932-37)	Army	Lieutenant
J. D. Dunn	(1935-36)	Royal Air Force	Leading Aircraftsman
R. J. Dunseith	(1929-33)	Royal Artillery	Lieutenant
J. R. Dymond	(1936-40)	Royal Air Force	Sergeant Pilot
J. A. Esler, D.F.C.	(1928-33)	Royal Air Force	Pilot Officer
S. H. Farley	(1940-44)	Royal Air Force	
W. H. Farley		R.A.S.C.	Lieutenant
J. I. Fawcett	(1934-39)	Royal Air Force	
F. Ferguson	(1936-41)	Royal Air Force	Flying Officer
J. F. Ferguson	(1934-35)	Royal Air Force	Sergeant
R. Finlay	(1930-32)	Merchant Navy	Radio Officer
G. B. W. Fisher		R.A.M.C. (India)	Major
I. H. Fleming	(1930-33)	Royal Air Force	Flight Lieutenant
E. Fletcher	(1930-34)	R.A.M.C.	Major
R. D. Fletcher	(1935-38)	Royal Air Force	Sergeant
E. A. Forbes	(1938-43)	R.E.M.E.	
P. Ford-Hutchinson	(1933-35)	Army	Corporal
R. F. S. Ford-Hutchinson	(1936-37)	Royal Air Force	Sergeant Pilot
W. R. Ford-Hutchinson	(1936-41)	Royal Air Force	Pilot Officer
D. H. Freeland	(1929-32)	Royal Air Force	Flight Sergeant
J. W. V. Fulton		Royal Artillery	Sergeant
W. C. Furey	(1927-30)	Royal Ulster Rifles	Corporal
W. H. Furey	(1927-30)	Merchant Navy	Engineer Officer
E. M. W. Garstin	(1927-28)	Merchant Navy	Wireless Operator
G. K. Garstin, O.B.E.	(1927-29)	Merchant Navy	Radio Officer
J. H. Garstin	(1927-29)	Royal Air Force	
R. E. Garstin	(1927-28)	Royal Air Force	
H. N. Gilbert	(1939-45)	Royal Navy	Cadet
J. S. Gilmore	(1929-30)	R.A.M.C.	Captain
W. J. Glenn, D.F.M.	(1932-37)	Royal Air Force	Flying Officer
G. B. Graham	(1939-42)	Royal Air Force	
G. F. Graham	(1934-37)	R.E.M.E.	
H. D. Gribbon	(1932-34)	Royal Navy	Ordinary Seaman
J. C. G. Groves	(1927-31)	Royal Air Force	Flight Lieutenant
T. A. Groves	(1926-30)	R.A.M.C.	Major
R. A. Halliday	(1932-36)	Army	Cadet
R. F. Halliday	(1935-39)	Royal Navy	Ordinary Seaman
A. A. Hamilton	(1936-41)	R.A.S.C. (Indian Army)	Lieutenant
E. L. Hamilton	(1927-34)	Royal Artillery	Lieutenant
H. C. Hamilton	(1929-37)	R.A.M.C.	Captain
D. J. Harper	(1936-41)	Indian Army	
E. J. S. Harper		North Irish Horse	Trooper
T. K. Harper	(1936-42)	Royal Air Force	
J. A. G. Harte	(1930-35)	Army	Captain
S. D. Hartness	(1938-43)	Royal Air Force	
D. C. Henderson	(1926-30)	Army Chaplain	Major
C. J. C. Hinnrichs	(1930-32)	R.A.M.C.	Captain

I sincerely hope you will not think I am trying to blow my own trumpet by giving you all these items - that would be useless at my age - now in my 80th year. These items are meant to be preliminary to what follows:-I propose, with your sanction and the sanction of the Board of Management of the C.A.I, to contribute a sum of £500 (five hundred pounds) to establish a Mathematical Prize Fund. This sum when invested in 3½ % War Loans or 3% Defence Bonds (or other safe investment) will produce about £15 annually. This will provide three (or four) prizes which may be very acceptable to the winners. The subjects would be Arithmetic, Algebra, Geometry and probably Trigonometry. Chemistry and Experimental Physics might sometimes be considered. But I think it would be wiser for me to leave the choice to yourself and your Mathematical Master.

If you and your Board agree to this offer, I am prepared to send you a cheque at any time. One stipulation I make is that I be allowed to "set" the first paper in Geometry. May I suggest that this be mentioned in the School Magazine (but not any of the personal items I have given you above). My object in asking you to do so is that it may act as a stimulus to some other old boy (or boys) to do something similar to what I am proposing now. I enclose a photograph which represents me about the age of 40. I cannot send you a more recent one as I have not been photographed since. You will kindly return this at your leisure. I hope you will pardon the length of this communication. With my deepest respect for yourself and my earnest wish for the continued success of the School.

Name	Years	Service	Rank
B. Henry		U.S. Army	Sergeant
G. N. Henry	(1926-31)	Royal Air Force	Leading Aircraftsman
R. N. Henry, O.B.E.		Royal Artillery Controller of Supplies, Cyprus	
S. Henry		Royal Artillery	
P. J. R. Heyland	(1939-41)	5th Gurkha Rifles	Lieutenant
C. O. Hezlet, D.S.O.		Royal Artillery	Lieutenant Colonel
W. J. C. Hill	(1932-37)	R.A.M.C.	Captain
F. Holley	(1933-37)	Royal Air Force	Aircraftsman
R. A. Holley	(1928-32)	Royal Air Force	Aircraftsman
W. M. Holley	(1930-34)	Royal Navy	Surgeon Lieutenant
C. Holmes	(1926-29)	R.A.M.C.	Corporal
T. D. Hope	(1933-35)	Royal Air Force	Sergeant Observer
T. Q. Horner		Royal Air Force	Group Captain
P. W. Hunt	(1942-44)	Indian Army	Cadet
D. J. Hunter	(1926-31)	Royal Navy	Sub-Lieutenant
G. Hunter		Royal Air Force	Aircraftsman
R. B. Huston	(1931-35)		
G. B. Hyndman	(1932-38)	Royal Air Force	Flight Sergeant
S. D. Haslett	(1939-45)	Royal Navy	Ordinary Coder
J. J. K. Irvine	(1931-34)	Royal Air Force	
J. A. Irwin	(1931-36)	Royal Air Force	Pilot Officer
R. B. Wylie Irwin, M.C., O.B.E.		Army	Lieutenant Colonel
R. J. T. Irwin	(1936-39)	R.A.C. Transvaal Scottish (South African Forces)	Major
T. W. Jamison	(1938-42)	Royal Air Force	Sergeant
H. C. Johnston	(1922-28)	Royal Navy	Surgeon Commander
J. Johnston	(1931-36)	Royal Artillery	Captain
W. R. Johnston	(1927-32)	R.A.M.C.	Lieutenant Colonel
A. C. Jones	(1932-33)	R.A.O.C.	Major
C. S. Kane	(1933-39)	Royal Artillery	Sergeant
Colin Kane	(1922-27)	Royal Air Force	Flying Officer
G. A. Kane		R.A.M.C.	Lieutenant
G. W. Kane	(1931-36)		
H. Kane	(1936-40)	Royal Air Force	Aircraftsman
H. S. Keatings	(1940-44)	Fleet Air Arm	Cadet
G. R. C. Keegan	(1940-41)	Royal Air Force	Cadet
C. R. Kelly	(1929-35)	Royal Air Force (Commando)	Sergt.
E. Kelly	(1930-32)	Royal Artillery	
J. G. W. Kelso	(1933-36)	Royal Air Force	Cadet
K. J. Kemp	(1931-36)	R.N.V.R.	Sub-Lieutenant
D. M'M. Kennedy	(1933-36)	R.A.M.C.	Captain
J. S. Kennedy	(1929-33)	Royal Air Force	
R. H. Kennedy	(1925-29)	Royal Artillery	Lieutenant
A. I. K. Kerr	(1930-36)	R.A.M.C.	Captain
R. B. Kiernan	(1934-37)	Royal Air Force	Aircraftsman
J. G. Kilbride	(1942-44)	Royal Navy	Writer
E. M. H. Kilpatrick		R.A.S.C.	Captain
C. W. P. King	(1941-43)	Irish Guards	Guardsman
F. S. B. Knox	(1933-38)	Royal Air Force	Sergeant Pilot
F. Y. C. Knox, D.S.O. (and Bar)		Royal Ulster Rifles	Brigadier
P. R. H. Knox	(1931-36)	Royal Engineers	Lieutenant
W. A. Knox	(1929-34)	R.A.M.C.	Captain
W. R. M. Knox	(1937-42)	Royal Engineers	Cadet
C. F. Kyle	(1936-40)	Royal Air Force	Cadet
S. K. Lecky	(1939-43)	R.E.M.E.	
A. E. Lenane	(1936-40)	Royal Air Force	Aircraftsman
H. O'H. Logan	(1937-41)	Royal Air Force	
L. Logan	(1935-40)	Royal Navy	Sub-Lieutenant
R. S. Love	(1934-36)	Royal Air Force	Leading Aircraftsman
T. Lowry	(1919-23)	Colonial Admin., Hongkong	
W. D. M'Afee		Army Intelligence Corps	Captain
J. M'Aleely	(1931-36)	Royal Air Force	
J. H. M'Cahon		Royal Marines	
J. K. M'Candless	(1923-29)	Royal Air Force	Leading Aircraftsman
J. H. M'Candless	(1938-41)	Royal Navy	Able Seaman
E. T. M'Cartney, M.C.	(1922-31)	R.A.M.C.	Lieutenant Colonel
R. S. M'Clelland	(1930-35)	R.A.M.C.	Major
D. H. M'Collum, M.C.	(1930-35)	R.A.M.C.	Captain
J. K. M'Collum		R.A.M.C.	Lieutenant Colonel
John K. M'Collum	(1923-28)	R.A.M.C.	Major
W. K. M'Collum		R.A.M.C.	
C. H. M'Conaghy	(1936-41)	Royal Air Force	Sergeant Pilot
A. M'Connell	(1930-34)	R.A.M.C.	Captain
J. R. M'Cullough	(1938-41)	Army	

Name	Years	Service	Rank
W. W. M'Cullough	(1940-44)	Army	
R. M'Dermott	(1929-34)	Fleet Air Arm	Lieutenant
R. M'Donald	(1929-33)	Royal Artillery	Gunner
G. R. C. M'Dowell	(1936-41)	Royal Air Force	Pilot Officer
S. G. M'Dowell	(1937-41)	Merchant Navy	
W. A. M'Fadden	(1937-39)	Royal Air Force	
C. J. M'Farlane	(1931-37)	R.N.V.R.	Sub-Lieutenant
R. H. S. M'Gimpsey	(1936-42)	Royal Air Force	
D. M'Grath	(1932-33)	Royal Ulster Rifles	Corporal
D. D. M'Grath	(1933-38)	Royal Air Force	Flight Lieutenant
W. M'Grath, D.S.O.	(1929-36)	Royal Engineers	Captain
W. W. M'Grath	(1925-31)	Royal Air Force	Squadron Leader
A. M'Gugan	(1941-42)	Royal Air Force	
F. M. N. M'Ilwaine	(1935-38)	Royal Air Force	Leading Aircraftsman
A. J. M'Intosh	(1930-34)	Army	
R. R. M'Intosh	(1931-34)	North Irish Horse	Trooper
J. W. M'Kay	(1934-39)	Royal Engineers	Lieutenant
R. J. M'Keag	(1929-32)	Royal Artillery	
J. E. M'Math	(1929-34)	Royal Air Force	Pilot Officer
N. I. M'Mullan		A.D.C.	Major
J. W. G. M'Mullan	(1935-39)	Fleet Air Arm	Sub-Lieutenant
G. A. M'Murray	(1924-29)	Army	
H. Y. M'Nabb	(1938-42)	Royal Air Force	Cadet
R. M'Neill	(1937-42)	Royal Artillery	Cadet
C. H. Macaulay	(1929-34)	Royal Air Force	
G. G. Mackey		Irish Guards	
F. A. Mackey	(1929-30)		
N. J. Mackey	(1934-38)	Royal Air Force	
T. Madill, O.B.E.		Royal Navy	Surgeon Commander
I. Malcolm	(1935-41)	Royal Air Force	
C. S. Malcolm	(1935-38)	Royal Air Force	
J. A. Mark	(1925-28)	R.A.M.C.	Captain
J. F. Mark	(1931-36)	R.A.M.C.	Major
J. D. Martin		Irish Guards	Sergeant
R. N. Martin	(1922-28)	R.A.M.C.	Captain
S. B. Matthews	(1929-34)	R.A.M.C.	Captain
J. S. Y. Mathewson	(1936-43)	Royal Air Force	Pilot Officer
B. G. Meharg, A.F.C.	(1927-35)	Royal Air Force	Squadron Leader
J. H. W. Millar	(1932-37)	Merchant Navy	Radio Officer
J. H. Millen	(1930-35)	Royal Air Force	Squadron Leader
F. W. Milliken	(1929-32)	Royal Air Force	
M. M. L. P. Minford	(1932-38)	Royal Artillery	Captain
W. A. H. Mitchell		Royal Irish Rifles	Corporal
I. Monteith	(1938-41)	Royal Air Force	Pilot Officer
R. A. C. Montagu	(1932-33)	Royal Air Force	
J. Montgomery	(1928-32)	Royal Artillery	Sergeant
T. E. Moody	(1929-33)	R.A.M.C.	Captain
K. M'G. Moore	(1926-33)	Royal Air Force	Leading Aircraftsman
R. T. Moore	(1935-39)	Fleet Air Arm	Cadet
E. T. Morrison	(1929-31)	R.A.M.C.	Captain
H. F. Morrison	(1933-39)	Royal Air Force	
G. G. Morrow		Royal Canadian Air Force	Fl. Lieut.
O. S. H. Mulholland	(1927-30)	R.N.V.R.	Lieutenant
S. Nevin	(1924-28)	Royal Artillery	Sergeant
A. R. Nicholson	(1937-42)	Army	Lieutenant
J. C. Nicholson		R.N.V.R.	Surgeon Lieutenant
W. Nicholson	(1932-38)	Royal Corps of Signals	Major
J. E. O'Fee	(1933-36)	Royal Air Force	Aircraftsman
R. D. Owen	(1932-34)	Army	
H. D. Patrick	(1928-34)	North Irish Horse	Lance Corporal
J. W. Patrick		Royal Air Force	Wing Commander
M. S. Patrick	(1925-29)	R.A.M.C.	Captain
L. J. Patterson	(1930-34)	Royal Air Force	Sergeant Pilot
R. M. N. Patrick	(1926-32)	R.A.O.C.	Major
R. J. F. Patton	(1936-41)	Royal Air Force	Flying Officer
J. L. Pinkerton	(1926-32)	Royal Corps of Signals	Lieutenant
T. C. Pinkerton	(1930-36)	Royal Air Force	Flight Lieutenant
R. W. M. Pollock	(1929-35)	Royal Artillery	Captain
A. C. Preston	(1928-30)	R.I.F.	Lieutenant
W. G. Rankin	(1937-41)	Merchant Navy	
A. C. Reid		Royal Air Force	Flying Officer
J. C. Reid	(1932-37)	Royal Air Force	Flying Officer
A. Ross	(1938-40)	Merchant Navy	
J. M. Ross	(1929-30)	Merchant Navy	Wireless Operator
P. J. G. Ross	(1933-39)	Royal Air Force	Aircraftsman
A. R. Ross	(1929-34)	Merchant Navy	

Appendix 3:
Further memories of Edward Simpson

War was declared only a fortnight after the Senior results. The Chief urgently advised my parents and me that, rather than enlisting in some infantry regiment, I should get to Queen's at once and join in the War later with a science qualification, which would make me more useful both to the country and to myself. He fixed it that I was accepted into the Mathematics Department that October although only 16, and I graduated in 1942 at 19. This was so far removed from the English age-pattern that in my final year I was still young enough to sit for (and win) a Cambridge Entrance Scholarship. I was greatly encouraged and helped to do this by an Old Boy in Cambridge, Robert J. Getty, Professor of Classics and Fellow of St John's College. Cambridge deferred the Scholarship while the War was on and I took it up at Christ's College (rather unusually as a post-graduate) in 1945.

While at Queen's, outside of lectures, I spent much time in the Signals detachment of the O.T.C. After

A. J. Russell	(1938-44)	Indian Army	Lieutenant
R. A. Russell	(1940-45)	Indian Army	
R. D. Russell	(1936-42)	Royal Air Force	Pilot Officer
E. Sandford	(1926-33)	War Reporter	
W. W. Sayers	(1929-35)	Fleet Air Arm	Sub-Lieutenant
R. A. Seymour	(1941-43)	6th Gurkha Rifles	Lieutenant
E. H. Simpson	(1934-39)	Special Service	
T. A. M. Small	(1939-41)	Royal Navy	Cadet
W. A. S. Small	(1933-40)	R.I.F.	Lieutenant
W. A. W. Small	(1930-36)	R.A.F.V.R.	Flight Lieutenant
W. H. C. Smith	(1937-42)	Merchant Navy	Radio Officer
A. M'I. Smyth	(1931-38)	Army	Lieutenant
F. C. Smythe	(1928-31)	Royal Artillery	Bombardier
R. A. Sproule	(1925-31)	Army	
T. J. Stanley		Royal Air Force	Leading Aircraftman
P. Steen	(1928-33)	Army	Captain
J. W. Stewart		Indian Medical Service	Lieut.-Col.
S. V. Stewart	(1938-43)	R.E.M.E.	
T. M'D. Stewart		Royal Air Force	Squadron Leader
F. R. Stirling	(1931-36)	Army	
J. Stirling	(1940-45)	Indian Army	Cadet
R. K. Sutherland	(1928-29)	Royal Artillery	Lance Corporal
J. Tannahill	(1930-32)	R.C.S. (N.Z. Forces)	
W. Telford	(1928-30)	R.N.V.R.	Lieutenant
A. D. H. Thompson	(1933-38)	Royal Air Force	Flight Lieutenant
J. A. R. Thompson	(1932-38)	Canadian Army	
W. A. B. Thompson	(1935-40)	R.N.V.R.	Sub-Lieutenant
W. D. Thompson		Royal Navy	
I. M'C. Todd	(1935-41)	Royal Air Force	Cadet
A. R. R. Torrie	(1930-37)	Royal Artillery	Gunner
E. C. Torrie	(1929-34)	Royal Navy	Surgeon Lieutenant
T. E. Tunnell	(1937-43)	Army	Cadet
K. E. Vogan	(1932-37)	Fleet Air Arm	Sub-Lieutenant
R. F. Walker, O.B.E.		R.A.M.C.	Brigadier
J. R. Watson	(1933-36)	Royal Navy	Ordinary Seaman
J. J. Watts	(1934-38)	Merchant Navy	Sub-Lieutenant
W. J. Watts	(1939-42)	Merchant Navy	
D. W. Wauchob	(1931-36)	Royal Air Force	Flight Lieutenant
D. A. Wheeler	(1936-41)	Royal Engineers	Corporal
R. Wheeler	(1936-39)	Royal Air Force	Sergeant
J. D. White	(1927-32)	R.H.A.	Lieutenant
D. Whitley	(1928-30)	Royal Air Force	Flying Officer
P. B. Williams		R.A.M.C.	Major
C. S. Williamson	(1925-28)	Royal Air Force	
F. G. S. Williamson, D.F.M.		Royal Air Force	Squadron Leader
W. Wilson	(1938-41)	Parachute Regiment	Private
H. Woodhouse	(1941-43)	Buffs	Lieutenant
R. Wray		Royal Artillery	Major
N. A. K. Wren	(1933-35)	Royal Air Force	Sergeant Pilot
E. Wright		North Irish Horse	Corporal

STAFF ON SERVICE.

Daniel Cunningham		Royal Air Force	Flight Lieutenant
N. E. Hoey		Army Intelligence Corps	Captain
J. A. Irwin		Royal Air Force	Pilot Officer
J. O. H. MacKenzie		Army Intelligence Corps	Captain
V. W. Smith		Royal Artillery	Lieutenant
R. E. Thompson		Royal Air Force	Flying Officer
G. B. Wheeler		Royal Irish Fusiliers	Lieutenant

KILLED OR DIED ON SERVICE.

N. A. Anderson		K.S.L.I.	Private
R. Barr		Royal Air Force	Sergeant
F. V. Beamish, D.S.O. (and Bar), D.F.C., A.F.C.		Royal Air Force	Group Captain
J. H. Bell		Royal Air Force	Sergeant
H. C. Caldwell		Royal Navy	Sub-Lieutenant (E.)
A. N. Campbell		Royal Air Force	Flying Officer
D. M. Campbell		Royal Air Force	Pilot Officer
T. Campbell		Royal Air Force	Sergt. Air Gunner
T. C. Clarke		Royal Air Force	Flying Officer
G. M'F. Clarke		Royal Air Force	Pilot Officer
H. Crawford		Royal Air Force	Sergeant
C. J. Crozier		Royal Air Force	Sergeant
P. Day		Royal Air Force	Cadet
A. A. B. Douglas		Royal Navy	Ordinary Seaman

J. A. Esler, D.F.C.		Royal Air Force	Pilot Officer
W. H. Farley		R.A.S.C.	Lieutenant
R. D. Fletcher		Royal Air Force	Sergeant
R. F. S. Ford-Hutchinson		Royal Air Force	Sergeant Pilot
D. H. Freeland		Royal Air Force	Flight Sergeant
G. B. Hyndman		Royal Air Force	Flight Sergeant
J. A. Irwin		Royal Air Force	Pilot Officer
K. J. Kemp		R.N.V.R.	Sub-Lieutenant
F. S. B. Knox		Royal Air Force	Sergeant Pilot
J. S. Kennedy		Royal Air Force	
T. Lowry		Col. Admin., Hongkong	
C. H. Macaulay		Royal Air Force	
C. H. M'Conaghy		Royal Air Force	Sergeant Pilot
D. M'Grath		Royal Ulster Rifles	Corporal
W. M'Grath, D.S.O.		Royal Engineers	Captain
K. M'G. Moore		Royal Air Force	Leading Aircraftman
L. J. Patterson		Royal Air Force	Sergeant Pilot
A. M'I. Smyth		Royal Irish Fusiliers	Lieutenant
J. Tannahill		R.C.S. (N.Z. Forces)	
K. E. Vogan		Fleet Air Arm	Sub-Lieutenant
D. Whitley		Royal Air Force	Pilot Officer

MISSING.

| J. E. O'Fee | | Royal Air Force | Aircraftman |

PRISONERS OF WAR.

R. A. Ardill		Royal Irish Fusiliers	Lieutenant
W. J. Glenn		Royal Air Force	Flying Officer
J. H. M'Cahon		Royal Marines	Captain
G. A. M'Murray		Army	
J. A. Mark		R.A.M.C.	Captain
J. A. R. Thompson		Canadian Army	
J. Monteith		R.A.F.	Sergt. w/o P/o

DECORATED.

M.C.	R. A. Ardill	Royal Irish Fusiliers	Lieutenant
D.F.M.	S. C. Bateman	Royal Air Force	Flying Officer
D.S.O., bar to D.S.O., D.F.C., O.B.E., American Legion of Merit, Royal Order of George I of the Hellenes (with swords), C.B.	F. V. Beamish, A.F.C.	Royal Air Force	Group Captain
D.F.C.	G. R. Beamish	Royal Air Force	Air Commodore
M.C.	C. E. St. J. Beamish	Royal Air Force	Wing Commander
D.F.C.	R. G. Boyd	R.A.M.C.	Captain
D.F.C.	J. A. Esler	Royal Air Force	Pilot Officer
O.B.E.	G. K. Garstin	Merchant Navy	Radio Officer
D.F.M.	W. J. Glenn	Royal Air Force	Flying Officer
O.B.E.	R. N. Henry	Controller of Supplies, Cyprus	
M.C.	R. J. T. Irwin	R.A.C. (S.A. Forces)	Major
D.S.O., bar to D.S.O.	F. Y. C. Knox	Royal Ulster Rifles	Brigadier
M.C.	E. T. M'Cartney	R.A.M.C.	Lieutenant Colonel
O.B.E.	T. Madill	Royal Navy	Surgeon Commander
D.S.O.	W. M'Grath	Royal Engineers	Captain
A.F.C.	B. G. Meharg	Royal Air Force	Squadron Leader
D.F.M.	F. G. S. Williamson	Royal Air Force	Squadron Leader
O.B.E.	R. F. Walker	R.A.M.C.	Brigadier

MENTIONED IN DESPATCHES.

	D. J. Christie	Royal Artillery	Major
	S. C. Craig	Royal Air Force	Warrant Officer
	C. R. Downey	Royal Air Force	Flight Sergeant
	F. Ferguson	Royal Air Force	Flying Officer
	F. V. Beamish	- -	Group Captain
	J. W. Patrick	- -	Wing-Commander
	J. J. Mark	R.A.M.C.	Major
	G. Montgomary	Anti-Aircraft	Sergt
	S. Nevin		Sergt
O.B.E.	R. H. N. Patrick	Army	Lt/Colonel
O.B.E.	L. C. Lynd	Merchant Navy	Chief-Engineer
M.C.	D. H. M'Cobern	R.A.M.C.	Captain
O.B.E.	R. B. Leslie Irwin	Army	Lt/Colonel
O.B.E.	G. A. Kane	R.A.M.C.	Lt/Colonel
M.B.E.	G. S. Cunningham	R. Navy	Surgeon-Lieut.
O.B.E.	Maclean		

---

graduation I was therefore on course for the Royal Corps of Signals O.C.T.U. at Catterick. But this was interrupted by my being called to London for interview by C.P. Snow and Harry Hoff and being sent at once as a Foreign Office employee to the Government Code and Cypher School at Bletchley Park. Its existence and its purpose - the breaking of German, Italian and Japanese codes and ciphers - were totally secret.

When I was back on leave in Northern Ireland and visiting the School, The Chief dropped an oblique reference (tactfully oblique so that I did not have to answer) to Room 40, the Admiralty's code breaking team in World War 1. I was disconcerted that he obviously knew where I was working and what I was doing, and wondered what hand he had had in my being sent there. For he was a much respected man of influence in many directions. I remember him with admiration and I owe him much.

Another boarding school groups, again undated. Boarding school photographs seem to have been taken much more regularly than those covering the whole school.

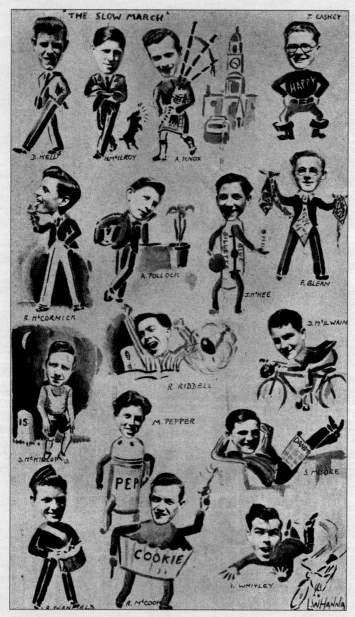

As others see us!

In the late 1940s, the magazine carried montages of some the better known characters in the senior school. Perhaps some readers may recognise themselves in these reproductions?

Major W. White

George Humphreys was a native of Donacloney, and was educated at Lurgan College. To his primary degree in mathematical physics from Queens University Belfast he added an M.Sc and Ph.D., as well as a Fellowship of the Institute of Physics. At Queens he played rugby and cricket, gaining a cricket blue of which he was justly proud. His teaching career began at his old school in 1938, and by the time he was appointed Head of Physics at Campbell College Belfast in 1947 he had become senior science master and acting Vice Principal at Lurgan. With a characteristic zest for both academic work and practical adminstration, he became not only a head of department, but also housemaster of Ormiston, and the College's Estates Bursar. In 1954 he was short-listed for the headmastership of Campbell College, and the following year he was chosen to succeed William White as Headmaster of Coleraine Inst. From the outset, this relatively young man felt that he had achieved his lifetime's ambition, and during the next twenty four years he set himself to the transformation of the school he had taken over.

The new headmaster, pictured in his study not long after his arrival.

George Humphreys: The Man

Humphreys burst upon Coleraine Inst in a whirlwind of restless energy which characterised both his entire headmastership and his life in retirement: not long before his death, in his eighty first year, he had bought the latest computer and was coming to grips with current developments in I.T. He was an instinctive planner, more than ready to share his vision with any audience, be it the prefects in their Study, the resident staff at the dinner table or the Governors in the Board Room. He had as keen a grasp of finance as many a bursar, and as enthusiastic a fascination with machinery as any clerk of works. By nature he was cautious about other people's requests or suggestions, though staff often learned that a bluntly negative response might be followed some weeks later by the familiar: "Ah, I was thinking the other day that what we might do is..." It was often just a question of patience!

To the end of his days at Coleraine Inst he relished any opportunity to get his hands on machinery. He often told against himself the story of how he and Eddie Norris, his faithful clerk of works, struggled with a defective heating boiler one Sunday morning just before church. The tussle ended with Humphreys' best suit being sprayed with heating oil, and he himself being seriously chastised by his wife when he went home to change. Another former member of the resident staff recalls being swept along with him to discover the source of a leaking pipe – and then left for some hours with his thumb in the hole after the Doctor himself had solved the problem and gone on to busy himself with something else!

He was a familiar, and greatly respected, figure among the groundsmen around the school estate, though sometimes a rather less than welcome one at site meetings during the big building schemes of the 1960s and 1970s. No suspect timber, no row of bricks out of true, escaped his penetrating gaze, and any contractor who tried to assert that: "nothing can be done now, Dr Humphreys", was likely to be reminded whose signature was required to release bills of payment. Indeed, six months before his retirement he triumphantly brought to the builder's attention a list of 104 matters requiring attention in the new Games Hall!

A typical morning in his study might have begun with the Bursar on the state of the school's investments, followed by a discussion with Willie Bradley about the health of the school tractor, and with Eddie Norris about a tripping fuse. ("Try a nail instead of fuse wire" was rumoured to have been the advice once!) Next might come an interview with a mother about her son's progress, a few minutes with Miss Moore analysing the price of potatoes and vegetables and then a phone call to the Ministry of Education to arrange another barn-storming visit to Belfast in search of more grant-aid for the next building project. At the Ministry, it should be added, he knew exactly who he needed to see, and he established a particularly good rapport with the Chief Building Officer. In their turn, officials soon found they were dealing with a man who had anticipated all their questions, and who knew exactly how to get what he wanted. Who but he, for example, could have persuaded them to fund new furniture as well as canteen extensions in 1967 - and then allow the school to use the existing tables and chairs to furnish the new library! Attempts to fob him off with anyone but his regular contacts would be met with a peremptory: "I haven't come all the way from Coleraine to see a clerk... If he's not available now, I'll just wait here until he is!"

Interviews with prospective staff could appear more like monologues about the greatness of the school – until the candidate realised just how much Humphreys had found out about him in the unguarded moments of the interview. "I don't ask for testimonials", he once said: "They aren't worth the paper they're written on – did you ever see a bad one?" He was never one to mince words either: one candidate for a History job was shown a sheaf of applications and told: "Historians are two a penny these days", while another was informed: "If I take you, your appointment will have to be ratified by the Governors – but round here they do what I tell them!" Some of the major reforms in university education towards the end of his career left him unimpressed. "I was interviewing a young man today and he told me he had modules of education and sociology... I told him I only employed people with proper degrees"!

Throughout his time in Coleraine he was actively connected in First Presbyterian Church where he served as an elder and latterly as Clerk of Session. A convinced evangelical, he involved himself enthusiastically in evangelistic outreach and was particularly supportive of The New Life Campaign of 1967. He was an accomplished and passionate preacher too, whom the Rev Brian Liddell could always call on to deputise in an emergency. On one such occasion, Humphreys was called on at short notice to lead the annual Remembrance Service. Momentarily forgetting that he was in the pulpit rather than the dais of the Assembly Hall, he concluded the formal act of remembrance with a peremptory: "Thank you – sit down," to the congregation!

His style was vigorous, occasionally ruthless, but there was a much softer side too. A member of the ancillary staff who had been through a difficult time was summoned to the office, given the keys of the Humphreys caravan in Donegal, and told to go and take a couple of days off. A young housemaster who had become rather too emotionally involved in a crisis was called over to the house early one Saturday morning, sat down by the Headmaster (in his pyjamas and dressing gown!) and given kindly advice about maintaining professional detachment. Parents of a promising boy who had their own family crisis were assured by Humphreys that, come what may, the boy's fees would be taken care of by "the pig fund". A vulnerable colleague in another school with personal problems found in Humphreys both a friend and a protector.

"If you knew all, you would forgive all," was his summary of this and similar cases. Just four situations, and they could be multiplied many times. He was also, of course, a devoted family man, and was inordinately proud of his two sons, his two daughters and of the growing family circle. In the latter years there would be big family gatherings every Sunday in the house, and the autocratic Headmaster would rapidly metamorphose into an indulgent grandfather. The gatherings continued at his retirement home in Portstewart, and at his last birthday celebration – a surprise party organised by the Governors to mark his eightieth – he was particularly touched by the presence of every single member of the wider family.

In relation to his teachers, he had a concept of professional development based on one of his favourite phrases – "a real professional schoolmaster", and he encouraged the staff to make the school as central to their lives as it was to his. Many of those he appointed cut their teeth in the expanding boarding school. Although burdened by a weight of duties which contemporary teachers would find nearly incredible, they were extremely well fed, and – even more important – they began their careers in a supportive community which helped many a young man find his feet and build his confidence. His vision of the staff was, admittedly, rather idealistic at times. One Sunday morning, he was most perturbed to find several clear marks of a football on the ceiling of the resident staffroom, and left instructions that the boys responsible were to be dealt with. It was just as well he didn't know how his young masters released some of their excess energy at lunchtime! On another occasion he rather astounded prospective parents during a tour of the school by exclaiming: "None of my young teachers either smoke or drink". A boarding school housemaster on the fringes of this conversation was heard to mutter discreetly in the ear of the visitors: "I think what the Headmaster means is, not during class."

Humphreys was very much a man of his time, a member of probably the last generation of heads who were captains of their own ship. His contemporaries were very much of the same mould – men like Victor Peskett of RBAI, John Frost of Sullivan, Louis Lord of BRA, John Cook of Campbell College, Randall Clarke of Bangor Grammar School and William Mol of Ballymena Academy. In the mellowness of retirement, he acknowledged that his skills were honed at a time when money was freely available and Principals unencumbered by equality legislation. He said more than once that in the atmosphere of the 1980s and 1990s he couldn't have survived – though one suspects that if he'd been put into such a situation at the start of his career, he would have coped with it well enough!

A Town And A School On The Verge Of Expansion

Although their personalities and management styles were very different, George Humphreys and William White had some things in common. Both had scientific backgrounds, both came as newcomers into the town from prestigious Belfast grammar schools, both were natural leaders, both created their own distinctive ethos within which they moulded and motivated their staff, both attached great importance to the boarding community within the school, and both came to personify Coleraine Inst within the local community. There were, of course, differences. Coleraine Inst from the 1920s to the 1950s saw itself very much as 'the town school' in a compact community, and William White managed a relatively small establishment in which he was able to combine teaching – which remained his first love – with personal supervision of the school's daily life. During White's headmastership the school expanded very significantly - from 129, including twenty-nine boarders, in 1927 to 408 including ninety-two boarders in 1955 – but the greater part of this expansion occurred as a result of the 1947 Education Act. As retirement approached, White felt vaguely uneasy about the increase in numbers, the quality of the intake and the whole brave new world of post war education.

In contrast, George Humphreys was primarily a manager and a builder who came to Coleraine at a time when the town was expanding. From

An aerial view of the school in the early 1950s, just before the major expansions of the Humphreys era began.

1. The handball alley.
2. Two storey science lab, demolished 1958: associated for some years with George Wilson and Arthur Nicholl.
3. Tennis courts.
4. The New Line, as this portion of the Castlerock Road was then universally known.
5. The vegetable plots. Some account of their productivity is included in this book.
6. The Headmaster's house.
7. The Sergeant's house, on the site of the present administration block.
8. The boarding school Matron's sitting room.
9. Major White's office, adjoining his classroom.
10. "The Gods". The top floor housed the biggest dormitory in the boarding school. Below were classrooms and the school's library.
11. Rooms 1 to 5. Room 3, in a central position, was for many years the venue for morning assembly.
12. The Ballycairn Road. At that time a leafy lane, it was substantially widened in 1971.
13. The old gymnasium, built in 1883 and demolished in the early 1960s to make room for extensions to the boarding school.
14. The piggery.
15. "Sausage Park". The major recreational area of the old school.
16. Dan Cunningham's physics lab.
17. A wooden classroom, where Tom Ryan and Maurice McDevitt taught competitively on either side of a thin partition wall!
18. "The Plaza". Nicknamed after the Belfast ballroom on account of its wood block floor, this was almost the first of the 1950s extensions to the school. For many years it was associated with Dr George Wilson.
19. The Sergeant's workshop – not only a maintenance facility, but also a teaching venue for junior woodwork.
20. Queens Park under construction.

his days at Campbell emerged one overarching desire, to build a very large school to equal anything in Belfast. Significantly, towards the end of his career, and with a school of some 1200 boys, he described The Inst to his Governors as 'big business'. Throughout his time the population of the Borough of Coleraine was expanding, with a steady increase in house building on the fringes of the town. During his first decade, housing along the Castlerock Road, the Ballycairn Road, Riverview Avenue and Queens Park was developing a large community virtually on the school's doorstep. By the time of his retirement in 1979 a much smaller proportion of the dayboys came from traditionally 'old Coleraine' families. Coincidentally, the boarding school enjoyed similar expansion, attracting a cosmopolitan intake and a particular link with Malaysia from the late 1960s onwards. At the close of his headmastership in 1979, a boarding school of almost 300 included forty-one Malaysian boys, four Arabs, one Indian, one Rhodesian and four boys from the United States.

Business and small industry were also expanding in the Coleraine of the 1950s and 1960s, and the school's development was intertwined with theirs. In the first years of Humphreys' headmastership B.K.S. Aerial Surveys was set up near to the school (and for a time rented two vacant huts on school premises for staff training), while the Chemstrand Factory negotiated way-leave through the school for an underground pipeline to the River Bann. Co-incidentally, one of his most outstanding appointments among the ancillary staff was Miss Anne Moore, of the family who owned the eponymous Foundry in Brook Street.

The twenty-four years of Humphreys' headmastership were also an expansionary period for Northern Ireland education, and we have already seen that the 1947 Act created a rising tide which launched many vessels. Across the Castlerock Road, Coleraine Intermediate School began operation in 1948 in the rather cramped buildings of the old Coleraine Model School. By 1955 it was in process of moving to a new campus which grew over twenty years into the Boys' and Girls' Secondary Schools, the former presided

over at its peak by Jack McDonald – himself an old boy of The Inst. Just over a decade after George Humphreys' arrival, the Christie Memorial Primary School opened in 1967 and rapidly became one of the Inst's biggest feeder schools. Further up the Castlerock Road, The Loreto Convent Grammar School was steadily growing, though as a girls' school it presented no direct competition to The Inst until the late 1970s when it became co-educational. For some years in the 1970s and 1980s, both Politics and German were taught to students of both schools at The Inst: so, strictly speaking, it could be claimed that for a short time Coleraine Inst was coeducational! At the far end of the town, and in many ways complementing The Inst, is Coleraine High School. Over many years there has always been friendly co-operation between the two, though even Humphreys trod carefully in his contacts with its formidable Principal, Miss Lilley. Both White and Humphreys would have been intrigued by the prospect of closer relations between the two schools which lay far away in the future. Most significantly, Coleraine became a university town during the 1960s, with important consequences for the school that will be touched upon later.

Expanding The Premises: A Fifteen Year Revolution

What, then, of the school which George Humphreys took over on the first day of term in September 1955? William White bequeathed him a healthy legacy. Numerically, the day school was growing, and, but for lack of space, many more boarders could easily have been enrolled. The post war problems with staffing had been solved, and the staff room had a solid core of well-qualified and experienced men. On the other hand, a growing school was in need of substantial capital investment after the shortages of the war years, and their brief experience of Schedule B semi-independence proved to the Governors that the school's financial needs were beyond their unaided resources. With the reversion to Schedule A status, Ministry of Education approval had already been granted for substantial extensions, and George Humphreys clearly relished having a major building scheme on hand as he

It might be too much to claim that the Model was loved by all those who boarded there, but during the peak years of the boarding department it provided much-needed space for up to 100 boys.

took office. Few but he could have foreseen the transformation of the following fifteen years, and not even he could have predicted that a change in Ministry of Education rules in 1968 would eventually give the school eighty per cent rather than sixty per cent of approved capital expenditure in return for Ministry nominees on the Board of Governors.

It might be added in parenthesis that some quite important changes were made to the constitution as well as the construction of the school in the 1960s. The traditional right of Institution members to nominate pupils for free places finally disappeared. In 1968 members as defined in the original Scheme were finally abolished, and Institution Governors were thereafter re-elected at Annual Meetings by Old Boys who qualified for membership by subscription to the school's funds. It was also stipulated that the President and Vice President of the Board must be former pupils of the school.

Realising that even the extensions already in hand were insufficient, the new Headmaster arranged to inspect the Model School, which Coleraine Intermediate School planned to vacate at Easter 1956. Further discussions with

the County Londonderry Education Board centred on Dr Forbes' substantial residence just across the Ballycairn Road from the school. The outcome was an agreement to rent the premises for two years as an extension to the boarding school, quickly followed by an agreement to rent four classrooms at the Old Model School – at a total cost of £100 p.a. including rates! With these temporary arrangements, the boarding school was increased to 130 in September 1956, and relocation allowed for a school library to be created in the bottom floor of the New Wing. Within a year the whole of the Model School had been acquired, giving the school nine additional teaching rooms and dormitory space for fifty-eight boys. The expansion of the boarding department in 1957 freed the old rooms six and seven in the New Wing as a dedicated school library, a facility recommended some years previously in a General Inspection Report. When the new library opened in 1968 the old library reverted to being a classroom, and in a slightly different configuration became the school's first drama studio in the 2003 rebuilding.

The foundation stone of the new assembly hall and classroom extension was laid on 4 June 1957 – one hundred years to the day since a

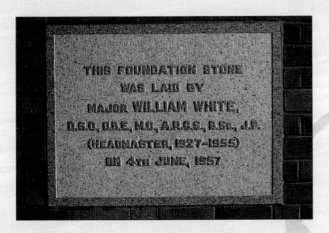

By the start of the new school year in September 1957 the boarding school had almost doubled in size during the first two years of the new headmastership, standing at 162 in a school community of 520 boys. On the first day of the new term a new school book room, directed by George Wilson and Irwin Rainey, distributed books and stationery to the value of £3000, although because of the non-completion of the new science labs the projected new school library had to be pressed into use as classroom accommodation.

similar ceremony for the foundation stone of the original school. Very appropriately, the ceremony was performed by Major White, wielding the same silver trowel used by Charles J. Knox, the local agent of the Clothworkers' Company, to lay the foundation stone of the original building a century earlier. He also unveiled two bronze plaques in the War Memorial Pavilion commemorating those who served and gave their lives in the two World Wars. Today these are located in the foyer between the Humphreys and Templeton Halls, and a further plaque unveiled within the Pavilion on the same day now resides in the School Museum. The same day also saw the formal unveiling of a clock on the War Memorial Pavilion commemorating the life of Dr S.J. Hunter.

The real headache at the start of the school year in 1958 was the late completion of the assembly hall and the new classroom block. The opening of school had to be put back by one week (to the later annoyance of both boys and staff this was not counted as part of the new term!). The new extension was opened on 18 September 1958 by Air Marshal Sir George Beamish. In addition to an assembly hall, the suite of buildings comprised a dayboys' kitchen and canteen, nine classrooms, three science labs and a bookstore. Rather less permanent than the buildings opened that day was the new school song which concluded the proceedings. Hugh Montgomery's words and James Moore's music were, sadly, not destined to join the established school songs of comparable institutions.

Major William White returned to Coleraine Inst on 4 June 1957 to lay the foundation stone of what was to become the office block and assembly hall – today the library.

Phone : Coleraine 497.

35 CHURCH STREET,

Coleraine, Sept 1st 1950

Mr Grant

TO MISS WOODS, DR.
BOOKSELLER AND STATIONER.

Concise School Arithmetic	6	0
School Algebra	5	6
Latin for today	4	9
Physical Basis Geography	2	9
Geog for today	4	9
Draw Flints &c Printing	4	6
Exercise Bk		7
Science ExerBk	3	6
Atlas	8	6
	1 0	0

With Thanks
1/9/50

Paid
Awbods
H.K.

**A reminder of the days before the school set up its bookroom, and boys had to go
Miss Woods' bookshop in Church Street (where Easons is today)
and make their own arrangements!**

During the same summer a large area of ground between the Manor House and Grove Shore pitches was drained and levelled to form an additional rugby pitch.

Reorganisation of dining facilities allowed the former day boys' canteen underneath the boarding department to be converted into a boarders' locker room, the availability of the science labs allowed the new library to come into full use, and further along the subterranean depths of the New Wing, some old store rooms became music practice rooms. As mentioned earlier, the newly-established B.K.S. Aerial Surveys company was granted permission to use two redundant huts at the Model for staff training: The Board was pleased to facilitate this, as they hoped B.K.S. might in time become a significant employer of former pupils.

The existence of an assembly hall made it possible to enhance the school's profile. In November 1958 it replaced Coleraine Town Hall as the customary venue for Prize Distribution. At Christmas 1958 there was a Festival of Nine Carols and Lessons, directed by Mr James Moore. This continued for over three decades, and in its time was one of the musical highlights of the Christmas period in the town. In February 1959 the school play "Badgers Green" was also performed in the assembly hall, and the annual Remembrance Service – formerly held in the open outside the War Memorial Pavilion – was transferred to the new hall. The British Association for the Advancement of Science held a public lecture for pupils from sixteen local grammar schools in the assembly hall, addressed by Sir Lawrence Bragg, a world famous physicist and Nobel laureate. During the first half of 1960 the BBC recorded "Sunday Half Hour" in the new hall, as well as "Top of the Form", a popular schools' quiz programme of the period. Coleraine Inst lost narrowly to Dungannon Royal School, but Humphreys reported that "the fee was used to buy two more paintings for our picture gallery in the library"!

An undated 1960s photograph of the choir, ready for the annual carol service.
The Director of Music, seen at the far right, was Mr James Moore,
organist of First Coleraine Presbyterian church and a noted figure
in the wider world of music in the town and the Province.

Introductory Music ..... "Christmas Pasterale"

Congregational Hymn – "Once in Royal David's City"
(Words on Separate Sheet)

PRAYER   – The Headmaster .

1st LESSON :: God announceth in the Garden of Eden
His plan for a Saviour.

  READER   : N.P. Williams – LIA

  CAROLS   : Question Carol (Appalachian)
Soloists – R. McNeill   LIC
          R.A.J. Stuart IIID

         : The Truth from above (Trad)
Soloists – D.A.L. Miller LIIA
          R.A.J. Stuart   IIID

2nd LESSON :: Isaiah the Prophet foretelleth the
coming of Messiah.

  READER   : S.C. Black – LIIA

  CAROLS   : "A Silver Bell" (Irish)
: "Ding dong, merrily on high" (French)

3rd LESSON :: The Prophet Micah foreseeth the
Glory of Little Bethlehem.

  READER   : D. McClarty – IIIB

  CAROLS   : "How far is it to Bethlehem" (Modern)
: "Whence is that goodly fragrance?"

4th LESSON :: The Angel Gabriel announceth to
Mary the birth of her son Jesus.

  READER   : D.R.O. Redman – IV

  CAROL   : Gabriel's Message (Basque)

5th LESSON :: St. Luke's record of the Birth
of Christ.

  READER   : R.W. Burns – V

  CAROLS   : Still the Night (Gruber)
: Cradle Song   (Schubert)

6th LESSON :: The Angel announceth to the
Shepherds the birth of Jesus.

  READER   : S.E.J. Henderson – UVI

Congregational Hymn – "While Humble Shepherds"
(Words on separate sheet)

7th LESSON :: The Shepherds come to the manger.

  READER   : Mr. K. Cushion, M.A.

  CAROLS   : O Hasten ye Shepherds. (German)
: Shepherds Rejoice   (French)

8th LESSON :: The Wise Men are led by a Star
to the Infant King.

  READER   : Mr. T.D. Surgenor, M.A.

  CAROL   : "We Three Kings of Orient are"
(Hopkins)
Soloists – M.J. Doherty LIIA
         D.A.L. Miller LIIA
         A.J.W. McConaghy LIIA

9th LESSON :: St. John unfoldeth the great
mystery of the Incarnation.

  READER   : The Headmaster

  CAROL   : The Cowboy Carol (arr. Sargent)

PRAYER   – The Headmaster

Congregational Hymn – "Hark the Herald Angels
Sing."

BENEDICTION

RECESSIONAL MUSIC .... Christmas Processional
(Moore)

One of the major innovations of the 1960s was the annual Carol service, which regularly
attracted audiences which more than filled the school assembly hall on the Sunday before
Christmas. This is the programme for the 1966 service.

The centenary service was held in the school on 12 May 1960. In the front row of this official photograph are Mrs Humphreys, The Rev. Dr John Legate, Dr George Humphreys, Mrs White, Major William White and Mr Bill Henry, President of the Institution.

As the 1960s approached, it was clear that Humphreys was only warming to the task. Two additional classrooms were now planned for the Model School, and during the summer holidays, room 5 was also converted into a general science lab, largely through the efforts of the ever-resourceful Willie Vincent. Additional tennis courts and rugby pitches were also under construction, and by January 1960 the decision was taken to build a new gymnasium, with a new boarders' dining room on the site of its predecessor. With future boarding extensions in mind, Humphreys had the old gym's foundations surveyed, and concluded that they could probably support a two-storey building. Willie Vincent was appointed clerk of works for the gymnasium and boarding extension schemes, which would eventually comprise a dining hall with a new dormitory and sick bay block above, as well as accommodation for the resident catering staff. Due to slippages in the builders' schedule, the gym and the new boarding extensions – including three dormitories, a sick bay and a dining hall — were not opened until 18 October 1962, by the Rev Dr D.C. Henderson, Deputy Chaplain General to the Forces, and a former pupil of the school. In the meantime, some of the unfinished dormitories had to be pressed into use in September to accommodate

the 226 boarders whom Humphreys had enrolled. Optimistically he claimed this figure was "optimum" and that he would now begin turning applicants away. Those who knew their man seriously doubted this one, and sure enough, in late 1962 The Board authorised Humphreys to take soundings in the overseas market for the recruitment of even more boarders!

The Rev Dr D.C. Henderson, officially opening the boarding school extensions including a new dining hall.
18 October 1962.

Even after a six year surge of building, the school was still bulging at the seams. Two further science labs were urgently needed. The dayboys' canteen, built to hold 250, was now feeding 320 each day, with room 13 being used as an overflow, and extensions to the dining area and kitchens were needed within two years. In 1964 the two redundant huts at The Model were back in use as classrooms. Ministry authorisation was agreed for two new biology labs, a lecture theatre and a staff room. In 1965 the boarders' dining hall was expanded by the creation of a long alcove to seat 100 boys, additional dormitory accommodation was created at The Model, and the biology block was in use. Parallel to these developments, plans were in the pipeline for a new pavilion and boat house, the acquisition of land for additional sports pitches, and the construction of a groundsman's bungalow.

In parenthesis, it might be noted that in the more relaxed 1960s, the bungalow was mostly built by the school's maintenance men under Willie Vincent's direction, and both the Water Commissioners and the N.I. Electricity Board readily agreed to their mains supplies being diverted to service the new house! Equally helpful were three local builders. When the school acquired thirty acres to lay out new pitches, Kennedy's, Maxwell's and Doherty's all agreed to dump excavated soil *gratis*, to facilitate levelling of the new playing surfaces, and Joe Kennedy went as far as promising to fill one deep hollow and level the new pitches, free of charge. The familiar topography of the top plateau, middle terrace and bottom plateau testify to this day to the quality of the work. Further recycling assisted the foundations of the river pavilion, with hard core from demolished houses being dumped into reclaimed swampland.

Also at this time the main driveway was widened and paved on each side, though a proposal to widen the Ballycairn Road drive, and re-site the sandstone Memorial Arch at its entrance, was turned down. Also rejected on the Headmaster's advice was a proposal in 1962 to purchase Holm Lea, the substantial house adjacent to the school, and establish a Prep School. Only once again did the idea

Opening of the new classroom block and swimming pool by Dr N.A. Burgess, Vice Chancellor of the New University of Ulster. 9 Feb 1967.

of a Prep School resurface, though as a last resort in connection with the threat of major educational change in the late 1970s. This will be explored further in the next chapter.

By the end of 1964 proposals for a new ten classroom block, including a language laboratory and an indoor swimming pool, were in the hands of the Ministry of Education, and building started in 1965. Delays in the completion of this project caused short-term problems at the start of the school year in September 1966, with the two faithful Model huts pressed into use again, classes being held in the assembly hall and on its stage (leading to the cancellation of the school play), and even the staff room and the gymnasium having to be taken out of use to store equipment arriving for the new projects. An increase in the pace of work may have had something to do with the Headmaster's intervention at the end of the summer holidays. As he reported to the Governors: "No overtime was being worked until the middle of August when I went to a site meeting and threatened the imposition of a penalty clause if the building was not finished within a reasonable period."! By the beginning of 1967 the new classrooms were ready, and although the river pavilion and boat house were not complete, the oarsmen were using the new training tank. The official opening of the classroom block performed by Dr Allan Burgess, Vice Chancellor of N.U.U., took place on 9 February 1967, and as an indication of the school's growing status, the Duke and

Three views taken during the visit of the Duke and Duchess of Kent to the school on 2 May 1968. The royal visitors signed the visitors books of the school and the Borough of Coleraine, and following the naming ceremony for the new rowing 8 "Slieve na Mona", the Duke tried his hand in the rowing tank of the newly opened boat house.

Duchess of Kent officially opened the River Pavilion during a Royal Visit to the Borough of Coleraine in December. Restrictions following an outbreak of Foot and Mouth Disease led to the postponement of the Visit in December 1967, and the opening took place in May 1968. In the midst of this building, still further extensions were progressing from the planning to the building stage. Agreement was reached in 1967 with the Ministry of Education to grant-aid a new assembly hall including a Board Room (a hard-driven bargain, with the Governors having to find only £5.600 of the estimated cost of £52.500) and the conversion of the existing assembly hall into a school library. The first steps were taken towards the building of four new science labs – all the more necessary since in September 1967 the school had achieved its first six stream entry of 158 first year boys. As the boarding school also showed every sign of continuing expansion, Humphreys produced possibly his boldest proposal - a block of thirty-three bed-sit studies for the senior boarders, after the fashion of university halls of residence. Even as the plans were being drawn up, it was decided to add a further storey, to give a total of forty-four studies and two staff bedrooms. In addition, a simpler piece of internal conversion turned the old boarders' dining hall into six new studies. Intriguingly, the only scheme which Humphreys planned but never executed was one to partition the huge "Gods" into three smaller dormitories. In later years, many a young resident master trying to keep order among twenty-eight lively adolescents in one huge communal bedroom might have wished this plan had been implemented! One less well-known scheme in 1967 was the building of an animal house "to remove the smell from the Biology labs". This rather curiously named building harks back to the days when it was still legal for schools to breed their own rats and mice for eventual dissection practice by A level students.

Almost inevitably, with two different firms handling the contracts for the library and the assembly hall, perfect synchronisation was not quite achieved and at the start of the school year the new library was in operation before the assembly hall was complete. "I found it

Dr Humphreys with the Prime Minster of Northern Ireland, Capt. Terence O'Neill, who officially opened the Assembly Hall, Sixth Form Centre and Library, 25 October 1968.

very difficult to start the school year, with so many new arrangements, without being able to address the boys. However by many and devious methods we were able to transmit the gist of the new rules and regulations consonant with the changes taking place", reported the Headmaster to the Governors! Those changes involved the addition of three small classrooms along a new balcony in the library, the conversion of the old stage into a classroom and library office, the conversion of the old library into a classroom, the reconfiguration of the general office and the Vice Principal's office, the creation of an upstairs waiting room, and the relocation of offices for the Headmaster and his secretary and the Bursar and his administrative staff. An ingenious hands-free intercom system (now preserved in the school museum) allowed the Headmaster to communicate with the entire administrative area, while access to his study was guarded by a mini traffic light with three coloured push-buttons lettered "Enter", "Wait" and "Engaged". Most callers, though, simply knocked and waited to hear what response came from the familiar voice within! On 25 October 1968 the school welcomed another distinguished guest, in this case the Prime Minister of Northern Ireland, the Rt.Hon. Terence O'Neill, who officially opened the new assembly hall, canteen extensions, sixth form study area and library.

Before the 1960s ended, the next stage of building began with plans for a new science corridor to link the biology labs with the classrooms in the swimming pool block, and a block of twenty-two new studies down the side of the gym. Its completion created a total of 130 study places and forty-four bedsits, and guaranteed every boarder in the fifth and sixth forms, as well as some fourth year boarders in The Model, either a personal or a shared study to work in. Few other Irish boarding schools had such a generous proportion of studies. The new labs and studies were officially opened on 28 October 1970 by Mr Ronald Groves of Dulwich College. In not much more than ten years the school had been totally transformed, and a new decade began with 975 boys, 316 of them boarders. The era of "Sausage Park" now seemed very ancient history indeed!

Getting Results

Those familiar with the pace of curriculum change in the 21st century might be surprised to discover that even in the 1950s and 1960s there was an undercurrent of change. In these decades there were major changes in the certificate examinations and in the awarding of university scholarships, and within the school the new Headmaster sought to diversify and improve. In those far-off days, representatives of local companies regularly toured the school to encourage boys to apply for industrial scholarships, and when B.K.S. Aerial Surveys opened in Coleraine they were willing to employ up to ten boys each year with good A levels in the Sciences or Geometrical Drawing. Within three years of Humphreys' arrival boys were gaining scholarships awarded by British Thompson Houston, and the Pye Radio Company's factory in Larne. Following the implementation of the Anderson Committee report in 1962, all Northern Ireland university students qualified for a Local Education Authority grant, and indeed for the next two decades the universities relied on local and central government for almost ninety per cent of their funding. In 1955, just ten boys went on to university after leaving Coleraine Inst: by 1965 almost seventy sought university entrance on the basis of exam results. While the school regretted losing the kudos of State Exhibitions and Bursaries (and the universities at first feared that increased grants might affect the quality of their intake), L.E.A. scholarships enabled many more boys to go to University. On the other hand, the success of Boyd Mullan and Richard Bennett (later to become a member of staff at C.A.I. and finally Headmaster of Portora) in the 1961 Trinity College Dublin scholarship exams prompted Humphreys to express confidence that "these successes in the Modern and Classical sides are the first fruits of our policy to encourage more boys of the right aptitude in this direction."

In 1963 the Northern Ireland General Certificate of Education was introduced, and in the process the Ordinary Level syllabus was reduced from six years to five, and Advanced Level increased from one year to two – thus ensuring that the size of the sixth form was bound to increase. The Senior Certificate ceased to be necessary for university matriculations, so the focus in reporting results shifted to the number of credits and distinctions awarded in individual subjects. One consequence of the new exam system was that schools in the United Kingdom could enter candidates for any examining board they chose. Concern about pass-rates in a number of Northern Ireland GCE Board exams, led Humphreys to establish an examining centre in Coleraine for the Associated Examining Board from December 1965 onwards. This gave some boys the chance of a repeat exam in January (a facility not offered in the Northern Ireland system), and this, coupled with the creation of "Lower 6 Remove", a small class of boys repeating the entire O level exam in their sixth year at the school, further enhanced overall pass-rates.

At the other end of the scale, award of the Junior Certificate examination at the end of form 3 automatically qualified fee-payers who had failed the eleven plus, and as Humphreys pointed out in 1961: "This will save their parents an aggregate of £1350 in fees for the rest of their school careers". This was no small issue, given that during the first five years of the new Headmastership the percentage of qualified boys in the school rose to eighty per cent. As the Junior Certificate declined

An early 1960s view of a growing staff,
many of whom spent their entire careers at Coleraine Inst.

in importance, it became possible for boys to review on the school's recommendation, based on the results of internal exams. In 1963 Humphreys reckoned that the exam would gradually disappear, and indeed in 1964 the decision was taken to abandon it. As the school expanded, the annual certificate examinations became a logistical problem, and as early as 1959 the assembly hall, gym, workshop and junior school canteen, in addition to some classrooms, were in use for Junior and Senior Certificate exams. By 1965, though, the days of the Junior Certificate were numbered, and as it became little more than a subject examination the decision was taken to phase it out in the school altogether.

Within the school, the 1960s saw an increase in the non-qualified intake. From the early 1960s dates an internal test given to the whole form 1 intake in English and Arithmetic in the first week of the term, on the basis of which boys were be streamed into sets. Humphreys was always interested to see how well these results correlated with the qualified or non-qualified status of the new boys. When the examination was introduced he told the Governors: "We will make an analysis of our own results and compare them with this year's qualifying exam results. We expect to find some interesting anomalies." Anomalies or not, the September classification examination continued for the rest of his headmastership.

"My Young Men..."

Reference was made earlier to George Humphreys' "young men", and in the 1950s and 1960s he built up a team of masters who either stayed for lengthy periods or went on to hold very senior positions in other schools. John Leslie, Robert Riddell and David Todd came in 1956, Cecil Henderson, Trevor Surgenor, Jim Brennan and Denis Jagoe the following year, and Bob McIvor, Donald McKay and R.G. McKay (no relation) in 1958. Jimmy Shaw, David Caskey and Ian McNeill came in 1959. 1960 brought Robin Semple (like Donald McKay and Robert Riddell, a former pupil) back to Coleraine Inst from a position in Omagh Academy.

Existing members of the staff room won recognition in various fields. In 1960 Bob McIvor and Hugh Montgomery were adjudged by Sir Tyrone Guthrie to be the Ulster best amateur actors of the year, an accolade later also bestowed on Denis Jagoe. In 1961 Arthur Nicholl, that famously innovative and highly successful head of department, spent the summer vacation with a team of Ulster teachers who travelled to Nigeria to instruct local teachers in A level teaching methods. The white suits which Arthur purchased for his trip attracted much attention around the school on his return in September!

A group of young staff at the 1958 Prize Distribution.
Left to right are Edgar Charlton, Bob McIvor, Normal Maxwell (who supplied the photograph), David Todd, John Leslie and Trevor Surgenor.

In 1962 Brian McGarvey, yet another former pupil, was appointed to the Chemistry Department, and Bob Caswell, with experience both of the Presbyterian ministry and the principalship of Belfast Bible College, assumed the headship of the R.E. Department – a position he retained until his retirement. The third new member of staff that year was George Hanns. Outstanding academic ability and an engaging eccentricity of character made him both a popular colleague and a highly respected teacher. In 1963 came Jim Flanagan and Eric Hayes, two Collegians who were also to spend a lifetime in the service of Coleraine Inst. 1964 brought John Birch, Ken Cushion and Sam McClements to the staff, and in 1966 came Richard Bennett and Des Giffin (both Old Boys) along with Tom Moore and Harold McCullough, and the legendary Jim Foote as head of P.E.

Jim came from the 'other' Inst, and devoted the rest of his career to the school and also to the sporting life of the town, particularly to Coleraine Amateur Swimming Club. Not the least of Jim's lasting contributions to school life was the institution of an annual swimming gala in 1967, which became possible with the opening of the new swimming pool. 1968 saw the first appearance of CAI at the Ulster Schools' Swimming Championships, and the story of competitive swimming will be taken further in the next chapter.

In 1967 Joe Brown, Dermot Jennings and Jim Archer joined the staff, and the following year Jimmy Gordon came from Royal School Dungannon, along with Jack Rowbottom, Wesley Ferguson, Sid Grey and Nevin Taggart. As the 1960s drew to a close, Brendan Drummond arrived in 1969 to begin many years of distinguished work as the School's Director of Music, along with Tommy Blair, Gavin Craig and Jimmy Stewart. Other men came for brief periods, but all save nine of those named above spent the greater part of their careers at the school, and of the others, five became Headmasters, one a head of department in Cookstown High School, while two others moved to positions in university education and the Schools' Inspectorate. At the other end of the scale, Gordon Mahony officially retired in 1959, but when the present authors joined the staff in 1971 he was still doing some part-time teaching. George Humphreys, like William White before him, had a soft spot for "Caesar", particularly after the death of his wife. Until his final illness in 1970s the old man continued to toddle happily in for his lunch each day as the school's guest and to delight the staffroom with his outspoken views on history and politics!

The staff in 1965.

Boarding School Organisation

As the boarding department expanded and developed on a split site, it was reorganised into three main areas in 1957. Junior House had fifty-seven boys, staffed by Edgar Charlton and Norman Maxwelll; Middle House with fifty-eight boys run by Donald McDonagh and Robert Riddell; and Senior House of forty-six boys under the direction of John Leslie and Davie Todd. The former sick room and the south dorm were now rather grandly termed "The School Hospital" (a name which, like its location, didn't last very long), and the Model School comprised four classrooms and four dormitories. As boarding numbers increased, the house system gradually consolidated. By the mid 1960s, New House (Arthur Nicholl), Junior House (Donald McDonagh), Middle House (Jim Brennan) and Senior House (Denis Jagoe) were operational, under the control of a Housemaster, two resident staff and a group of prefects. As the boarding school reached its peak size, the number of Houses was increased and the Houses renamed after local beauty spots and tourist attractions. Benone and Kenbane (forms 1 and 2), Dunluce and Runkerry (forms 3 and 4, in the Model School) and Rathlin and Ramore (forms 5

and Lower 6) was an attractive set of names: strangely, the new bedsit block was known only as "Senior House". The original Housemasters were Arthur Nicholl, Jim Brennan, Donald McDonagh and David Todd. Denis Jagoe, Robin Semple and Donald McKay were added to the team later in the 1960s as the boarding school expanded, and Sam McClements became the first Housemaster of the new Senior House. Jim Brennan, David Todd and Denis Jagoe were in turn replaced by John Leslie, Bob McIvor and Jim Flanagan. At the start of the 1970s the team of Housemasters comprised Donald McKay, Arthur Nicholl, Robin Semple, Donald McDonagh, John Leslie, Jim Flanagan and Sam McClements.

1960 saw the formation of the Fifth Coleraine Scout Troop (C.A.I.). Mainly associated with the boarding school over many years, it was founded by Mr Roy McKay, and staff involved over the years included Bob Caswell, Jim Flanagan, Eric Hayes and Dermot Jennings, latterly with help from former pupil Ken Boyd, of a family intimately associated with the school. For the record, Coleraine Inst's first two Queen's Scouts were Jimmy McArthur and "The Milky Bar Kid" Ferguson. The demise of scouting in the 1990s mirrored the

Boarding School 1960.

gradual decline of the boarding department, but many boarders still look back to those Friday nights of "The Wide Game" and the long summer evenings of camps in the Scottish Highlands and the Isle of Man.

One of the boarders' rare opportunities to leave school (legitimately!) during the week was on Saturday evenings. From 1956 until the school's own swimming facilities opened in 1968 Coleraine Inst reserved the pool at the Northern Counties Hotel on Saturday evenings for a "swimming club", initially supervised by Dan Cunningham and Maurice MacDevitt. Resident staff had mixed memories of accompanying a double-deck bus of lively adolescents to Portrush and back, and of supervising them for the hour they were in the water. One teacher the boys did not trifle with was the late Robert Riddell, a strong swimmer who took some exercise himself during the sessions. On one occasion, an unwise boy attempted to pull Robert under, only to find himself being held below the surface for rather longer than he preferred! Until the mid 1960s, the club's sole non-recreational activity was in preparing boys for the Royal Life Saving Society's awards, supervised for many years by Dan Cunningham. With the building of the school's own pool, competitive swimming began around 1968, and more is recorded later on this.

Keeping The Place Running

At the beginning of his headmastership, Humphreys relied on a small group of people to run the office and the ancillary services. The matron was effectively responsible for the running of every aspect of the Boarding School, there was a small office staff of three girls, and a supervisor for the dayboys' canteen. The school's accounts were managed by the school accountant, Mr R.F.Steedman, from his office in the town, and indeed Board Meetings were held, and most decision making done, in the Town Hall. As the school expanded, so did the need for additional staff and broader structures, and the building of a new administration block in 1958 allowed a thorough re-vamping of services. Following R.F. Steedman's retirement in 1956 a bursar's department was set up within the school, initially managed on a part time basis by Albert Clarke. Albert was, of course, Vice Principal, but when he retired from the teaching staff in 1965 he became full-time bursar, retaining this position for a further five years. He was succeeded as bursar and estates manager by Colin Beck, himself a former pupil. Albert and Colin also filled the position of Clerk to the Board of Governors, a responsibility that to this day devolves upon the school's bursar. The Headmaster's secretary had her own (albeit tiny) office adjacent to a small upstairs waiting

**Albert Clarke's retirement in the 1960s
ended an era in our history.
This picture captures Albert's
tranquil equanimity!**

Between 1957 and 1959 Miss Eleanor Logan was the boarding caterer. "Greater variety in menus and improved quality of cooking" were soon apparent, as was a more settled attitude among the domestic staff who, it will be recollected, had been rather unsettled towards the end of the White era. In 1959 Miss Anne Moore was appointed boarding school caterer. A former pupil of Coleraine High School, she first came to Humphreys' notice as catering superintendent at Ormiston House in Campbell College, and at the time of her appointment she was House Keeper to Queens Elms Hostel at Queens University Belfast. Her appointment brought to Coleraine Inst a formidable manager, and by the mid 1970s her small kitchen was turning out upwards of a thousand meals a day for the boys, as well as three cooked meals of superb quality for the resident staff. A year after Miss Moore's appointment, Miss Doreen Stinson assumed responsibility for dayboy catering. To her fell the responsibility of managing the huge increase in dayboy lunches over the following three decades.

room outside the Headmaster's office. The cosy seclusion of their premises did not, however, prevent two of Humphreys' secretaries from being successfully wooed by a couple of his 'young men'!

In relation to the ancillary staff, some very long-lasting appointments were made during Humphreys' first two decades. Along with Willie Vincent, men like Willie Bradley, Eddie Norris, James Black, Edwin McCloskey, Joe Moffatt, Bertie Vance and Willis Glass developed a tradition which kept the school grounds, buildings and science labs in immaculate condition. At the beginning of an auspicious new year 1958, Miss E.M.Gilmore, formerly of Portora Royal School and with 14 years' experience of boarding school management, succeeded Miss Johnston as matron of the boarding school. It is an indication of inflation over the succeeding years that the Governors agreed to pay Miss Johnston a pension of £2 a week! Miss Gilmore proved to be a highly successful and very long-term appointment, and by her retirement in 1984 she had served for almost the whole of two Headmasterships.

At the other end of the scale, Hugh Murdock, one time coachman to the Headmaster, retired in 1956, the same year that Miss A.S. Boal, boarding school matron from 1926 to 1942, passed away.

**Willie Vincent – the last school Sergeant
– receives a presentation from Dr George
Humphreys following his retirement.**

Tug of war team 1959.

The Sporting Explosion Of The 1950s And 1960s

Rugby and cricket were the school's founding sports, joined after 1928 by rowing. We have already seen that during the 1930s cricket had a long period in the doldrums, and for many years the more athletic boys played rugby during the winter, and rowed during the summer months. The first fifteen years of the Humphreys headmastership saw not only a physical expansion of the school campus, but also a broadening of the range of sports available to the boys. He had three simple criteria for 'new' sports activities: they should be coached by dedicated men; they should be successful; and (it has to be said) they should be seen to pose no threat to the 'established' sports of rugby, cricket and rowing. While the relationship between 'new' and 'old' sports was sometimes strained, the provision of a wide variety of sporting activity greatly enhanced the school's reputation and was – of course – a major selling point as the school expanded. On 21 March 1962 an Honours Committee was established to fix the conditions for the award of a new – and very distinctive – blue honours blazer. The original eligible sports were rugby, cricket, rowing, athletics and tennis, and later harriers (formerly cross country) was added to the list. The original regulations governing the honours system is reproduced here, and it is salutary to note the prices obtaining at that time for honours blazers and ties!

Inevitably, individual staff put their own stamp on particular activities, none more so than the school's rugby directorate. Tom Ryan,

Ronnie McPherson, John Birch, John Leslie and Jim Foote led a dedicated team of rugby coaches during a period which, by 1968, saw the game being played competitively right down to Under Twelve level (some years before Coleraine RFC began the mini rugby experiment). Although the Schools' Cup eluded Coleraine Inst for the entire duration of Humphreys' headmastership, there were semi-final appearances in 1956 and 1957, and in 1966 a narrow defeat in the final by Campbell College. Among many hundreds of boys who wore the cardinal red jersey, many names stand out, of whom there is space only for a skimming. Brian Fillis captained the First XV for three successive seasons from 1964 until 1967 – a record equalled only by one D.Ogilvy in 1888-91. His rugby career was unique in another respect, in that he also captained both the only Medallion team to win the Shield (in 1963), and the only Coleraine Inst squad ever to win the prestigious Roehampton Sevens in 1965. The team coach on that occasion

Brian Fillis, one of only two boys to have captained the First XV for three successive seasons.

For many years the tug of war between present and past pupils was a keenly contested event. These pictures from the 1959 sports day, supplied by Mr Jim Cameron, illustrate something of the atmosphere of the event.

From the Summer of 1962, a new School Blazer, to be known as an "Honours Blazer", together with a matching "Honours Tie", may be worn by Boys and Old Boys who have represented the School at Rugby, Cricket, Rowing, Athletics or Tennis.

Design.   **Blazer:**   Plain, Single-breasted, Hopsack material.
Colour - Light Royal Blue.   Two chrome buttons.

Badge: Three Shields embroidered in White, Red and Black silk thread.

Date and Club: The year of first award, and team or Club embroidered in Silver Wire.   (See below).

Total Cost: Approximately £8. 15s.

Tie: Terylene.   Light Royal Blue ground, with narrow Red, White and Navy stripes.

Cost: Approximately 8s. 6d.

Conditions of Award.   The Honours Blazer and/or Tie may only be worn by Boys recommended by the Captain of the sport involved, and approved by an Honours Committee, consisting of the five masters in charge of games, under the chairmanship of the Headmaster.

The minimum qualifications, (except in exceptional circumstances) for the award of Honours, are as follows:-

Rugby: 75% of all matches played by the 1st XV;

Cricket: 75% of all matches played by the 1st XI;

Rowing: All races in one season for the 1st VIII, *Amended to 75% of all races for 1st VIII + 1st or 2nd IV* or Two seasons as Cox of the 1st VIII; *1 meritorious season as Cox if a large no. of races were involved.*

Athletics: Two Seasons representing the School at County *at least one of which must be* level in the Open Class as a full member of the Athletic Club;

Tennis: Each year's team will be considered on its merits.

Harriers: *75% of all Senior Races: Finished in first 6 in 3 inter-school races or third of field in 2 AHA Senior Races*

In every case the Honours Committee will have the final say, and fulfilment of the above qualifications may not necessarily result in the award of Honours.   *normally to be considered only after 2 seasons with the Senior Team.*

Old Boys.   Any Old Boy who considers himself entitled to wear an Honours Blazer and/or Tie must apply to "The Secretary of the Honours Committee", c/o the School, stating the Year and Game in which he satisfied the necessary conditions.   The Committee will then decide whether or not the claim should be recognised.

Supply.   Each Boy or Old Boy whose Honours Claim is approved by the Honours Committee will be issued with an official certificate authorising the purchase of a Blazer and/or Tie. This certificate should be presented to Messrs T.D. Macready & Sons, Bridge Street, Coleraine, who will supply the Blazer and/or Tie, at the applicant's expense, and retain the certificate.

NO HONOURS BLAZER OR TIE CAN BE SUPPLIED WITHOUT

AN OFFICIAL CERTIFICATE.

Lettering on Pocket :   The letters "C. A. I." will be across the top of the pocket, with the Year of the first award immediately underneath, and just above the Badge.   The Initial Letters of not more than two of the Games Clubs, for which Honours have been awarded, will be below the Badge.   The Clubs are "R.F.C.",   "C.C.",   "R.C.",   "A.C.",   "T.C."   *"H.C."*
Oarsmen may have Crossed Oars behind the Badge.

The honours system, with its distinctive blue blazer, was introduced in 1962. This is the original specification, with handwritten additions by Mickey Eyre following the extension of the system to cover the Harriers Club.

Coleraine Inst won the prestigious Roehampton Schools' Sevens tournament in 1965. Captained by Brian Fillis, the team included Tim Stewart, Ivan Archibald, Alex Gibson, Terry Smith, Adrian Mencarelli, Sam Holley, Victor Outram and Joe Sweeney.

was John Birch, who only five years earlier, in his last year at school, had captained the victorious RBAI team of 1960. One of many congratulatory messages received by Brian Fillis was a letter from one H.A.Cox, a member of the Schools' Cup winning team of 1896!

Of several boys who achieved Ulster selections, Johnston Redpath in 1962-3 and Keith Patton in 1968-69 achieved the captaincy of Ulster sides. In 1956-57 no fewer than four boys - A.L.C. McCarter, G.C. Spotswood, B.T. Ferguson and A.C. McElhinney – donned white jerseys, and in 1959 – 60 there were three: John Nicholl, George Crawford and Samuel Moore. Finally, in 1966-67 no fewer than five Coleraine Inst boys played together for the Ulster schools: Brian Fillis, Timothy Stewart, Iain McDonald, George Crilly and Jimmy Leitch – a record not equalled again for many years. Rather surprisingly, in view of the school's very high reputation in the world of rugby, Coleraine Inst had no schoolboy international selections in this period, nor did any Old Boy ever achieve an Irish cap.

Tragically, untimely death claimed two of the school's most talented players during their sixth form days at school. Sammy Moore, who played three successive seasons on the First XV, died after a short illness, on 6 August 1961. Kenneth Morrison, who had moved

directly from the captaincy of the Medallion to a place on the First XV, died very suddenly on 18 March 1968. The loss of two popular and talented boys cast a shadow over the whole school community.

Samuel Lyons Moore was still in the sixth form when he died suddenly in 1961. He was in his third year as a member of the First XV and his passing stunned the entire school community.

211

Two glimpses of the action in the 1967 Schools' Cup quarter final between
Coleraine Inst and Rainey Endowned School Magherafelt.

GPO ⬤ GREETINGS TELEGRAM

6. GTG 9.38 ARMAGH PO 34/32=   GREETINGS=

BRIAN FILLIS CAPTAIN COLERAINE A1   1 ST FIFTEEN
RAVENHILL RUGBY GROUND BELFAST=

BEST WISHES FOR A GOOD GAME AND A CLEAR WIN
HOPE TO SEE SAM DROP A GOAL= J I BRENNAN

A piece of communications history in itself, this is the telegram which arrived at Ravenhill for Brian Fillis on the day of the 1966 Schools' Cup final. The sender was Jim Brennan, who had recently moved from Coleraine Inst to be Headmaster of the Royal School, Armagh.

For the rowing club this period began quietly, but developed quite dramatically. The school's oarsmen rowed from Bann Rowing Club's boathouse, and some of the school's small fleet of boats dated back to the 1930s. Maurice MacDevitt did some coaching and administration, and the school was greatly indebted to two particular friends for help with training: Johnny Leonard, and Mr Henry Clarke M.P. – a flamboyant character if ever there was one. The stream of lively instruction flowing from his bicycle along the riverside was characterised as a mixture of "advice, condemnation and even at times damnation"! To this enthusiastic mixture was added one essential ingredient: a new member of staff young enough to have recent experience of rowing for the school, and totally committed to its development. That man was R.A. ("Mickey") Eyre, and he rapidly put his own stamp on the developing club. His death in May 2010, as this book was going to press, was in many ways the end of an era in the school's history. In 1958 a new clinker eight "Ballycairn" was launched. In the following season winter training was inaugurated, assisted by an ingenious two seater tub – the product of lab technician Edwin McCloskey's

inventive genius – which was installed in the boarding school plunge. Further additions came to the fleet in the shape of the clinker eight "Ballysally" in May 1962, a fine eight "Cooldarragh" and a clinker four "Ratheane" in May 1964 and a fine four "Slieve na Mona" in 1968. The naming of "Slieve na Mona" coincided with the opening of the school's own boathouse, bringing to an end almost forty years of sharing Bann boathouse.

Hard training and new boats accelerated the pace of success. On 20 May 1961 The Wray Cup was won for the first time in seventeen years – albeit in "Kitty", one of Bann's boats! Wray Cup victories were recorded again in 1965 and 1968, and the elusive Craig Cup was captured in 1969. The tally of regatta trophies began to mount year on year, and some particular successes will long be remembered. In 1963, Coleraine Inst sent a crew to Henley Royal Regatta for the first time. In 1964 the First VIII became the first ever recipients of the I.A.R.U. Schools Union Trophy, and in the same year the First IV were victors in the schools fours race at Dublin Metropolitan Regatta. Finally, in 1968 and again in 1969, the first eight was chosen to row for Ireland in the Quadrangular

International. They didn't win, but the sight of eight oarsmen wearing their green vests, with oars specially repainted to match, set the seal on fifteen years of development.

Largely under John Leslie's guidance, cricket retained its historic position within the school during this period. Surprisingly, the first ever cricket tour – to Dublin, playing St Andrews College and Sandford Park – did not take place until May 1960. There were two inter-provincial selections: T.C.Stewart in 1965 and David Meharg in 1969. Each season, though, saw an extensive programme of fixtures.

During the 1950s and 1960s, tennis consolidated its position as a small, but successful, activity. Provincial honours were awarded to T.W.K. Fulton in 1956 and John McAllister in 1964, and a major breakthrough came in 1966-67 when school teams reached the finals of the Ulster Schools' Tennis Championships at Senior and Junior levels. The enthusiastic leadership of Arthur Nicholl and Jim Flanagan had much to do with this dramatic progress, and the next chapter will focus on Jim's contribution to school Badminton from the 1970s onwards. The Badminton Club was, in fact, founded in 1959 by Jimmy Shaw. Jimmy was soon to throw himself wholeheartedly into cross country and athletics, and badminton's rapid expansion was largely inspired by Jim Flanagan and Arthur Nicholl. In 1968 CAI won the North West League and reached the finals of the Ulster Schools' Badminton Championships. In 1969, described at the time as the best season to date, North West League victory was accompanied by reaching the semi finals of the Schools Cup. In each year, Percy McCloskey achieved Ulster Schools selection.

The traditional road race – a 'previously decided' event in the annual school sports - has already been mentioned, and indeed in 1958 the start and finish points were again changed so that the race began on the Ballycairn Road and ended in front of the War Memorial Pavilion. The prospect of several hundred boys spread across the full width of the road, and flowing around the (albeit exiguous) traffic as they made their way up to the Mound and down again, would be enough to induce cardiac arrest among today's Health and Safety executives. Amazingly, in all the years the event was run, there were neither casualties nor traffic collisions! From this annual one-

During the 1960s the Harriers became well-established, and Jimmy Shaw chose this team photograph of the year 1964-65 as one of the more memorable of the decade.
Back row: C.A.R. Lyle, J.H. Henry, D.S.B. Meharg.
Middle row: Mr Ken Cushion, C.D. Woodside, W.R.L. McFaul, B. Scott, D.A. Adams, R.M. Smyth, A. McCarter, Mr Jimmy Shaw.
Seated: I.J. Wilson, W.S. Henry, D.M. Hinnrichs, A.N. Johnston (Capt), W.T. Moffatt, B. Brewster, A.J. Longman.
On the ground: D. Uprichard, P.S. Bentley, I.M'G. Henderson, V. Christie.

off, however, something more significant developed. Norman Maxwell had won a cross country half-blue at Queens University, and for two years he encouraged boys to run and train. Although he never saw it, the seed sown was to bear much fruit, and from 1958 onwards, under the enthusiastic supervision of Ronnie McPherson and later Jimmy Shaw, Bob Caswell and Ken Cushion, a cross country club developed. In that year the school began competing in the Co. Londonderry Inter-Schools' Cross Country Championships, and in 1961 hosted the North West Schools' Cross Country championships for the first time.

By the early 1960s their level of success was such that George Humphreys' initial misgivings about the sport soon dissolved into enthusiastic praise in his quarterly reports to the Governors. 1964 was a proud year for this relatively new sport. Its title was officially changed to the Harriers Club, the Club was given representation on the Honours Committee, and its members were made eligible for award of the blue Honours blazer. By the mid 'sixties, members were representing the school at upwards of forty race meetings during the winter months, and in 1967 the formation of the Ulster Schools' Athletics Association witnessed to the general expansion of track and field events among Northern Ireland Schools. By the end of the decade, the school magazine listed almost sixty fixtures in the junior, intermediate and senior age groups. The harriers had arrived with a vengeance!

Related to cross country was athletics. Supervised by Ronnie McPherson and Norman Maxwell, a team was entered for the Co. Derry Schools Championships on 19 May 1956. Despite having had no practice in either discus or javelin events (the school at the time owned neither a javelin nor a discus), the fledgling team broke 11 of the 28 records at the Meeting. At the 1958 championships Coleraine Inst and Coleraine High School made a clean sweep of the boys' and girls' events, and – significantly – Dr Humphreys was President of the Meeting. The first fixture against Foyle College took place in 1961, to which was added another with Portora in 1964. Regular participation in the Ulster Grammar Schools' Championships began after 1966, and in that year two senior athletes – W.F. Adams and Terry Smith – were selected for the Triangular International in Belfast. The inauguration of another new competition, the Ulster Schools Athletics Championships, added a further regular competition to an expanding schedule of events after 1967, and in the same year a number of boys entered the Northern Ireland Youths and Junior Championships. 1969 produced the club's best set of results ever, the highlight of which was Arthur Kerr's gold medal (and new record) in the Senior Javelin at the Irish Schools' Championships. Kerr's selection to represent Ireland in the Schools International in Dublin in July 1970 set the seal on a decade of remarkable progress in the school's newest sports club.

Appendix: How It Was In The 1950s – One Boarder's Memories.

While this book was in preparation, the authors made contact with Mr Rodney Evans of Radcliffe on Trent, Nottinghamshire. Whilst recuperating after surgery, Rodney very kindly jotted down his memories of boarding in the 1950s. As reproduced here, we are certain that they will strike a chord with many readers of his vintage!

My first recollection is of my parents packing a large cabin trunk, including items of uniform, casual clothing and bed linen, all of course duly labelled with my name. My recent visit revealed that the main school building was not greatly altered, though the grassed area we called "Sausage Park", the two storey science laboratory and the old physics lab had gone. I remember also a geography room where "Paddy" Ryan taught, with "The Boss" McDevitt's art room on the other side of the wall. On Sausage Park itself was a wooden building where Irwin Rainey taught us English, with Sergeant Willie Vincent's workshop at the other end. I remember too the old gymnasium, and the pigsty behind it.

Within the boarding school I remember six dormitories: south, middle, north, near and far new and gods. I remember 'the gods' particularly, with its twenty seven beds covered with regulation red blankets. We were taught to make our beds, with

**The boarding school at the beginning of Dr George Humphreys' time.
This picture is dated 1955-56.**

the sheets tucked so tightly that you had to remove the pillow, slide into bed and then replace it. If your pals tipped your bed over, you were trapped inside it, but that was all part of the fun we had. 'Lights out' was as early as 8.45pm: in theory thereafter was strictly 'no talking', but since the resident masters were at the other end of the school conversation was usually safe enough. At 7.30am next morning, our alarm clock was Willie Vincent, shouting "get up!", pulling out the end of your bed and banging your feet for good measure. Then it was down to "The Plunge" underneath room 3 for a morning cold dip, preceded by an invigorating warm water wash at the basins around the shallow tank. It was great in the summer term – but definitely character forming in the winter!

Suitably washed, we went down to the Common Room to await the summons to breakfast in the dining room under room 1. In my early years, at the end of Major White's time, meals were plain and sparse. On the breakfast table was what looked like a washing up bowl filled with porridge, although there was plenty of brown bread and rhubarb jam – not always totally fresh either! If you wanted an egg with your tea, you provided one for yourself, wrote your name on the shell and handed it in to be boiled and then presented to you like a tribal offering! Under Dr Humphreys, we all noticed a major improvement in the quality and quantity of our meals. Any letters which arrived were distributed after breakfast, and then the ringing of a hand-bell heralded morning assembly in room 3 and the start of our day's lessons. After tea was 'prep' –

two hours of supervised homework, six nights a week. The weekends gave us some freedom, for on Friday and Saturday afternoons we could go down town. Our one shilling (5p!) of pocket money was doled out on Friday at lunchtime, and it was surprising just how far it went in those days. Most of it was spent on the delights of The Palladium cinema, and on sweets chewed and crunched during the performance. As I got older, I was introduced to rowing at Bann Rowing Club, and retained an active interest in this excellent sport until the ripe old age of 54!

The Sunday routine was certainly a strict one, and before the first of our two visits to church we climbed into the Sunday uniform of white shirt, black tie, pinstripe trousers, black waistcoat and jacket, and black socks and shoes. Inspection was after breakfast, our shoes made a little more shiny by rubbing them against the back of our trouser legs! The lines then wended their way down to the town churches and back, and on the dark evenings the boy at the back of the line would carry a red torch. In between times, of course, there was lunch followed by the famous three mile walk around the Ballycairn Road.

Though discipline was firm, it was generally fair. My time at The Inst helped me a great deal in later life, and certainly encouraged me to be resolute and independent. Strange as it may seem from this description of the rather austere regime we followed, in June 1957 there were tears in my eye as I left the school for the last time.

In some respects the final years of George Humphreys' headmastership were strangely similar to those of his predecessor. The last decade of White's career unfolded against the backdrop of world war and post-war austerity. The last ten years of Humphreys' headmastership coincided with serious economic recession in the United Kingdom generally, as well as an upsurge of community unrest which was to change permanently the nature of the Northern Ireland state. Educationally, whereas White had to come to terms with the consequences of the 1947 Education Act, Humphreys became embroiled in a vigorous struggle with a Labour government intent on imposing a comprehensive system of education in Northern Ireland. It was a struggle that George Humphreys relished, and it ensured that his career finished at least as vigorously as it had begun twenty-four years previously.

An Unsettled Decade

The expansion of the Northern Ireland economy in the 1950s and 1960s brought significant benefits both to the town and to the school during the first half of his headmastership. The 1970s were a very different proposition. In Northern Ireland, 'The Troubles' did not affect Coleraine as seriously as Belfast, Londonderry or the border areas, though the town experienced a serious bomb attack on 12 June 1973. The overall situation remained tense, though, and several former pupils, and at least one parent, lost their lives in terrorist attacks on the security forces. A number of members of staff had part-time service with the Ulster Defence Regiment, the Territorial Army and the R.U.C. Reserve throughout these dangerous years, fortunately without injury. Devolved government was suspended in 1972, and with the imposition of Direct Rule, ultimate control of education policy passed out of local hands. Twice, in 1974 and in 1977, communal protest merged into political stoppages which became, effectively, general strikes. For the United Kingdom as a whole, the seventies were a period of economic difficulty, high unemployment, severe inflation and political instability which saw four general elections between 1970 and 1979 and periods of minority or small majority government at Westminster.

These circumstances affected boarding in many ways. In 1971 Humphreys reported to the Governors that "in the boarding school we have lost twelve boys mainly due to parents emigrating to Australia, New Zealand and Canada. A number of our English boys have also withdrawn, the parents expressing concern about travel through Belfast at this time." Two years later, news of an explosion at Aldergrove Airport led to the withdrawal of four European boarders. With the onset of the troubles, soldiers sent to Northern Ireland were serving much shorter tours of duty, and this had its effects on a boarding school with a traditional services clientele. Economic and inflationary pressures made other parents think seriously about the cost of boarding, even in a school which offered the best value for money in Northern Ireland. In 1973, for example, fees had to be raised to reflect a twenty-five per cent wage increase authorised to ancillary staff by the Ministry of Education, and an eighteen per cent rise in the cost of foodstuffs. Even the nationalisation of the Iraq oilfields had a link with the school through at least one expatriate family who were unable to keep their son at Coleraine Inst. In common with all other establishments, the boarding department was advised about the security of the sons from families linked to the armed forces, and in 1973 security barriers were installed around the school estate. Other issues had to be considered, and in 1972 it was reported that "The problems for teams travelling arising out of the troubles have not diminished, and the risks involved in taking buses to certain parts of Belfast and Londonderry have to be carefully considered".

The two most junior boarding houses were Kenbane and Benone, and during the 1970s the Housemasters were Donald McKay, Arthur Nicholl and later Joe Cassells, who revived the tradition of annual house photographs.

Kenbane House 1974 - 75.

Kenbane House 1973 - 74.

Kenbane House 1977-78.

Richard Bennett, along with rather grim-faced Robert Park and Len Quigg, feature in this early 1970s photograph of Ramore House. One young man in the front row would never have dreamt then that one day he would be minister of Portrush Presbyterian Church!

Staff photographs were generally taken to mark significant occasions, on this occasion the retirement of Jim Edwards as Vice Principal in 1973.

In 1974, the Ulster Workers' Council strike brought normal life in Northern Ireland almost to a standstill. Always a good forward planner, Humphreys had foreseen this situation, and installed a generator capable of delivering heat and light to the boarding school, as well as stockpiling essential foodstuffs – though the boys were to become rather weary of the *ersatz* blue-grey mashed potatoes produced by mixing sacks of a proprietary powder with boiling water! Eggs and milk were not a problem, though: local farmers were happy to provide the school with what they were unable to sell to their usual customers, and one producer even delivered large quantities of mushrooms which Miss Moore characteristically put to all manner of creative culinary uses. Electricity was in short supply during the worst of the three-week action, and when the boys had gone to bed, the nightly shutting down of the generator was followed by an eerie silence, the darkness broken only by the speckled light of torches and candles in the Senior House studies and the staff bedrooms. School attendance did not suffer unduly, as the local strike organisers were keen that young people should be kept off the streets: anonymous telephone calls to the Headmaster threatening violence if he did not close the school were put down to

disaffected pupils who felt that the stoppage should have been even more widespread! A strike by Ulsterbus drivers later in the year – totally unrelated to what had gone before - actually had a far more significant impact on school attendance.

A Thriving Community In Troubled Times

Paradoxically, although times were difficult, the 1970s were strong years for the school and for its reputation both locally and further afield. In the darkest years of the decade, the boarding school's Malaysian community held steady, and the eventual decline of this sector of the market was due to factors totally unrelated to the troubles. Following the imposition of Direct Rule, the Westminster government encouraged foreign industrialists to explore Northern Ireland's economic potential, and industrialists from Japan, West Germany, Finland, Sweden and Switzerland were among those who visited both the Coleraine area and the School. Her Majesty the Queen included Coleraine in a tour of the United Kingdom during the Silver Jubilee of her reign in 1977. It was a source of great pleasure to the school that the Mayor of Coleraine, Alderman John White, a former pupil and a member (and later President) of the Board of Governors, was a luncheon guest of Her Majesty. The school's educational prestige was enhanced by George Humphreys' election to the Headmasters' Conference in 1974, thus conferring on the Inst the status of a public school, and in 1978 he served for a year as President of the Ulster Grammar Schools Headmasters & Headmistresses Association, eventually receiving the O.B.E. for services to education in the year of his retirement. The Governors marked the twentieth anniversary of his headmastership in 1975 by commissioning a portrait in oils, which was formally presented at a private dinner party in January 1976. Today that painting hangs in the school library. It remains a most striking likeness of its subject, and many who walk along the library balcony are almost conscious of those piercing eyes following them as they go! 1976 also marked the end of an earlier generation in the deaths of William White and Albert Clarke. Albert's length of service to the school - fifty years as a member of staff, Vice Principal and, from his retirement until his final departure in August 1970, Bursar and Clerk to the Governors – was exceeded only by that of Dr S.J.Hunter.

Like many other Headmasters of his generation, Humphreys preferred to deal with parents individually rather than through Parents' Associations or regular meetings of parents at the school. Strange as it seems, the holding of a meeting for parents of boys in Form 1 in September 1975 "to let them know how the school operated and discuss with them our mutual problems" was the rather hesitant outcome of long debate and much thought. It has to be said that the Headmaster was not at his most relaxed during this evening, but the attendance of some 240 parents (the last of whom did not leave until 11.20pm!) showed him the value of the exercise, which became an annual event. By 1977 an annual Third Form parents meeting was also being held, and the format was gradually modified into its current shape. The formation of a Parents' Association, however, would have to wait for almost three decades.

The pace of expansion continued unabated throughout the decade. On 28 October 1970 twenty two new boarding studies, a further suite of science labs and an engineering workshop were officially opened by Mr Ronald Groves, the Master of Dulwich College, and formerly Principal of Campbell College during Humphreys' time on the staff. During the next two years there were further extensions and improvements: the stage area of the former assembly hall was converted into a two-storey study area with individual carrel places; a purpose-built laundry was installed in the boarding school, and the original dining hall of the old Model School was converted into studies for fourth year boys. By the mid 1970s, every boarder from Form Four upwards had access to at least a shared study, and every boarder in Upper Sixth had a personal bed-sit, a facility which few boarding schools of the time could emulate. On 27 February 1973 the Phase Five extension, numbering 14 new classrooms including two art rooms, a new language laboratory, a technical drawing office and a pottery workshop, was officially opened by the Vice Chancellor of the Queens University of Belfast, Sir Arthur Vick. Although further additions were to be made, Phase Five essentially completed the Humphreys vision of a school big enough to cater for over a thousand boys, and indeed by the end of his tenure of office the school population had passed the 1200 mark, with a full-time teaching staff of seventy-five.

But although retirement was now looming on the horizon for George Humphreys, there was still unfinished business. Against a background of educational as well as political uncertainty, the Governors and the Old Boys' Association launched a Consolidation and Development Fund Appeal, aimed at underpinning the school's finances even further, and providing the school with an all-weather athletics track, an extension to the Boat House, two new tennis courts and a Games Hall. Within a year of its launch, the Fund stood at £27.000, and eventually well over £40.000 was raised.

Each development was enthusiastically supported by the school community. Jimmy Shaw, a pivotal figure in harriers and athletics throughout his career, has contributed his own memories of the running track which was officially opened in October 1974 by Prof. H.G.Lamont, President of C.O.B.A.

"Characteristically, the Headmaster returned the request for a new all-weather hard core track as a challenge to those involved. Athletes, especially harriers, raised over £2000 through sponsored runs supervised by Ken Cushion, who also acquired substantial funds from local businesses. Duly impressed, the Governors provided the balance so that work on the track could begin. It was decided that the track should be located in front of the War Memorial Pavilion, where bad drainage had rendered the rugby pitch almost perpetually unplayable.

Although it could only hold a 300 metre track, the site was a compact and fairly well sheltered amenity which was for many years the best equipped and most often used school track in the Province."

Within four years, there was further development in this part of the school estate. On 30 September 1978, the Games Hall was officially opened by Bill Henry, who the previous year had retired as Chairman of the Board of Governors, to be succeeded by John White, whose knowledge of the school, the local community, and the world of local and national politics was as legendary as it was immense.

Mr W.E. Henry
Chairman, Board of Governors 1953-1977

Even as he retired, George Humphreys left behind him a final building scheme. In the late 1970s, a Mrs Irene Templeton contacted the school. Her late husband, William Templeton of Bushmills, had briefly been a pupil at the school in the early years of the century. Following his emigration to Canada, he went on to a distinguished career in civil engineering, and designed the Templeton International Airport in Vancouver. With no surviving close relatives, Mrs Templeton generously gave the school almost £67,000 to fund a prize in her husband's memory and to build a small auditorium to complement the main Assembly Hall. The whole scheme, which included a suite of music rooms in the basement below, was completed by the beginning of Dr Robert Rodgers' principalship, and it was most appropriate that George Humphreys was invited back to the school on 29 October 1979 to see the new building officially opened.

Amazingly, though, the boarding school remained resilient throughout the 1970s, and with over 300 boys was one of the biggest in the Province. The relative peace of the Coleraine area was a strong point for parents of boys in other less safe parts of Northern Ireland, and the day school also continued to expand. By 1977, with almost 300 boys in the lower and upper sixth forms, Humphreys could claim – with only slight exaggeration – that he had "the equivalent of a Sixth Form College at the top of the school".

The Last Generation Of "My Young Men": the Staff In The Seventies

The school's expansion throughout the seventies allowed Humphreys to appoint large numbers of new teachers each year, some destined to spend their entire careers in the service of the school. Among them were the late Allan Gilmour (1971), whose career finished as Head of Geography, Joe Cassells (1971) , the co-author of this book, John Martin(1973), later to become Head of History, Sam Turtle (1973) and Mike McNay (1976) who in their early years might have been surprised had they known they would both finish their careers in the Vice Principal's office, and Len Quigg (1971) who would have been even more shocked to know that one day

Few photographs exist of the staffroom during a working day, but this shot taken in the early 1970s conveys the atmosphere. You may recognise Dermot Jennings, Donald McDonagh, Gordon Donaldson, Robert Park, Edgar Charlton (back to camera), Jimmy Gordon, Jimmy Shaw (seated on table) and John Martin.

he would be Headmaster! John Patterson returned to his old school in 1974, remaining there for his entire career until retirement in 2008. The following year, Ronnie Bryson came from Portora to take over the headship of the Art Department. With his white hair and flowing beard, there was only one possible nickname for this genial Scotsman, and "Santa" he remained until the day he retired. Other arrivals in 1975 included David Harkness who eventually succeeded Arthur Nicholl as Head of Biology, Jim Knight who served for many years in the English Department and finished his career in charge of Form One, and the formidable Luther Hopkins, just retired from the RAF, and famously disinclined to take prisoners in the classroom! Among the longer-serving men of the 1977 intake were Leslie Robinson of the Modern Languages Department, and John Brown who eventually succeeded Ronnie Bryson as head of what became Art and Design.

Humphreys' final appointments in 1978-79 included a group destined to have a major input into school policy into the twenty first century: the names of Richard Adams, Robert Simpson, Phil Blayney, Victor Boyd, Willie McCluskey and Stephen Graham are still fresh in the memory of recent former pupils. Along with these newly-qualified practitioners came a highly experienced maths teacher from Mountcollyer Secondary School in Belfast. Alan Breen was an outstanding teacher who gave many years of service both in the classroom and in coaching golf, bridge and association football. His sudden death on the squash court, literally within days of his retirement at the end of the summer term in 2005, stunned the entire school community.

Long before the phrase was ever in common use, the boarding school housemasters of the 1970s formed a kind of senior management team under the leadership of the formidable Richard Bennett. Movements and promotions within the staff in this decade and the next brought Joe Cassells, Robert Park and Dermot Jennings into middle management as Sam McClements left the school and John Leslie, Arthur Nicholl and Donald McDonagh moved into other areas of school responsibility.

Although he prized his best men highly, Humphreys was proud of the achievements of all his staff, the more so when promising young men sought greater responsibilities in other schools. He was wont to say that "My young men are running most of the schools of Northern Ireland". If this was a slight exaggeration, it was none the less true that Dennis Jagoe left in 1970 to be Head of Ballycastle High School and later of Ballymena Academy, Harold McCullough to be Head of Physics at Bushmills Grammar School, Bob McIvor to be Head of English at Coleraine High School, Sam McClements to be Head of Science at Kirkcaldy High School in 1972, Gavin Craig to be Head of Economics at Bushmills Grammar School in 1974, John Blayney to be Head of Maths at Ballycastle, and later at Lurgan College, in 1978, and Gordon Donaldson to be Vice Principal of Wallace High School in 1978. In addition John Birch and Wesley Ferguson both left, in 1975 and 1977, to follow distinguished careers in The Schools' Inspectorate. Among former members of staff who went on to prominence in University education departments were Dr Brian McGarvey and Dr Ron McCartney – the latter still serving well into an active retirement as a Maths teacher in Forman Christian College, Pakistan. Although it is not strictly within the scope of this chapter, it should be recorded that within a few years of Humphreys retirement, two of his other "young men" had also gone on to higher things: Clive Jackson to be Head of Classics at Ballymena Academy in 1980, and Richard Bennett to be Headmaster of Portora Royal School in 1983. In a gesture of affection and respect for his old Headmaster, Richard invited George and Emma Humphreys to Enniskillen as guests of honour at his first Prize Day. There were others who decided on a change of profession: in 1972 Ian Woods left to pursue a career in accountancy which eventually took him to Canada, while Griffith Boreland returned to University to retrain as a medical doctor. Four of Humphreys' appointees – John McCammon, John McClean, Ian Mairs and Robert Simpson – eventually left teaching for ordination in the Church of Ireland, the Presbyterian Church in Ireland and the Church of Scotland. Nor was the attraction of ministry confined to the staff

A Coleraine re-union in Enniskillen. For his first Prize Distribution as Headmaster of Portora Royal School, Richard Bennett invited George and Emma Humphreys as the guests of honour. Here they are pictured with The Rt. Rev. Gordon McMullan, Bishop of Clogher.

at this time. At the sesquicentenary service in January 2010 the Rev. Frank Sellar, the guest preacher, recalled that he was one of no less than five of the "class of 1976" who eventually became clergymen.

At the other end of the scale, Humphreys' last decade saw the departure of men whose careers stretched into their fifth decade of teaching, and in the case of Albert Clarke covered exactly fifty years both as full time teacher and part-time bursar. Jim Edwards stepped down as Vice Principal in 1973. Jock Mackenzie followed in 1975 and Dan Cunningham in 1977, both men having been the first to occupy the positions of Senior Master (the ancestors of today's Senior Management Team) following changes in teachers' salary structure in 1972. The same regulations allowed a school of the size of Inst to appoint a second Vice Principal, and R.A. ("Mickey") Eyre became the first Second Vice Principal (!) in 1972. Tragically, Maurice Macdevitt ("The Boss" to a generation of boys) died very suddenly following a heart attack in 1974, and only three years after being appointed Second Vice Principal following Jim Edwards' retirement, George Wilson suffered a serious stroke in 1977 which was to curtail

his career prematurely. Tom Ryan, another White appointee, replaced George in the Vice Principals office after a lengthy spell as master in charge of rugby and head of Geography. Finally, 1978 was also marked by the sudden death of Irwin Rainey, the legendary Master in charge of the Book Room. As his friend

A priceless view of three men of the White era, still at work towards the end of the Humphreys years: Jock McKenzie, Tom Ryan and Gordon 'Caesar' Mahoney.

George Wilson's premature retirement on health grounds left the staffroom a less colourful place. When Jimmy Shaw and Joe Cassells went out to his house to photograph him for the school magazine, the appearance of the faithful old dog turned a formal portrait into a real gem!

and colleague Hugh Montgomery wrote at the time: "For this school, he did patient and unremitting work which contributed much to our corporate life, which required thoroughness, and which not many of us could have shouldered so graciously."

A volume could be filled with stories of men some of whom, in ways which would scarcely be possible today, balanced exceptional teaching ability with more than mild eccentricity. Many have memories of Jock Mackenzie exhorting his French classes to "sing it, fat head!", or once teaching an entire lesson from the front seat of his car whilst the boys shivered in an obedient line outside one of the huts at the Model. Others will remember Dan Cunningham's rigorous Physics classes, no less than his ability to recite

all the colours of the spectrum in one breath, with only a slight gasp before "… and indigo..". Arthur Nicholl's gravelly Belfast accent ("Now watch the board, and I'll go through it again.") was as distinctive as Jim Edwards' clipped and polished tones, Tom Ryan's lilting brogue ("Did ye hear de one about…?") or George Wilson's Aghadowey cadences. One occasion comes to mind when a new sixth form pupil, just arrived from Kuala Lumpur, found himself in George's A level Chemistry class. Student and teacher rapidly found themselves on either side of a wall of incomprehensibility, though George's exasperated cry of: "Man dear, can ye naw speak the Queen's English?" eventually cracked the tension as the whole class – teacher included – saw the funny side and burst out laughing. Nor should we leave the 1970s without a reference to those two stalwarts of the Art Department, Irwin Rainey and "The Boss" Macdevitt. One memorable morning, both men's classes were at work – Irwin's, as always, totally silent, and Maurice's rather less so – whilst their teachers enjoyed a quiet smoke in the connecting store. All of a sudden came the sound of a class shuffling to its feet, followed by the familiar stentorian command: "Ah, siddown, siddown. Where's your teacher?" In the ensuing confusion the disposal of Irwin's cigarette burned a hole in the lining of his coat, whilst "The Boss" jammed his finger down the sink whilst dealing with his own. This was as nothing when Maurice dashed into his room to be confronted by a gale of laughter, and a visiting sixth former who specialised in imitations of the Headmaster. The story ended in even more disorder, with the boy racing down the corridor, pursued by an irate Maurice, vigorously belabouring him with a rolled-up newspaper.

Before moving on, a word ought to be said about the ancillary staff of the 1970s, for Coleraine Inst has traditionally been very much a community rather than a hierarchy. The decade began with the death of William Vincent in December 1971. His early career has been mentioned elsewhere: his passing – active to the end in helping collecting dinner money each week – very much marked the end of an era. Jamie Black also retired, and the year 1977 saw the passing of Andy Kerr and Willie

Although he had retired by this time, Willie Vincent did some odd jobs around the school, and this 1971 picture of the ground staff was taken not long before his death.

Back row: James Black Jr, Bertie Vance, Victor Callaghan and Willis Glass.

Middle row: Bobby Grierson, Eddie Norris, Willie Bradley, Willie Murdock, Ted Dadswell.

Front row: James Black Sr, Willie Vincent, Andy Kerr.

Murdock. The very fine picture reproduced here of the ground staff in 1971, taken for the school magazine, uncannily captures the personalities of a diverse but supremely happy group of men.

Making The Grades

The format of public examinations changed radically in the 1960s, and in the 1970s there were further modifications as the Senior Certificate with its marks out of 400 was replaced by the General Certificate of Education and grade boundaries expressed in terms first of numbers, and then the familiar letters A to E, in 1975. The creation of a network of examination boards gave Humphreys the opportunity to shop around, particularly in the cases of Maths, French and English, the standard of whose Northern Ireland examinations he felt was not always fair to weaker boys. For many years until the introduction of the present modular exam system at the end of the twentieth century, selected candidates were

entered for the Associated Examining Board's resit exams at Christmas time. This, along with the creation of a "Lower Sixth Remove" to allow boys to repeat all their GCE exams in a post-O level year, enhanced the reputation of the Inst as a school where the middling and weaker candidates received at least as much attention as the scholarship high-fliers. Non-qualified boarders particularly thrived under a regime where nightly prep was not an option, and the system then in place allowed the school to recommend boys for review (and thus exemption from paying further tuition fees) on the results of the school's internal examinations. A particularly satisfied customer was one little boy whose parents worked overseas, and whom Humphreys enrolled as a boarder at the unusual age of ten. In consequence of his two years in Form One, a year in Lower Sixth Remove and a repetition of his Upper Sixth year, he left school with a sound set of A levels, and was probably unique in our history by having been a pupil for a complete decade under the care of no fewer than three Headmasters - George Humphreys, Robert Rodgers and Stanley Forsythe!

A mark of the growing overseas community was the first entry of pupils in 1978 for the Joint Matriculation Board's test in English, designed specifically as a University Entrance qualification for candidates whose first language was not English. Then, as now, the vast majority of upper sixth leavers sought a college or university place, and one consequence of the ongoing troubles in the Province was the increasing number of boys who chose to go to Great Britain for their third level education. As early as June 1971, Humphreys noted that for the first time in his headmastership, none of the year's top scholars had applied for either Queens University Belfast or Trinity College Dublin.

At the risk of invidious omissions, some flavour can be offered of our students' successes in University Scholarships during this decade. In 1970 J.R.Cameron was awarded an exhibition to Peterhouse Cambridge, and the following year D.T.Gault and W.N.Chestnutt won open scholarships to Edinburgh. In 1972 Mark Ferguson, destined to achieve international fame in the world of dentistry, was awarded a Major Scholarship by the General Dental Council, while H.H.Lee took first place in Physics and the Silver Medal of the Physical Society of Great Britain. In 1973, there was a trio of Open Scholarships: John Fitzgerald to Imperial College, David Stewart to Edinburgh and Samuel Tanner to Queens University Belfast. In 1974 James McFarland won an Open Bursary to Glasgow, and in 1975 David Christopherson achieved a Scholarship to Corpus Christi College Cambridge. 1976 saw Stephen Brown scoring the highest marks in the Further Maths exam, and an Open Scholarship to Peterhouse, Cambridge, while David McKay won a Scholarship to Corpus Christi, Cambridge. 1977 was a particularly successful year, with Terry Blain taking a Bursary in Modern Languages at Corpus Christi, Cambridge, Rory Seaton a Bursary in Natural Sciences at Peterhouse, Alistair Haire a Major Bursary at St Andrews, and Ian Jess gaining entrance to Peterhouse.

"That Trendy Socialist Lord..."
An Epilogue To The 1970s

The final year of George Humphreys' reign at Coleraine Inst was in many ways the most exhilarating, as it brought to a head a long battle between the Northern Ireland voluntary Grammar Schools and the Labour government. Their particular target was Lord Melchett, a Junior Minister at the Northern Ireland Office with responsibility for educational development. Melchett's opponents, Humphreys among them, were quick to point up the ironies of his past career. An old Etonian and Cambridge graduate, Peter Mond, Fourth Baron Melchett, was the son of Sir Julian Mond, Chairman of the British Steel Corporation, and the heir to the Mond family fortunes. It hardly helped his cause that this youthful Peer had recently been chairman of a House of Lords Working Group on Pop Music. Melchett's attempt to bring comprehensive schools to Northern Ireland was unsurprising, given the development of education policy in the 1970s. After the introduction of Direct Rule in 1972 control of education policy passed from Stormont to Westminster, and a new Labour government rapidly made its intentions clear. The 1973 Burgess Committee recommended a review of the eleven plus transfer system, and in 1976 the newly established Education and Library Boards were instructed to draw up plans for a comprehensive replacement to the existing system of secondary education. Three working parties were also set up to study the implications of a comprehensive system, chaired respectively by Prof. Alan Astin (on school management), Dr John Benn (on the voluntary sector) and Dr R.J. Dickson (on preparatory and boarding schools).

To Coleraine Inst, as to voluntary Grammar Schools generally, the dangers seemed threefold. First there were financial concerns, relating both to investments and income from fees. Second, there was the issue of structure. There was much interest at the time in the so-called Dickson Plan, which had recently introduced two-tier secondary education in the Craigavon area. This involved transfer at eleven plus from primary schools to junior high schools, then again at fourteen plus to senior high schools, including former all-through Grammar Schools like Lurgan College and Portadown College. Humphreys' view was that if such major changes were to be imposed throughout Northern Ireland, the establishment of a prep department might be necessary to safeguard the boarding school. On the other hand, the option of turning Coleraine Inst into a Sixth Form College was reckoned as totally impracticable. Thirdly, even without any structural change to secondary education, there was the issue of a non-selective intake at eleven plus and its implications for traditional Grammar School education.

On the transfer issue, the voluntary schools opted for flexibility, and the Alternative Transfer Procedure produced few problems for Coleraine Inst. In September 1978, the first year of the new system, ninety-three per cent of dayboys and seventy-five per cent of boarders were non fee-paying. On the issues of finance, school structures and a comprehensive ethos there would be no such compromise. Despite his emollient protestations in June 1977 that the government would give ample time for the evolution of the best possible system, Melchett could have been under no misapprehension. The Governing Bodies' Association, backed by a Parents' Union which mobilised grass roots support for the voluntary sector around Northern Ireland, kept up unrelenting opposition until the defeat of Labour in the 1979 general election brought this round of the contest to an end.

In September 1971 the school's enrolment passed the one thousand mark and Humphreys, with the Governors' approval, continued to inflate the school, which in the five years after 1974 grew by almost 100 to around 1200 boys. In a confidential briefing to the Board on 7 February 1978 (a tape of which, in the school archives, is possibly the only extant recording of his voice) Humphreys outlined his thinking and his long-term strategy. First, he was anxious to establish a claim on a large intake if a quota system was imposed on the school at the time of eleven plus transfer. Second, he was aware that some local Catholic voluntary schools were beginning to safeguard their own numbers by becoming coeducational rather than single-sex in intake, and that in consequence up to ten per cent of the Inst's

In this view of the school, the phase 5 extension is complete, but the Templeton Hall still lies in the future.

dayboy intake might disappear. Third, and longer term, he hoped by the early 1980s to pay off all the school's existing loans and debts, against a worst-case scenario that a future government might undermine voluntary schools by restricting or abolishing their income from fees.(It was generally understood that the Benn Committee, mentioned earlier, was in favour of abolishing the right of voluntary schools to charge any fees).

Coincidentally, as the big building schemes continued through the 1960s and 1970s, the Governors had been borrowing competitively from the banks rather than solely from the Department of Education, and keeping sufficient short-term investments to guarantee ready capital for sudden emergencies. The Consolidation and Development Fund, mentioned earlier, had also generated some useful capital for the school. In the 1970s, voluntary schools qualified for 85% capital grants, had fifty per cent of salary grants paid direct, and could charge a per capita fee for all pupils to cover overheads including the servicing of existing loans. As Humphreys contemplated his retirement, he was fairly certain that Coleraine Inst's financial position could be secured, even if the right to charge fees was modified or withdrawn. His thinking about the boarding school was similarly realistic, and indeed he anticipated the effects of any future decrease in numbers. His own private – and very radical – view was that if numbers ever fell below the 260 mark, it would make best sense to abandon the Model School, reduce the total boarding number immediately to around 220 and thus keep the boarding fee relatively stable through cutting running costs.

The defeat of Labour in the 1979 General Election prematurely ended what might have turned into an epic struggle. This was a relief for Humphreys in two ways. First, a serious threat to the school had now been lifted. Second, he had by this time decided to retire in August 1979, and after the depth of his involvement in the struggle of the previous few years, he might have found it rather difficult to walk away from the battlefield while the war was going on!

The Board Of Governors In The 1970s

Throughout his twenty four years at Coleraine Inst, Humphreys enjoyed the total confidence of the Governors, and between the Headmaster and the Board a rare bond of mutual respect was forged. In the 1970s some changes took place in the composition of the Board, notably the increase of its size by the appointment of Ministry of Education representatives as part of a deal which increased financial assistance with Capital Spending Schemes from sixty-five per cent to eighty-five per cent. During this period death removed from the Board Messrs J.H.T. Reid, James Jackson, Knox Caldwell (at the time of his death in 1974 the oldest serving Governor), Garth Anderson and Alec McCurdy, while retirements and clerical removals saw the departure of the Rev. R.J. Pentland, Pastor W.J. Rowell, Canon W.R..J Benson, and Messrs R.A. Dalzell, E.L. Hamilton, and Dr W.J.C. Hill. Following the retirement of Albert Clarke, Colin Beck was officially appointed Bursar and Secretary to the Board of Governors in September 1971. Finally, at the Annual General Meeting in February 1978 there was a significant change in leadership of the Board as Bill Henry and Gordon Crawford announced their retirements as President and Vice President. John White was elected to succeed Mr Henry, and Ernest Morrison Mr Crawford. This, almost as much as George Humphreys' retirement the following year, marked the end of an era, as Bill Henry's presidency began in the last years of William White, and the Crawford family's links with the Governors stretched back to the nineteenth century.

"Half Past Three : School's Just Starting."

As well as underpinning the school's physical expansion, a large boarding school also contributed to the school's extra curricular activities, and in particular sports and games. There may have been an element of exaggeration in the remark, quoted above, which Humphreys made to a visitor as the bell rang at the end of a school day, but there was no doubting the number of boys passing his office on the way to the pool, the

Another Harriers' year on which Jimmy Shaw looked back with particular nostalgia.

Back Row: Mr Jack Rowbottom, A. Watson, J. Davis, G. McIlwaine, D. Martin, C. McClean, J. Mairs, W. Baxter, N. McKay, D. McKay, Mr Ken Cushion.

Middle row: Mr Jimmy Shaw, J. McIlwaine, P. Kitson, E. Carson, P. Crossley, R. Henderson, N. Annett, R. Seaton, N. Baxter, R. Watson, Dr George Humphreys.

Front row: K. Woodrow, J. Dawson, K. Mullan, C. Black, I. Adams, H. McFaul, J. McKee, D. Dinsmore, M. Windebank.

pitches or the track, rather than directly to the buses or the town centre. During the late sixties and early seventies there was a further expansion of what used to be called 'minor' sports, to which Humphreys continued to give wholehearted encouragement. In the 1974-75 season, history was made when fourteen boys achieved schools international, and twenty-two provincial, selection in rugby, rowing, athletics, cricket, swimming and badminton. To mark the occasion the Governors hosted a celebratory dinner for the coaches, the boys and their families at the Carrig na Cule Hotel in Portstewart. Though not strictly a school sports club, permission was given in 1978 for "A ski-ing course in North Italy", and the annual ski trip has continued to be part of the school calendar ever since.

Travel to away fixtures is a subject in itself, and today's Inst boys might be surprised to learn that it was only in the 1970s that hired buses rather than the train from Coleraine station became the normal mode of transport. As the smaller sports increased, the school bought its first minibus in 1975 (at a cost of £3000!), and later a school car, originally intended to pull the Rowing Club's boat trailer to regattas. There is room in this section only for a flavour of what Coleraine Inst boys achieved.

It was rather unfortunate that, in spite of the large numbers of players and coaches, rugby's reputation depended in the popular estimation on success or failure in two competitions. Winning the Schools Cup eluded Humphreys altogether (though he was present at the victorious 1992 final, characteristically disregarding the reservations of his doctors!) Most years of the 1970s, though, saw Coleraine boys taking representative provincial honours. Thus Campbell Malseed, R.H. Patterson and S.J. Ferguson achieved Ulster places in 1970-71, Campbell Malseed, Davie Cromie, Taylor Dinsmore and Syd Parker in 1971-2, R.J. Marshall, Michael Williams and Peter Geary in 1972-3, Michael Williams and Davie Smith in 1973-74, Marshall Donaghey in 1974-5, Alan Gardiner and Uel Moore in 1975-6, John McConnell and John Erskine in 1976-77 and 1977-78, and David McCurdy and Roger Anderson in 1978-79. The 1974-5 season at least saw a victory in the Medallion Shield, while the Second XV won their tournament in the 1974-5 and 1978-79 seasons. Two long-serving coaches stepped down during the 1970s. Though he continued to coach, after 18 years as Master in Charge of Rugby Tom Ryan handed over overall responsibility to Jim Foote in June 1975, and two years later John Birch left teaching to join the Schools

Inspectorate. John was involved with the First XV throughout his career at Coleraine Inst, and to mark his departure the 1st XV played an Old Boys XV representative of the teams John coached throughout his thirteen years at school.

In cricket, the 1971-2 season was described as among the best in the history of the sport at CAI. The First XI lost only three of their twenty-three games, and Archie and Chris Fullerton, W.R.Forsythe and David Moorehead were selected for Ulster schools trials. In the 1974-5 and 1978-79 seasons the Colts XI won the North West Schools' Trophy. David Johnston and Craig Lapsley were selected for an Ulster Colts XI in a two-day match against the Welsh schools in 1975, and David had the honour of captaining the side. In the following season, he became the first CAI boy to be selected for an Irish Schools Cricket Team against Wales in Dublin. In 1976-77, both Johnston and Paul Kitson represented Ulster and Ireland, while at junior level, Stephen Beveridge was selected for the Ulster Under 15s against Wales. In 1977-78 Paul Kitson achieved selection for Ulster and Ireland, joined in the Ulster squad by Barry Clements.

The harriers enjoyed conspicuous success, and in the first year of the decade won the Senior and Intermediate Schools Championships of Ireland – the first time one school had won two Irish Championships in the same year. In the following season, they had an excellent record in local competition, finishing second in the All Ireland Championships. The 1974-5 season was hailed as the best in the club's history, with twelve major trophies and no fewer than 148 individual awards. Senior and Intermediate teams took first places at the Ulster Schools Championships, and the Junior team not only represented Ulster Schools at the Irish Championships but also won the Irish Junior Schools Trophy. The 1976-77 season brought victory in the Ulster Schools Championships at Senior and Intermediate levels, during a season in which 144 individual awards were gained, and ten trophies won or retained. 1977-78 was a quieter year, though in 1978-79 the club won ten trophies, and the Intermediate team became Ulster champions and finished second in the Irish finals.

In athletics, the 1970-1 season was one of great success, and the boys won the Co. Derry Schools Championships, retaining the Blackmore Trophy. In the Ulster Schools Championships, Coleraine athletes won three Ulster titles and were second in seven other events. A.M. Kerr was selected for the Irish Schools team in the Quadrangular International Athletics Championships. Following the 1972 Irish championships, Maurice Eakin and Clifford Carruthers were selected to represent Ireland. In the 1973 season Maurice Eakin again achieved international status, and in 1974 the Club won the Ulster Schools Senior Team Championship as well as the Senior Relay Trophy. The following year CAI athletes won the junior and senior sections at the District Championships, and the overall trophy. At the Ulster Championships the senior team won the Perpetual Challenge Cup. To crown an outstanding year Roy Henderson and Nigel Annett were selected to represent Ulster and Ireland, while Marshall Donaghey and Jarvis Weir were selected to compete with the Northern Ireland 3As. In the following season five boys – Ian Condron, H.E.A. Carson, N. Jackson, Davie Logan and Keith Barton – were selected for the Ulster Schools team. In the 1976-77 season sixteen boys represented Ulster schools in inter-provincial matches, and David Logan, Gregor Hewitt, Norman Richmond, Sam Richmond and Barry Mulholland were selected for the Ulster Schools team. The 1977-78 season was no less outstanding for the club: Stephen Allen, Jonathan Bloomfield, Mark McCormick, Paul Cunning and Robert Watters all competed in the Schools Inter Provincial, while Robert Watters had the honour of selection for the Irish Schools team in javelin, and produced the best Ulster performance of the meeting. In 1978-79 a very strong squad represented Ulster Schools at the Irish Schools Athletic Championships in Dublin. At Senior level the club won the Royal College of Science Cup, which had seldom come north before, and the Intermediate team was placed second. The senior relay team was placed first, winning the championship silver baton.

Swimming and life saving have existed as a competitive sport for many years, and records exist of occasional galas against other schools as far back as the 1930s. With the arrival of Jim Foote as Head of P.E., and the opening of the school's own swimming pool, the 1970s saw a virtual rebirth of the Club and the foundation of a tradition of excellence which has lasted until the present day. Jim Foote, the redoubtable Con O'Callaghan of Belfast Inst and Fred Parkes of Campbell College were largely responsible for the creation of the Ulster Grammar Schools and Ulster Secondary Schools Championships, which along with the Minor Schools Championships and (following Coleraine Inst's admission to the H.M.C.) the annual Public Schools Relays in London shaped an arduous swimming season which lasted from September until May. Jim's enthusiasm rubbed off on at least two of his junior colleagues, and under his careful supervision, Joe Cassells and Robert Simpson were in due course to succeed him as masters in charge of the sport. Also through Jim, close bonds existed with Coleraine Amateur Swimming Club, and almost all the school's swimmers, including the boarders, were linked with both clubs. Two senior swimmers achieved selection to the Irish Schools team for the annual Quadrangular International gala: Barry Johnston in freestyle in 1972, 1973 and 1974 and Jeremy White in breaststroke in 1979. Hal Fitzgerald, the best backstroker of the decade, was chosen as an intermediate for an Ulster team which toured the USA in 1976, and during this tour he set a new Ulster Schools' backstroke record. Every year saw relay team gold medals in all age groups at each of the Ulster Schools competitions, and particular strength in the Senior section gave Coleraine Inst victory in the coveted Queens University Cup at the Ulster Schools Championships for four successive years between 1976 and 1979. Annual appearances at the Public Schools Relay Races began in 1974, and from 1976 until 1979 Coleraine Inst teams were placed either second or third in the two main events, the Bath Cup and the Otter Trophy. 1979 was the most outstanding: the Senior Team winning the Medley Relay in the Irish Schools Championships. The same squad had the satisfaction of being runners-up in the two premier U.K. public schools relays: they were beaten – in each case at the final touch – in London by R.B.A.I.!

Badminton was another club which was still fairly new in the 1970s and which in this period was associated with that formidable combination of Jim Flanagan, Donald McKay, Allan Gilmour and Robert Blair. The decade opened with a clean sweep of the North West League, the Ulster Schools League and the Ulster Schools Cup in 1970-71. Percy McCloskey, who captained the club, was chosen on three occasions to represent Ulster and selected to play for Ireland against Scotland at under fourteen level. The following year saw victory in the Ulster Schools Cup and League, and in the All Ireland Championship. David Balmer and Alan Oliver were selected for Irish Schools in two international events. In 1974-5 the club won all but four of the fifty-eight matches which comprised its season. The senior team was defeated in the final of the Schools Cup, but at junior level there were victories in the Junior Cup and League. As Northern Ireland champions they entered the All Ireland Championships, and won matches against the three other provinces to emerge as undisputed Irish Champions. David Mills was the outstanding individual – in both under sixteen and under eighteen age groups – and he and Peter Ferguson won the Ulster Under sixteen doubles. David and Ron McKay were chosen to represent Ulster against the English Counties at under sixteen level. 1975-76 was no less auspicious. The seniors won the Ulster Schools League, and the minors (under fourteen) won their first Ulster Trophy. David Mills again emerged as the outstanding player, representing Ireland in the Under seventeen team against the Home Countries in Bristol, and Ulster under eighteen against the other provinces. Peter Ferguson, for his part, was selected for the Ulster under sixteen team against the English Counties. 1976-77 continued the relentless rise in the club's fortunes. The Ulster Schools' Cup and League were won without the loss of a single game, and the club became Irish Schools' Champions with scores of six – nil against the other provinces. David Mills represented Ulster and Ireland at under eighteen level, and Peter Ferguson the Ulster Schools. As if this were not enough, the 1977-78 season was described as 'phenomenal'. Coleraine Inst teams reached all eight possible finals, and won five trophies. The senior team

Rowing at the start of a new decade. Mickey Eyre and Sam McClements are pictured with the full club at the boathouse.

won both Cup and League, and went on to win the Irish finals, again by six – nil scores. The club captain Peter Ferguson was the Ulster Schools 'Champion of Champions', a member of the Irish Under 18 team, and the choice of the Milk Marketing Board as 'Top Sporting School Leaver' of the year. Scott Henderson also played for the Ulster under eighteens, Stephen Beveridge for Ulster under sixteens, and John Ferris for Ulster under fifteens. The following year saw the club reach six out of seven Ulster Schools' Finals, winning three Cup and one League competitions.

One is hesitant even to begin a summary of the Rowing Club's achievements in this decade – anything less than a book in its own right would be almost a distortion. In this decade Mickey Eyre continued to be one of the most respected rowing coaches in the United Kingdom, was nominated for the Olympic Games umpiring panel in 1976, and umpired at the F.I.S.A. Junior World Championships in Austria in the same year. Joining him in the coaching team were Sid Grey, and Ian Mairs, (themselves former competitive oarsmen), Sam McClements, Richard Bennett, Steen Anderson and Robert Blair.

The 1970s began with a marathon row, which raised £1950 for new boats, and the 1971 season brought thirteen regatta trophies and mainly unbeaten Junior Schoolboy and Colts crews. Two restricted fours were launched on

June 1973: launch of the "Coolnasillagh", which was named by Mr and Mrs Stanley Stewart. The bow section of this boat is now on permanent display in the school museum.

The Craig Cup-winning Junior C8 of 1978, with their coach, Richard Bennett. Back row: Michael Wilson, Stanley Elder, Ian Gourley, Paul Taylor. Front row: Conal Austin, Murray Brown, Alan Anderson, Kenneth Ferguson and Robert Angell.

Old Boys' Day, 25 September 1971, named by Mrs McClements and Mrs Grey. In 1972 came victories in the Eights and Fours Championships of Ireland, the first time any northern school achieved such a distinction. The first eight was again chosen to represent Ireland in the Quadrangular International Championships in Dublin, and their second place in this event helped Ireland win the schools International Trophy for the first time for many years. This year also saw victory in the Wray Cup. 1973 produced a first eight which Mickey Eyre judged to be one of the best crews in the history of the club: no Irish crew came within three lengths of it all season, and at the Blessington Regatta it broke the 2000 metre course record by no less than thirty-four seconds. There were victories in both the eights and fours races at the Irish Schools Championships, and C.A.I. again represented Irish Schools at the Quadrangular International in Nottingham, with the four winning and the eight coming second in their respective events. A quieter 1974 season none the less brought eleven trophies to the club

cabinet, and on 28 September 1974 Mr R.L. Kennedy named a new pair "Crevenagh" in memory of his wife. The School Magazine also noted the names of eighteen former pupils still involved in competitive rowing throughout the British Isles, and three Old Boys – Mickey Eyre, Ian Kennedy and Willie McCahon – involved in I.A.R.U. administration as Chairman, Hon. Secretary and Hon. Treasurer.

In 1975 pressure on space was alleviated by the extension to the boathouse, and the Club entered the world of high technology with a video camera presented by a parent for use in coaching. Joining forces with Bann, the club won the Senior Schools Youth Eight Championship of Ireland. This entitled them to represent Irish Schools for the third time at the Home Countries International Regatta, where they came second to England. The cadets clinched the title of being the best cadet crew in Ireland by winning at five regattas, including Dublin Metropolitan. The cadets and colts also dominated the 1976 Irish rowing season, with a virtual clean sweep of their

Pictured at the naming ceremony for three boats on Old Boys' Day 30 Sepember 1978, are the three members of the Irish Coxed Pair: David Gray (Bangor G.S.) and Coleraine old boys Noel Graham (1959-1964) and Iain Kennedy (1961-1969). These men formed the first Irish crew to contest a world final in New Zealand in November 1978, where they finished 6th. Also in the picture is Dr George Humphreys, Headmaster, and Mr Mickey Eyre, head of rowing at Coleraine Inst.

events at all the Irish regattas. The cadets recorded ten wins in ten races, and the colts tally of wins included the Craig Cup. In this season a new fine four, named "Slieve na Mara" was launched, the gift of a parent, and former pupil Iain Kennedy was selected for the Irish Olympic Team. In 1977 the Wray Cup and the Craig Cup were among 41 trophies won in a season where the colts were almost undefeated on the rivers of Ireland. Seniors and colts also achieved six trophy victories at Chester and Northwich. A new eight —"Kildollagh" — was launched. Old boys Iain Kennedy and Noel Graham represented Ireland at the World Rowing Championships in Amsterdam, finishing eighth in the world. In 1978 the Wray and Craig Cups were retained and the First IV selected to represent Ireland in the Wales International, where it came in second to England. Otherwise, damage to boats and bad weather made for a rather frustrating season. On 30 September 1977 "Cooldarragh II", replacing the boat seriously damaged earlier in the year, and the coxless pair "Sandelford" were officially named, while "Kildollagh", re-skinned after damage at Derry Head, was re-launched. Iain Kennedy and Noel Graham, who

named the boats, continued their international career at the 1978 World Championships in New Zealand. The 1979 season brought a total of twenty-eight trophies and the Club were the first recipients of the D.B.McNeill Trophy. Brian Russell and Neil Dennison won the Double Sculls Championship of Ireland, and were selected to represent Ireland in international competition.

Two other sports might be briefly mentioned. In 1974 Hugh Boyd won the Lowry Cup for the best performance in the Ulster Schools Golfing Championships. In 1976 the tennis club had a particularly good season, reaching the finals of the Ulster Schools Tennis Cup. The outstanding players of their year were Peter Little and Willie Noteman, who were selected for the Ulster Schools tennis team. In the following season they won the Ulster Schools' Tennis Cup, and Peter Little became the top under eighteen player in Ulster, being selected for the Irish Schools' team, and for an Irish Junior Team.

On 20 March 1976 a sponsored rowing event to raise funds for the IARU produced the rare spectacle of Rowing Club fours and eights going up through the locks at the Cuts. This event will be remembered as bitingly cold, and stormy enough to have made Mickey Eyre wonder whether or not to curtail it. In the end he didn't, and no-one died of exposure either!

The staff photograph taken to mark the retirement of Dr George Humphreys in 1979.
It was historic also in being the last staff photograph taken by the late Mr Jim Moore,
a well-known local commercial photographer who had a standing contract
with the school over many years.

End Of An Era

Although he had originally intended to stay for a little longer, George Humphreys eventually decided to retire at the end of the summer term in 1979. For one who, no less than his immediate predecessor, had placed his mark on the school, retirement was a significant milestone in our history. Happily, he was spared any slow decline of his powers, packing a long and vigorous retirement with service as Chairman of the Northern Health Board and President of the Boys' Brigade in Northern Ireland, as well as active membership of the Kirk Session of First Coleraine Presbyterian Church. In retirement he was an invited guest at the opening of the Templeton Auditorium, a project he saw almost to completion before

G. Humphreys with canteen staff.

his departure, and Stanley Forsythe invited him to distribute the prizes on Speech Day 1984. He was also delighted to be the guest of honour at Portora Royal School in 1983, at the invitation of Richard Bennett, newly appointed Headmaster and previously Head of Boarding at Coleraine Inst.

To the end of his life his new home in Portstewart remained the focal point of his family circle, and he was of course particularly proud of his grandson's meteoric rise to fame in Ulster and Irish rugby. He was an assiduous student of Information Technology, and shortly before his death he had acquired one of the most up-to-date computers on the market. Let the last word on a formidable character go to his successor, Robert Rodgers. Shortly after the transition, a caller to his office inadvertently, and totally by force of habit, addressed the new Headmaster as "Dr Humphreys." Rodgers looked up and smiled as he quickly replied: "Oh no, not quite." Unique indeed, in every way!

Dr G. Humphreys

Appendix: A Day In The Boarding School.

In 1976, the co-author of this history thought it might be a good idea to record for posterity what a day in the boarding school was really like. Long-lost, the pictures re-emerged recently, and nine out of a large selection give a flavour of an age long past.

The community centre of the boarding school was the dining hall, managed by the redoubtable Miss Moore. This is how it was before 'going in' was shouted and 300 boys arrived to be fed.

Each Friday at lunchtime the junior boarders queued in room 3 to get their pocket money and, if they were going on pass, their Saturday chits.

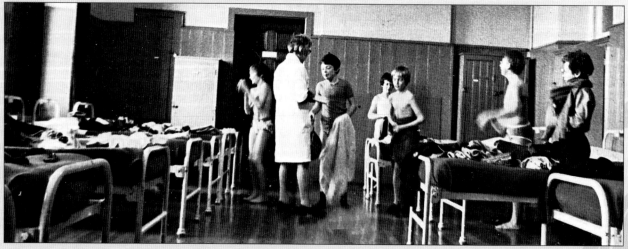

After school on Fridays the junior boarders showered, and then put on clean clothes. Supervising this operation is Miss Gilmore, for many years matron of the boarding department.

Prep – supervised homework – was strictly non negotiable! Here Jimmy Gordon has rooms 1 and 5 well under control and is about to take his roll around the rest of the boarding department.

Getting books for afternoon school – possibly not the kind of image which the prospectus would have wanted to picture!

During the wintertime, there was often little to do on a rainy afternoon but convert room 3 into an impromptu badminton court. To the left two boys can be seen on their way back from Tommy Allen's tuck shop.

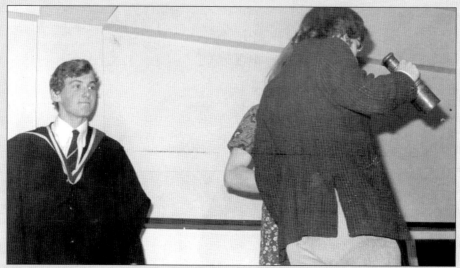

By tradition, the boarders produced a Christmas revue which gently (and sometimes not so gently) sent up the school and the staff. This 1976 representation of prize day features as Headmaster a young man later to become a distinguished surgeon as well as a Governor of the school!

Traditionally, the end of prep at 8.15pm was the signal for impromptu cricket matches on the front field which lasted until bedtime – or even beyond, if the duty master was in good form!

Suppertime marked the end of prep for the small boys, and a break for the seniors before work recommenced – in theory anyway – until 9.30pm.

Chapter 10

The Rodgers Years:

1979 - 1984

To replace George Humphreys the Board of Governors turned, for the first time in the school's history, to a serving Headmaster. Dr Robert James Rodgers was Principal of Bangor Grammar School, and therefore already a member of the Headmasters' Conference. An historian by training, it was most appropriate that his Doctoral research was on the Rev. James Carlyle – a nineteenth century figure who, like Rodgers himself, was well known both in Irish Presbyterianism and the world of education. Robert Rodgers was a Belfastman, a product of 'the other Inst' which in later years he was proud to serve as Governor, Chairman of the Board and latterly as its most recent historian. His teaching career began in Grosvenor High School, and he often spoke with great fondness of his days in the classroom. He moved from teaching to teacher training as Principal Lecturer and Academic Registrar at Stranmillis Training College, going on to become Headmaster of Bangor Grammar School in 1977. In a very short time he acquired a formidable reputation, and his appointment in Coleraine was of particular pleasure to George Humphreys, who regarded him as one of the best Headmasters in the Province. Like his predecessor, he was an elder in the Presbyterian Church, serving on the Kirk Session of Hamilton Road Bangor, and co-opted after his arrival to the Kirk Session of New Row. He and his wife Mary had two children: Colin was a medical student, while Jennifer was in the sixth form of Sullivan Upper School.

Robert Rodgers, The Man

Within a very short time of his arrival, the new Head was regarded with a mixture of respect and awe. It was widely believed that, in the words of the Psalmist, he neither slumbered nor slept. From the outset, he was to be seen around the campus at all hours of the day and night, and nothing around the school escaped his notice. Every detail of the Inst community was rapidly committed to his memory, and the staff were particularly fascinated by a mysterious small card, covered in miniscule script and figures, which he occasionally drew from his top pocket to consult, if something of interest arose during a conversation. In addition to a customary presence on the touchline each Saturday morning, he gave equally regular support to competitors in what at that time were termed the 'minority sports'. It was not unknown for him to spend a January Saturday morning in Belfast, watching the First XV playing an away game, before driving on to the McCallum Hall to greet the badminton team and then finishing at Castlereagh Pool to spend time with the swimmers at the Ulster Schools' Championships. On one such occasion he arranged to come back to Coleraine in their minibus: characteristically, when they emerged to find that dense freezing fog had closed the M2, he insisted on driving the bus via the Antrim Road, to give some relief to staff who had spent the whole day officiating at the poolside. Typically, too, when the swimming club staged a 24 hour relay swim for the school charity, he simply regarded it as his duty to be there throughout the night to support the boys and the staff in their effort.

In the day school, it soon became clear that he had rapidly put names to the sea of faces which confronted him in morning assembly, and those who thought that distance from the stage was a guaranteed cloak of anonymity soon found out otherwise, to their cost. In the boarding school he used a small pack of cards to learn the name of every boarder, though the boys felt slightly uneasy as that piercing gaze scanned every table at each mealtime! Serious breaches of discipline were memorably dealt with, and often the sting of the Headmaster's tongue was found to be far more devastating than any cane. He rarely raised his voice, and was at his most effective in tones barely louder than a whisper. On one occasion a group of senior boarders, who at least had the wit to plead guilty as charged, stood trembling in his study to be given the choice either of an extensive range of sanctions, or of a one-way journey home. When one had the temerity to break the silence with: "Sir, we need time to think about this", Rodgers' icily menacing reply was: "Young man, I offered you two choices, not three"!

This was, of course, only one side of the coin. Although a formidable disciplinarian, Rodgers was also a consummate encourager. Early in his headmastership he expanded the Honours Committee and had the school honours system broadened because he believed it should recognise areas of school life other than sport, and include colours as well as full honours awards. It gave him particular pleasure in 1983 when Dan McMullan became the first pupil to wear the coveted blue blazer with the word "Music" under the badge. He ran weekly tutorials for boys of clear ability who were considering Oxford or Cambridge among their university applications, and at the other end of the spectrum he had a particular concern for boys – especially boarders – who were academically weak. He put great stress on the responsibility of Prefects within the system, and introduced an application, self-evaluation and interview process for the appointment of boarding school prefects which was far ahead of the practice of most other schools.

Immediately after his arrival he asked each member of staff to provide him with a written C.V. and within three months of his arrival he had watched all seventy three of them in their classroom environment. A problem, or a parental complaint, could sometimes lead to a pointed, if salutary, private interview - but though a teacher might have emerged from the Study feeling rather shaken, he could be confident that in public he would have the Headmaster's total support. That support was shown in other ways too. One master who had spent his summer holidays working in a mission hospital overseas, arrived home, two days into the school year, to find the Department of Education threatening to dock him two days' pay. The verbal tornado which Rodgers unleashed against the bureaucrats of Bangor was more than enough to have this petty decision rescinded!

He had no time for hearsay, innuendo or generalised criticism of the school or its employees. Those rash enough to allege that: "...people around the town are saying..." would be stopped in their tracks by a quiet: "Name six!". He feared no-one either. During a General Inspection, it came to his notice that one of the inspection team had breached the established ground rules. The hapless Inspector was quietly ushered out of the class he was observing, to be enlightened in the Office about basic professional courtesies. It should be said that the eventual Inspection Report was a glowing one, and Rodgers even allowed himself some whimsical humour in his report to the Board: "They described us as one of the best Grammar Schools in the province, and I modestly did not question their qualifications or indicate that I was already convinced of this"!

Very much the traditionalist, he was privately critical of the Department of Education's new contracts for teachers, and told the Governors: "I am convinced that the extensive detailing of specific duties will only encourage a less than professional attitude of mind which impairs rather than generates good working relationships." Put simply, Rodgers, like his predecessor, valued and encouraged any member of staff who showed himself willing to go the second mile in the service of the school - not just in academic or co-curricular activities either. Two such examples can safely be quoted from his quarterly reports to the Governors: At the start of the school year in 1981 he reported that "the bursar and Mr Shaw heroically and successfully undertook the felling of two trees pronounced to be in a dangerous condition. Not only did this anticipate the storm of the following week, but it also provided a spectacle for new boarders on their first Saturday here, and helped allay the pangs of homesickness."

He was equally pleased to note that "one of the young resident masters has acquired a driving instructor's qualification and has his own dual control car in which to give instruction." To avoid the risk of being accused of free advertising, the present authors note only that the same young resident master is now a very senior Departmental Head, and has long since 'retired' from the profession of driving instructor!

Rodgers would surely have been familiar with Charles 1's celebrated dictum: "Sir, a sovereign and a subject are clean different", and he made it clear from the outset that 'collegiate government' was not his model of headmastership. That said, he believed in clear communication, and rapidly established regular meetings of Form Masters, Departmental Heads and Boarding School Housemasters to discuss and progress school policy. Attention to detail was the hallmark of his style, of which his memorandum on Report Writing was a classic example: "Remarks should begin close to the left hand margin of the appropriate column, and should terminate with a full stop." introduced a comprehensive set of directions which left nothing to chance! It should be added that he invariably set an example of clear and accurate communication. The almost universal misuse of the word "incredible" today recalls the inflexion of that quiet voice saying: "Really... you don't believe it?" That word "incredible" almost – but certainly not quite – describes the influence that one man had in such a short period, and it is to that period that we now turn in greater detail.

Community Development

Robert Rodgers took command not just of a school but also of a sizeable community, for Coleraine Inst in September 1979 comprised 1205 boys, seventy-five teachers and an amazing (no, not incredible!) ninety-four ancillary staff. By any standard, C.A.I. was a significant employer of labour in the area, and the total 'family circle' of employees, their families and dependents would have gone into hundreds. In our own day of cutbacks and contracted-out services, it requires some mental effort to grasp that Coleraine Inst employed not only a resident ancillary staff, but also a team of craftsmen including joiners and painters, and even a small team of night cleaners in the day school!

The men who kept the school running in the 1980s: Back row: Alec McKinney, Des McCorriston, Kenny McBride, Brian Holmes, inset Cecil Callaghan.

Front row: Jimmy Craig, Denny McAleese, Willis Glass and Victor Callaghan.

Throughout his time, Rodgers sought both to develop the school and to link it more closely to the wider local community. During his first year as Headmaster he held a reception in school for all the local school Heads in an attempt to co-ordinate school holiday dates, and in 1983 developed this into a local forum "in response to the problems anticipated of declining enrolment in the secondary sector, and to pressure from the Department of Education to encourage co-operation among schools." In consultation with Miss Enid Carson of the Girls' Secondary School he arranged a "Survival cookery course" for Upper 6 boys preparing to go off to University, and other links with the Girls' Secondary School included a joint school quiz team and the co-operative production of three successive school plays. In 1980 pupils from the Boys' Secondary School joined the C.A.I. Ski Trip to Bulgaria, and the following year Dalriada pupils joined the Easter modern languages trip to Spain. As noted later, Head Prefects from all the local schools were invited to the annual Boarding School "Christmas feast." In 1981 a Parents' Union was formed to provide " a means for generating more of a community interest among our parents through social functions", though in the longer term this concept really only developed with the foundation of the Friends' Association in 2006.

Brendan and Hazel Drummond, and Prunella McCausland made a formidable team (or perhaps trio?) in the Music Department. These pictures of choir and orchestra in 1980 were taken following considerable success in several classes at Coleraine Musical Festival.

He was equally aware of developments in educational technology, though this extract from the Board minutes dated January 1982 shows just how great is the gap between even the recent past and the present day: "The Chairman welcomed to the Board Mr Ian Mairs, who in turn introduced Keith Bradley, Bryan Semple and Adrian Huston. Mr Mairs gave a brief history of the development of computers and explained the functions of the apparatus to be demonstrated. The boys gave demonstrations, and spoke of the possibilities for use in school and commerce." That one demonstration notwithstanding, it was to be many years before the click of the typewriter disappeared from the office, or every financial transaction – including the monthly staff salary advice – ceased to be recorded in pen in heavy ledgers, with a backup using sheets of flimsy carbon paper!

In troubled times, Rodgers had an acute ability to read the mood of the school community, and, at least once, to give wider community leadership. A dark moment in the troubles came with the murder of The Rev. Robert Bradford in his constituency office in 1981. Aware of a widespread mood of anger, which gave rise to a province-wide Day of Action on 23 November 1981, Rodgers drafted a letter

calling for an improvement in security policy, made it available for governors, staff and senior boys to sign, and personally accompanied a group of senior pupils to a an open-air service in The Diamond during the action day.

Within the school community, as has already been mentioned, he expanded the Honours System to include music and the arts as well as the established school sports. In pastoral care he instigated the system of class tutors which continues in the school to this day. In 1980 he encouraged the school Scripture Union to run a Summer Camp for boys starting in Form 1 in September, and this too has continued to grow in popularity ever since. He enlisted the help of one of the authors of this book to prepare a slide presentation entitled "Twenty Four Hours at Coleraine Inst", which continued to be the centrepiece of the June evening for new parents until digital technology finally made it obsolete! Although he ran regular tutorials for the academic high-fliers contemplating Oxbridge entrance, he also convened a staff working party on the needs of academically challenged boys and introduced the Certificate of Secondary Education for weaker candidates who would otherwise have been unclassified in the GCE examinations. Under the dynamic leadership of Arthur Nicholl, he established

Choir 1980.

a Health Education Committee which anticipated modern curriculum practice by many years. During these years also the late Donald Girvan consolidated an already excellent careers department using the intriguingly named JIGCAL system. Few were aware what this acronym represented: Job Ideas and Information Generator / Computer-assisted Learning system. The computer in question was a huge and cumbersome device, producing printouts on continuous rolls of paper perforated down each side!

In December 1982 he laid before the Governors a series of development options, some of which were still ongoing at the time of his departure. Among them were schemes for the continued refurbishment of the boarding department, the expansion of the administration block, the provision of better accommodation for the office staff and the Vice Principals, the extension of the careers department and the creation of an interview room. Two schemes which, sadly, failed for want of Department of Education funding were the conversion of the gymnasium into a two-storey sixth form centre and the building of squash courts adjacent to the Sports Hall. They would have been most valuable assets, but a severe cutback in central funding ensured that they never progressed beyond being tantalising possibilities.

In the wider world of education, Robert Rodgers was invited in 1981 to join a combined working party of representatives from the Headmasters, The Governing Bodies Association and the Bursars Association set up to survey the financing of voluntary Grammar Schools. The following year he joined the executive committees of both the GBA and the Ulster Heads' Association, and in 1983 he served a term as the Association's President.

"Co-Curricular Activities"

"Co-curricular activities", was a favourite Rodgers term to describe the full range of out of classroom activities, and his period had much to record. During his time nine boys – Rodger L Anderson, Roger C Anderson, Robert Barry, Allen McDowell, Colin Adams, Mark Lennox, John Nicholl, Wayne Pollock and Johnny Caskey – represented Ulster Schools in rugby, and Rodger Anderson won a full Irish Schools' place in 1981. 1982 was notable as the year of the first-ever overseas rugby tour to British Columbia. Rodgers himself toured with the team, and to deal with the complex finances of this tour, the Governors' permission was gained for the school to acquire a Barclaycard!

One significant event in the rowing club was Brian Russell and Neil Dennison's 1979 victory in the Double Sculls Championships of Ireland, and their selection for Ireland. Another was the retirement, in 1983, of Mickey Eyre as Head of Rowing, to be succeeded by Ian Mairs. The Cricket Club won the McCullough Cup in 1981 – their first major schools competition victory for some years – and also boasted a run of Ulster selections: Clifford Forsythe and Michael Clements in 1981, Alan Nicholl in 1982 and David Forsythe in 1983. In badminton, James McFetridge was by far the most remarkable player of his day, crowning a run of international appearances with selection for Ireland at the European Championships in Helsinki in 1983. He was, of course, not alone: Stephen Beveridge played for the Irish Under 18 squad in 1979, John Ferris achieved international honours in 1980, and Gary Henderson in 1984. With regular successes in the major Ulster and Irish competitions, C.A.I. became one of the leading badminton schools in Ireland during the 1980s. 1980 itself was a notable year, when the capture of all nine schools trophies established a record never emulated by any other school.

The Harriers and the Athletics Clubs also continued a run of considerable success. In 1977 Paul Cunning had the distinction of being the first C.A.I. harrier to be selected for an Irish Schools Team at an international event, while Philip Tweedie (today a Governor of the school) was selected to represent NIAAA at the New York World Championships in 1984. The Swimming Club, regularly successful in each age group at all the major Ulster and Irish Schools Galas, staged two particularly successful internal events: a twenty-four hour relay marathon in 1980 to raise money for the school charity, and another charity marathon – this time a twelve hour event involving the senior relay squad only – in 1982. Successes in the smaller sports included table tennis, where Tim McLennan, Roger Duncan and John McFaul achieved Ulster rankings in 1983, and Squash, where C.A.I. were the under ninteen Northern Schools' League Champions in 1982.

This record of school team successes was complemented by the achievements of individuals in their own right. Ashley Moore was selected for the Irish Surfing team in 1979,

Some of the staff involved in the 1981 school sports. From left to right Phil Blayney, John Mathers, Bob Caswell, Stephen Graham, Sam Turtle, Willie McCluskey and Donald Girvan.

Never let it be suggested that sportsmen lack a sense of poetry! On their way to the 1981 Irish Schools Championships in Claremorris, the C.A.I. Swimming Club pay their homage to the grave of W.B. Yeats at Drumcliffe. Left to right are Adrian Troy, Grant Kennedy, Michael Ho, Patrick Dark, Jeremy White, David Bones, Chris Kennedy, Andrew White, Adjay Bedi and Alistair Carson.

the same year that Ali McGarvey was selected for the Irish Youth Soccer squad; while LJ Yeoh was selected to represent Malaysia in the 1981 Junior World Squash Championships. Ranald Smith became a member of the British Under Nineteen Judo Squad during his final year at school. Finally, among the annual list of university places were two to American universities which were, at the time, unique in the history of the school. In 1982 Declan McSheffrey won a soccer scholarship to the University of Alabama, while Clifford Forsythe was offered a Volleyball Scholarship to Pepperdine University, South Carolina. To complete a rapid review with some reference to other activities, the Bridge Club shared first place with Campbell College Belfast in the Ulster Schools' Bridge Cup in 1982, and in the following year the club represented Northern Ireland at the International Tournament in Wales.

In the realm of music and drama, two traditional events were slightly modified during the Rodgers headship. One was the Christmas service of Nine Lessons and Carols, which continued to take place on the last Sunday afternoon of term. Rather than one reader from each year group in the school, plus a member of staff and the Headmaster, the format now included representatives of the boys, teaching staff, ancillary staff and governors. The other change was in relation to school plays. After many years as producer, Hugh Montgomery handed this responsibility to Robert Simpson from 1980 until 1984. As noted earlier, these productions were in collaboration with Coleraine Girls Secondary School. An exceptionally talented group of Inst actors at this time included Mark Carruthers, Robert Taylor and Jimmy Nesbitt, and few readers will need to be reminded that all three followed careers which have brought them considerable media exposure.

Pictured in 1980, David Bones hands over a substantial cheque to the Headmaster after the Swimming Club had completed a 24 hour continuous swim in aid of the school charity, Ulster Cares.

The annual tradition of school plays ended – almost accidentally – in the early 1980s. After a lifetime of school play production, Hugh Montgomery had gone into semi-retirement, but in the Spring Concert of 1983 he was tempted by the request to direct a performance of Gilbert & Sullivan's "Trial by Jury", the shortest of the Savoy Operas and the only one without spoken dialogue. With a rather basic sound system at his disposal, and without any radio mikes, Hugh improvised gloriously: the Judge's faithful tipstaff, for example, followed his master around the stage with a microphone concealed in the end of his wand!

"Trial by Jury" was a huge success, and the positive reaction it generated persuaded him to tackle a full-length Gilbert & Sullivan the following year. "H.M.S. Pinafore" paved the way for a run of musicals which were to continue without a break until 2000. More will be said about these lavish productions in the next chapter.

The Human Side Of The School

During even a brief headmastership there were some significant changes in staff. Among the longer-serving appointments were Noel Crooks and Norman Cully in 1980, Ian Crown and Mark Reavey in 1981 and Robert Kane and Mark Gray (later to become a minister in the Presbyterian Church in Ireland) in 1983. Cive Jackson left in 1980 to become Head of Classics at Ballymena Academy, and in 1982 Jimmy Stewart was appointed Vice Principal of Ballymoney High School and Richard Bennett Headmaster of Portora Royal School. Ian Wilson, another Humphreys appointee, left in 1983 to set up the North Down Heritage Centre. An expert on matters to do with the sea, and the author of the authoritative "Shipwrecks of the Ulster Coast", Ian had an encyclopaedic knowledge of football and cricket which inevitably earned him the staffroom nickname of "Wisden". Among those who completed twenty-five years service during Rodgers' headship were John Leslie, Robert Riddell and Jimmy Shaw.

Taken on the last day of Dr. Robert Rodger's Headmastership, the staff in 1983.

Sadly, these few years saw a disproportionate amount of illness among the staff. Dessie Giffin, Nevin Taggart, Joe Brown, Mickey Eyre, Cecil Henderson, Ian Mairs, Robin Semple, Donald McDonagh and Robert Riddell were all absent for extended periods. Donald McDonagh's tragic death is referred to elsewhere, and Cecil Henderson was compelled to take premature retirement on health grounds. Cecil was a formidable linguist, who in his time had lectured at Magee College Londonderry, and his departure was a great loss to the Modern Languages Department. Robert Riddell returned, but with a much lighter teaching load before his final retirement in 1988. In a similar fashion to Albert Clarke in a past generation, he had been responsible for everything concerning staff salaries. A man of total discretion, few realised, in the days before Freedom of Information legislation, just how extensive was his knowledge of the school's finances. A former pupil and a talented Mathematics teacher, he was totally fascinated by anything to do with finance and taxation, and on Budget Day each year he could be found

during free periods with a small transistor radio at his side in order to miss not a single pearl from the lips of the Chancellor! His illness left a big gap in the administration of the school, and was one factor in the appointment of Donald Cormac as full-time Assistant Bursar in 1984. One other retirement in these years was of Luther Hopkins in 1984. Luther came into the profession after a lifetime in Royal Air Force: small of stature but commanding in voice and presence, he was a genial teacher, but one whom boys rapidly learned not to cross! In December 1981 Gordon Mahony, one of the great characters of the past, died at the age of eighty-nine – almost certainly the oldest surviving former member of staff, and one of its greatest characters.

Among the ancillary staff, 25th anniversaries of service were marked for Edwin McCloskey and Willie Bradley, as well as Miss Stinson and Mrs Steele from the dayboy canteen and Miss Gilmore the boarding school matron. Notable retirements were of Frank Richardson, lab technician, in 1982 and

251

A much respected pair! Tommy Allen and Davie Pringle managed the school office, and a good deal else around the school, during the 1970s and 1980s.

of Davie Pringle and Tommy Allen, office assistants, in 1983. Tommy and Davie were well known both in the town as well as the school community, and not least of their many duties around the school were the operation of the school tuck shop, the management of the bus queues each afternoon, and (in Tommy's case) the supervision of boarders' swimming on Saturday mornings. Jimmy Black left in the spring of 1982 to become Clerk of Works at Ballymena Academy, in the same year that James Black, senior, passed away.

One very generous, and rather imposing, character of these years was the late Mrs Irene Templeton. Shortly before George Humphreys' retirement, Mrs Templeton contacted the school with a view to establishing a permanent memorial to her late husband, William Templeton (1905-1908). He emigrated to Canada with his family in 1908, and became famous as the designer of the Templeton Airport, Toronto. She not only paid the entire cost of building the Templeton Auditorium, but also installed an organ in the building and

made several very generous cash donations to the school. Although she only visited Coleraine Inst once, at the opening of the Auditorium in October 1980, she kept contact with the school until her death, aged ninety-four, in February 1989.

The Boarding School In Difficult Times

Every Headmaster since the Second World War has had to cope with changes in education policy, and Rodgers had his share. Even during his brief tenure of office, issues arose which were to have a long-term impact on the size and structure of the school. Although the threat of comprehensive education had now receded, Grammar Schools were now subject to a dayboy intake quota, though in his time the boarding school was exempt.

Of the 1205 pupils on the first official day of his headship, 291 were boarders: forty-one Malaysian, four Arab, four American, one Indian and one Rhodesian (albeit with a home

A 1981 view of Senior House, under Jim Flanagan's command.

address in the Orkney Islands!). In ability terms there was some disparity between the dayboy and boarding communities, with ninety-seven per cent of dayboys, but only fifty-three of boarders, exempt from fee-paying – though this figure included almost all the overseas boys, who would not have sat the Qualifying Examination. Remedial education for the weakest boarders seemed an immediate issue, and he certainly considered the possibility of a pre-first form year, taught by an experienced remedial teacher. A year later, the total of boarders again crossed the 300 mark, but the imposition of quota limits on the dayboy intake meant, paradoxically, that his staffing allocation was for the first time reduced – albeit only by one. Throughout the Humphreys

years, an expanding Common Room always guaranteed plenty of 'young men' for resident duty: Rodgers faced a potential shortage of staff as boarding numbers stayed buoyant. One immediate solution was the recruitment of postgraduate university students – a policy followed by some of the Belfast boarding schools. One of the first of these was Michael Clendinning, himself a former boarder, who not only undertook resident duties but also put much time into establishing a highly successful Bridge Club in the school. As a qualified teacher, taking a course in Applied Linguistics at the then N.U.U., he was doubly valuable as a temporary member of staff during a time of difficulty in the Modern Language department. A longer term possibility was the provision of "suitable accommodation for married teachers who might become resident staff." For the rest of Rodgers' time, and long into the time of his successor, staffing the boarding school was to become an increasing problem.

The first year of Rodgers' incumbency saw a very gratifying increase of the boarding school to 301 – the highest total since 1977 – but enrolment in September 1981 dipped quite sharply to 284. The turn of the 1980s – remembered now as the beginning of the Thatcher era – was a difficult time economically. Parents, who reckoned a boarding education was beneficial for their sons, were now finding it difficult to afford it for the full seven years. As Ulster Grammar Schools generally were being squeezed, more and more of Rodgers' colleagues were eager to enrol fee-payers from CAI's boarding department, in some cases even before they had completed the review period. On the other hand, boarding numbers held up remarkably well during the rest of Rodgers' headmastership, partly due the admission of several local boys who, because of the quota restrictions, could not have been admitted as day pupils, but even more to the continued influx of overseas boys. Rodgers was particularly heartened by a revival in Malaysian interest, following the U.K. government's introduction of economic university fees for overseas students, and the imposition of stricter quotas on those who sought places in Australian universities.

1980 was a peak year for boarding, and although CAI did better than most boarding schools, the trend in numbers led relentlessly downwards thereafter. Towards the end of his time, Humphreys had foreseen this, and had even given confidential advice to the Governors about the point at which the Model should be closed, and a smaller boarding department consolidated on one side of the Castlerock Road. Rodgers was no less aware of the trends, and (probably arising from an accident on the Castlerock Road in October 1981) he was also privately concerned about "the disadvantages and hazards of a split site". On the other hand, he was reluctant to close the Model whilst overseas enrolment remained relatively buoyant, and the boarding account was still in surplus. One possibility for development arose when two adjacent houses, on Ballycairn Road and Queens Park, came on to the market in late 1982. In a development plan considered by the Board in December 1982, the case for buying both properties was noted thus: "Could provide for possible consolidation if the Model were to close with declining numbers; could offer accommodation for partly resident married staff". The two properties and the adjoining land were purchased in 1983, the Ballycairn Road house being turned into accommodation for the resident domestic staff, and 23a Queens Park becoming the new sick bay and matron's residence. The former sick bay and domestic quarters were turned into additional studies and bedsits, both particularly necessary in view of a temporary expansion of boarders in Forms Five and Six. The Governors were also moving towards the concept of a smaller boarding school with more modern facilities, and the 1982 development plan encompassed "Major boarding department refurbishment", including "suspended ceilings if floors will support these" and "smaller dormitory or bedsit units as numbers decline."

Although he had no personal experience of boarding schools, Robert Rodgers instinctively identified with the community life of the boarding department, and introduced some sensitive innovations. As mentioned earlier, the selection of boarding prefects was altered to a process including self-assessment and an interview panel. He insisted that the entire boarding community attend the Sunday evening epilogue service – including the overseas boys from a non-Christian background – on the basis that it was a community meeting for the dissemination of information! In 1981 he installed a microphone in the dining hall for the benefit of the duty master, whose duties included the recitation of first and second grace at the beginning and end of meals. The Head Prefects of the Boys' and Girls' Secondary Schools, of Coleraine High School and of Loreto College were invited to the annual boarding school "Christmas Feast", though this did little to civilise an occasion which usually exemplified the more boisterous side of an all-male boarding community.

More sadly, during his time the boarding department suffered the loss of three of its best-known and loved staff. In 1981 Mrs Bessie O'Connor – "Chips" to a generation of junior boarders – passed away. Very much a larger than life character, and far more than just a member of the domestic staff for the previous twenty years, she had a pastoral influence which was the equal of many a 'professional'.

On 24 May 1982, Donald McDonagh finally succumbed to a long struggle with cancer. Best known to boarders as the Housemaster of Runkerry, and the genial chairman of the Friday evening Debating Society, "Bomba" was a man of rare character. Mathematician, musicologist and Methodist local preacher, his gentle and civilised approach to life was much appreciated by the whole school community. In a poignant tribute to his memory, the whole school lined the Ballycairn Road as the funeral cortege passed by on its way to Coleraine Methodist Church. Within four months Mrs Sweeney, the equally well-respected Matron of the Model School, had also passed away. For the first three years of his headmastership, Rodgers continued to have the benefit of the highly-experienced Richard Bennett as Senior Boarding Master: following his appointment as Headmaster of Portora Royal School in January 1983, David Harkness succeeded to this important position.

Robert Rodgers' own departure co-incided with the retirements of two of the boarding school's best known personalities. Miss Beryl Johnston was for many years Miss Moore's assistant in the boarding school canteen, and her retirement left a big gap in the team of ladies who daily produced almost a thousand meals with what was by any standards limited facilities. But it was the retirement of Miss E.M.Gilmore, after twenty-six years service as Matron, which really signalled the end of an era. Rodgers perfectly summed up this highly professional and totally dedicated lady: "She has old fashioned standards, and an authoritative air, which both commands respect and instils a certain awe."

Quotas And Qualifiers: Educational Change In The Early 'Eighties

With previous experience both of headmastering and of College lecturing, Rodgers was well aware of the politics of education. At the time of his appointment, the Dickson and Benn Reports had turned the spotlight on the enrolment policy, organisation and financing of voluntary schools and their associated boarding departments, and the Astin Report was to recommend the restructuring of the Board of Governors to include Teacher and Parent representatives. Some of the resultant changes were relatively minor: for example, the textbook allowance to each non fee-paying pupil became a lump sum paid to the school, and in line with the practice of the controlled sector, textbooks became the property of the school. The school's finances were now largely based on an annual block grant, and CAI in fact participated in a pilot scheme when this change was made in 1982. Other small acorns of the 1980s were later to proliferate into huge educational oaks: in 1980 the school was required to produce a Health and Safety Policy, and the Headmaster and Bursar attended a seminar on the then-new Industrial Relations Order. In 1983, following a landmark decision of the European Court of Human Rights, the death-knell of corporal punishment in schools was sounded by a Department of Education Policy Document on the subject. Its final disappearance was, however, a matter for Rodgers' successor.

More seriously, admissions of dayboys were now capped by a quota, and when a new formula was introduced in 1981 CAI's permitted dayboy intake was reduced from 135 to 125. This contributed significantly to a drop in dayboy numbers from 919 in 1980 to 902 in 1981, and although the quota was restored to 130, before falling again to 120, the dayboy enrolment never again reached the 900 mark. Within the quota restrictions, Rodgers suspected a 'hidden agenda' at the Department of Education, aimed at pressuring Grammar Schools into admitting only 'qualified' pupils. The NEELB position was that twenty per cent of the school's dayboy intake could include fee-payers - but only if 'qualified' boys were

Group photograph of the Governors taken with Robert Rodgers, before his departure for
Stranmillis College, Belfast.

turned away to make room for them. In 1984 the simple quota was abandoned, but intake figures were hedged about with caveats which were of little help to the Grammar Schools, and dayboy numbers again dipped sharply from 881 in 1983 to 864 in 1984. In October 1983 Rodgers reported to the Board that "a trend concealed in the global figure is the predicted decline in numbers enrolled in Form One – dayboys and boarders – and in both cases this would seem likely to continue, with a consequent shrinking of the school population and the number of staff employed." That prediction turned out to be absolutely correct in relation both to boys and to staff. It was even then becoming clear that the great days of unlimited expansion were gone beyond recall, and in retrospect September 1978 – with the appointment of no fewer than eleven new members of staff – had been a watershed. There was more. During the remainder of the 1980s the School Magazine recorded the retirements of a sizeable group of long-serving staff: in reality, those "retirements" were almost all voluntary redundancies which saved the jobs of younger colleagues as falling pupil numbers began serious erosion of the staffroom.

The other major administrative change was in the Board of Governors. The Board of C.A.I., in common with almost every other Grammar School, was unanimously opposed to the principle of Teacher and Parent Governors for a number of reasons, one of which was that The Scheme (the Constitution of the school) as it then existed prohibited from the office of Governor any salaried official of the Institution except the Treasurer and Secretary to the Board. Despite their opposition, legislation was passed, The Scheme was altered, and the Board was soon to be completely reconstructed to comprise fourteen Governors elected by The Institution, six appointed by the Department of Education, three Governors elected by parents and three by staff, and one Governor representing the Irish Society – the latter the only remaining ex officio member of the Board. The new arrangements also ended the principle of ex officio clerical members of the Board, but nine local ministers (the incumbents of First Coleraine, New Row and Terrace Row Presbyterian churches, of St Patrick's and Killowen Parish churches, of Ballyclabber Reformed Presbyterian Church, and of the Baptist, Methodist and Congregationalist churches) were designated ex-officio members of The Institution upon whom the Board could call "for counsel and assistance in matters appertaining to the pastoral oversight of the boys." This was, in effect, a neat way to keep the link with the town ministers, who remained on the Board, but no longer with the right to vote.

After a relatively short Headmastership, Robert Rodgers was appointed to the principalship of Stranmillis Training College Belfast, where he was destined to spend the rest of his professional career. In the staffroom and the boardroom at Coleraine Inst there was both regret at his departure, and also realistic acceptance that a man of his calibre was exactly the right choice for such a significant position in Northern Ireland education. Bob Rodgers was and remains a man of two Institutions, for on his return to Belfast he became first a Governor and then Chairman of the Board of Governors of his old school, R.B.A.I. His most recent achievement has been the publication of a history of the school, ably taking up where John Jamieson's monumental sesquicentary history of R.B.A.I. left off in 1960 and continuing the story down to 2007.

Mr R.J. White
Chairman, Board of Governors 1978-1997

Dr R. Rodgers

To replace Robert Rodgers the Governors again turned to a serving Principal, Stanley Forsythe of The Royal School Dungannon. His tenure spanned a period of rapid change, and he was fated to preside over the school during some of the most unsettling years in the history of modern education. A Belfastman, and a pupil of Belfast High School, the young Stanley Forsythe developed three major interests: rugby football, with the legendary Jack Kyle as an early object of hero-worship; the Church of Ireland (he was the first non-Presbyterian Headmaster of Coleraine Inst in living memory!); and the study of Chemistry. The Kilwaughter Medal in his pass degree at Queens University, followed by First Class Honours in Chemistry a year later, seemed to point towards an academic career, but instead of continuing to a Ph.D., he opted for teaching, first at Armagh Royal and then as Head of Chemistry at Portadown College. When he was appointed Headmaster of The Royal School Dungannon in 1974 he was the youngest principal of any Ulster Grammar School. When he came to Coleraine Inst ten years later, one of his departmental heads was Arthur Nicholl, who had also been short-listed for the Dungannon job!

Uniquely among the Headmasters of Coleraine Inst, Stanley Forsythe was a keen singer with a fine tenor voice and a love of church music, and Reggie Patterson lost no time in recruiting him into the choir of St Patrick's Parish Church. He brought a quiet Anglican dignity to assembly each morning, and more than one boy testified to being impressed by his careful and reverent reading of the Scripture portion and the Prayer Book collect each day. He valued the friendship of his rector, the Rev Kenneth Clarke, and when "Fanta" Clarke in due course became Bishop of Kilmore & Elphin, Forsythe was delighted to welcome

The new Headmaster pictured before his first Prize Distribution, October 1984.

him back as chief guest at Prize Day. Within the school he gave every encouragement to a Parents' Prayer Group, an unobtrusive but effective body which continues to meet weekly throughout each school term, and to the Scripture Union Summer Camp which is still a valued part of the induction process for new pupils in Year 8.

Stanley and Joan were exemplary parents, and their young family brought life and colour to the Headmaster's residence. Karen and Catherine went to the High School, but after their days at the Christie Memorial Primary School, there was no debate about where Colin, Peter and finally Jonathan would be educated. All three boys – popular and very gregarious – managed to enjoy their school careers to the full without causing themselves or their father any undue embarrassment! As the son of a father who in his time had played for the First Fifteens of Belfast High School, C.I.Y.M.S.

and Queens University, it was no surprise that Colin Forsythe finished his school career as a member of the victorious Schools' Cup team of 1992.

If pressed to sum up the Forsythe style in two words, 'genial' and 'personable' seem very appropriate. He was at his best one-to-one with people. At parents' evenings or prize distributions few people would go home without an individual greeting from the Headmaster. A good deal of informal contact around the school was made in the corridors or outside classroom doors, and he regularly dined with the resident staff, effortlessly drawing the younger staff around him into the conversation. In the privacy of the office, a formidable range of skills was deployed on staff, boys and parents as he mollified the angry, comforted the distressed, advised the perplexed and affirmed the discouraged. Teachers who went to him with a professional problem often received not only sympathy and good advice, but also the reassurance that the Headmaster had, in his time, been in the same place himself.

As a public speaker his style was homely and direct, and the sharpness of his wit was particularly appreciated in his annual speeches at the Old Boys' Association dinners. There was originality as well, and as each year's Prize Day approached there was always speculation about the theme around which he would weave his report. Possibly the most ingenious was in 1996, when the annual musical production was "The Wizard of Oz". His speech that year was woven around the names of all the principal characters, and the munchkins as well!

Shortly after he came to Coleraine, a joint Marketing Partnership, aimed at East Asia and the Far East, was formed by the Northern Ireland Boarding Schools. Stanley Forsythe was a guiding light in the Partnership from its inception, and represented it on more than one overseas visit. In the wider sphere of Headmasters' Conference meetings he was no less at home. In the group photograph taken at the end of the last Conference he attended before retirement, now on display in the School Museum, he is to be seen right in the centre of the front row!

A young lady who was destined to serve five Headmasters, and at the time of this book's publication, is still the Headmaster's Secretary. Mrs Gwen Reavey in the old school office, beside a piece of cutting edge telephone technology. The date is Wed. 13 June 1984.

Behind the easy informality, there was an insistence on old-fashioned courtesy and, when necessary, a steely determination which the boys instinctively respected. Although he rarely raised his voice, he could communicate displeasure in much more effective ways. A Sixth Form class once arrived in the author's class straight after assembly, to report some minor disturbance. One student caught the atmosphere very perceptively: "We all started to laugh, but Mr Forsythe gave us his 'death' look, and we all went quiet again"! Death looks apart, he enjoyed his leadership of the school community, and as retirement approached he frankly admitted that he would miss terribly his daily contact with the boys. When the Staff Committee sounded him out on a retirement present, he made the rather unusual request of a barometer. For a man with a keen ability to read the mood and temperature of the school – and the instinct to know when to act, and when to say (in a characteristic phrase) "leave it with me" – it was perhaps an appropriate gift at the end of the last lengthy headship recorded in this book.

"The Past Is Another Country. They Do Things Differently There."

This famous dictum could be applied as much to the early days of Forsythe's headship as to those of any of his more distant predecessors – in fact, even more. It is worth pausing at this point to highlight the sheer pace of change, both in Coleraine Inst and in the community, during so short a time as the twenty five years since the young Headmaster of Dungannon Royal took charge at the Inst. 1 January 1984 began one of those significant years, though its world was not quite the one that readers of George Orwell's eponymous novel might have anticipated four decades previously. For Headmasters, the Department of Education was not (quite) the Ministry of Fear. Although admission quotas had lately arrived, employment practices were still fairly straightforward, and league tables, health and safety procedures, safety cases, equal opportunities provisions, disability access requirements, child protection regulations, discipline and exclusions policies were yet to come. With them came names, titles and descriptions: by the time of his retirement Stanley Forsythe was all too familiar with Staff Performance and Development Review, Local Management of Schools, School Development Plans, Performance Indicators and - yes - the full panoply of the Common Curriculum!

For the boys, credit cards and 'holes in the wall' were in their infancy, and junior boarders were still collecting their pocket money each Friday from their housemasters, while seniors were advised to open either a bank account, or an account with Mr Millen at the Waterside Post Office. (Many will remember, of course, that when withdrawals reached the bottom of a page in the Post Office Book, it was retained for accounting and posted back to the holder a week later.) Some older members of staff were still insisting on a monthly pay cheque being put into their hands rather than a direct transfer made into their bank accounts. The school had only recently obtained a Barclaycard, and that because of the 1982 Canadian rugby tour. The school accounts were still managed by human brain, biro pen, the Kalamazoo System and the old-world courtesy of Miss Ruth Woodhead. The basilisk eye of the computer in every corner – and even the name Classroom 2000, which eventually brought the scheme to fruition in 2004 - would have been regarded as an Orwellian fantasy. In classrooms chalk and the blackboard were still the primary media of communication, and the overhead projector a novel concept. Whiteboards (even non-interactive ones), digital projectors or the intranet, would have been regarded as simply adumbrations of the popular TV programme "Tomorrow's World". Far in the future lay the collapse of the last bastion of the ancien regime – the hand written termly report to parents. Photocopying was almost unknown, apart from a small heat copier in the Bursar's office which produced single copies of documents on semi-transparent paper whose images faded within a few days. Scanning of course was as yet unknown. Class notes and exam papers were mostly written on to carbons or stencils and duplicated either on Banda machines (whose products, reeking with methylated spirit, were eagerly sniffed by the recipients) or on the Gestetner which incontinently squirted black ink over the hands of those venturing too near its working parts. Those staff who were well ahead in modern developments were using portable typewriters to cut their stencils, and bottles of nail varnish-like fluid to correct their mistakes.

For entertainment, each boarding house had its own television set, hired on a termly basis from one of a number of local dealers – like Dempseys in Portstewart or Willie Walker in New Row - who rented out television sets as well as selling them! Communication with the outside world was still by a single pay telephone in the boarding department – the familiar Coleraine 3579 - used by resident staff and boys alike. Considerable discussion preceded the installation of a direct line to the Senior Resident Master's room. The first mobile telephone to appear in the school – the size of a brick and with a telescopic aerial – was purchased largely to facilitate contact with the bursar during his peregrinations around the school estate. (As late, indeed, as the year 2000 the Governors were asked to provide a mobile telephone to help teachers driving school vehicles keep contact with the school!) Modernity was represented by the transistor radio and the cassette tape recorder, the age of the record player and the vinyl disc was still far from over, and chart-toppers from "Top of the Pops" could still be bought as "seventy eights" over the record counter in Woolworths. Fast food outlets existed only in the United States of America, and hungry boarders going down town at the weekend still relied on the chip shops, the Lombard Café or Morelli's Coffee Bar to sustain them before the rather exiguous Friday or Saturday tea. Within the school, both dayboys and boarders ate cooked lunches served to tables in containers: the cash cafeteria concept was first introduced to the day canteens in 1986. In one respect, though, the revolving wheel came full circle: today, as in the 1980s, gas is once again widely used as a domestic power source. In the mid 1980s, however, the school was forced to alter the kitchens to take account of the rundown and closure of Coleraine Gas Works. Healthy eating, and the vilification of junk food, of course, lay in the future. Without a qualm of conscience the school was quite happy for Tommy Allen and Davie Pringle to run their tuck shop daily at break and lunchtime, and after school for the boarders – selling the boys what they liked, rather than what was good for them!

Finally, and more sombrely, Northern Ireland seemed intractably mired in a stalemate which was certainly one factor in the decline of the boarding department and the continuing gravitation of talented leavers towards university education 'across the water'. Political progress was minimal, and the return to Belfast of any devolved power, least of all in regard to education, seemed a very long way off. In this respect, if not in the politics of Northern Ireland education, things were rather more settled by the end of the Forsythe era than they had been at the beginning.

The School Community Over Two Decades

William White, George Humphreys and Stanley Forsythe all enjoyed lengthy terms of office, but of the three, Forsythe arguably faced the most rapid pace of educational change. Not least of these was a very marked alteration in the staffroom profile, and this is worth a brief historical reflection.

During the Humphreys era, the expansion of the school and the increase in promotional opportunities encouraged men to commit themselves to a lifetime's service in unprecedented levels.

The distinction of forty years' service is a very considerable rarity in the history of CAI, and can be claimed by only eleven of the several hundred people who have served the school over its 150 years. Dr S.J. Hunter's forty-eight years of service could never now be equalled, but during the Humphreys era Albert Clarke retired after forty-five years (including a short period as Bursar after the end of his teaching career), and Jock Mackenzie with a similar period of service. Jim Edwards and Dan Cunningham, who retired in the 1970s, were the last men to serve for forty-two years. The remaining five – Tom Ryan, Arthur Nicholl, Edgar Charlton, Trevor Surgenor and Jimmy Shaw – ended their service during the Forsythe years. Trevor Surgenor, with forty-one years' service at his retirement in 1998, was the last to serve for over four decades.

Over the last twenty-five years a much more mobile approach to career patterns can be discerned within the teaching profession. Despite a steady fall in staff numbers as the size of the school declined, Forsythe still made thirty-two appointments during his term of office, although twenty-six of his original staff were still there at the time of his retirement. As the school celebrates its sesquicentenary, the tradition of long service in a predominantly male staffroom is disappearing, and anecdotal evidence would indicate that Coleraine Inst is not alone in this respect. By the beginning of David Carruthers' headmastership in 2007, the average age of the staff was considerably lower, the average period of service shorter, and the proportion of female staff much higher than had been the case in the mid 1980s.

To begin with the departures of the period, no fewer than twenty-eight of those who left the staff had served for at least twenty years, and a significant proportion for thirty years or longer. A fair number of these retirements reflected the shrinkage of staff numbers, and the willingness of the more senior men to seek voluntary redundancy in the interest of their more junior colleagues. They also included the last group of men to have continued teaching well into their sixties – although with changes in government policy and pension arrangements, this trend may well revive in the coming decades!

Five of the White generation - Tom Ryan, Hugh Montgomery, Mickey Eyre, Jack Farrell and Arthur Nicholl – and a very large number of Humphreys' "young men" ended their teaching careers working for Stanley Forsythe. Most of their names will be familiar to former pupils of a particular generation: Robert Riddell, Donald McKay, Donald Girvan, John Leslie, Edgar Charlton, Ian Knox, Jim Foote, Sid Grey, Trevor Surgenor, Eric Hayes, Jim Archer, Robin Semple, Jimmy Shaw, George Hanns, Ken Cushion, Des Giffin, Dermot Jennings, Jim Flanagan, Tommy Blair, Jimmy Gordon, Ken Ford, Colin Beck, the school Bursar,

**John Leslie and Robin Semple –
a formidable team in the Vice Principal's
office, and not a computer terminal in sight!**

and Dr Brendan Drummond all had service of twenty-five years or more. Since eleven of these were departmental heads, and three finished as Vice Principals of the school, the middle and senior management of the school was very different by the end of the Forsythe years from it had been at the beginning. Many others moved on to teach elsewhere, and no fewer than four men – Mark Gray, John McClean, Robert Simpson and the late Ian Mairs – left to train for ordination in the Presbyterian Church in Ireland, the Church of Scotland and the Church of Ireland. Finally, Stanley Forsythe's retirement coincided with that of Miss Prunella McCausland, for almost twenty-five years an instrumental tutor in the Music Department. Her retirement, together with that of her brother-in-law Brendan Drummond, and a year of later of her sister Hazel Drummond, after thirty years' service, ended a unique family network within the staffroom.

The CAI Staff Marathon relay team.
Left to Right: Mr. M.McNay, Mr. M. Irwin, Mr. R. Beggs, Miss J. Davis, Miss K. Poots

There is no truth whatsoever in the rumour that Mr. McNay was passed by a 70+ year old man dressed as a lollipop man who was doing the whole Marathon on his own.

Miss Davis opted for the "Glory" leg. She set off at snail pace but she was just saving herself for a fine flourish at the finish line in front of the cameras. She was particularly strong on the stretch outside Campbell College and retook with ease the lollipop man who had not passed Mr. McNay.

All in all, a great day's fun was had by everyone involved and the interest generated through the school in the weeks before the big day was tremendous. About £1000 was raised for the Northern Ireland Cancer Fund for Children, most of it very willingly contributed by the traditionally generous pupils of C.A.I.

The team is determined to better its performance next year but this has nothing to do with Miss Davis' move to Campbell College! This year they finished in 552nd place out of nearly a thousand entrants in a time of 4 hours, 7 minutes and 32 seconds. The lollipop man's time is not known. Honestly!

64

Article from the June 2002 issue of the school magazine.

As the school's enrolment declined, departing staff were not always replaced. Following a Province-wide trend, newcomers were becoming more inclined to stay only briefly before seeking promotion elsewhere, and in some cases the school was able to offer only short service contracts. These trends were to intensify in the following years. During Forsythe's entire headship, thirteen members of staff served for five years or fewer before moving on: significantly, in the seven years since his retirement, departures in the same category have now almost matched this number.

Continuity does still exist, though on a smaller scale: twenty-six staff at the time of Forsythe's appointment were still in post when he retired. Thirteen of his own thirty-two appointees were still in service at the start of the sesquicentenary year, the most senior of them Mark Irwin (1989), John McCully (1991), Patrick Allen (1992), Ken Peden (1993), the 1997 trio of Richard Beggs, Lynn McClure and Trina Reid, and David Stewart (1998). As this chapter was being written, the entire staff was still aged on the right side of sixty – possibly for the first time since the founding years of the school. The comparative youthfulness of the staff was exemplified by the entry, for the first time ever, of a staff relay team in the 2002 Belfast Marathon. Michael McNay, Mark Irwin, Richard Beggs, Jill Davis and Karen Poots deserve their niche in the history of the school – and for the record, their time of 4 hours seven minutes and thirty-two seconds gave them 552nd position in a field of over a thousand entries!

In a period of retrenchment there was still some expansion. Reference will be made later to the development of technology in the school: here it is sufficient to note that under Gareth Clarke (1986 – 1999) a completely new department was evolved, and that its staff included not only the present Head of Technology, Mark Irwin, but also Martin Edwards (1988-1989) and Robert McGregor (2002 to date). A subject which began in room 24, the old library, using cardboard and drinking straws as constructional materials, today occupies a purpose-built Technology Centre with state of the art facilities which – as will be seen later – have produced literally world-ranking construction and design.

On the other hand, and again following a Province-wide trend, Ancient History, Latin and Greek were all gradually phased out during the Forsythe years. When Bob Caswell retired in 1985, after twenty-three years as Head of R.E., Ken Cushion moved from Classics to lead the R.E. department, and with the retirements of Donald Girvan in 1991 and Trevor Surgenor in 1998, Robert Simpson became the sole remaining teacher of Latin and Greek. His own departure in 2002, to seek ordination in the Church of Ireland, brought 142 years of Classics to a close, although during the year 2002-2003 Trevor Surgenor returned to see the fifth form class through to the last GCSE Latin results that CAI would ever record. When they sat in their first Latin class at Coleraine Inst, Neal Griffith, Jeff Haslett, Alan Kershaw, Seamus Fleming and Mark Gilfillan would never have thought that five years later they would make their own little piece of history as the last Classics scholars!

Stanley Forsythe's staffing policy was innovative in another respect. Apart from the Music Department, where Prunella McCausland, Heather Drummond and Joy Clyde were at first mainly instrumental tutors with some class teaching, Coleraine Inst must have been one of the last Northern Ireland Grammar Schools with a virtually all-male staff. His headmastership began to redress the balance, and saw the appointment of eighteen ladies. Two of them, Mrs Alison Blackwell, appointed Head of English in 1999, and Mrs Suzanne Cameron, who became Head of Music in 2002, were not only the school's first two female Departmental Heads but also the first two HODs to be externally appointed. His other female appointments were Lynn Jeffers, Ruth Millar, Lynn Montgomery, Trina Reid, Jill Davis, Jennifer Bell, Lesley Orr, Karen Poots, Heidi Giffin, Tonia Hunter, Julie Stevenson, Joanne Mace, Stephanie Hollinger, Heather McCarroll and Melanie Bell. Although never a full-time member of staff, Angela Kavanagh spent lengthy periods in the Geography department from 2000

THE END OF CLASSICS AT COLERAINE INST

In a bygone age Latin and Greek were an essential part of Grammar School education, and they certainly featured from the foundation of Coleraine Inst in 1861. Our first three Headmasters- appointed at a time when only Arts graduates were eligible to hold the position - were all in this tradition. There are surviving old boys, too, with memories of Dr S.J.Hunter – a former vice principal who was a distinguished classicist, some of whose books are still in the school library's collection, and whose name is commemorated in one of the prizes presented each year at Speech Day.

Some years ago the Inst, in common with many other grammar schools in Northern Ireland, took the decision to phase the Classics out. Greek and Ancient History disappeared from the curriculum in recent times, and Mr Robert Simpson, who retired last year, was the final Head of Classics. The GCSE class he taught in form 4 now becomes the final Latin class in the school's history.

Neal Griffith, Jeff Haslett, Alan Kershaw, Seamus Fleming and Mark Gilfillan would scarcely have thought such a transformation would take place in their school lifetimes, since when they came in 1997 Latin was still a compulsory subject throughout the Junior School. Fortunately, Mr Trevor Surgenor, himself a former Head of Classics for many years, was prepared to come out of retirement to enable this class to complete their GCSE studies. Mr Surgenor was associated with Classics at Inst for some 41 years before his retirement in 1998, most of them as head of the department in succession to Mr J.I.Brennan, later to become Headmaster of the Royal School, Armagh. The Classical tradition will not be completely lost, as some of the resources of the department have gone to Ballymena Academy, where Mr Clive Jackson [a teacher here from 1971 – 1980] is currently Head of Classics. But Coleraine Inst will retain one link with the past. In his early years at the school Mr Reavey taught Latin as well as French: so along with the last Latin class, we can also identify the last current member of staff to have taught Latin!

Mr. T. Surgenor and the last GCSE Latin class.

42

Another article from the June 2002 issue of the school magazine.

onwards. Mrs Trina Reid was in due course to make history by becoming the first Year Head (the gender neutral equivalent of Form Master!) in the school's history.

The Board of Governors itself saw considerable change during Stanley Forsythe's time, and there were significant changes between the group of men who appointed him, and the men and women who appointed his successor. During his headmastership he worked with three Presidents of the Board - John White (1978 to 1997), Jim Tweed (1997 to 2001) and Ken Cheevers (2001 to 2004) – as well as two Bursars, Colin Beck and his successor Gordon Knight who currently holds the position of Bursar and Clerk to the Board of Governors. Colin's connection with the school as pupil and employee totalled a massive forty-four years, thirty-seven of them as Bursar. At the time of his retirement the school magazine recorded:

"his detailed knowledge of the school site and services was unsurpassed, and architect and surveyor alike frequently sought his advice on solutions to the problems they encountered during the many stages of upgrading that Inst has enjoyed over these past years."

Some very long-standing members of the Board retired or died during this period. Ernest Morrison and Dr George Kane resigned in 1988. The retirement and death in 1989 of Bill Henry – the man who chaired the Board which appointed George Humphreys - broke yet another link between the White and the Forsythe eras. Three years later, Gordon Crawford's retirement brought to an end a family connection with the Board and the school stretching back almost to the time of TG Houston. At the time of his retirement he had served as governor since 1947, and was thus the last member of the Board to have served

Mr J.S. Tweed

Chairman, Board of Governors 1997 - 2001

The Board of Governors, pictured shortly after Stanley Forsythe's arrival at Coleraine Inst.

Colin Beck served as Bursar from 1965 until 2002, serving three headmasters, though his connection with the school as pupil and Bursar spanned a total of forty-four years.

during William White's headmastership. In 1993 Edwin Conn and T.B.F. Thompson retired, while in 1994 death removed another long-serving governor, Jim Balmer. David Edmiston, a flamboyant character and a loyal supporter of the school and the Old Boys' Association over many years, retired in 1996. The Board was particularly shocked by the sudden and premature death of Mr Alan Hamilton in 1998. Towards the end of this period the Rev Tom Donnelly, at the time the senior serving governor, died in 2002, and in the same year Leslie Morrell stepped down from the Board. In line with developments in the staffroom, Miss Margaret Boyce's appointment in 1994 ended the male domination of the Board, and four years later she was joined by Mrs Alison Millar.

During Stanley Forsythe's headship, parents and staff gained representation on the Board for the first time. The background to this has already been explained, and on 27 February 1986 three teacher governors (Jim Flanagan, Jim Foote and Robin Semple) with three parent governors (William King, the Rev Sam Millar and Mr Mervyn Patterson) took their seats in the boardroom for the first time.

While some of the older governors were not entirely happy about this development, the long-term effect has been very beneficial to the Board's operation. In addition, the unwritten convention that these elected governors do not seek a second term of office has allowed an increasing number of staff and parents to gain insight and experience. Coincidentally, an Executive Committee was set up in 1985 to handle some areas of Board business "without embarrassment to either the existing Board members or the parent and teacher governors", and each Board meeting now receives a report from the Executive for discussion.

Tragedy touched the school community in these years. The summer holidays in 1987 had scarcely begun before the tragic death of James Fulton, a sixth form student and a loyal member of the Harriers Club. A year later, the school community lost a much younger member, fourteen year old boarder William Evans. In 1990 his parents presented a trophy in his memory to be competed for in the Triathlon Event. Although no longer a pupil, Christopher Danton, a boarder from 1975 until 1983, died at a tragically early age, and the family generously provided the school with an all-weather cricket square in his memory. Other recent former pupils whose lives were cut short prematurely were John Nichol and Christopher Johnston, the latter during his first year as a Cambridge undergraduate. In the summer of 1990 fifth year student Gareth Hutchinson, a promising sportsman and member of the Shield-winning Medallion team of 1989, was killed in a traffic accident. A cup in his memory was added to the list of Prize Day awards for the fifth former judged to have made the greatest contribution to the sporting and academic sides of school life.

In September 1985 Miss Audrey Dempster was appointed as office receptionist, immediately establishing herself as a good-natured and highly efficient practitioner in public relations. Tragically, fourteen months later she was fatally injured in a traffic accident whilst driving home after her day's work. In July 1989 the school maintenance men were stunned by the sudden death of Bertie Vance, a painter for 24 years and one of the most popular members of the school community. Mrs Grace Foote, wife of Jim Foote and one

of the boarding school matrons, died in the summer of 1994 after a long illness. Less well known to the wider school community, but the faithful servant of three Headmasters, was Mrs Craig, housekeeper of the Headmaster's residence, who also died in 1994.

The staffroom suffered loss through the sudden deaths of George Hanns in the summer of 2000 and Kevin Davis in the following year. George will be remembered as an engagingly eccentric character as well as a fine classroom teacher of formidable academic ability. Many of his mannerisms were noted and imitated by his colleagues as well as his pupils – the gentle voice, the rhythmical swaying which accompanied his most profound utterances, and the inevitable cardboard box under his arm, conveying exercise books to and from the classroom. His sudden death within weeks of retirement (he was still technically in employment) was a numbing shock to his family and to his colleagues. The Hanns Memorial Cup for Poetry was presented by the family in his memory, and fittingly its first winner was one of George's former pupils,

George Hanns's retirement in June 2000 proved, sadly, to be only a matter of months before his death. John McCully, Len Quigg, Victor Boyd and Robert Simpson, along with Jill Davis and Alison Blackwell, made this light-hearted presentation on the last day of the school term in June 2000.

Michael McAllister. Equally abrupt was the passing of a much younger man, Kevin Davis. Though gruff in manner and uncompromising in discipline, Kevin was a good-humoured classroom natural for whom teaching was a very congenial calling, and he was heavily involved in the development of I.T. in the school. After a sudden and brief illness, he died on 26 December 2001, and the huge turnout of staff at his Requiem Mass in Ballymena demonstrated both the popularity of the man and the strength of school community feeling. In two very fitting tributes to his memory, the staff and boys raised the sum of £2000 for the Chest, Heart and Stroke Association, and the Davis family donated a cup for annual presentation to the top mathematician in form five.

Beyond the staffroom, the wider school community saw some significant changes during the Forsythe years. In 1986 Mrs Anne Guy became an assistant matron in the boarding school, retaining that position until the boarding department closed. Heather McShane joined the boarding catering staff in 1987, eventually succeeding Miss Moore as the last boarding school catering manager. Additions to the technical and maintenance staff included Peter McLaughlin and Kenny McDowell in 1987, Denny McAleese in 1988, Des McCorriston in 1993, James Stevenson and Paul Magill in 1995 and Stuart Scott in 2000. For a short time in the late 1990s a trio of gap year students from Australia worked in the school office and the boarding department. Joe Healey, James Gay and Simon Doherty were intensely sociable and extremely good humoured: long after their departure they left many happy memories behind them.

Some well-known personalities among the secretarial and ancillary staff retired or left during this period, including office receptionist Miss Ruth Woodhead in 1986, lab technician George Knight, (senior), and boarding school caterer Miss Anne Moore in 1987, head groundsman Willie Bradley and Clerk of Works Eddie Norris in 1988, Miss Mary Colhoun, assistant matron for 16 years, in 1989, Assistant Bursar Donald Cormac and master craftsman Willie Lake in 1990, day school Caterer Miss Doreen Stinson and groundsman Jimmy Craig in 1995, Billy Ferris from the school office in 1997, and Alec McKinney from the ground staff and Edwin McCloskey – with forty one years' service to the school - as chief technician in 1998.

Edwin in particular became a legend in his lifetime. As a young lab technician, at his own request and in his own time, he successfully sat the Certificate examinations in the sciences, and by the time of his retirement would have been well able to teach a class himself. The science department stores bore the stamp of his formidable organisation – row after row of shelving, with equipment logically arranged for easy access and where necessary properly labelled. In his tiny workshop, everything from carpentry through metalwork, plumbing

The retirement of loyal servants of the school is always a matter of sadness: here Willie Bradley and Willie Lake receive gifts to commemorate their service to the school.

and electricity to glass-blowing was tackled without fuss or difficulty, and as the pace of Information Technology quickened, he effortlessly kept himself ahead of the computer revolution. Nor were his skills limited to the science department: back in the 1950s it was he who set up the first inter-com connecting the Headmaster's office with the rest of the administration block, and advised Mickey Eyre on the construction of a purpose-built training tank for the oarsmen. Even retirement did not end his service to the school, for when the school museum was established in 2006 he not only donated a vast range of scientific apparatus, but also advised on its positioning, labelling and display.

George Humphreys' 80th birthday in 1996 was marked by a surprise birthday party organised by the Governors, and attended by the entire Humphreys family connection as well as past and present staff.

With the closure of the boarding department, the last two matrons, Mrs Hilda Orr and Mrs Anne Guy and the caterer Mrs Heather McShane were declared redundant in 1999, while painter Willis Glass and lab technician Roy McQuilkin retired in 2000, the year that receptionist Jacqui Monroe emigrated to Canada.

Several deaths among former members of staff during the Forsythe years signified the ending of an era. Jock MacKenzie, that memorably flamboyant character with forty-five years of service, passed away in 1987, and Jim Edwards, whose connection with the school stretched back to 1931, died in July 1992. Well known to generations of Old Boys, Jim was blessed not only with a long and active retirement, but also with a happy second marriage following the death of his first wife in 1973. 1993 saw the passing of Robert Riddell, and in 1995, following a long retirement, latterly in very poor health, George Wilson was taken from us. George Humphreys died in January 1997, followed almost within the year by his wife Emma, in February 1998. Not long before, the Governors had marked his eightieth birthday with a surprise celebration in the Humphreys Hall – a delightful occasion attended by the entire family circle, the Board of Governors, and a number of guests who brought the greetings of each decade of his headmastership. The years seemed to fall away that night, as he replied to the greetings with a speech of rare eloquence and passion.

It was in many ways appropriate that Jack Farrell, a convinced Christian and lifelong Wesleyan, died suddenly in his pew during evening worship in Coleraine Methodist Church in January 1991. His son Jeremy, who followed his father into the teaching profession, presented the J.P. Farrell String Cup both in memory of his father and in recognition of his own very considerable contribution to school music as a pupil. Finally, the death of Dan Cunningham in March 2003 at the age of 91 removed the oldest surviving former member of staff, whose connection with the school as both pupil and teacher spanned almost fifty years.

Two possibly unique circumstances for the school community were recorded in the June 1989 and June 1998 school magazines. That of 1989 included a group of ten boys and a very proud lady, in a photograph which will possibly remain unique for all time in the school's history. Mrs H.S. Millen of Knockmult already had a connection with Coleraine Inst through

Rather surprisingly, there has been little in the way of year reunions in the history of the school, but the enterprising class of '74 staged a twenty year reunion in 1994.

her brothers Harry and Jack Crawford both of whom were Old Boys. Harry joined the RAF in 1936 and was killed in action in 1941, while Jack left in 1944, studied medicine at Queens University Belfast, and spent the rest of his life in Canada, dying in Victoria, British Columbia, in 1976. Mrs Millen was in time to be blessed with ten grandsons, every one of whom was on the school rolls during the academic year 1989-90. The ten young men featured in this unrepeatable group were Andrew (Upper 6), son of Eleanor and Glenn Kerr; Russell (form 2), son of Anne and William Millen; Thomas (Upper 6), Ronald (form 5), Stephen (form 3) and Alan (form 1), sons of Millicent and Harry Millen; Malcolm (Upper 6), Stuart (form 3) and Neale (form 1), sons of Hester and Colin Beck; and Greg (form 1), son of Gladys and John Henry. To widen the connection slightly further two of the fathers – Colin Beck (1955-62) and John Henry (1958-65) were themselves Old Boys. Colin himself, of course, was the school's bursar.

Nine years later, the magazine again featured a family represented by four brothers at the school at the same time. Steven, Alan, Colin and Neil McCracken spanned the complete range between Year 8 and Year 14, and were quite taken with the idea of being – in their own way – history makers!

A New Educational Landscape: Headmastering After 1984

As hinted earlier, not even the most prescient observer could have foreseen the changes which Forsythe was called on to implement, or the environment in which they occurred. Throughout the United Kingdom, education began to feel the gathering pace of central government scrutiny and direction, and the revolution in information technology ensured that every aspect of a school's performance could be instantly accessed and analysed on the web.

Following in the footsteps of OFSTED in Great Britain, the Schools' Inspectorate in Northern Ireland developed much more rigorous procedures than the rather more gentlemanly encounters of a bygone era, and inspection teams demanded huge amounts of paperwork in advance of their appearance. In 1992 'league tables' of A level and GCSE examination results were first published.

After two decades, the General Certificate of Education and its younger cousin the Certificate of Secondary Education, were combined in 1988 into the General Certificate of Secondary Education Ordinary Level. The 1989 Education Reform (Northern Ireland) Order began the most far-reaching curriculum upheaval in living memory – a process which

Mrs Millen and her ten grandsons.

twenty years later is still ongoing. Areas of study, contributory compulsory subjects, 'cross-curricular' and 'educational' themes rapidly gave birth, and among their firstborn children were Education for Mutual Understanding, Cultural Education, Economic Awareness and Health Education: by the new millennium they had in their turn begun to breed such sturdy grandchildren as Learning for Life and Work. Alongside curriculum change came major changes in assessment. Programmes of study, focussed on assessment targets across key stages, introduced new levels of bureaucracy into the most straightforward of classroom encounters. To supervise them came the Northern Ireland Curriculum Council and the Northern Ireland Schools' Examination and Assessment Council. The first year of the new century saw the end of the traditional two year Advanced Level structure, and in the last three years of his headmastership, Forsythe had to oversee the transition to AS and A2, and a complete modular restructuring of the examination system. At the junior end of the syllabus, 1992 saw the beginning of the Northern Ireland Common Curriculum covering what were now known as years 8 to 10, though the concept of a major external examination system at the end of Year 10 eventually – and thankfully – died a death.

Following a review of pastoral care in the school Year 8 Mentoring was established in September 2002. This picture shows the first-ever mentors in a scheme which has continued to prove its value over the intervening years.

Back Row: Nigel McCloy, Terry Forgrave, Neal Griffith.
Middle Row: Alan Kershaw, Philip Braithwaite, Andrew Cummings.
Front Row: Jeff Haslett, Stephen Kirkpatrick, Alex Humphrey, Peter Topping.

Also in this period, school principals increasingly found themselves walking in a legal minefield. In 1982 a case relating to corporal punishment in schools went all the way to the European Court of Human Rights: its determination ended schools' freedom to impose their own codes of discipline, and heralded a new emphasis on the rights of children. Within a decade, very proper concerns about institutional child abuse created a small industry of bureaucracy as schools were required to produce written policies on child protection, to have designated teachers responsible for its delivery, and to implement codes of practice for dealing with allegations. A Parents' Charter for Education was unveiled in 1993, and from 1996 all schools were required to produce detailed policies and strategies to identify and implement Special Educational Needs provision. From 1987, and not without some eyebrow raising among older staff, the school was legally required to have a written policy on Sex Education. By 1990 the staff were receiving Information Technology training, and staff Committees had been established to develop Curriculum Change, Pastoral Care, Records of Achievement and the Teaching of Lower Ability Groups.

In legal terms, contracts for teaching and ancillary staff had to be revised in the light of changes in employment law. Revisions of this law, and the law on expulsions and exclusions, gradually circumscribed the traditional autonomy of head-teachers to 'hire and fire' as they saw fit. Far gone were the days when a Headmaster advertised for staff, shuffled the letters of application, held one-to-one interviews and finally presented his choice to the Governors for ratification. By 2001 the Early Professional Development Scheme had transferred the latter part of postgraduate teacher training to schools, and the Headmaster and Chairman of the Board were required to monitor the first two years of employment and certify the successful completion of a range of assessments.

Further gone too were the days when the same Headmaster could terminate a boy's education by a curt "pack your bags!", and by the end of the Forsythe era, expulsions had turned into a protracted process involving the Board of Governors, the Education and Library Board and legal representatives of the boys concerned. Even a successful process could be reversed on appeal to a Tribunal. A further problem concerned the financing of school travel. Legislation passed in 1991 prevented the school from charging for any activity directly related to a course of study, and this led to the principle of a voluntary contribution from parents to cover travel costs. Finally, after 1992 the school was required to hold an annual meeting of parents: it is only fair to say that this rarely attracted more than a handful of attenders, nor did it last more than a few minutes. Early in the new millennium the legal requirement to hold this rather pointless annual meeting was finally removed – but not before attendance had declined to zero anyway!

The Northern Ireland Voluntary Grammar Schools had their own particular problems. In common with all post-primary schools, their right of admission was restricted by intake quotas which were first imposed, then modified and finally scrapped. The basis of their funding was altered, and in economically difficult times approval for capital schemes became harder to gain. Sweeping changes were imposed on the structure and powers of Boards of Governors. Towards the end of Stanley Forsythe's time the 2002 Burns Report proposed the replacement of the 11+ examination and the establishment of local school collegiates – issues which are far from final resolution as this book is being completed almost eight years later!

Coleraine Inst was affected in many ways, not least a decline in pupil numbers from an all-time peak of 1220 in 1980 to 845 in 1990, and a shrinkage of the boarding school during the same period from 301 to 109. A transformation in the landscape was taking place, and an end to the calmer and simpler age in which George Humphreys had been able to triple the size of the school within two decades.

The Last Years Of Boarding: 1984 – 1998

Closing the boarding school in 1998 was without doubt the most difficult single decision of Stanley Forsythe's headmastership. In retrospect, there was an inevitability about it: boarding in Northern Ireland was in sharp decline, and Coleraine Inst had outlasted several of its contemporaries. Boarding numbers peaked as far back as 1971 with 319 boys, though in percentage terms the peak year had been 1964, when the boarding department accounted for 36.45% of the school population. From 1971 onwards numbers had been drifting slowly down, year on year, broken only by slight increases in 1976, 1977 and 1980. The decline accelerated relentlessly after 1982, exacerbated by a number of factors, notably difficult economic conditions, changes in government policy on Grammar School intake (not least the imposition of the 'full economic fee' on fee paying pupils) and a contraction of our international clientele. A further problem was staffing. As the school's overall enrolment declined, it became increasingly difficult to guarantee a flow of young resident masters to run the boarding school. The employment of post graduate students as resident staff was a qualified success, but it was truthfully only a stopgap. Gender issues in employment presented a further challenge, and near the end of the boarding school's existence Forsythe did indeed appoint the school's first ever female resident teacher.

The traditional ethos of boarding education was changing too. In the past, boys were not infrequently enrolled as prospective boarders at birth (the last instances of this at Coleraine Inst occurred as late as the 1970s). Parents believed that their sons' interests would best be served by spending their full school careers in a boarding environment. They expected that weekend passes would be few and far between. They accepted that conditions would be more austere than at home, and in an age when discipline and authority were less questioned than they are today, they believed the overall boarding package would be character-building. Not all parents, however, went as far as one father who in 1974 addressed a curt note to a Housemaster: "My son has not written home for three weeks. Please beat him.", or a mother who deposited her tearful offspring one September with the observation: "This'll make a wee man of him!" Coleraine Inst had a better record than many

Another of the boarding school traditions was the decoration of dormitories before Christmas. The dormitories were 'judged' by the Headmaster's wife after the Christmas feast, but in truth everyone won a small prize!

boarding schools in relation to the standard of accommodation and the provision of pastoral care, and generations of boarders contributed to a sense of community which in some cases nourished lifelong friendships. Two positive spin-offs of this closed community spirit were the disproportionately large contribution that boarders made to the sporting life of the school, and the very considerable academic success of boarders – particularly those who began from a very modest base.

In the 1980s and 1990s, however, perceptions and expectations were changing. By 1991 it was becoming clear that the overseas market was in terminal decline: symbolically this was the last year in which a Malaysian boarder was enrolled. Forsythe's frank estimate was that the survival of boarding would depend on a local market that no longer had potential for growth. Boys were becoming less rather than more likely to remain as boarders for their entire school careers. Austere living conditions and rarely granted weekend passes were no longer acceptable as once they had been. Forsythe worked hard to make boarding more attractive, and by the early 1990s most dormitories had been thoroughly refurbished. Bunk beds and duvets replaced the old iron bedsteads,

and carpeted floors, suspended ceilings and double-glazed windows gave dormitories a cosiness they had never had before. Individual study accommodation spread further down the age range. Latterly boarding became virtually a five day week commitment, with day-boarding as an additional option. Real effort was put into developing the quality of pastoral care, and to marketing the school both locally and overseas: Stanley Forsythe's involvement in the Northern Ireland Boarding Schools Partnership has already been mentioned. Paradoxically, in its latter years a much smaller boarding department was an extremely happy environment for the shrinking group of boarders who enjoyed a greater sense of space than any of their predecessors. In the latter years too, contracting numbers made the traditional "Christmas feast" a much more intimate (and, in all honesty, a much more mannerly) occasion.

To some extent also, the boarding department was a victim of its own past success. Down-sizing would have been difficult, as a large suite of buildings needed to be maintained regardless of how many boys lived there. Indeed, even after the boarding department closed, upkeep of empty buildings – which were integral to

FOR SALE

The Model School

Castlerock Road, Coleraine

on instruction from The Coleraine Academical Institution

Occupying a prestigious elevated position, overlooking the Castlerock Road, the above property occupies a site of approximately 1.25 acres and is ideally suited for residential development or various Institutional uses.

Preliminary discussions have already taken place with the Department of the Environment — Planning Service, regarding redevelopment, and outline planning permission has already been granted for demolition.

Nationwide Anglia Estate Agents

Daniel Henry & Son

22 New Row, Coleraine. BT52 1AF Telephone: (0265) 53777/8

The disposal of the Model School was a sign that the tide had turned for boarding, not just in Coleraine but among many other Ulster schools.

The last-ever boarding school group photograph, taken on the evening of the 1995 Christmas feast at the request of Joe Cassells who that year completed 25 years' unbroken service in the Boarding Department.

the school's structure and therefore could not be demolished – continued to be a significant drain on resources. One obvious, and easy, option was to close the Model School. As far back as 1978 George Humphreys had privately advised the Board to close the Model if numbers began to fall sharply, and after 1985 there was no further capital expenditure on the other side of the Castlerock Road. The Model closed in 1988, and following a successful application to de-list the main building, the site was sold. Today Old Model Court, much quieter by day than its predecessor, perpetuates the name in a pleasant residential development. Ironically, even the disposal of the Model was of limited benefit to the school, as it coincided with the introduction of new and very strict fire regulations for boarding schools, the implementation of which consumed a good deal of the sum generated from the sale.

The writing was on the wall. Due to falling numbers, the boarding school Scout Troop was closed in 1992. More seriously, the boarding account went into deficit in 1993, and in 1997 the annual losses began to outweigh the interest from accumulated investments. At this point the Governors commissioned Price Waterhouse to review the options, and their report made bleak reading. Projections indicated that on current trends the annual loss was likely to be a six figure sum by the millennium. There was really only one conclusion, and in 1998 one hundred and thirty eight years of history came to an end. The community tradition survived right to the last. Indeed in 1992, a boarding department of 93 boarders could still provide over half the squad of that year's victorious Schools Cup team, including its captain, Darryl Callaghan. The year before its final closure, Joe Cassells ended a record twenty five year association with the Boarding Department as its final Head of Boarding, and the last three Housemasters at closure were Dr Norman Cully, John Martin and Phil Blayney. Much of the main Boarding Department was eventually rebuilt and reconfigured into new classroom accommodation along with a School Museum: this significant development, opened during the final year of Forsythe's headship, will be mentioned later. Appropriately, his retirement in 2003 was also the year when Anthony Davis and James Dillon, the last remaining boys to have begun their school careers as boarders, left at the completion of their A level studies. The school magazine duly pictured Anthony and James along with Mr John Patterson, who by that time was the last serving member of staff to have been a boarder. Changed times, indeed!

Two years before the closure of the boarding school, 'down-sizing' led to the closure of the separate catering facilities for the boarding department. Resident staff, housemasters and Headmaster Stanley Forsythe have just finished the last-ever lunch in the old dining hall.

By 1998 boarding had finished.
On the day the Boarding School finally closed Mrs Hilda Orr (Matron) and Mrs Anne Guy (Assistant Matron) are pictured with Joe Cassells (former Head of Boarding) and the last three Housemasters: John Martin, Phil Blayney and Dr Norman Cully.

BOARDING AT C.A.I. –
THE LAST SURVIVORS!

Coleraine Inst was founded as a boarding school, and at one stage boarders formed over 30% of the school population and had a heavy input into all the major school sports. Those days are now passed, but the new school year should see the reopening of the refurbished boarding department, albeit in a new guise.

Though dormitories, studies and common rooms are now gone, many of its human resources remain. Four of our technical staff – Kenny McDowell, Brian Holmes, Kenny McBride and Mary Bredin – began their employment in the boarding school, while Victor and Cecil Callaghan's general responsibilities included the boarding department as well as the day school. No less than 28 of our present teachers served time as resident staff. Seven of these - Dr Cully, Mr Breen, Mr McCluskey, Mr Blayney, Mr Martin, Mr Harkness and Mr Cassells - are all former Boarding Housemasters, and Mr Harkness and Mr Cassells are also former Heads of the Boarding Department.

In the world of rugby football, so long associated with boarding, there are also final connections. Jonathan Bell will certainly go down in history as the last ex-boarder, and Jeremy Davidson as the last former member of the resident staff, to be capped for Ireland.

But of the thousands of boys who have passed through the Boarding Department, only two now remain on the present school rolls. Anthony Davis, whose late father Kevin was also a resident master in the 1990s, came in September 1995 as a day-boarder, and James Dillon has the distinction of being the last boy to have begun his school career as a full-time boarder. James' Housemaster when he came in September 1996 was Mr Martin, now Head of History and coincidentally still one of his teachers.

Pictured with Anthony and James is Mr John Patterson, who has the distinction of being the last member of staff to have been a boarder [between 1964 and 1968]. Though now unique in this respect, Mr Patterson is by no means the only former pupil among the staff. There is of course his own son, who joined us this year, as well as Mr Adams, Mr Kane, Mr Allen, Mr Beggs and Mr Smith, all of whom were pupils here between the 1970s and the 1990s, and all of whom should be with us for many years to come!

Anthony Davis, James Dillon and
Mr. John Patterson

41

Article from the June 2002 School Magazine.

Into The Age Of The Net: The I.T. Revolution

In a fairly traditional, indeed rather hierarchical, establishment, it was really quite remarkable that such a large amount of long-term change probably began in a totally new department headed by a very young man. Known almost from the outset as "Boffin", Gareth Clarke arrived fresh from Stranmillis College in 1986 to set up the Technology Department almost from scratch. Over the next thirteen years he oversaw the creation of a new department housed by 1990 in a Technology Block at the cutting edge of classroom design, while his knowledge of computing greatly assisted the installation of the original ISDN line Internet system in the school. As mentioned earlier, the first computer had arrived in the school slightly before Gareth's time, but it must be admitted that most staff looked on the whole IT concept with some scepticism. The initial staff training in 1990, working on Apple Macs with nine-inch monitor screens, would today seem antedeluvian – but the die was cast. A year later CLASS (Computerised Local Administration for Schools) came to CAI, though the Board of Governors may not have been much the wiser when informed that "we have received ten terminals, a disk driver, three printers and training for staff in utilising the system. Initially it will assist the school's administration, but it will also be used by staff as the associated hardware and software develops". To a school and a boardroom for whose older members "hardware" was still something they bought in McCandless's shop in Church Street, these were heady days indeed! By 1997, not without some pressure from the late Kevin Davis, the school had a website. A lot more pressure was needed, this time by the school on the Department of Education, before a major I.T. upgrade, including the establishment of an intranet, became available. Few schemes can have been more unfortunately named than "Classroom 2000", for this scheme was not fully completed until 2004, the year after Stanley Forsythe retired.

Not least of the Technology Department's achievements was in the enhancement of the school's global reputation, and this ongoing story will be taken up later. In 1995, Computer Aided Manufacture was added to the Technology syllabus, and three GCSE and A level students, Ben Carter, Michael Ross and Richard Castle, took up the challenge of creating their own unit. Branded CAISAM (Computer Assisted Image Scanning and Manufacture), they developed a computer controlled milling machine which won international awards in Hamilton, Ontario, where the boys represented Ireland in an International Science and Engineering Fair, and at a further international exhibition in Santiago, Chile. Fulfilling a long-term ambition, Gareth Clarke and his wife Sylvia emigrated to Canada in 1999, but people like Mark Irwin, Mark Adair, Robert McGregor, Mike McNay, the late Kevin Davis and Paula McIntyre have ensured that Coleraine Inst continues to develop as a leading player both in technology and in the ongoing computer revolution.

Stanley Forsythe, headmaster, greeting Dr John Reid, at that time Northern Ireland Secretary, during a visit to the school in 2002. Dr Reid held an audience of Upper 6 politics students spellbound, and completely over-ran his schedule!

Expansion And Improvement: Building In The Forsythe Era

Although numbers were shrinking, the school's amenities and facilities continued to improve from the mid 1980s onwards. Early in Forsythe's headmastership the administration block was expanded to provide better office accommodation and a more pleasant reception area. Included in the scheme was a completely new boardroom, and the first Governors' meeting was held there on 10 December 1986. The seamless appearance of the extension was, though, rather artificial: in the interests of aesthetic continuity, weathered roof tiles were transferred from the Gymnasium to the new extension, whilst the Gym roof got the benefit of the new tiles!

The 1980s programme of refurbishments in the boarding school has already been described, though declining numbers led to the closure of some of these areas within a very few years of their transformation. For a short time in the early 1990s, the sick bay and Matron's flat were moved to 23a Queens Park, but as boarding numbers continued to decrease these facilities moved back whence they came during

The last major event of Stanley Forsythe's headship was the official reopening of the refurbished 1860s building in June 2003. Mark Carruthers unveils the commemorative plaque.

Left to right Stanley Forsythe, Mark Carruthers and Mr Ken Cheevers, President of the Board of Governors.

the last years of boarding. Following the end of boarding in 1998, the very small number of boarders who elected to finish their education at Coleraine Inst were accommodated in 23a Queens Park for one year after the official closure.

The turn of the millennium saw the completion of several refurbishment projects including a thorough re-vamp of the school's library facilities. The Technology Centre has already been mentioned, but a word should also be said about Science provision. A rolling programme of improvement, beginning in 1999, led to the refurbishment of all nine science laboratories, complete with digital projectors, interactive whiteboards and the most up to date data logging equipment and internet access. The completion of this project was marked by an opening ceremony on 11 December 2001.

By far the biggest scheme, though, was the complete transformation of the original boarding department, declared open in June 2003 within a few months of Stanley Forsythe's retirement. There had long been a need for additional classroom accommodation, and the creation of a drama suite and a school

museum had been long-term aspirations. From 2000 onwards, a committee of Governors planned the scheme, which was certainly the most ambitious since the Humphreys years. Almost two years of continuous upheaval followed, with temporary classrooms located in the quad, and parents advised that there was simply no room to bring cars into school to collect boys at the end of the school day. The result was striking and attractive, and as the most recent expansion of the facilities, the project is described in detail as an appendix to this chapter.

A Gold Mark School: Beyond The Curriculum In The Forsythe Era

"Sports Mark: Gold" is an appropriate way to introduce a survey of the sporting life of the school during Stanley Forsythe's headmastership. The Department of Education and The Sports Council regularly monitor all aspects of sports' provision in schools, and in 1997 Coleraine Inst was one of only three Northern Ireland schools to earn the ultimate accolade of the Gold award. The citation spoke of the standards attained across the range of

Pictured at the time of the 1997 Gold Mark presentation, referred to in the text, are Jim Foote, Ronnie McPherson and Stanley Forsythe.

Ulster Schools' Cup Winners, 1992.

Back Row: Mr A. Sherrard, Mr R.S. Forsythe, Mr S. Graham.
Back Row Group: G.J. Wilmott, G.H. Waugh, K.D. Johnston, G.A. Robinson,
M.V. Hyndman, M.A. McLornan, C.S. Forsythe.
Middle Row Group: B.M. Know, D.M. Kirkpatrick, T.R. Young, J.A. McKee,
G.A. Campbell, J.R. Hutchinson, R.W. Kettyle, M.A. Waugh.
Front Row: P.C. Curry, J.C. Bell, D.H. Callaghan (captain), R.A. Wilson, A. Redpath.
(Missing: B.R. McConnell).

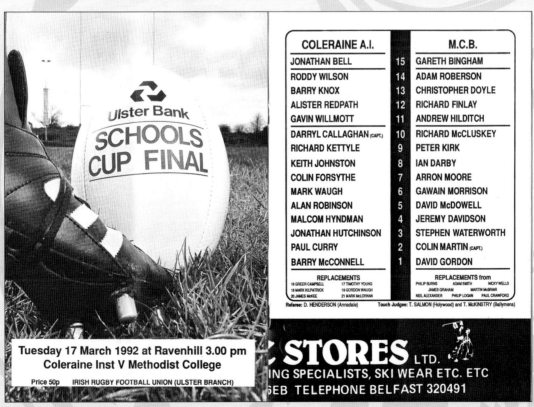

COLERAINE A.I.		M.C.B.
JONATHAN BELL	15	GARETH BINGHAM
RODDY WILSON	14	ADAM ROBERSON
BARRY KNOX	13	CHRISTOPHER DOYLE
ALISTER REDPATH	12	RICHARD FINLAY
GAVIN WILLMOTT	11	ANDREW HILDITCH
DARRYL CALLAGHAN (CAPT.)	10	RICHARD McCLUSKEY
RICHARD KETTYLE	9	PETER KIRK
KEITH JOHNSTON	8	IAN DARBY
COLIN FORSYTHE	7	ARRON MOORE
MARK WAUGH	6	GAWAIN MORRISON
ALAN ROBINSON	5	DAVID McDOWELL
MALCOM HYNDMAN	4	JEREMY DAVIDSON
JONATHAN HUTCHINSON	3	STEPHEN WATERWORTH
PAUL CURRY	2	COLIN MARTIN (CAPT.)
BARRY McCONNELL	1	DAVID GORDON

REPLACEMENTS
16 GREER CAMPBELL   17 TIMOTHY YOUNG
18 MARK KILPATRICK   19 GORDON WAUGH
20 JAMES McKEE   21 MARK McLORNAN

REPLACEMENTS from
PHILIP BURNS   ADAM SMITH   NICKY WELLS
JAMES GRAHAM   MARTIN McBRIAR
NEIL ALEXANDER PHILIP LOGAN PAUL CRAWFORD

Referee: D. HENDERSON (Annadale)   Touch Judges: T. SALMON (Holywood) and T. McKINSTRY (Ballymena)

Ulster Bank
SCHOOLS
CUP FINAL

Tuesday 17 March 1992 at Ravenhill 3.00 pm
Coleraine Inst V Methodist College

Price 50p   IRISH RUGBY FOOTBALL UNION (ULSTER BRANCH)

C STORES LTD.
...ING SPECIALISTS, SKI WEAR ETC. ETC
...6EB TELEPHONE BELFAST 320491

Darryl Callaghan's fifteen were the most recent to have won the Ulster Schools' Cup, in a
thrilling final still remembered almost twenty years later. Uniquely, the team included boys
who played for two schools' international teams: Jonathan "Dinger" Bell for Ireland and
Roddy Wilson for the Scottish Schools.

Action from the 1992 Ulster Schools' Cup Final.

sports provision, the number of staff involved and the degree of success at all levels. But there was something more. Though not directly connected to any criteria, this honour was actually a most fitting recognition of the thirty-one years' service of Jim Foote, who retired that year as Head of P.E. In acknowledging the Gold Mark award, Jim characteristically and modestly referred only to the staff and boys who had created and sustained the school's sporting success. It fell to his colleague Jimmy Shaw to record Jim's own massive contribution to CAI in the School Magazine. One extract from that most perceptive of tributes summed up the man: "As he moved gently but firmly among us, Jim Foote was an organiser, a reassurer, an inspirer and a great example whom people emulated even if hardly conscious of doing so." As we begin a summary of the activities covered by the huge umbrella of his Department, it is important not to forget a man who by his very nature was supremely competent, and totally self-effacing.

Although Stanley Forsythe's scrupulously fair Prize Day Reports customarily dealt with the sports in alphabetical order, it is probably best to begin with the one which involved most members of the school community. Despite a 1987 policy change in Schools' Rugby which reduced the age limit for school representation to 18, successive senior teams had much success, with Schools' Cup final appearances in 1988, 1990, 1992 and 1998 and a victory in 1992 which at the time was reckoned as one of the highest-scoring finals in the history of the competition. Not to be outdone, the 2nd XV had a sustained run of successes in the annual 2nd XV Schools' Tournament, while the Medallion team won the Ulster Schools Sevens in 1985, and the Medallion Shield twice: outright in 1989, and shared with Methodist College in 2000. The 1st XV Canada tour of 1982 was followed by visits to South West France in 1985, to Japan in 1988, to Paris in 1990, to Chile, Argentina and Uruguay in 1993, to the Cook Islands, New Zealand and Fiji in 1999, and to South Africa in 2002. Among those who represented Ulster were Paul Chambers, John Nicholl, Wayne Pollock, Dessie Smith, Brian Swinson, Johnny McCartney, Trevor McCallum, Keith Johnston, Andrew Hutchinson, Stephen McConnell, Andrew Kirkpatrick, Russell Harte, Angus Monteith, Gillan Carruthers, Robert Conway, Leslie George, Wayne McAfee, Neill Patterson, Paul Roxborough, Richard Beggs, Kevin Beattie, Jonathan Bell, Roddy Wilson, Paul Currie,

Darryl Callaghan, Alastair Redpath, Allen Robinson, Barry McConnell, Nicky Brown, Jonathan Dobbin, Russell Harte, Philip Kirkpatrick, Graham Turner, David Burns, David Willmott, Ian Gilchrist, and Andrew Trimble. The honour of Irish representation was held by Paul Chambers, Wayne Pollock, Brian Dean, Jonathan Dobbin, Stephen McConnell (who played in Australia), Gillan Carruthers (in France), Jonathan Bell, David Willmott, Ian Gilchrist and Robert Conway (both Irish Schools and under 19) and Andrew Trimble. Andrew and Jonathan Bell, also of course gained full international caps after leaving school. Uniquely, due to his family ancestry, Roddy Wilson became certainly the only Coleraine Inst boy ever to have donned the blue jersey of the Scottish Schools International Team in 1992!

**Jonathan Bell (Irish Schools) &
Roddy Wilson (Scottish Schools).**

There was also a remarkable continuity of service among rugby coaches, and men like Jim Foote, John Leslie, Edgar Charlton, Dermot Jennings, Sam Turtle, John Patterson, Mike McNay, Willie McCluskey and Stephen Graham all accumulated periods of over twenty five years of coaching.

The Rowing Club achieved success in these years in spite of losing four highly experienced coaches. Mickey Eyre had of course retired in 1987, but illness prematurely ended the teaching careers of Steen Anderson in 1992 and Sydney Grey in 1997, while Ian Mairs had left in 1986 to train for ministry in the Presbyterian Church. Coaching assistance was supplemented by Ronnie Bryson, Paul Livingstone and Robert Blair and by Simon Hamilton and Neil McClements, both of them experienced oarsmen who worked for some time as assistants in the boarding school whilst pursuing postgraduate study at The University of Ulster. A particularly useful overseas visitor was Australian gap year student James Gay of Scots College Melbourne, who stroked the Coleraine Inst crew rowing at Henley in 1996. At the other end of the age range, Pat Erwin and the evergreen Bobby Platt contributed a lifetime of experience to helping the Inst Club, and coached the crew which rowed at Henley in 1998. In 2003 a group of oarsmen quietly arranged for him to feature on a local television programme entitled "Making a Difference" – a fitting tribute to a man who would have had every reason to stay in quiet retirement. International oarsmen in these years included Stephen Medcalf, Richard Boomer, Colin Campbell, Jonathan Todd, John Millar, William Wright, Jonathan Coulter, Geoff MacDiarmaid, Edward Grey, and Alan Campell – a name which was to become world-famous, and will recur in the next chapter. John Millar and Geoffrey MacDiarmaid achieved selection for the Irish Coupe de Jeunesse Squad in 1997, winning gold medals at the European Junior Rowing Championships in Bosbaan, Holland.

At home, the Wray Cup was won in 1987, 1988 and 1999, and the Craig Cup in 1996. Further afield, 1990 marked Coleraine Inst's return to Henley Royal Regatta for the first time since

1967. Three members of this crew – Richard Boomer, Colin Campbell and Andrew Todd – were selected to row in the Irish crew at the Home Countries International at Nottingham. In the mid 1990s, Coleraine crews again made names for themselves at the London H.O.R., and at Henley in 2001, a Coleraine crew achieved a first round victory in the Princess Elizabeth Cup for the first time in the history of the Club. Additions to the fleet of boats came in 1990 with a new eight named by Mr David Boomer, and in 1996 an enthusiastic team of fundraisers led by Mrs Alison Millar raised almost £25,000 to buy new boats and ergometers. Mr Billy Huston, one of the oldest surviving former oarsmen, travelled to Henley that year to encourage the crew and to name one of the new boats "W.C.Huston".

The formidable Badminton Club machine kept Coleraine Inst at the forefront of this sport throughout the period. Jim Flanagan, Allan Gilmour, Donald McKay, Robert Blair and Paul Livingstone formed a tight coaching team of long service and great experience. The number of Ulster and Irish championship victories would fill a chapter in themselves: it was noted with some satisfaction that at the 1991 Championships the club had completed exactly 100 Ulster and Irish titles since 1970! In June 2002 a large contingent of past and present players of the whole of his career entertained Jim Flanagan to a celebratory dinner to mark his retirement after thirty-eight years service to the school and the sport. Very sadly, as will be mentioned in the next chapter, death prematurely claimed both Allan Gilmour and Paul Livingstone only a few years later. Among the leading players of the time were Colin McBride, Gary Henderson, James McFetridge, Geoffrey Oliver, Richard Kinghan, David Ilsley, Ruari Hatrick, Gary Anderson, Reid Moody and Bryan Henderson. Some of these boys represented both school and country at the highest levels. James McFetridge represented Ireland at the European Junior Championships in 1984. Colin McBride played at the European Championships in Warsaw in 1987 and was selected to train with the Commonwealth Games Squad in 1988. Gary Anderson played at Ulster and Irish level, was Ulster Champion

of Champions and school champion from 1994 to 1997. Reid Moody won the Champion of Champions Tournament in 1998, and played for Ulster under nineteen.

The closely connected Athletics and Harriers Clubs continued successfully. Among those who competed successfully in Athletics at Irish level in 1984 was Matthew Gordon, while Philip Tweedie (who went on to compete in the world Junior Championships in New York) and Roger McKay represented the Northern Ireland AAA under nineteen team in the Home International. Roger himself also won selection for N.I. AAA teams competing at the British Junior National Indoor Championships and the Home Countries International at Meadowbank, Edinburgh, in 1985. Other boys who achieved success at Irish level included Christy O'Neill in 1986, Philip Pollard in 1988, Richard Kerr in 1993, Glenn McMurray, Mark Darragh and Gary Bellingham in 1995 – the same year that David Matthew achieved full international representative honours – and David Matthew and David Willmott in 1996. In 2000 Ashley Gilchrist, Daniel Kerr, Robert Conway, Jonathan Adams, Aaron Rankin and Gillan Carruthers represented Northern Ireland at the Commonwealth Youth games in Edinburgh, and Gordon Clarke achieved Ulster representative honours. In 2001 Greg Walton, Ian Purcell, Gillan Carruthers and Robert Conway also achieved Ulster and Irish selections.

The Harriers continued successful competition at home and in annual visits to the prestigious inter-school events in Glasgow and Coventry. Their ultimate success came in 1994, with victory in the King Henry VIII Coventry Relays. Coleraine Inst had competed here since 1973, and the success of Russell Watson, Mark Tosh, Richard Kerr, Nathan Hansford, David Kerr and Stuart Beck confirmed Coleraine's position as the unofficial British Schools' Champions. Greg Walton was selected for the Irish team for the Schools' International in Wales in 2002. Once again, a solid core of loyal and long-serving staff underpinned many years of success. The names of Ken Cushion, Jimmy Shaw and Richard Adams deserve special mention in connection

The only Coleraine Inst team ever to win the King Henry VIII Coventry Schools relays – the British schools' relay championships. With Mr Richard Adams are pictured Stuart Beck, Nathan Hansford, Russell Watson, Richard Kerr, David Kerr and Mark Tosh.

particularly with Harriers. These men, along with Stephen Graham, Dessie Giffin and Jim Foote, were also associated with Athletics in season. Finally, and probably never noticed, was a small but important detail. For many years Tom Blair, Head of Geography but no mean calligrapher, must have produced the immaculate copperplate on many hundreds of winners' certificates at schools events. Following his retirement, the tradition was continued by John Brown, Head of the Art Department.

Reference was made in an earlier chapter to what Jimmy Shaw, the founding father of Harriers at Coleraine Inst, once described as "an institution within the Institution". For generations, the Annual School Road Race involved every boy in the school around the traditional Ballycairn circuit of 2.6 miles – some taking it more seriously than others, and many probably rather enjoying the experience of blocking the traffic on what in the 1980s was still a rather quiet thoroughfare. 1990, however, was the year the Road Run ended.

A combination of factors led to this: increasing road traffic; the expanding ramifications of health and safety legislation; a deterioration of interest in distance running. The spectacle of several hundred boys making a mass start from the Ballycairn entrance, with the same Jimmy Shaw – megaphone in hand - towering above them from his stance on top of the gatepost, faded into folk memory. And although the Harriers Club continued to run the familiar course competitively, it was never quite the same again.

Under John Leslie and Clive Jackson, and later Tony Lee's, supervision, cricket continued to be enjoyed throughout the school. Ulster Schools selections included Derek Forsythe in 1984, Stephen Lusk in 1989, Francis Ward in 1991 (the latter travelling to Canada with an Irish under nineteen team in 1991) and Stephen Kelly in 1997 and 1998, while Philip Kirkpatrick played for Ulster Schools in 1994 and Irish Schools at a cricket festival in Holland in the summer of 1995, and his brother Andrew achieved Ulster selection along with Stephen

Kelly the following year. Although not quite as far travelled as the rugby club, there were regular fixtures in Dublin and in 1990 the First XI was entertained at Aras an Uachtarain by the Irish President, Mrs Mary Robinson. From the 1998 season onwards, the club had the benefit of an all-weather wicket, the generous gift of the Danton family in memory of their son Christopher, who died tragically of illness at the beginning of his professional career.

Arguably the greatest resurgence came in the area of schools golf, much of the credit for which went to the late Alan Breen. In 1985 the senior team won the Ulster Section of the Aer Lingus Schools' Championship for the first time, while in 1987 and 1989 the senior golfers won the Ulster Schools' Winter League, followed in 1990 by first victories in both the Ulster and Irish Schools' Championships. Michael Sinclair was a significant figure in these years, playing for the Irish Youth Team and continuing his professional career after leaving school. In 1993 Richard Elliott achieved the distinction of becoming Irish Junior Champion and in 1994 Richard Elliott, Chris Brown and Mark Hemphill won the Ulster Section of the Golf Foundation of Ireland tournament and the Irish title. Most significantly, this gave the trio the right to represent Ireland in the

international finals held at the famous Royal and Ancient at St Andrews, where Coleraine Inst finished in seventh place – in the world! Richard Elliott's school career finished in 1995 with selection for the Irish Schools' Golf team. In 1996 the seniors won the Ulster Schools' Winter League and the Golf Foundation Irish finals, and Kenneth Allen, Chris Brown and none other than the young Graeme McDowell played in the International finals at Blairgowrie. Here they finished in fourth place with the best performance of the home countries and the second best in Europe. Further Ulster and Irish successes were recorded in 1997 and 1998. Before his school career ended, Graeme McDowell went on to play for an Irish boys' team in Slovenia in 1997 and the following year in an Irish Junior team which won the Nations' Cup in Belgium. As this book was going to press, Graeme's historic victory in the U.S. Open in June 2010 was making world headlines. It was an honour for the school to be associated in a small way with the first European golfer in forty years, and the first Northern Ireland player since Fred Daly in 1947, to have won one of the most prestigious competitions in the world of professional golf.

Other smaller clubs punched far above their weight in successes at home and beyond. Under

Pictured at the 1984 Irish Schools' Swimming Championships at Tuam are Patrick Allen, Kenneth Collins, Jeremy Bolton, Amit Bedi, and the brothers Grant and Dean Kennedy.

Robert Simpson's dynamic leadership in the 1980s and 1990s, the Swimming Club retained its position as an Ulster leader. Hadden Page, Johnny Keys, Alistair Nimmons and Adrian Eakin's victory in the 1988 Irish Schools' Freestyle Team Relay was a first for the club. In 1993 Chris Lees achieved Irish Schools' selection, while the following year Keith Morrison was selected for the Ulster men's squad at the Interprovincial Championships. In 1997 Martin Boddie was selected for Ulster Schools. The Tennis Club produced a Junior Ulster Championship team in 1986 and an Intermediate one in 1987. A member of both teams, Richard Beggs (later to return as a member of staff) was selected in 1988 for the Under 18 International Squad, playing as no. 1 on the Ulster Schools team. In the early 1990s the school competed briefly in the then popular discipline of Triathlon, and in 1992 Mark Tosh represented Ireland in Spain at the European Junior Championships, finishing as top Irishman.

One school sport that never quite took off was Men's Hockey, which was introduced as a games option in the 1990s. Despite the enthusiastic leading of two female staff – Karen Poots and Trina Reid – Coleraine Inst has yet to produce a schools' trophy victory, or a provincial or national selection!

A Multi-Faceted Community: Other Extra-Curricular Activities

Coleraine Inst in the 'eighties and 'nineties may have been in numerical decline, but the sheer variety of activity beyond the classroom or the sports pitches more than compensated. For want of space, an impressionistic sweep must suffice. To begin with, by far the biggest events of the year between 1984 and 2000 were the annual musicals which for almost two decades replaced the traditional school play.

The tradition of musicals began in Hugh Montgomery's last years at the school, with five of the Gilbert & Sullivan Savoy Operas staged between 1983 and 1987. The last of them, "Iolanthe" in 1987, even brought Hugh out of retirement for one final production. Under Len Quigg's and Brendan Drummond's direction the repertoire broadened, and two of the greatest spectaculars were "Oklahoma" in 1994 and "South Pacific" in 1997. Two shows were repeated: "Oliver!" in 1988 and 1995, and "Joseph and the Amazing Technicolour Dreamcoat" in 1989 and 2000. Playing for three nights to audiences totalling well into four figures, and involving upwards of 120 boys, these ambitious performances involved girls from Coleraine High School, and were justly regarded as the high point of the Easter term. Len's appointment as Vice Principal ended

A reminder of the huge and lavish productions which ran annually during the 1990s: a climactic moment in "Annie Get Your Gun".

Joseph 2000.

thirteen years of direction, and there was to be only one more – "Camelot" in 2001 directed by Mrs Heidi Giffin. Heidi's departure, and Brendan Drummond's retirement, marked a natural pause, and the musicals have been replaced by a series of spring concerts and dramatic productions.

Former pupils and staff members of this era have been particularly generous in leaving special awards behind them for annual competition in the spheres of music and the arts. From two former Heads of Department came the Dr Brendan Drummond Cup for Junior School Music, and the Blackwell Cup for A Level English Coursework, while Richard Tullett and Vijay Sharma donated the Sharma-Tullett Cup for Senior Debating, Jimmy McAleese the McAleese Cup for Drama, and Mark Carruthers and Robert Taylor the Burbage Cup for acting.

Although not strictly a school production, some dramatic history was made in 1984 when the late George Hanns chartered a special train - itself probably a unique event in the school's history! - to take 280 boys to a production of "Twelfth Night" at the Lyric Theatre in Belfast. There was a further coincidental Inst connection in that the train driver was the father of an old boy, Willie McCahon, at that time Head of Modern Languages at Armagh Royal.) Described by George as "a triumph of

logistics", the crowning moment of the entire operation was the delivery of 280 Kentucky Fried Chicken suppers to Botanic station literally minutes before the arrival of the last train back to Coleraine!

One casualty of changes in examination timetabling was the traditional Christmas Festival of Nine Lessons and Carols. Non-availability of the Assembly Hall led to the cancellation of this service after 1999, and it was replaced by an internal school service on the penultimate day of term. Among the noteworthy musicians of the period may be noted Dan McMullan, leader of the Ulster Youth Orchestra in 1984.

For a time in the 1980s a group of A level economists made a name for themselves, setting up a Young Enterprise Company marketing metronomes (and declaring a modest dividend to their shareholders!) in 1987 and winning the Northern Ireland interschools "Running the British Economy" competition in 1988.

Debating developed as a serious interest in these years, and Robert Park (1985), Julian McComb (1986), Brian Moss and Colin Murray (1999) achieved high levels of success at provincial and national levels. In design work David Blair became a national personality in 1996 when he won a car design competition sponsored by BMW. The car he designed made a guest appearance at the school, and David himself became something of a media star. Seven years later, a Year 11 team took first place locally in a Jaguar Formula 1 Model Car Competition, and went on to the United Kingdom finals. In 1989 a Quiz Team was entered for the Irish News/Ulster Television Schools Quiz. The following year's team won the Irish News Cup – a fitting conclusion to the career of Donald McKay, whose retirement from the staff began with the expenses-paid trip to Paris which was part of the prize!

Further media success was achieved in "Blockbusters", a popular television schools quiz of the 1980s screened by Central Television. The success of John McIvor and David McIlroy in 1987 won the school a video recorder (which survived in the History department into the new millennium!), and in 1992 Martin Aiken and Matt Ekins also appeared on the show. Kyle Martin, Neil Morrison and Andrew Robinson entered in the 2000 Worldwise Quiz, won the Geography Association's Northern Ireland Schools finals, and finished with representation at the United Kingdom finals in Birmingham. In 2002 The Letts School Challenge involved Coleraine Inst in an internet entry-based general knowledge competition. The team won the Northern Ireland qualifying round and came third in the grand final at Cambridge.

From the 1990s, some of our science students excelled themselves in high-level competition. In the Royal Society of Chemistry's "Top of the Bench" competition in 1991, David Dunwoody, Dara Henry, Dickson Ward and Alastair McIntyre won the Northern Ireland heats and went on to become British Isles Champions. In 1999 David Connor and James Elliott won silver medals at the Irish Physics Olympiad and James travelled to Padua, Italy, for the summer Olympiad. The following year the school was represented in the U.K. National Physics 2000 competition. David Connor and Andrew Millen achieved bronze and silver in the Under Twenty Physics section, and Andrew represented Ireland at the International Olympiad in the summer. In 2003 at the Irish Science Olympiad, Gareth Callaghan and Timmy Martin achieved silver

and gold distinction. Although a large number of Science teachers were involved in preparing students for these competitions, particular mention should be made of Robert Blair and the late Paul Livingstone. Further reference to these men will be found in the next chapter.

The Bridge Club brought considerable success to the school at Ulster and Irish level. Possibly the peak year was 1999, when Gary Bellingham and James Cummings won representative honours on the Ireland Under 20 bridge team, while Sam Duddy and Peter Chan joined them among the award winners at the Irish Schools' Bridge Championships. The selection of Peter Chan and David Dickson for the Northern Ireland under 20 team in 2000, and Jonathan Fillis and Seamus Fleming in 2003, continued the tradition right through to Forsythe's retirement.

During Stanley Forsythe's years considerable stress was put on charity fundraising. Hardly a Saturday passed without our boys being active in street collections for various charities, and in 2000 Junior and Senior Charity Committees were set up in the school by Miss Karen Poots. The annual 'no uniform' day for charity began early in the Forsythe period: the most eye-catching of these was in 2002, when Karen managed to persuade a large number of her colleagues to dig out their old school uniforms for the day. The school's energetic activity in charitable work was recognised in 2001 by the award of the Rita Roden Cup of Achievement, presented at Hillsborough Castle in response to fund raising for the Mozambique Disaster Fund of that year. Certainly the most colourful of the charity projects was a tea towel produced in 2001 featuring wickedly accurate representations of most of the teaching staff, drawn by sixth form artist David Anderson. Not lacking in commercial *nous*, David capitalised on the success of this venture by persuading his victims to buy the original cartoons of their likenesses! Another noteworthy form of fundraising was through the annual Readathons, introduced in 2002 by Alison Blackwell, then Head of English, which in its first year raised almost £2.500 for The Roald Dahl Foundation and Sargent Cancer Care.

David Anderson, Lower Sixth

Many old boys of the past decade will remember the dynamic Karen Poots, and her many fundraising activities in aid of school charities. David Anderson produced a series of wicked caricatures of the staff, and they were made up into a unique teatowel which sold in quantity. One of the authors of this book has a central position, along with his iconic kettle and coffee mug!

Non-uniform days for charity became regular features of school life after the 1980s, but only once did the staff make an effort in this direction – a 'uniform' rather than a 'non uniform' day. The brainchild of the then Charity Organiser Karen Poots, this aspect of these days was – rather sadly in the opinion of the authors – never repeated!

Throughout the Forsythe years, Coleraine Inst was prominently involved in the Seven Schools Project, a cross-community grouping of the seven local secondary schools aimed at promoting links between young people of different political, religious and academic traditions. Similarly cross-cultural links were maintained through involvement in the Ulster Project Delaware, which each year gave eighteen teenagers and four leaders the experience of travelling together to the U.S.A. Finally, a mention should be made of the twinning link between Coleraine and La Roche sur Yon in France. A number of staff, including Mark Reavey, Eric Hayes and Tony Lee were prominently involved in the Twinning Association, and periodic exchange visits were organised between Coleraine Inst and the Lycee Kastler in La Roche.

Any Headmaster's retirement is marked in a variety of customary ways, but few have had the distinction of a musical composition.

Not long before the end of the term, Stanley Forsythe was lured to the Boardroom, to find a lone drummer awaiting him. Aaron McClean, even in First Year a champion drummer with Finvoy Pipe Band, launched straight into "The Forsythe Retreat", a drum solo he had composed specially to mark the occasion! Some days later, Forsythe conducted a more conventional final school assembly, not just the last of the year but also of his career. His response to a generous gift, and a rousing ovation, from the boys was a speech of characteristic warmth and charm. It may have registered with them as heartfelt though rather brief, and he had probably intended to say more. But, in truth, unseen except by those nearest to him on the stage, the Headmaster was – for the only time in nineteen years - struggling to retain his composure.

Taken on the last school day of Stanley Forsythe's headmastership.
Standing with him is his successor Len Quigg.

The Head Boy, Andrew Trimble (far right) and Deputy Head Boys, Iain Giffin and
Stephen McElnay present the Headmaster with his retirement gift,
a gas barbecue, on behalf of the School.

Appendix: The Rebirth Of The Boarding School: The 2003 Renovations

First and most obviously, the facade of the old boarding department received a thorough face-lift. The exterior stonework was sandblasted and repainted, and the installation of floodlighting has turned it into a most spectacular sight at night. All the Georgian-glazed windows were replaced, though the purist would note that, in the central tower, the original double window over the door had coupled round-headed sashes rather than a rectangular frame. In the early 1990s – strictly speaking in breach of the listed status of the building - the exterior windows of the Gods Block had been renovated with PVC double-glazing: their replacements were similar but not identical to the originals, which of course had metal frames.

At the north end of Isaac Farrell's main building of 1860, the 1960s boarding school extensions were demolished. The removal of the dining hall, the sick bay, dormitories 1 to 3 and the resident domestic staff accommodation allowed the main building to be seen once more in its original state, with the bricked up windows in the north bay restored and reglazed. Also thankfully demolished was the huge chimney and girder casing which for some years defaced the front of the building. Moving to the south end, there was some extensive remodelling where the original building joined the Gods Block. Demolition of an upstairs toilet and the former coal store below, resurfacing of the former ramp, and removal of the glass-topped passageway that once led to a series of boarders' studies below the steps at the south end created a pleasant courtyard area. The wall and distinctive archway at the ramp also disappeared – along with a deep well, latterly covered over by a huge slate slab. This has now disappeared under a new tarmac surface. Between the gym and the west side of the main building the 1960s study block – which had latterly fallen into very severe disrepair – was demolished and the opportunity taken to provide ramps for disabled access. There were some completely new additions, so sensitively done that future generations may well mistake them for the original design! Chief among them was a completely new north end, built on to the corner of the main building and incorporating the old room 4 (more recently room 5). This forms a quite spectacular entrance from the quadrangle, with a wide stairway to all floors. Three sash windows in the new walls, again in original Georgian-glazed style,

preserved the architectural balance, and the new area was given a hipped and slated roof in the style of the original building. Internally the main building has been extensively re-ordered, and following the great boarding tradition of saints and scholars, it currently houses the English and R.E. departments.

In the old main hall, the wood panelling was retained, - though now painted over - and extended to cover the entrance to the old room 1. Stanley Forsythe had hoped that a large school crest could have been incorporated here, but this proved not to be possible. To the left, the old room 2 was enlarged by the demolition of the Focus Room, extended backwards and merged with one of the former Ramore dormitories to the left and the Senior Resident Master's room to the right. In the original school this was the drawing room of the Headmaster's residence, and it retained both a rather grand marble fireplace, and the original wooden window shutters in working order, until the boarding school closed. These three rooms together now form the museum complex, opened in 2006, which includes much material relevant to the old boarding department.

The former boarding prefects' study – previously the main staff room until the building of the present office block in the late 1950s –disappeared altogether, and the space was been turned into an extension of the entrance lobby. To the left of the main hall, new stores and toilet facilities were built along the corridor which once housed the Model House Locker Room.

The huge expanse of the former room 3– once associated with nightly prep, and the school's assembly hall in the days of Major White – finally disappeared. Between 1994 and 2002 this room was divided into two with a corridor down the side, and the rooms numbered 3 and 3a. In 2003 the whole area was completely reconfigured, and the former rooms 3,5 and 1 became the new rooms 1, 2 and 3. A purpose-built drama studio with tiered seating and a small stage area was created inside a room which, depending on their generation, past and present pupils would remember as room 4, room 24 or the School Library. Above the drama studio – and indeed connected to it by a new back stairway – is the new room 8, which occupies the middle floor of the Gods Block. Until the 1950s this floor was divided into three classrooms – one of which was the school's first ever science laboratory when the Old Boys Wing (as it was first known) opened in 1894. As the boarding school expanded, the area was converted into two small dormitories and two even smaller staff bedrooms.

Moving to the upper floor of the main building, the configuration of the former boarding department was changed beyond recognition. The resident staff room on the main landing is now an English department office. The old South Dormitory has become the new room 7, though the doorway leading through to the Ramore House studies in the attic of the original Headmaster's residence was sealed up, along with the doorway from the landing into the former Middle and North dormitories The entrance to the new rooms 4, 5 and 6 is now through a lobby where there was once a staff bedroom, and a stairway to the former Near and Far New dormitories. Room 4 is largely the old Middle Dorm (later dorm 5), room 6 is the former North Dorm (dorm 4) and room 5 has been created from part of the old Near and Far New Dormitories

(dorms 6 & 7). The remaining part of this dorm now forms the wide corridor along this floor. The corridor leading from rooms 4, 5 and 6 to room 8 was also refurbished, with toilets and storage space formerly occupied by the Rathlin House linen room. Sadly, its ancient hand-cranked laundry lift to the ground floor was one of the casualties of the refurbishment! The demolition of the 'flyover' from the matron's department to the Senior House marked the start of the refurbishment process. The two buildings are now physically separate, but the old tuckshop and drying room were turned into the school's first purpose-built sixth form centre. The former Senior House Common room became, for a short time, an interview room for year heads: more recently it has become a recreational area for senior students.

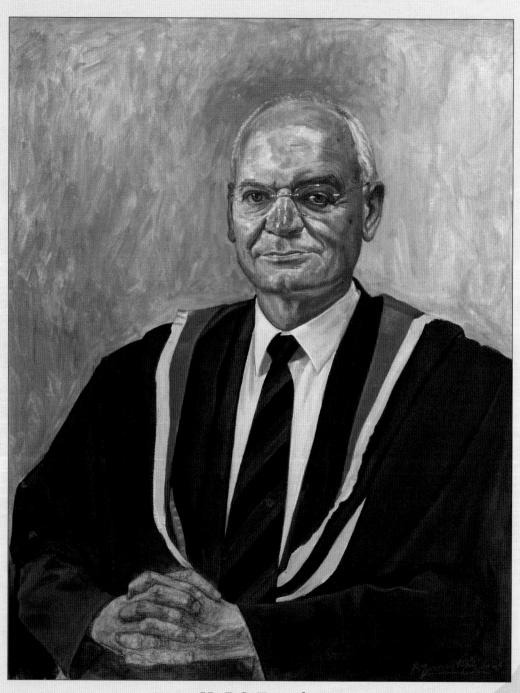

Mr R.S. Forsythe

Chapter 12

2003 to 2010

Len Quigg And David Carruthers

The transition from one headmastership to another, usually a straightforward matter, was rather different in 2003. The sudden withdrawal of a Headmaster-designate only days after his appointment provided our version of Harold Macmillan's famously understated 'little local difficulty', and as Stanley Forsythe began a well-earned retirement, the school faced a unique challenge. In difficult circumstances, the Governors were exceptionally fortunate that, within the school community, they found exactly the man for the hour.

The Latest Two Headmasters

Leonard Francis Quigg joined what was then termed the day staff in September 1971, and was a resident master from the following Easter until his marriage to Joan in 1977. A countryman, and a lover of the 'hamely tongue', Len delighted – and still delights – in his North Antrim roots. Educated at Ballycastle High School, he was marked out early in his career by outstanding classroom qualities as well as administrative gifts, and was the natural choice to succeed the formidable Hugh Montgomery as head of English in 1986. As a departmental manager he excelled, something which was recognised beyond the Coleraine Inst community. A focussed inspection report on the English Department in 1994 spoke of "the vigorous leadership of the head of department", and in time Len became a senior GCSE examiner and the co-author of three standard textbooks for GCSE English, widely used throughout Northern Ireland. An inspiring A level teacher, with a particular scholarly interest in the works of Thomas Hardy, Len was no less committed to the academically less-gifted. By his own choice he taught at least one bottom set in every year of his career, and his kindly but uncompromising approach encouraged many boys to a new confidence in themselves and a greater pride in their work. In 1999 he moved naturally from the headship of the English department to the Vice Principal's office, as Robin Semple's successor. From 1987 onwards he produced annual school musicals which regularly involved upwards of 150 pupils and staff, and even during his time as Vice Principal and Headmaster he could be found of an evening, hammer in hand, building the set for the forthcoming production. Such spare time as he had in a totally disciplined lifestyle was filled by his joy in the countryside, his skill as a 'labouring man', his interest in local dramatics – with many years' experience of set building and stage management in Ballycastle Choral Society – and his involvement in the Vestry affairs of Drumtullagh Parish Church, of which he wrote a delightful history over twenty years ago.

Nor was this all: the sense of duty which motivated his professional career led him into part-time membership of the Ulster Defence Regiment from 1972 until 1985, where he eventually attained the rank of Captain.

For a man nearing the end of his career and supremely happy as a second in command, the summer of 2003 was a time of heart-searching for Len Quigg. But the Board of Governors' request that he act as Headmaster pending the re-advertisement of the post was unanimous and persuasive, and he felt that in conscience he could not evade the challenge. Three months later, he was an applicant for the re-advertised post, and his appointment in November 2003 as the eighth Headmaster of Coleraine Inst surprised no-one in the school community – except, possibly, the man himself.

Stanley Forsythe's retirement coincided with that of Jimmy Gordon as Vice Principal, and he was succeeded as Vice Principal by Sam Turtle, of whom more later. During the interregnum of September 2003 to January 2004, Robert Blair and Michael McNay shared the responsibilities of the second Vice Principal, and Len Quigg's confirmation as Headmaster coincided with Michael McNay's appointment as the new Vice Principal.

Pictured at Len Quigg's retirement dinner in June 2007.
Left to right: Len Quigg, Jimmy Gordon, Jim Foote, Dermot Jennings, Jimmy Shaw,
John Leslie, Robin Semple, Robert Blair and Joe Cassells.

Although his tenure of office was, of necessity, brief, the record of this chapter will show that the Quigg period was both determined and decisive. On Len's own retirement in June 2007, after thirty-six years of service, the Governors were faced, for the third time in less than four years, with the appointment of a Principal. Their choice fell on Dr David Carruthers, Head Master of the Mathematics Department at The Royal Belfast Academical Institution. Dr Carruthers was educated at Belfast Royal Academy, and, after a gap year, studied Mathematical Physics at Nottingham University before completing a Ph.D. at Queens University Belfast. Following his father's footsteps, he became a schoolmaster, teaching Maths in his old school for three years before moving to RBAI. During his years at Inst he completed the Professional Qualification for Headship (NI), the now desirable qualification for aspiring heads. When his appointment was announced, many members of the Coleraine Inst community – not just the boys either! – had recourse to a well-known website for enlightenment about their new Headmaster from his former

pupils in Belfast. One anonymous posting spoke for many: "He's a big loss for us, and he'll be a big gain for Coleraine". David and Nicola Carruthers have two young sons, Harry and Jamie, who have already made their own very distinctive contribution to the school community!

The Community, Aged 150

One item of business from David Carruthers' first meeting with his Senior Management Team encapsulates the difference between the worlds of 2000 and 2010, never to speak of 1860 or 1984 - a school policy on the use of MP3 players, iPods and mobile phones on campus. Perhaps readers over the age of eighteen should be warned that a review of the last seven years is likely to contain language and images which are, if not disturbing, perhaps barely comprehensible!

The seven years since Stanley Forsythe's retirement have continued the trend of staff turnover which was remarked on in the last chapter. In this very short period some twenty nine people have either retired or moved on, balanced by twenty four new appointments, as the staff room continued to become younger and more gender-balanced. Not all of the departures, sadly, were happy occasions. Alan Breen had been looking forward to a productive early retirement: tragically he died suddenly on the squash court during the first week of the summer holidays in July 2005. Allan Gilmour, with thirty-five years' service, latterly as Head of Geography, succumbed to a long illness a month later. Their names are permanently commemorated in three trophies now awarded each Prize Day in their memory: the A.J. Breen Award for Sportsmanship; the

A.J. Breen Cup for Endeavour in Mathematics, and the Allan Gilmour Cup for Geography Coursework. As if these numbing losses were not sufficient for a close-knit staffroom, Paul Livingstone died as the result of a brief but lethal illness during a summer holiday abroad in 2006. A relatively young man with twenty-two years' service, Paul had just been promoted as Head of Physics and Senior Teacher, and had also thrown himself wholeheartedly into the work of the newly-formed Coleraine Inst Friends' Assocation. In characteristic gestures of respect to a mutual personal friend and of loyalty to the school, Robert Blair postponed his retirement, and Robin Semple returned

Mr L.F. Quigg

301

several years after his own, to deputise until Paul's position could be re-advertised. In the same year Mrs Joy Clyde, a part time teacher in the Music Department, passed away after a brief illness. Tragedy had also struck the family of a much younger member of the community through the sudden death, in September 2005, of Brian Darling, very shortly after he had left Upper Sixth to continue third level education.

More happily, recent years have been marked by convivial functions to mark the departure of senior figures in the school. Leslie Robinson, Richard Adams, Joe Cassells, Robert Blair, Len Quigg, John Patterson, Phil Blayney, Sam Turtle and John Martin all enjoyed good send-offs at functions organised by their own departments and by the staff room generally. John Patterson's retirement brought to an end a short period – rare in any school – when a father and son taught together in the same department: equally remarkably, for good measure Stephen Patterson succeeded his father as Head of Year 13! John Martin's retirement as Head of History took another thorough professional into retirement, and also coincided with the end of one of the school's oldest academic departments: in September 2009 Sarah Pinkerton – now Mrs Sarah Taggart - replaced him, not as Head of History, but of the new Department of Society and Government.

Of all these retirements, perhaps that of Sam Turtle should be singled out for further comment, not only because he retired as Vice Principal of the school with thirty six years' service, but also because he was – and remains – a truly larger than life character. The 2009 School Magazine drew attention to his "genuine interest in each pupil, impressive knowledge of his subject and charismatic delivery of his subject." The same retirement tribute neatly defined the hall mark of his classroom discipline: "a sweetly-timed, gentle put-down, followed by a two phase clearing of the throat, the second part of which was barely audible in the ensuing merriment." Beyond the classroom Sam coached cricket from 1973 until 2000, and the Medallion XV from 1981 until 2000. The latter period included six Shield final appearances, and most appropriately

Sam Turtle – a legend in his lifetime!

concluded with the Medallion Team of 2000 sharing the Shield with Methodist College. "Sammy T – a legend!" So said one of his students, and right he was, too!

As the school approaches its sesquicentenary, only a handful of George Humphreys' "young men" remain – all of them, alas, far past the time when the adjective was appropriate - and the departures mentioned above really signify the ending of a generation. There have been corresponding changes in senior positions. Six years after her appointment as an inspirational Head of English, Alison Blackwell moved on to Ballymena Academy, to be replaced by Mrs Karen Taggart, herself the wife of a former pupil, Robin Taggart. In 2006 Ms Pauline Murphy was appointed as Head of Geography, while Ms Paula McIntyre became the school's first Head of Information Technology. In 2008, in a curriculum development which would have totally amazed our founders, the genial Mrs Amanda Cooper became the first-ever Head of Home Economics, and in the summer of 2009 the first purpose-built accommodation for her department was erected – appropriately near

Len Quigg's retirement staff photo 2007.

the site of the old boarding school kitchen! At the end of the same year Sam Turtle was replaced as Vice Principal by Patrick Allen, whose connection with the school as pupil and teacher stretches back to the era of George Humphreys. The most recent departures of senior staff have been Phil Blayney after thirty-one years' service in the Biology Department, Gary Spence who resigned as Head of R.E. to take up a vice principalship in his native Scotland, and Tony Lee, another of the Humphreys generation. Tony's name will always be associated with his two great loves in education: the study of Geology and the First XI cricket team.

Home Economics arrives at the Inst.

2008 is an historic year for Coleraine Inst as it has opened it doors to a new academic subject for Years 8 & 9 - Home Economics!

Most pupils whom I have met, so far, think H.E is about "cooking, eating, and shopping" but it is much more complex than that: Home Economics is about the home, living in local and global societies, looking after your body and being part of a family. Through studying Home Economics, you will learn how to think critically, make informed choices and develop practical food skills.

At the moment H.E. can be found in room 17, the old chemistry lab., and as of yet we haven't had our make-over but not to be overcome by adversity we have had practical lessons with smoothies, sensational dips, wraps and heavenly breakfasts featuring on the menu for the first term. For the year 10 students considering GCSE Home Economics as an option for next year but not too sure where it will take you - a qualification in the subject can lead to many interesting and rewarding careers in:

Teaching, Dietetics, Consumerism, Product Development, Environmental Health, Food Technology, Nutrition, Marketing, Journalism, Social work and Catering.

Mrs Cooper

This picture shows the delivery (in sections) of Coleraine Inst's first ever
Home Economics Centre, 2009.

Career breaks have become more common within teaching in the new millennium. In 2004 the late Alan Breen spent a year teaching in The Archbishop Spalding Senior High School, Maryland, USA. Tim Smith, a former pupil who taught for nine years in the Art Department, spent two years in Uganda, and Stephanie Hollinger and Julie Stevenson broadened their experience in Australia and Canada. Neither of the two ladies returned to Coleraine Inst, and Julie in particular discovered not only a new country, but also the man she was later to marry! Most recently, Victor Boyd spent the school year 2008 – 2009 working at Xia Academy, in North West China, under the auspices of the Overseas Missionary Fellowship.

In the Board of Governors, an era has now totally passed. Not one of today's governors was a member of the Board during the era of George Humphreys, though fourteen of them were pupils in his time, and his son-in-law, Prof. Scott Brown, is the Irish Society's representative on the Board. Mr Ken Cheevers retired from the Board in 2003 at the end of a four year term as President, to be replaced by the current President, Mr James Smyth.

Among the visitors to the school in its 150th
anniversary year was the Moderator of
the General Assembly of the Presbyterian
Church. Dr Stafford Carson toured the
school and fielded questions from a senior
R.E. class.

Mr K.H. Cheevers

Chairman, Board of Governors 2001 - 2004

Three years later came the departures of five senior members. Miss Margaret Boyce, as recorded earlier, had made history as the first lady Governor in 1994. Mr James Tweed was a former President of the Board, with a Coleraine Inst connection going back to his schooldays in the 1930s. Of a similar vintage was Mr Ronnie Cameron, whose service on the Board of Governors spanned three decades. Mr Lane Macfarlane, another senior member, was not to enjoy a long retirement: his passing in 2006 was mourned not only by his family and by the school, but also by the Coleraine business community of which he was a prominent member. The Rev Fergie Marshall, the 'father' of the Board at the time of his retirement, was one of the last members of the 1939 Schools' Cup team. His death in August 2009 came not long after that of his fellow team-member Mr Brian Smyth of Totnes, Devon, and their passing finally severed one of the longest surviving threads in the sporting history of the school.

Among the administrative staff, recent appointments have included Mrs Barbara Davey as the school's first full-time library administrator, Mrs Diane Armstrong as the office receptionist, and Mr Kenny Cox as technician in succession to Mr Kenny McDowell. After fifteen years as the school joiner, the efficient and totally unflappable Denny McAleese retired in 2004. Denny's major project – completed almost single handedly – was the partition of the old room 3 into two separate classrooms in the early 1990s. His departure also ended a long school tradition, for he was the last maintenance man to live in the school residence in Queens Park. Sadly, Denny enjoyed a retirement of only four years, and his passing was mourned by many in the school community. In 2005, the retirement of George Knight – 'young' George to a particular generation – ended a father and son succession in the Science Department which stretched back to the 1960s. In 2007 Mrs Kay McGrath retired from the cleaning staff after thirty-two years' service, ending a three decade partnership with her sister, Mrs Pat Kennedy, and in 2008 Kenny McDowell retired as Chief Technician after twenty-one years' service. Other lengthy spells of service have been recorded in this period too: in our sesquicentenary year groundsman Cecil Callaghan will complete thirty-three years in the employment of Coleraine Inst, while Victor Callaghan has already made school history by a spell of unbroken service to the school dating back to April 1965. Since 2006 Joe Cassells, having retired from the teaching staff, has sought in a small way to entertain himself, and to inform the wider school community of its past, by taking on the voluntary position of Curator of the School Museum.

"Constant Initiatives And Changes."

"The world around us is changing at a pace we have probably never seen before, and it is important that schools respond to that in order to meet the needs of pupils." David Carruthers' judgement at the time of his appointment has been amply reflected in the developments even of the short period since Stanley Forsythe's retirement.

Within the school, Len Quigg began his headship with a series of initiatives, and under his successor they are being expanded and developed. The 2003 Costello Report, which as will be noted later, began the process of ending the traditional 11+ transfer, also recommended

Mr J.I. Smyth

Chairman, Board of Governors 2004 - Present

In recent years, the special guests at Prize Distribution have been younger Old Boys. In October 2009 we welcomed Dr Alan Barr of Merton College, Oxford.

"local collaboration and partnerships between schools and Further Education Colleges" in order to provide "a broad menu of courses." Coleraine Inst is currently involved along with Coleraine High School, Coleraine College, and other local schools in Coleraine Area Learning Partnership, whose aim is to provide the widest level of subject choice across the whole Borough area. Within school, Citizenship, Learning for Life and Work, Journalism, Motor Vehicle Studies and Home Economics have taken their places in the curriculum, while the European Computer Driving Licence, later succeeded by GCSE Information Technology, was incorporated into the new I.T. Department. An elected School Council has, since 2004, given boys in each year group a sense of ownership of the development of school policy. Parent involvement has been encouraged through the foundation of Coleraine Inst Friends' Association. Contacts with local primary schools have been enhanced. Celebration of success at every level has been encouraged by displays within school. During his time on the Senior Management Team Willie McCluskey led new initiatives in marketing and promoting the school within the community, and more recently Robert McGregor has continued his pioneering work. The 2005 Rugby Tour to Australia and New Zealand was a joint initiative with St Mary's College Dublin. The

most momentous development, whose final outcome still lies in the future, is an ongoing round of negotiations with the Department of Education and Coleraine High School in relation to a possible future merger.

In the wider world of education, the flood of change continues. The introduction of Common Funding of Schools in April 2005 led to Coleraine Inst (in common with forty-seven other voluntary Grammar Schools) suffering a loss of funding, and the great recession of 2008 led to the further tightening of strings on the educational purse.

Performance Review and Staff Development became compulsory from September 2005, and was substantially revised in 2008 – even Headmasters and Vice Principals were not exempted from performance targets! The Early Professional Development Scheme, which replaced the more informal probationary year for newly qualified teachers, began towards the end of the Forsythe era, and is now firmly established.

The regulations governing Special Educational Needs provision have become much more stringent: Patrick Allen and Lynn Magee have developed the school's provision to a high standard of excellence, and in 2009 Mrs

BBC BLAST - Radio Broadcast

BBC Blast is a selection of creative workshops which goes on tour throughout the UK to give young people a chance to get involved in activities ranging from radio presenting to sports photography.

Research

On Wednesday the 13th May the Year 11 Journalism class were given the opportunity to participate in a Radio Presenting workshop. When we arrived at the Dunluce Centre, where BBC Blast was being held, we were ushered into a big yellow bus. This would be our "classroom" for the next three days. We were introduced to Anita Miah (BBC Radio Presenter) and the rest of the crew on board the bus. They helped us brainstorm ideas for packages on our radio show. We came up with some interesting ideas to cover such as the obvious choice, the North West 200 and focusing on Portrush as a tourist destination. After this we spent some time compiling contact details for potential interviewees.

Interviews

On Thursday we set out to get those all important interviews. We split into two groups, Paul and Mark captured the voice of the people of Portrush, with interviews from local surfers, business people and the general public. Meanwhile Daniel and Sam went out to tackle the crowds at the North West pits. Although we were slightly nervous and self-conscious at first, the interviewing turned out to be pretty enjoyable

and soon we were throwing ourselves into it. t was a fantastic opportunity to use the recording equipment and really felt like an authentic journalistic experience.

Editing and Production

Friday was the most important day of the course with a live broadcast to the Web looming in front of us. We put together the script for the show with the help of Elham Rizi the Assistant Producer. We did a couple of practice runs but when 3 o'clock came it was time for the real thing! We were all apprehensive as we walked into the on board studio, but when the on-air light came on the show just seemed to fly by and was great fun.

Thanks must go to the BBC Blast crew on board the bus for making it such a great experience and to our teacher, Miss Magee for organising the whole thing.

By Mark McFetridge, Sam Steen, Paul Milliken and Daniel McColgan.

An Information Technology Class in 2009.

Kathleen Thompson became the school's first part-time Learning Support Assistant. For all pupils, cold print has replaced sometimes eccentric handwriting on school reports, and from 2009 the reporting format was required to include assessments of Communication, Use of ICT and Use of Number. Assessment as well as delivery of the curriculum has developed no less exponentially. Even staff who have retired in very recent years (and for whom 'benchmarking' had connotations more of graffiti in science labs than of the nferNelson Cognitive Ability Tests) would struggle to recognise the new world of assessment for learning, residuals and tracking, never to mention the Revised Curriculum's overarching concept of "The big picture". The ghost of William White would be amazed to contemplate the world of 2010 – he who was wont at times of staff shortage during the 1940s to "put all the classes into room 3 after assembly, and starting from the factors of the difference of two squares, to work right through to the binomial theorem before break."!

The most recent, and at the time of writing ongoing, issue in education concerns transfer at 11+. The 2003 Costello Report began a process which was to lead to the scrapping of the traditional 11+ exam. From a situation which can most charitably described as untidy have emerged a number of approaches to unregulated

transfer from 2010. Coleraine Inst, in company with many other voluntary grammar schools, is now a member of the Association for Quality Education, and in November 2009 over one hundred P7 pupils came to Coleraine Inst for the first time to sit the AQE's transfer tests. No doubt in the future – assuming that books have not by then been replaced by more modern communications media - the historians of the school's bicentenary may be able to assess their long term significance!

In 2004 a generous and anonymous donation, from a friend of the school with family connections, made possible the award of annual bursaries to the value of £4000. Named "The Kelmor Bursaries" at the request of the donor, these awards are based on A level results in Physics, Chemistry, Maths and Engineering.

"Outstanding Opportunities And A Wide Range Of Activities"

...Not our own judgement, but that of the Education and Training Inspectorate in 2006, and an appropriate way to introduce a review of the school beyond the classroom at the age of 150. 2008 marked the twenty-fifth anniversary of the Christian Union Summer Camp for boys transferring from primary schools to Inst. One of Robert Rodgers' initiatives, it has developed over the years as

The pre-Christmas Charity Fair has become one of the more recent regular events in the school year. Staff and boys take part in a wide range of fun events for charity at the end of the Christmas term.

One of many charity events each year is the shoe box appeal in aid of Romanian children.

an important part of our induction process. Outsiders have been frankly amazed by the number of staff (and their spouses) and senior boys who are prepared give up a week of their holiday each year in the familiar environment of Castlewellan Castle.

The theme of support for charities has been touched on earlier, and its creative expansion over the past decade has brightened school life as well as benefiting good causes locally and nationally. The 2009 School Magazine listed ten separate initiatives within the previous year, involving activities as varied as a charity bun sale for Children in Need (confections produced 'in house' by a junior class!), a rugby match in support of the IRFU Charitable Trust, the third annual Charity Fair inside school, and a team from Inst and Dominican College who worked on a building project in Belfast on behalf of the Christian cross-community charity Habitat for Humanity. Almost every Saturday of term time, Coleraine Inst boys are on the streets of the Borough,

and last year almost £13000 was collected in support of a range of charities. Sponsorship enlivens giving, and in recent years money has been raised through an annual Readathon, with even a sponsored silence for the Tsunami Appeal in 2005. The staff have made their contributions too – most spectacularly in 2004 when Julie Stevenson, Patrick Allen, Mark Palmer, Mike McNay, Damian McDonnell and David Stewart abseiled down the front of Belfast's Europa Hotel, and Gwen Reavey, Diane Armstrong, Barbara Davey and Cecile Forgerit (that year's French Assistant) swam in the Butlin's Swimathon in support of the Marie Curie Cancer Foundation. Selfless giving has other aspects, and in 2004 two junior boys were honoured for their personal bravery. Peter O'Hara, himself only in Year 9, saved a younger boy from drowning at the Drumaheagles Marina, while Christopher Campbell was one of three local boys honoured by the Royal Humane Society for their part in rescuing a man in danger of drowning in the Camus River.

A recent new venture for The Inst has been participation in Habitat for Humanity, a cross-community Christian charity aimed at eliminating poverty housing and homelessness. In 2009 eleven boys joined a similar group from Dominican College to assist in 'building a house' on the Shankill Road, Belfast.

An intrepid group of teachers prepare to abseil down the north face of the Europa Hotel, Belfast for charity in 2004. Left to right Mark Palmer, Dave Stewart, Mike McNay, Damian MacDonnell, Paddy Allen and Julie Stevenson.

Further afield, rugby and cricket tours and modern language and ski trips have long been a tradition in the school calendar, augmented in the last decade by English Department trips to Stratford on Avon, and in 2005 a Technology Department tour. Its itinerary – including the Corus Steel Plant, and the Jaguar and Land Rover factories in Birmingham – already has a slightly dated air! By far the most newsworthy event began with a Technology Department entry in the Formula 1 in Schools design competition. At first sight this was a competition to design a model racing car; in fact it was a complex, and extremely prestigious, computer design competition which took Alistair Adams, David Anderson, Aimal Khan, Jonathan Steen and Philip Taylor through Northern Ireland and United Kingdom finals in 2006, and on to the world championships in Melbourne, Australia, in March 2007 in the company of Technology staff Mark Irwin, Robert McGregor and technician Chris Thomas. Their victory not only gave the school world-class status, but also a trophy received at the hand of none other than Bernie Ecclestone. For good measure, and by amazing coincidence, the trophy itself was designed by an old boy of Coleraine Inst! There was considerable local and national newspaper and television coverage, and a civic

reception for the boys and the technology staff on their return. The following year Colin Henry, Andrew Avery, Tom He, Michael Wallace and Matthew Adams travelled to Kuala Lumpur. Unfortunately the world trophy went elsewhere, but the Coleraine Inst team gained second place in the world in engineering, third fastest time in trials, and overall fifth position in the World Championship Finals. For good measure, two of the group were invited to Belfast in 2009 to meet the crew of the U.S. Space Shuttle Discovery.

The World Beating Car.

The school achieved world renown in 2007 when a group of young engineers won the Formula 1 in Schools World Championships in Melbourne, Australia. The trophy was presented by Formula One supremo, Bernie Ecclestone himself.

Even more academically oriented visits included the participation of our best young scientists in the periodic Irish Science Olympiads. Described by one participant as not so much a holiday as a chance to do exams somewhere else, these encounters brought a gold medal in Chemistry for Gareth Callaghan and a silver in Physics for Timmy Martin in 2003, bronze medals for Alex Humphrey and Alan Kershaw in 2004, and most recently a silver in Physics for Tom He. A rather less strenuous A level Physics visit to Geneva in 2006 allowed the boys to meet Dr Alan Barr, an Old Boy closely involved in the CERN project, and who was the guest of honour at Prize Distribution in October 2009.

The tradition of music and drama has continued under Suzanne Cameron, with the collaboration in recent years of Melanie Bell, Damian McDonnell, Stephanie Hollinger and most recently Lynn Magee. The last full-scale musical was "Camelot" in 2001, directed by Heidi Giffin. Since then there have been lively annual concerts and plays, some of them involving junior boys as well as more experienced senior actors. "Blood Brothers" and Tom Stoppard's "Fifteen Minute Hamlet" have alternated with equally entertaining but less well-known productions such as "School Daze", "Mission Impossible" and "Ernie's Incredible Illucinations". The school orchestra continues to expand its repertoire – "we do everything from Vivaldi to the Beatles!" in the words of one enthusiastic member – and it led the praise most impressively at the 150th anniversary service in Terrace Row Church on 31 January 2010.

Two scenes from the most recent school play. "Ernie's Incredible Illucinations" was presented on 1 April 2009, directed by Lynn Magee.

Cast of Ernie's Incredible Illucinations.

"A Long And Proud Sporting Tradition"

So said David Carruthers in his 2009 Speech Day report, and as we approach our sesquicentenary, this is no less true than it was in the past. In rugby the honour of Irish Schools' representation since 2003 has gone to Joe Burns, Andrew Trimble, Chris Smyth, Chris Cochrane and Jason Bloomfield, and to these boys' names can be added those who were selected for Ulster Schools' teams: Peter Budina, Peter McNay, Angus Warwicker, Josh Christie, Jonny Shiels, David Dorsett, James Cromie, Jason Bloomfield and Conor Gaston. In 2007 Jonny Shiels was nominated as Ulster Bank Ulster Schools' player of the year, and in 2008 Stephen Graham, veteran coach of the First XV and long-time Ulster schools selector, was deservedly awarded a Coach of the Year accolade at the annual Coleraine Sports Awards Ceremony. Sadly the sesquicentenary year will not be marked by a Schools' Cup victory, but the rugby tradition is as deep-rooted as ever, and the 2008-9 season ended for our year eight players with victory in the NEELB ten a side tournament.

137 years after it started, Rugby is still alive and well at Coleraine Inst. The under 12 rugby tournament of 2008.

The Rowing Club continues to maintain a premier position. In 2003 the club captain Iain Giffin was selected for Junior Ireland in the Home Internationals in Cork, and the J18 four – Iain Giffin, Jason Taggart, Connor Campbell and Philip Braithwaite, coxed by Drew McNeill – won the bronze medal at the Irish Championships. Michael McNaul rowed with the Irish squad at the 2008 Home Internationals and in 2008 and 2009 Jonathan Mitchell was selected for the Irish 4- crew competing in the Coupe de la Jeunesse (the Junior European Rowing Championships.) Also in 2008 the school Junior 18 coxless quad - Jonathan Mitchell, Robert Hart, Michael McNaul and Jamie McBurney - were named Junior Sports Team of the Year at the Coleraine Sports Awards after winning a silver medal at the 2008 Irish Championship Regatta. The names of coxes feature less prominently in the annals of the rowing club, but in 2009 Peri-Jake Stynes was selected to travel to Vichy in France as a cox to the Irish squads in the Coupe de la Jeunesse.

At the other end of the age-range, veteran coach Bobby Platt, MBE, won his most recent award as Coach of the Year – aged eighty-six! The same ceremony concluded with the annual award traditionally presented at the Chairman's discretion. In 2008 it went to three men, all old boys of the school, who are currently household names in world rowing – the Olympic trio of Richard Archibald, Richard Chambers and Alan Campbell. Richard Archibald has recently retired from world-class action after competing in the Irish Men's Lightweight Four at the Beijing Olympics. The other two were also in China in 2008, Chambers in the Great Britain Lightweight Four and Campbell representing Team GB in the single sculls, achieving a creditable finals place only weeks after serious injury and while still recuperating from surgery. Chambers, a gold medallist with the GB lighweight four in 2007, was out of action through injury in 2009, but Campbell won the silver medal at the 2009 World Championships. Stephen Feeny, another notable former pupil, has recently broken into

Peri Jake Stynes and Jonathan Mitchell following their Irish selections for the
June 2009 Coupe de la Jeunesse in Vichy, France.
Also pictured are Dr David Carruthers and Mr Bobby Platt.

the GB lightweight squad, with three World Cup final appearances so far. 2003 also saw the naming of a new racing 8 "Camus", while the Craig Cup was won in 2001, 2003, 2004, 2005 and 2007. After a seventeen year gap, the Wray Cup was contested between the Portora and Coleraine Inst 1st fours in 2007, and Coleraine Inst secured a comfortable three length win. In October 2007 the club took delivery of four new boats.

In April 2009 Bobby Platt MBE and
Jonathan Mitchell meet Sir Steve Redgrave
at a seminar in University of Ulster,
Jordanstown.

Over recent years very close links have developed between the Rowing Club and Coleraine Inst Old Boys' Rowing Association, not least with the revival in 2002 of an annual race between the school and a COBRA crew. COBRA also maintain a website (www.COBRArowing.com) which includes an archive of encyclopaedic proportions. Readers in search of a full history of rowing at Coleraine Inst would do well to consult this site.

Representative honours have come the way of the Cricket Club too, with Alastair Handforth's selection for Ulster Schools in 2004, and – for the first time in the school's history – Scott Campbell's selection for the Irish Schools' under fourteen team in 2007, and the under 15 team in 2008. Also in 2007 Paul Douglas and Rishi Chopra were selected for a North West representative XI.

A key name in the harriers was that of Greg Walton, who won District and Ulster Schools' cross country titles, and ran in the team which came second in the 2003 Glasgow Relays. Similar success came with 3rd place in the Coventry Relays in 2004 and the Glasgow relays in 2004 and 2006, when the team of Stuart Fulton, Philip Gilliland, Mark Anderson,

Christopher Steen, Jason Bloomfield and Matthew Livingstone took silver medals. In athletics, Steven Morrow and Matthew Livingstone represented Ulster Schools in the 2003 Schools Inter Provincials, and Steven represented Irish Schools at the Schools International. In the following year, Steven's career reached its climax in his selection for Northern Ireland at the Commonwealth Youth Games in Australia. As the 150th anniversary approaches, the most recent success for the Harriers' Club has been at minor level. Victory in the 2009 Wallace Park Relays brought the McCue Shield to Coleraine for the first time since 1999. One of those involved was Brian Tweedie, whose father, Philip, was a well-known name in the harriers of a generation ago!

The Badminton Club maintained its status in these years. Bryan Henderson achieved Ireland Under 19 selection in 2003 and finished a luminary career with selection to train with the Commonwealth Games Squad in Sweden in 2004. In the same year Stephen Dobbin was selected for the Ulster under ninteen and Irish under seventeen teams, and in 2006 he was selected for the Ulster Under Seventeen team. Success followed the Tennis Club too, with the Senior team finishing as runners-up in the 2004 Ulster Schools indoor Tennis Cup, and Neal Griffith a finalist in the individual championships. The following year's Intermediate team (Chris Gowland, David Hanna, Alan Ewart and Howard Beverland) won the Intermediate Trophy in the Ulster Schools Championships. Most recently, Brent Haslett and Simon Curry have played in the Champion of Champions tournament.

The Swimming Club saw a major resurgence in the mid 2000s, with a growing club anchored in the talent of Chris Coils, Ciaran Sloan, Jaydee Ferguson, Christy McLaughlin and Conor Nicholl. The team won the Coleraine Sports Council "Junior Team of the Year" title in 2007, and as the sesquicentenary year begins, have achieved levels of success at the Ulster Grammar Schools, Ulster and Irish Schools and British Public Schools Championships not seen since the 1980s. A particularly satisfying victory, after an eighteen year gap, was in

the Senior Freestyle Team Relay at the Irish Schools Championships in 2009.

Recent consolidation has been seen also in the Squash Club. James Taylor, Peter Murphy, Andrew Avery and David McCluskey have been successively Ulster and Irish Schools Under Thirteen, Under Sixteen champions, and in 2009 the same team were Under Seventeen Squash Champions. As such they represented Ulster in the 2009 All-Ireland squash finals in Thurles. Most recently, Peter Murphy has had the honour of representing Ulster in the under seventeen interprovincial tournament, while the under thirteen team of Joe Spence, Angus Hamilton and Jamie Taggart came third in the Ulster Schools Novice Cup.

One completely new sport to emerge within the last decade was Association Football. Notwithstanding the misgivings of grammar school traditionalists, the Head of R.E., Garry Spence, took the first steps in this direction in 2004 with the blessing of Len Quigg and the Governors. Under Fifteen, Under Sixteen and Under Ninteen teams were soon competing, and success followed. In the 2005-6 season the under nineteens won the district league. In the next two seasons the under sixteens won their district league, and in 2007 the under eighteens reached the Northern Ireland Schools' Cup final, losing 1-0 to St Louis Ballymena before a large crowd at Ballymena Showgrounds. In the 2008-9 season the under fifteens won their district league, taking the historic Irish Society Shield. The most outstanding player of the period was Howard Beverland, who towards the end of his time at school was regularly playing for the Coleraine FC first team. History was made in March 2009 with the first-ever football tour by the Coleraine Inst Football Club. The boys played against a local team in Liverpool before watching Everton and Arsenal in the afternoon.

To complete this survey some other highlights must be recorded. In 2003 Jonathan Fillis was selected for the Northern Ireland under twenty-five Bridge Team, while in 2007 Thomas Patterson competed in the USA in the 2007 Open Karate Championships, winning two gold medals for Northern Ireland. In the

History was made in the 2008-2009 season, when the Under Fifteen association football team won the Coleraine and District Schools League, and the Irish Society's Shield. Coleraine Inst not only won the Shield for the first time, but also became only the second local Grammar School to do so.

Ben Cuckoo, Under Fourteen Northern Ireland Schools' Judo Champion. In the Under 14+50kg category. Very much a 'first' in the history of Coleraine Inst!

same year Jordan Milliken was nominated Best Overall Performer at the All Ireland Karate Championships in Dublin, and in 2008 Ben Cuckoo was the Under 14 Northern Ireland Schools Judo Champion. Golf continues to flourish, and in 2009 the senior team reached the final of the British Independent Grammar Schools Competition for the first time, narrowly losing to Campbell College.

McDowell's C.A.I. Master Class

On Wed 26th September 2007 European tour professional Graeme McDowell took time out of his hectic schedule to go back to his golfing roots.

Graeme, a former C.A.I. pupil, took a golfing master class for 35 members of C.A.I.'s golfing fraternity. The session started with Graeme giving a demonstration of 'how it should be done,' then the boys were given the opportunity to hit some balls with Graeme casting a critical eye over proceedings and offering some invaluable tips.

After the coaching session Graeme gave the boys the opportunity to ask questions, this gave them an insight into the life of a Tour Pro. The C.A.I. pupils also grabbed the opportunity to get their golf equipment signed!!!

Since then, Graeme has gone on to win the U.S. Open in June 2010.

Coleraine Inst Friends' Association

Apart from a short-lived organisation in support of the voluntary grammar schools in the 1970s, and a much longer-running regular prayer group for parents supportive of the school Christian Union, Coleraine Inst never until recent times had a traditional parents' association. One of a number of initiatives launched during Len Quigg's short but busy headmastership was the Coleraine Inst Friends' Association, aimed at consolidating links between staff, parents and supporting the school's ongoing development. A steering group representing the teaching staff, senior management, parents and Coleraine Old Boys' Association met first in June 2005, and from this emerged C.I.F.A., whose founding office bearers were Mrs Sharyn Griffith, Chairperson, Mrs Patricia Taylor, Secretary, and Mr Stephen Murdoch, Treasurer. The inaugural event was a dinner in the Academy Restaurant, Portrush, on 19 November 2005, and since then the Association has arranged a wide variety of activities including charity functions, dinners, table quizzes, fashion shows, film premier evenings, a family fun day with car boot sale and barbecue and a spectacular midsummer ball in June 2008. Through these and other activities, the Association has already raised some £10.000 for the benefit of academic departments and sports clubs in the school. In addition to fundraising events, C.I.F.A. continues to give practical support to a range of activities, including help with the running of junior discos and with catering at rugby tournaments and other events. Most recently, two committee members were co-opted to the group planning the school's sesquicentenary celebrations.

Two views of the CIFA Fun Day and Car Boot Sale in June 2007.
Sadly, persistent rain rather spoiled the day.

Senior musicians entertaining cinema goers at a premier of "Burn After Reading"
organised by C.I.F.A. at the Jet Centre, Coleraine in October 2008.

The interior of the school museum, opened in 2006.

The School Museum

The seed of this particular development was sown during Stanley Forsythe's headmastership, and former senior laboratory technician Edwin McCloskey was asked to select some historic pieces of science equipment for preservation. At the turn of the millennium further discussions took place between Stanley Forsythe, Colin Beck and Joe Cassells, and during the renovation of the 1860 building, provision was made for the creation of a school museum. For various reasons there was a time lag at this point, but following his retirement in 2006, Joe Cassells expressed an interest in reviving the project. With the encouragement of Len Quigg and Gordon Knight, and the support of many in the school community, enough historic items were unearthed to justify the informal launch of the museum after the 2006 Prize Distribution. Since then, it has grown exponentially, and particular thanks are due to Gordon Knight, the school bursar, and to the school's maintenance staff for much

practical help. The original single room has now expanded into a three-gallery complex, with memorabilia of all kinds continuing to flow into the hands of a delighted curator. The visitors' book presently contains almost 600 names, among them former pupils of every decade since the 1930s. It has been a particular pleasure that every one of them has found among the displays something related either to himself or to someone he knew – indeed one visitor found his own name carved on a desk! As well as visits by individuals, the museum has welcomed a number of community groups, has been used by television crews filming school-related events, has hosted a number of functions, and is visited each year by several junior classes. The museum and archive has now established itself as one of the most extensive of its kind in the country, and representatives of a number of other schools have visited it with a view to starting something of their own. New visitors are always welcome, and require only to contact the school office to arrange a visit.

When he left Coleraine Inst in 1942, Roy McDowell would never have thought he might return 66 years later – and find a photograph of himself in the school museum! In his last year Roy was school captain and captain of rowing.

To mark his visit in November 2008,
he met Jeremy Mitchell, Michael Griffith and Angus Warwicker –
respectively 2008 - 2009 captain of rowing, head prefect and captain of the first XV.

The 150th anniversary year began with a special service in Terrace Row Presbyterian Church on 31 January 2010. Pictured here: The Rev Frank Sellar, Mr James Smith, Dr David Carruthers, Alderman Sandy Gilkinson, Mayor of Coleraine, and Mrs Gilkinson, Mr Len Quigg and Mr Stanley Forsythe.

Conclusion:
From The Past To The Future

In the well-worn phrase, history is a seamless robe, but 31 January 2010 is probably the most appropriate place to make a final cut. In fifty years' time it might even make a convenient starting point for whatever is published to mark our bicentenary, though it is certain that neither of the authors of this book will be here to see it! The anniversary thanksgiving service in Terrace Row Presbyterian Church, which officially marked the beginning of the sesquicentenary celebrations, brought together several hundred employees and friends of the school, Old Boys and former members of staff representing every decade from which there are still survivors. Although it was a splendid celebration of the past, those taking part very properly included not only past and present members of the school community, but also Marcus McKeag from year 8 and the head prefect, Andrew Whitmarsh – a fitting confluence of the past, the present and the future. The Inst has always been a living community and – in the words of the school hymn at the start of the service – "this pause upon our way" brought the three ages vibrantly together.

The original fourteen boys who answered their names at the first roll-call on 1 May 1860, and the teachers who took responsibility for their education, could hardly have foreseen how far around the world their successors would spread the name and reputation of their school. If an institution is indeed the corporate shadow of its members, another history could well be written of the influence which Coleraine Old Boys continue to exert in the world of the 21st century. In The Pentagon, in Whitehall and at Stormont, their advice has shaped local, national and international affairs. They have made their mark in the world of sport, from the international golf circuit and the Olympic Games to the Rugby Six Nations and international Association Football. They continue to push back the frontiers of knowledge in the faculties of many universities, to alleviate suffering in the fields of medicine, surgery, psychiatry and dentistry, and to attend to the spiritual welfare of society

Andrew Whitmarsh, head prefect, with Mr Denis Desmond, Her Majesty's Lord Lieutenant for County Londonderry.

through ordained ministry. Many have carried their love of education into the teaching profession, some even into headmastering. They are to be found in all three branches of the armed forces, and at the highest levels of policing throughout the British Isles. They practise in the courts as judges and barristers - sometimes in cases which at times have made the front pages of the broadsheets, never to mention the tabloids. Some are well known in music, the arts, the theatre, the media and as professional broadcasters. One at least serves in the team responsible for compiling that press icon, The Times Crossword. Others have made their mark in almost every conceivable trade and profession. But even more important, many thousands of ordinary boys who passed quietly through the school without becoming particularly famous will still look back to their time at The Inst with some gratitude. Although they may not have felt particularly grateful at the time, they achieved the results they needed, gained self confidence, fulfilled their potential, tried something new, made friends whom they still meet on occasion - and even passed a few exams along the way.

Seen in this light, Coleraine Academical Institution is much more than the aggregate of 150 years of past history. It has been, and it remains, a dynamic community, proud of its past, confident of its future, and determined to meet whatever challenges may fall across its path.

Senior boys involved in stewarding at the service, pictured
with the Mayor of Coleraine and Mrs Gilkinson.

The school orchestra, directed by Mrs Suzanne Cameron led the praise at the service,
and the organist was Dr Brendan Drummond.

Among former staff attending the service were Richard Bennett, Jimmy Gordon, John Leslie and Robin Semple.

The first generation of the sesquicentenary year.

Each of the year 8 classes of 2009 – 2010 pictured on their first day at school.

Sesquicentenary Class 8Q.

Sesquicentenary Class 8W.

Sesquicentenary Class 8F.

Sesquicentenary Class 8R.

Sesquicentenary Class 8H.

Sesquicentenary Prefects.

Sesquicentenary Board of Governors.

Back Row: Mr Richard McDermott, Mr Robert McKeag, Mr Trevor Shiels,
Rev Robert McMullan, Mr Ivan Campbell, Rev Donard Collins, Rev Warren Peel.
Middle Row: Mr Stephen Murdock, Mr David McClarty, Mr Gordon Knight *(Clerk)*,
Mr Aubrey Taggart, Rev Philip Campbell.
Front Row: Mr Eric Boyd, Mr John Stevenson, Mr James Smyth *(President)*,
Dr David Carruthers *(Headmaster)*, Mr Archie Linnegan *(Vice-President)*, Mr Fred Mullan.

Dr D. M. Carruthers

Group photograph taken during the visit of The Honourable the Irish Society and The Clothworkers' Company, to mark the school's 150th annniversary. 2 June 2010.

As outlined in the early stages of this history, Coleraine Academical Institution's chief patrons and donors were The Worshipful Company of Clothworkers of London and The Honourable The Irish Society. Therefore, it is not surprising that the arms of these two historic bodies are incorporated into the school coat of arms, which was granted in 1870. The coat of arms basically consists of three symmetrically positioned shields.

The top left-hand shield in the school crest is the coat of arms of The Honourable The Irish Society. The left-hand side of this shield is the same design as the arms of the City of London, The Irish Society being a London company. The design features a quartered shield with an upright sword in the top-left quarter. On the right-hand side of the shield is the familiar Red Hand of Ulster, indicating the historic link between London and the province of Ulster.

The more complex design of the top right-hand shield is based on the arms of The Worshipful Company of Clothworkers of London and its symbolism has much to do with ancient processes used in cloth-making. In the upper part of the shield are two symbols which look like figure threes, but these are actually "habicks", instruments used for dressing cloth. In the middle of the shield is a "chevron", representing the rafter of a gable, and underneath is a thistle-like plant called a "teazle". The prickly heads of teazle plants, known as "burrs", were set in frames and used to remove small particles of wool from finished cloth.

The bottom shield is a composite design representing the school, quartered with what looks like a St George's Cross. The upper quarters contain symbols from the Coleraine arms, an upright sword and a salmon, while the lower quarters feature an hour-glass, warning of the passage of time, and an open book, representing knowledge.

The Greek motto (in English letters: Heos Hemera Estin) comes from John, Chapter 9, verse 4 and means "Work while it is day", a neat link with the hour-glass symbol. Underneath the word Hemera is a "heckle", an ancient cloth-working instrument similar to the teazle.

(This explanation of the school crest is based on an article entitled "The C.A.I. Coat of Arms", by the late Sam Henry, F.R.S.A.I., the full text of which can be viewed in the School Museum.)

J.C.Hall	1863	J.C.McMaster	1919	O.J.Johnston	1967
J.Huey	1864	W.Crawford	1920	R.G.R.Evans	1968
N.Forsyth	1865	A.F.Dalzell	1923	R.M.Smyth	1968
T.Lyle	1866	D.R.Michael	1924	P.R.Mullin	1969
J.McMaster	1868	R.J.Getty	1925	J.R.Cameron	1970
T.M.Greer	1869	T.E.Reade	1925	G.W.D.Eakin	1971
A.H.Rentoul	1869	T.R.Wright	1925	R.C.Buckley	1971
A.J.McElnaine	1870	G.A.C.Wilson	1926	D.T.Gault	1972
J.Clarke	1871	R.B.Hunter	1927	R.L.Tweed	1973
T.Brookes	1872	J.N.M.Legate	1928	W.A.Dadswell	1973
J.A.Wallace	1873	D.McKennan	1930	N.R.Todd	1974
M.Steen	1874	W.W.McGrath	1931	D.J.Christophersen	1975
J.V.Young	1875	J.M.Kennedy	1932	D.J.B.Mullin	1976
J.Moody	1876	J.I.Cunningham	1933	S.A.Brown	1977
H.Hunter	1877	H.M.Bennett	1934	R.McF.Seaton	1978
T.R.Lyle	1879	J.M.Cameron	1935	L.D.McKie	1979
J.McNeill	1879	J.A.Irwin	1936	B.W.Millar	1979
H.A.Irvine	1880	J.Anderson	1937	O.J.Yeoh	1980
W.C.Steele	1881	E.H.Simpson	1939	D.A.Nicholl	1980
W.J.Hardy	1882	J.H.Bruce	1939	M.Smyth	1981
S.J.Hunter	1883	L.Logan	1940	T.W.Murphy	1982
A.M.Bulloch	1892	D.A.Wheeler	1941	C.A.Hunter	1983
J.C.Davison	1893	A.R.Nicholson	1942	M.A.Gibbon	1984
J.M.Hezlett	1894	R.L.Smyrl	1943	Y.M.Ho	1985
A.Barr	1895	R.A.Eyre	1944	S.P.Forde	1985
W.W.Stewart	1896	R.G.Ussher	1945	J.D.J.McCabe	1986
J.G.Wallis	1897	I.McCausland	1946	S.Ward	1987
R.M.Houston	1898	D.M.Pollock	1947	N.P.I.Mooney	1988
W.J.Morrison	1899	D.H.McLain	1948	D.Hegarty	1989
D.G.Madill	1900	T.S.Wilson	1949	K.C.Tso	1990
T.May	1901	J.Hunter	1950	G.V.H.Ward	1990
J.H.G.Brookes	1902	R.H.Riddell	1951	S.P.Quah	1991
W.R.Browne	1903	M.W.McLain	1952	R.A.Harte	1992
J.A.Tomb	1904	W.H.C.Maxwell	1953	S.G.Kelly	1992
J.H.M.Madill	1905	J.B.Haldane	1954	S.A.Wright	1993
J.L.McFall	1906	J.I.Langtry	1956	G.J.McKeever	1994
R.McCahon	1907	G.C.Spotswood	1956	A.J.Barr	1995
G.R.Gilmore	1908	K.H.Edwards	1957	D.G.Dunwoody	1996
J.McKay	1909	I.McC.Torrens	1958	P.Ramachandran	1997
J.Murphy	1910	R.H.Martin	1959	S.Fleming	1998
J.T.Anderson	1911	I.C.Hunter	1960	S.Henry	1999
S.Fullerton	1912	W.N.B.Mullan	1961	D.M.Connor	2000
T.Madill	1913	N.K.Blair	1962	J.M.Hogg	2001
A.Gilmore	1914	R.E.Cox	1963	S.Martin	2002
F.W.Walker	1915	H.H.Clarke	1964	A.J.Davidson	2003
F.R.Franklin	1916	S.A.Rainey	1965	C.N.Griffith	2004
R.N.D.Wilson	1917	W.B.C.Walker	1966	A.T.Kirk	2005
J.F.Alexander	1918	I.R.Taylor	1966	M.I.Kerr	2005

The Honourable The Irish Society's Prize

First awarded 2006

S.Li	2006	J.D.Stewart	2008	Z.T. He	2009
N.C.Bleakly	2007	M.P. Griffith	2009	M.A. Taeubert	2009

Head Prefects / Head Boys

Head Boys (1)

This official title originated at the beginning of Dr Humphreys' headmastership in Sept. 1955 and the position was held by both dayboys and boarders before 1964. Previously the captain of the First XV was designated "School Captain". (Boarders = *)

M.J.MacQuillan	1955*
T.B.Ferguson	1956
H.F.Kissack	1957*
E.H.L.Christie	1958*
R.H.Martin	1959
P.V.Hadden	1960
M.McNicholl	1961
J.H.McCracken	1962*
J.J.H.Morrell	1963*

From Sept. 1964 until Sept. 1997 a separate Head Boarding Prefect and Head Dayboy Prefect was appointed each year. These two official titles were used in the prefects list published annually in the school magazine.

Head Dayboy Prefects

J.D.Hill	1964
G.S.Crilly	1965
W.T.Moffatt	1966
A.W.Marshall	1967
D.D.Barr	1968
J.H.Kerr	1969
D.C.Boyce	1970
R.C.Malseed	1971
A.S.Baxter	1972
M.R.R.Williams	1973
J.C.McKee	1974
M.E.Nicholl	1975
W.D.J.McKay	1976
T.B.Blaine	1977
W.D.B.Clements	1978

Head Boarding Prefects

A Head Boarding Prefect was appointed from Sept. 1964 until Sept.1997. Although this was the official title, The Head Boarding Prefect was often referred to unofficially as "The Head Boy" during Dr Humphreys' headmastership. (Brian Fillis was ,however, specifically listed as "The Head Boy" in 1966.) As mentioned below, this position was clarified by Dr Rodgers in 1979.

W.T.McCarter	1964
W.B.C.Walker	1965
B.F.Fillis	1966
("Head Boy" in prefect list)	
D.S.B.Meharg	1967
D.S.B.Meharg	1968
D.C.Gillespie	1969
A.T.Fullerton	1970
A.T.Fullerton	1971
S.T.Dinsmore	1972
D.B.Smyth	1973
R.J.Mitchell	1974
F.J.Mullan	1975
S.C.Monteith	1976
D.J.Mills	1977
P.M.J.Scott	1978
I.G.McCarter	1979
I.J.Murphy	1980
M.C.Hunter	1981
C.A.S.Danton	1982
P.S.Slaine	1983
J.Nicholl	1984
W.S.Brown	1985
M.W.Gordon	1986
G.W.Wilson	1987
A.R.Henning	1988
G.V.H.Ward	1989
("Head Boy" in prefect list)	
G.R.Houston	1990
R.R.Boomer	1991
A.E.N.Shannon	1992
D.C.Ward	1993
D.S.H.Brown	1994
R.G.McCracken	1995
P.A.Hollingsworth	1996
D.F.Cecil	1997

Following closure of the boarding department this office lapsed.

Head Boys (2)

From Sept. 1979 onwards, the Head Dayboy Prefect was officially termed "The Head Boy" - except for the year 1989 – 90 when G.V.H. Ward held this title.

S. Beveridge	1979
K.M.Ferguson	1980
A.R.Nicholl	1981
R.A.White	1982
G.M.Montgomery	1983
A.D.Irwin	1984
D.V.J.Millar	1985
T.C.McCallum	1986
D.W.Nicholl	1987
M.W.Nelson	1988
N.T.Graham	1989
F.Ward	1990
R.A.G.Truss	1991
R.F.Kerr	1992
B.R.McConnell	1993
P.D.Kirkpatrick	1994
S.S.McConnell	1995
K.S.Morrison	1996
K.W.M.Gamble	1997
A.R.Lynas	1998
P.S.Barr	1999
I.D.Hamill	2000
S.W.McCluskey	2001
A.D.Trimble	2002
P.R.Topping	2003
R.M.Boyd	2004
P.J.McElnay	2005
S.J.H.Dobbin	2006
J.D.Stewart	2007
M.P.Griffith	2008
A.J.Whitmarsh	2009
D.G.M.McCluskey	2010

Harriers Captains

1963-64	A.N.Johnston	1977-78	H.S.Burke	1993-94	D.W.Kerr
1964-65	A.N.Johnston	1978-79	D.F.Logan	1995-96	P.T.Boyd
1965-66	A.N.Johnston	1979-80	D.F.Logan	1996-97	P.T.Boyd
	W.T.Moffatt	1980-81	C.Brennan	1997-98	R.E.Jones
1966-67	W.T.Moffatt	1981-82	P.S.Smith	1998-99	P.S.Blair
1967-68	A.S.Anderson	1982-83	G.R.J.Donaldson	1999-00	G.A.D.Walton
1968-69	B.D.Uprichard	1983-84	P.J.M.Tweedie	2000-01	G.A.D.Walton
1969-70	M.Britovsek	1984-85	W.J.Witherow	2001-02	
1970-71	P.S.McNally	1985-86	M.W.Gordon	2002-03	
1971-72	P.S.McNally	1986-87	M.W.Gordon	2003-04	S.G.Morrow
1972-73	I.H.Adams	1987-88	A.S.Mallagh	2004-05	M.W.Livingstone
1973-74	J.Dawson	1988-89	M.R.McCurdy	2005-06	M.W.Livingstone
1974-75	P.B.Corr	1989-90	P.C.H.Pollard	2006-07	P.N.Gilliland
1975-76	P.B.Corr	1991-92	R.F.Kerr	2007-08	P.N.Gilliland
1976-77	G.C.McIlwaine	1992-93	R.F.Kerr		

Badminton Captains

1969-70	P.McCloskey	1983-84	D.A.Mulholland	1997-98	K.W.M.Gamble
1970-71	D.R.Balmer	1984-85	G.J.Henderson	1998-99	S.R.Moody
1971-72	D.R.Balmer	1985-86	M.A.Quigley	1999-00	G.D.Gault
1972-73	M.Holley	1986-87	C.McBride	2000-01	P.Magowan
1973-74	S.Foong	1987-88	C.McBride	2002-03	B.G.M.Henderson
1974-75	A.J.Mooney	1988-89	R.A.Kinghan	2003-04	B.G.M.Henderson
1975-76	D.J.Mills	1989-90	R.A.Kinghan	2004-05	B.G.M.Henderson
1976-77	D.J.Mills	1990-91	G.S.Oliver	2005-06	S.J.H. Dobbin
1977-78	P.R.Ferguson	1991-92	K.R.Crawford	2006-07	S.J.H.Dobbin
1978-79	S.C.Henderson	1992-93	D.Ilsley	2007-08	N.W.B.Haslett
1979-80	S.Beveridge	1993-94	V.A.Gault	2008-09	N.W.B.Haslett
1980-81	W.J.Ferris	1994-95	R.S.McAuley	2009-10	N.W.B.Haslett
1981-82	W.J.Ferris	1995-96	G.T.Anderson		
1982-83	W.J.McFetridge	1996-97	G.T.Anderson		

Swimming Captains

1968-69	C.S.Carter	1983-84	J.G.Kennedy	1998-99	P.A.Irvine
1969-70	E.H.Stewart	1984-85	J.A.D.Kennedy	1999-00	
1970-71	R.L.Dobson	1985-86	A.R.Nimmons	2000-01	C.L.Knight
1971-72	R.L.Dobson	1986-87	A.R.Nimmons	2001-02	A.J.Boyd
1972-73	B.H.G.McCann	1988-89	A.D.Eakin		C.P.Neill
1973-74	J.J.Glover	1989-90	H.McM.Page	2003-04	M.T.Neill
1974-75	B.N.Johnston	1990-91	G.O.Boddie	2004-05	R.M.Boyd
1975-76	J.D.Donaldson	1991-92	G.O.Boddie		M.T.Neill
1976-77	R.E.Fitzgerald	1992-93	A.E.N.Shannon	2005-06	D.A.Willis
1977-78	R.J.C.Foote		C.T.F.Thompson	2006-07	D.C.S.Flatt
1978-79	H.M.Fitzgerald	1993-94	G.W.Eakin	2007-08	M.J.McDowell
1979-80	J.J.White	1994-95	A.P.Turner	2008-09	C.A.Sloan
1980-81	P.J.Dark	1996-97	M.G.Boddie	2009-10	C.A.E.Coils
1982-83	R.A.White	1997-98	P.A.Irvine		

Cricket Captains

G.A.Jackson	1900	J.H.Duffy	1937	I.N.McMurray	1974
R.F.Seddall	1901	W.A.Condy	1938	S.J.Cole	1975
J.H.G.Brookes	1902	W.A.Condy	1939	J.M.Stewart	1976
J.Dickie	1903	P.W.J.Dimond	1940	D.J.Johnston	1977
E.R.Casement	1904	F.H.Collins	1941	M.C.Lapsley	1978
N.Morton	1905	R.J.A.Lindsay	1942	W.D.B.Clements	1979
A.Small	1906	S.W.McVicker	1943	S.Beveridge	1980
J.McIntyre	1907	J.B.Getty	1944	I.F.McIlgorm	1981
R.F.Walker	1908	W.B.Morrow	1945	A.R.Nicholl	1982
W.R.G.Breen	1909	W.B.Morrow	1946	J.K.Hillis	1983
W.R.G.Breen	1910	F.E.Anderson	1947	D.A.Forsythe	1984
W.McC.Sharpe	1911	B.McCrea	1948	R.D.Christie	1985
W.McC Sharpe	1912	A.G.H.Morrow	1949	S.P.Mawhinney	1986
	1913	D.H.Orr	1950	B.J.Rooks	1987
	1914	D.J.Wheeler	1951	D.B.Logan	1988
F.C.Knox	1915	D.Adair	1952	M.W.Nelson	1989
A.F.Henry	1916	D.Adair	1953	N.T.Graham	1990
A.Henry	1917	R.A.Semple	1954	F.Ward	1991
	1918	J.Freeman	1955	R.Millar	1992
	1919	R.N.M.Edwards	1956	C.A.J.Gore	1993
B.Henry	1920	R.N.M.Edwards	1957	A.V.McGonigle	1994
F.V.Beamish	1921	E.H.L.Christie	1958	P.D.Kirkpatrick	1995
G.R.Beamish	1922	C.E.S.McClure	1959	A.N.Kirkpatrick	1996
T.D.Raphael	1923	B.D.J.H.Moriarty	1960	A.N.Kirkpatrick	1997
W.E.Henry	1924	B.D.J.H.Moriarty	1961	S.C.Kelly	1998
	1925	S.J.McDonald	1962	J.T.Carson	1999
	1926	J.J.Redpath	1963	G.Shirlow	2000
R.A.Crawford	1927	P.J.Legate	1964	I.D.Hamill	2001
R.A.Crawford	1928	W.P.Smyth	1965	C.J.Gault	2002
M.S.Patrick	1929	M.K.Oakman	1966	J.Elder	2003
T.A.Groves	1930	D.W.Oakman	1967	M.Davis	2004
J.A.Mark	1931	T.N.Orr	1968	A.Handforth	2005
C.H.Beamish	1932	T.N.Orr	1969	G.T.F.Gaston	2006
J.A.Esler	1933	A.T.Fullerton	1970	S.A.Caulfield	2007
A.D.Kelly	1934	A.T.Fullerton	1971	P.J.Wallace	2008
K.J.Kemp	1935	A.T.Fullerton	1972	A.W.Douglas	2009
K.J.Kemp	1936	D.N.McCarthy	1973	A.W.Douglas	2010

Golf Captains

1979-80	K.J.Taggart	1989-90	R.G.Walls	2000-01	A.A.Rankin
1980-81	L.M.McKeever	1990-91	A.J.Lamont	2001-02	S.W.McCluskey
1981-82	W.J.Ferris	1991-92	A.J.Knight	2002-03	G.W.D.McGrotty
1982-83	D.A.Mulholland	1992-93	J.McCracken	2003-04	G.W.D.McGrotty
1983-84	D.A.Mulholland	1993-94	R.T.Elliott	2004-05	G.W.D.McGrotty
1984-85	M.Kilgore	1994-95	R.T.Elliott	2005-06	R.W.F.McCrudden
1985-86	P.N.Cameron	1996-97	G.McDowell	2006-07	R.W.F.McCrudden
1986-87	P.N.Cameron	1997-98	G.McDowell	2007-08	P.M.McAuley
1987-88	G.S.Patterson	1998-99	J.R.D.Todd	2008-09	A.G.Brown
1988-89	G.D.Stevenson	1999-00	J.R.D.Todd	2009-10	A.G.Brown

Rowing Captains

A.N.Clarke	1928	J.B.Fleming	1956	J.A.Paul	1984
G.A.McMurray	1929	J.B.Fleming	1957	M.R.White	1985
T.C.Clarke	1930	J.Doherty	1958	J.H.Boomer	1986
T.C.Clarke	1931	M.S.Hegan	1959	J.H.Boomer	1987
T.C.Clarke	1932	R.W.Woods	1960	S.G.Medcalfe	1988
P.J.Taylor	1933	R.R.B.Craig	1961	J.D.Bailie	1989
H.L.Gallagher	1934	J.H.Boyd	1962	B.Smyth	1990
W.McGrath	1935	J.H.Boyd	1963	R.R.Boomer	1991
W.McGrath	1936	J.D.Hill	1964	B.J.Steele	1992
A.J.Clarke	1937	J.D.Hill	1965	B.J.Steele	1993
A.J.Clarke	1938	M.T.Clarke	1966	R.D.Dysart	1994
J.W.McKay	1939	N.H.Hamill	1967	S.D.S.Morrow	1995
W.A.B.Thompson	1940	A.P.Millar	1968	J.K.Millar	1996
G.R.C.McDowell	1941	A.P.Millar	1969	W.T.Wright	1997
A.R.Nicholson	1942	J.M.Hill	1970	J.T.Coulter	1998
A.J.Russell	1943	W.D.Ferguson	1971	B.H.Dickson	1999
R.A.Eyre	1944	H.S.Curry	1972	S.C.Henry	2000
H.R.Cameron	1945	H.A.Pearson	1973	C.L.Bradley	2001
W.F.N.Black	1946	C.P.Service	1974	D.K.Martin	2002
D.M.Pollock	1947	M.E.Nicholl	1975	I.M.Giffin	2003
S.M.Young	1948	W.H.Clements	1976	P.J.Braithwaite	2004
J.W.Caskey	1949	G.W.Canning	1977	D.Ewart	2005
J.W.Caskey	1950	D.W.Anderson	1978	D.J.Taggart	2006
A.J.Pollock	1951	I.F.C.Hogg	1979	M.R.McNaul	2007
W.C.Collins	1952	B.McC.Austin	1980	R.Dinsmore	2008
W.N.Linton	1953	J.R.Dean	1981	J.A.McBurney	2008
W.N.Linton	1954	N.J.A.Leslie	1982	J.P.Mitchell	2009
F.S.J.McKee	1955	K.J.S.McConnell	1983	M.Stynes	2010

Tennis Captains

1996-97	P.W.Hutchinson	2003-04	C.N.Griffith
1997-98	R.A.Stewart	2004-05	A.G.Minihan
1998-99	J.I.Elliott	2005-06	C.M.Gowland
1999-00	D.M.Connor	2006-07	C.M.Gowland
2000-01	T.J.Stewart-Moore	2007-08	A.J.Ewart
2001-02	T.J.Higgins	2008-09	M.P.Griffith
2002-03	C.N.Griffith	2009-10	A.G.Brown

Association Football Captains

2003-04	A.A.Dobbin	2007-08	H.A.Beverland
2004-05	C.R.A.Dunlop	2008-09	C.J.Steele
2005-06	E.M.Taylor	2009-10	P.W.Milliken
2006-07	E.M.Taylor		

G.M.Irvine	1883-84	H.C.A.Johnston	1927-28	D.W.Oakman	1968-69
A.J.Irwin	1884-85	A.A.McMath	1928-29	J.H.Kerr	1969-70
R.Dunlop	1886-87	A.A.McMath	1929-30	R.C.Malseed	1970-71
J.K.Bresland	1887-88	J.C.Groves	1930-31	R.C.Malseed	1971-72
D.Ogilvy	1888-89	J.A.Esler	1931-32	G.I.McManus	1972-73
D.Ogilvy	1889-90	J.A.Esler	1932-33	M.R.R.Williams	1973-74
D.Ogilvy	1890-91	J.N.McKeary	1933-34	R.C.McIntosh	1974-75
J.L.Frazer-Hurst	1891-92	J.N.McKeary	1934-35	D.A.Gardiner	1975-76
T.McNeil	1892-93	W.McGrath	1935-36	M.F.G.McIntosh	1976-77
S.Smyth	1893-94	H.A.Crouch	1936-37	M.F.G.McIntosh	1977-78
S.Smyth	1894-95	A.J.Clarke	1937-38	S.McF.Seaton	1978-79
W.P.Ringland	1895-96	H.Hegan	1938-39	R.M.Connor	1979-80
G.Armstrong	1896-97	W.D.F.Marshall	1939-40	E.G.M.Davis	1980-81
B.Richards	1897-98	W.D.F.Marshall	1940-41	M.C.Hunter	1981-82
I.R.Headech	1898-99	G.R.C.McDowell	1940-41	W.T.McKeown	1982-83
R.H.Casement	1899-00	M.J.Wauchob	1941-42	J.D.Caskey	1983-84
W.Owens	1901-02	J.S.Y.Matthewson	1942-43	W.A.Pollock	1984-85
J.R.Jackson	1902-03	H.M.H.Morrison	1943-44	J.S.T.McCartney	1985-86
D.L.McCullough	1903-04	H.R.Cameron	1944-45	T.C.McCallum	1986-87
E.R.Casement	1904-05	A.J.Orr	1945-46	D.W.Nicholl	1987-88
A.Small	1905-06	J.N.M.Foster	1946-47	W.P.McBride	1988-89
W.C.Neill	1906-07	G.A.Tanner	1947-48	C.L.O'Neill	1989-90
W.C.Neill	1907-08	W.J.McVicker	1948-49	M.P.Dobson	1990-91
R.F.Walker	1908-09	H.C.Orr	1949-50	D.H.Callaghan	1991-92
R.R.Neely	1909-10	J.C.Graham	1950-51	M.A.McLornan	1992-93
R.J.Henry	1910-11	R.McGrath	1951-52	N.B.G.Brown	1993-94
W.McC.Sharpe	1911-12	G.Giffin	1952-53	A.J.Hutchinson	1994-95
T.Madill	1912-13	E.A.M.Johnston	1953-54	A.J.Monteith	1995-96
R.Davidson	1913-14	R.Scott	1954-55	A.N.Kirkpatrick	1996-97
J.E.McLarnon	1914-15	J.W.Mencarelli	1955-56	C.J.McClean	1997-98
A.F.Henry	1915-16	A.C.McElhinney	1956-57	A.R.Lynas	1998-99
A.F.Henry	1916-17	D.Giffin	1957-58	P.S.Barr	1999-00
F.C.Shaw	1917-18	E.H.L.Christie	1958-59	G.H.A.Carruthers	2000-01
H.McKee	1918-19	R.W.E.Stewart	1959-60	D.W.G.Burns	2001-02
B.Henry	1919-20	S.L.Moore	1960-61	A.D.Trimble	2002-03
F.V.Beamish	1920-21	S.J.McDonald	1961-62	J.Burns	2003-04
G.R.Beamish	1921-22	J.J.Redpath	1962-63	S.McCulloch	2004-05
W.M.W.Patrick	1922-23	A.M.Allen	1963-64	P.W.A.McAllister	2005-06
J.D.McClelland	1923-24	B.F.Fillis	1964-65	R.F.W.McCrudden	2006-07
J.D.McClelland	1924-25	B.F.Fillis	1965-66	J.G.Shiels	2007-08
J.W.Patrick	1925-26	B.F.Fillis	1966-67	A.D.Warwicker	2008-09
R.F.Phillips	1926-27	S.Roberts	1967-68	D.C.Rankin	2009-10

HEADMASTER: Dr. D.R.J. Carruthers, B.Sc., Ph.D., P.G.C.E., P.Q.H.(N.I.)

VICE-PRINCIPALS: Mr W.M. McNay, B.A., Dip.Ed.

                       Mr P.W.J. Allen, B.Sc., P.G.C.E., C.P.D. P.Q.H. (N.I.)

ART:
Mr J. Brown, B.A., P.G.C.E., Adv.Dip.H.T.A.D.
Mrs E. O'Neill, B.A., P.G.C.E.

BIOLOGY:
Mr D.A. Harkness, B.Sc., P.G.C.E., C.Biol., M.I.Biol.
Mr D. McQ. Stewart, B.Sc., P.G.C.E.

CAREERS:
Dr G. W. Hull, B.Sc., Ph.D., P.G.C.E.

CHEMISTRY:
Mr W.G. McCluskey, B.Sc., Cert.Ed., B.Phil.
Dr N. Cully, B.Sc., Cert.Ed., D.Phil.
Mrs T.D. Reid, B.Sc., P.G.C.E., C.P.D.

ENGLISH:
Mrs K.M. Taggart, B.A., Dip.Ed.
Mr J.V. Boyd, B.A., A.L.A., P.G.C.E.
Mrs L. Gibson, B.A., Cert.R.E., P.G.C.E.
Mr J.J. McCully, B.A., P.G.C.E.
Miss L. Magee, B.A., P.G.C.E.
Mr S.J. Millar, B.A., P.G.C.E.

GEOGRAPHY:
Ms P. Murphy, B.A., P.G.C.E.
Dr G.W. Hull, B.Sc., Ph.D., P.G.C.E.

SOCIETY AND GOVERNMENT:
Mrs S. Taggart, M.A., P.G.C.E.
Mr W.A. Gaston, B.A., P.G.C.E.
Mrs M.L. McClure, B.Sc., P.G.C.E.
Mrs R.E. Smyth, B.A., P.G.C.E.

HOME ECONOMICS:
Mrs A. Cooper, B.Sc., M.Sc., P.G.C.E.

SENIOR MASTERS: Mrs K.M. Taggart, B.A., Dip.Ed.
                                        Mr R.T. McGregor, B.Tech.Mech.Eng., P.G.C.E.

INFORMATION TECHNOLOGY:
Miss P.A. McIntyre, B.Ed.
Mr K.S. Freeburn, B.Sc., P.G.C.E.
Mrs L.M. O'Doherty, B.Sc., P.G.C.E.

MATHEMATICS:
Mr R.I. Crown, B.Sc., P.G.C.E.
Mr R. Kane, B.Sc., P.G.C.E.
Mr M.J. Palmer, B.Sc., P.G.C.E.
Mr S.T. Patterson, B.Sc., P.G.C.E.
Mrs C. Smyth, B.Sc., P.G.C.E.
Mrs A.M. Weir, B.Sc., P.G.C.E.

MODERN LANGUAGES:
Mr M. Reavey, B.Ed.
Miss V.J. Calvin, B.A., P.G.C.E.
Mr G.B.E. Knox, B.A., P.G.C.E.
Mr W.M. McNay, B.A., Dip.Ed.
Mr K.A. Peden, B.A., P.G.C.E.
Miss G.H. Watters, B.A., P.G.C.E.

MUSIC:
Mrs S.J. Cameron, M.Sc., B.Mus., Hons, M.T.D.

PHYSICS:
Mr W.S.A. Mitchell, B.Sc., P.G.C.E.
Mr S.D. Gault, B.Eng., P.G.C.E.

PHYSICAL EDUCATION:
Mr S.H. Graham, B.Ed., B.Phil., S.N.A.S.C.
Mr R.M. Beggs, B.Sc., P.G.C.E.
Mr R.D. Boyd, B.A. P.G.C.E.

RELIGIOUS EDUCATION:
Mr M.J. Dickie, B.D., P.G.C.E.

TECHNOLOGY AND DESIGN:
Mr M.W.C. Irwin, B.Ed.
Mr R.T. McGregor, B.Tech.Mech.Eng., P.G.C.E.

PRESIDENT: Mr. J.I. Smyth, B.Sc., C.Eng.
VICE-PRESIDENT: Mr. W.A. Linnegan, B.A.
HON. SECRETARY: Mr. F. J. Mullan, M.B., B.Ch., B.A.O., F.R.C.S.
HON. TREASURER: Mr D.A. Irwin, F.C.A.
HEADMASTER: Dr D.R.J. Carruthers, B.Sc., Ph.D., P.G.C.E., P.Q.H. (N.I.)

Mr. R.M. Beggs, B.Sc., P.G.C.E.
Mr. E.W. Boyd, B.Mus., A.L.C.M., M.A. (Hon)
Prof. J.S. Brown, M.D., F.R.C.G.P.
Mr. J.I. Campbell
Rev. P. Campbell, Th.Dip.
Mr. F. Farrell
Mr. J.D. Hill, B.A., D.L.
Dr. G.W. Hull, B.Sc., Ph.D., P.G.C.E.
Mr. P. Leighton C.B.E., Q.P.M., L.L.B.
Mr. D. McClarty, M.L.A.
Mr. R. McDermott, M.Sc., F.C.M.I., M.I.H.T., M.I.Q.
Mr. R.J. McKeag, L.B.I.P.P., L.M.P.A.
Mr. G. Montgomery, M.A. (Hons), Dip.Arch., R.I.B.A.
Mr. S.J.A. Murdock
Mr. W. Oliver
Mrs. A.K.M. Rowe, B.A. Hons, P.G.Dip., L.I.S., P.G.Dip. C.I.E.G.H.E.
Mr T.R.J. Shiels, M.A., A.C.A.
Mr. J.C. Stevenson, F.R.I.C.S.
Mr. A.J. Taggart, B.Sc., C.Eng., M.I.C.E.
Mrs K.M. Taggart, B.A., Dip.Ed.
Mr. D.H. Torrens
Mr. P.J.M. Tweedie, B.Sc. (Hons), M.R.I.C.S.

EX-OFFICIO MEMBERS OF THE INSTITUTION

Rev. Dr. D. Clarke
Rev. D. Collins
Rev. W.P. Corrigan
Rev. P. Fleming
Rev. R.S. McMullan
Rev. W. Peel
Pastor T. Watson

CLERK TO THE BOARD OF GOVERNORS

Mr. G.L. Knight, B.Sc.

BURSAR:	Mr G.L. Knight, B.Sc.
BURSAR'S SECRETARY:	Miss S.E. Anderson
HEADMASTER'S SECRETARY:	Mrs L.G. Reavey
ACCOUNTS CLERK:	Mrs R. Steele
RECEPTIONIST:	Mrs D.M. Armstrong
CAFETERIA SUPERVISOR:	Mrs N. Tannahill
COOK:	Mrs M.T. Bredin
ASSISTANT COOK:	Mrs H. Knox
CATERING ASSISTANTS:	Mrs L.J. Doherty
	Mrs E.A. Freeman
	Mrs M. Knight
	Mrs M.D. McCandless
	Mrs C. Ramage
	Mrs L.M. Tannahill
ESTATE MANAGER:	Mr V. Callaghan
MAINTENANCE ASSISTANT:	Mr B. Holmes
JANITORS:	Mr G.K. McBride
	Mr H.D. McCorriston
	Mr J.A.T. Stevenson
CLEANERS:	Mrs P.E. Kennedy
	Mrs M.J. Wilson
	Mrs C. Conley
	Mrs W. Boyle
GROUNDSMEN:	Mr C.W. Callaghan
	Mr P. Magill
LABORATORY TECHNICIANS:	Mr D.K. Cox
	Mr H. Canning
	Mr S.J. Scott
PRINT ROOM TECHNICIAN:	Mr W.J. Campbell
TECHNOLOGY TECHNICIAN:	Mr R.C. Thomas
LIBRARY ADMINISTRATOR:	Mrs B. Davey
MUSEUM CURATOR & ARCHIVIST	Mr J.A. Cassells
MODERN LANGUAGE ASSISTANTS:	Mrs V. Oliván-Vinué
LEARNING SUPPORT ASSISTANT:	Ms K. Thomson, M.A.(Hons). P.G.D.E.

SCHOOLDAYS

ON THE BANKS OF THE BANN

COLERAINE
ACADEMICAL
INSTITUTION

1860 - 2010